MODES OF INTERPRETATION IN
OLD ENGLISH LITERATURE

Sumum wordlaþe   wise sendeð
on his modes gemynd   þurh his muþes gæst,
æðele ondgiet.

Christ II 664–666a

Edited by
PHYLLIS RUGG BROWN
GEORGIA RONAN CRAMPTON
FRED C. ROBINSON

Modes of Interpretation in
OLD ENGLISH LITERATURE

ESSAYS IN HONOUR OF
STANLEY B. GREENFIELD

UNIVERSITY OF TORONTO PRESS
Toronto Buffalo London

ISBN 0-8020-5678-4

∞

Printed on acid-free paper

Canadian Cataloguing in Publication Data

Main entry under title:
Modes of interpretation in Old English literature
  "The publications of Stanley B. Greenfield, 1951 to
  the present": p.
  Includes bibliographical references and index.
  ISBN 0-8020-5678-4
  1. Anglo-Saxon literature – History and criticism.
  2. Greenfield, Stanley B. (Stanley Brian), 1922–
  I. Brown, Phyllis Rugg, 1949–   . II. Crampton,
  Georgia Ronan, 1925–   . III. Robinson, Fred C.
  (Fred Colson), 1930–   . IV. Greenfield, Stanley
  B. (Stanley Brian), 1922–   .
  PR176.M62 1986   820'.1   c86-093896-4

Contents

PART II: WORDS AND THE WORK

PART III: THE WORDS:
PHILOLOGICAL STUDIES

PART IV: SOURCES AND WORDS

Abbreviations

Akad der Wiss, Phil-Hist Kl	Akademie der Wissenschaften, Philosophisch-Historische Klasse
ASE	*Anglo-Saxon England*
ASPR	The Anglo-Saxon Poetic Records, ed G.P. Krapp and E.V.K. Dobbie
A SS	Acta Sanctorum ... supplementum, ed Joannes Bollandus and successors 1643 sequentia
Aufl	Auflage edition
Bayer	Bavaria, Bavarian
Bede *EH*	Bede's *Ecclesiastical History of the English People* ed Bertram Colgrave and R.A.B. Mynors
BGdSL	*Beiträge zur Geschichte der deutschen Sprache und Literatur*
BHL	Bibliotheca Hagiographica Latina Antiquae et Mediae Aetatis, ed Society of Bollandists 1886–
BL	British Library
Bosworth-Toller	*An Anglo-Saxon Dictionary* by Joseph Bosworth, ed and enlarged by T. Northcote Toller and *Supplement* by Toller 1882–98; 1908–21
BM	British Museum
CCSL	Corpus Christianorum, Series Latina
CHEL	Cambridge History of English Literature
CL	*Comparative Literature*

CLA	*Codices latini antiquiores: A Paleographical Guide to Latin Manuscripts Prior to the Ninth Century* ed E.A. Lowe 1934–71
Cl & Med	*Classica et Mediaevalia*
Crit I	*Critical Inquiry*
EEMF	Early English Manuscripts in Facsimile
EETS	Early English Text Society
es	extra series
os	original series
ss	supplementary series
EHD	*English Historical Documents c. 500-1402* 2nd ed; ed Dorothy Whitelock
EHR	*English Historical Review*
ELN	*English Language Notes*
ES	*English Studies*
E&S	*Essays and Studies*
ns	new series
E Stn	*Englische Studien*
Gmc	Germanic
JEGP	*Journal of English and Germanic Philology*
Landesbibl	Landesbibliothek
Leeds SE	*Leeds Studies in English*
MÆ	*Medium Aevum*
MED	*Middle English Dictionary* ed Hans Kurath, Sherman M. Kuhn, and others 1954–
MGH	Monumenta Germaniae Historica
MLR	*Modern Language Review*
MLN	*Modern Language Notes*
MP	*Modern Philology*
MS	*Mediaeval Studies*
Neophil	*Neophilologus*
NF	Neue Folge (new series)
NM	*Neuphilologische Mitteilungen*
NLH	*New Literary History*
N&Q	*Notes and Queries*
O Dan	Old Danish
OE	Old English

OED	*The Oxford English Dictionary ... on Historical Principles* ed J.A.H. Murray and others
OEM	*Old English Martyrology*
OEN	*Old English Newsletter*
O Icel	Old Icelandic
ON	Old Norse
O Sw	Old Swedish
OWN	Old West Norse
PBA	*Proceedings of the British Academy*
PELL	*Papers on English Language and Literature*
PL	Patrologia Latina, ed J.-P. Migne
PLL	*Papers on Language and Literature*
PMLA	*Publications of the Modern Language Association*
PQ	*Philological Quarterly*
PRIA	*Proceedings of the Royal Irish Academy*
RES	*Review of English Studies*
Rolls Series	Rerum Britannicarum medii aevi scriptores
sa	under this year
S Med	*Studi Medievali*
Sc	Scandinavian
SN	*Studia Neophilologica*
SP	*Studies in Philology*
sv, vv	sub verbo (under this word, head; words, heads)
TPS	*Transactions of the Philological Society*
TSLL	*Texas Studies in Literature and Language*
TRHS	*Transactions of the Royal Historical Society*
YES	*The Yearbook of English Studies*

Preface

A s WE BEGAN the love-labour of assembling this book to honour Stanley B. Greenfield, we confronted a considerable problem: how to narrow contributions to a size reasonable for a monograph. Stanley Greenfield's publications range widely, including an essay on nineteenth-century American fiction and a verse translation of *Beowulf*, and he regularly teaches survey courses as well as the Introduction to Old English Language and Literature, *Beowulf*, and Chaucer's poetry. Moreover, his students often have taken their training to other centuries, even other disciplines, or out of academe altogether. We limited our collection to studies illustrating useful interpretative approaches to Old English literature in order to reflect the deepest concentration of his work and something of his characteristic approach to literature. In his teaching and publications, always insisting on the primacy of a careful examination of the text, the words themselves, he opens up for students the rich world underlying the text. And thus we offer him a book which gives examples of different modes of interpretation.

We thank first Professor James L. Boren, who, assisted by Professor Carlisle Moore, is responsible for the 'tabula gratulatoria.' Paul Olum, President of the University of Oregon, Richard Hill, Vice-President for Academic Affairs and Provost, and Robert M. Berdahl, Dean of the College of Arts and Sciences, also at the University of Oregon, supported the volume with encouragement and funding. Professor Thelma Greenfield often assisted us, especially during the stages when preparation of the volume was not generally known. Donna Balderstone turned her exacting eye both to the proofreading and the preparation of the index. In addition we have had encouragement and advice from many friends and colleagues at Portland State University, the University of Santa Clara, and Stanford University. We all have shared in the pleasure of creating a book to honour our teacher and friend, Stanley B. Greenfield.

KIM R. STAFFORD

Foreword

OFTEN, WHEN THE HARP GOES ROUND, a traveller thinks back. In spring, when finally we drank raw mead together behind Stanley and Thelma Greenfield's house, the taste of the oldest English language itself had been our preparation. We had sipped and then drunk deep, had drenched our tongues from the first abrupt verse of Caedmon to the blaze of fire and resignation that follows Beowulf past mortality. I look back now. What had led us – a small tight company gathered with Stanley Greenfield – to commit our twenties to graduate study in medieval literature?

Enrolling for my first term, I remember, I had to choose between a linguistics course and Old English. To me then, they both sounded like hurdles preliminary to the long pursuit of finer things. By contrast, I fancied the modern poets. Old English? At least, I reasoned, that course might include some literature.

Then, that first day, there stood Stanley in our classroom's doorway, looking us over. Held against his heart, that copy of Klaeber's *Beowulf* was a brown talisman covered with battle scars – the book's spine worn utterly away by use, the boards and all bound together by a great rubber band. We could glimpse his own marginal notes in a neat and tiny hand – everywhere. Cotton Vitellius A.xv went through fire, but this book had been chafed to shreds by the sheer persistence of one man's devoted reading.

That first glimpse told me the truth about this man. Oregon rain shall fall; a teacher shall deal out gifts of seeing. Around the seminar table, we were a battle-ring turned inward, remembering. We lived in that Anglo-Saxon light of no colour, only intensity – the shine on each word chanted through octaves of poetry. We stood at Maldon, and leaned on the seafarer's starboard rail, listening. We dove through the dark waters, and we opened the real barrow of treasure, of a strange, bright language time did not tarnish. As the course approached its end, we hastened. We were quicker then. We saw things. Our own books began to wear the early signs of devotion. We were of Stanley's troop. Our strength should be more, as our time together grew less.

And then the mead, the celebration in that study rising like an observatory out of the roof of the Greenfield home. The walls hummed – or was it our bones? – as we thundered through the last four hundred lines of *Beowulf* in an afternoon. Then sunlight crosses the floor, and the good hawk of our voice through the hall swings. For me, and for other Greenfield students, a concluding session like that was not an end, but the beginning to a longer pilgrimage. Because of the tough beauty and articulate wisdom in those works he has helped us know, we turn back and back again to the native sources of English literature.

For one thing, as this volume clearly shows, Stanley Greenfield's teaching has gone far beyond the classroom through the kind of publishing he has always done. We have his survey of the field in *A Critical History of Old English Literature*, and the deeper probing of *The Interpretation of Old English Poems*. His work with Fred C. Robinson, *A Bibliography of Old English Literature to the End of 1972*, is another essential tool; and his translation, *A Readable Beowulf*, is both a critical tool and a joy in itself. Through these books and his many articles and reviews, Stanley Greenfield has held up the splendid works of the Old English canon, turning them glittering before us after the manner of poetic variation, so that we might see them more clearly by the multiple perspectives of his scholarship: literary history, criticism, bibliography, and translation. Through these publications, and through his steady organizational work and public appearances and his time in Regensburg, Cambridge, Los Angeles, and Berkeley, he has taught not only his students but the profession at large.

In this book lies a rich harvest in gratitude to Stanley Greenfield, but not all of his colleagues and students can be represented here. All of them do not now practise the particular craft of scholarship he has taught, for there are many modes of interpreting the wisdom and the sense of devotion he has given us. Some teach in other fields, some write poems, and one even builds well-tempered harpsichords. These translate what we learned from Stanley Greenfield to their own texts of wood and rhythm. The spirit demands, 'Sing me hwæthwugu!' and each shall sing. Our treasure and our gratitude take many forms.

After graduate school, when I had gone my way by teaching, research, writing, and travelling, after my class had left the room one day way out in Idaho I found on an old desk the heart of *The Wanderer*, lines carved with perfect accuracy: 'Hwær cwom mearg, hwær cwom mago?' My tongue twitched with the sweet taste of memory. That was like finding the singed, lucky manuscript of my own life in the ruins of the modern world. That was like this book, this talisman we bind together to give to our teacher and our friend.

PHYLLIS RUGG BROWN and
GEORGIA RONAN CRAMPTON
Introduction

SINCE EVERY TREATISE, every book, every essay, every remark about all literature, ancient, medieval, and modern, Anglo-Saxon or not, is necessarily a word about words, it may be asked why so particular an emphasis on the word should be remarked among the Anglo-Saxonists who have contributed to this volume. One reason surely resides in Stanley B. Greenfield's example, both in his writing and in his teaching. Words – their denotations, connotations, syntactical and grammatical relations, even their sound and rhythm – have been the centre of Mr Greenfield's work; and always his care about the words of the text has been fastidious and fierce.

Beyond that, however, Anglo-Saxon words give us, with corroboration from some archaeological finds, most of what we know about our mother tongue's ancestor and the culture of our forebears who spoke the language. Some of those words are muted now, nearly opaque to our speculations. We can only theorize about the meaning of 'thyle,' and the artifacts that come to light sometimes only deepen the mystery, as does the Sutton Hoo harp – we can only guess what it looked like and how it was played. Therefore the Anglo-Saxon words we do possess have the preciousness of their scarcity. The situation that Alain Renoir cites in his essay is emblematic: nineteen scattered words and a few letters are all that remain of Riddle 89 because the manuscript is worm-eaten. Not enough words survive to let us surmise the question let alone the answer. Daniel G. Calder writes, 'Before sweeping any item in our sparsely populated Anglo-Saxon corpus into the poetical dustbin, we must strive – heroically, I think – to love it.'

The extant words, then, are what we do have. They come to us in texts that are frequently stripped of the facts surrounding literature that usually inform our reception of it. Details about occasion, authors, the status, the identity, or even the nature of some personae, conditions of composition, the audience the author had in mind, even the degree of conventionality of verbal artifice, things readers cannot help knowing something about with later literature – all these may be obscure or blank, Professor Renoir and others remind us.

Beyond our need for the words, though, Anglo-Saxon vocabulary exerts its own strong coil of grace. Hedged against Podsnappery, Fowler's Rule No 5, 'Prefer the Saxon word to the Romance,'[1] still inspires and intimidates. To borrow and extend an emphasis in Peter Clemoes' essay, the Anglo-Saxon word is a 'tacen,' that is, in touch with that part of the outer world it tokens. Some words seem almost to be fragments from that world, cohering to it. 'Hafuc sceal on glofe,' ('Hawk shall be on the glove') and 'Rand sceal on scylde, // fæst fingra gebeorh' ('Shield shall have boss, tight finger-guard') from *Cotton Maxims* (17b and 37b–38a), words from a poem about which Mr Greenfield has written,[2] seem almost as tactile as the relations they designate. This tactile quality often gives even the more abstract concepts a poignant solidity: 'Wea bið wundrum clibbor' ('woe grips surprisingly').

The scholars represented in this volume belong to a generation which recognizes that edited texts may be misleading. Surely the presentation of Anglo-Saxon literary texts is a giant work for which all are grateful. Without that work Anglo-Saxon studies would not exist. However, reading texts as reported and emended by those who have preceded us can result in misconceptions about both the text itself and its manuscript contexts. Wonderful as the Anglo-Saxon Poetic Records are, those records are abstracted from manuscripts. Previous generations of scholars have left us, in the editions of Anglo-Saxon literature, a heritage containing both valuable and insufficiently examined suppositions. The still-purveyed idea that Danish invasions caused the ninth-century recession in Anglo-Saxon learning is an example of one such supposition, according to Helmut Gneuss, who re-examines the words of Alfred's *Preface to Pastoral Care* and evidence from library holdings and book production to confirm the king's own account. A too-facile willingness to bring striking historical events to bear upon a striking text is simply one way in which writers about earlier literatures may be led astray. Students of Anglo-Saxon literature are increasingly aware that we may not even be asking the appropriate questions of the texts that do silently survive, unaccompanied by an 'ars poetica' sufficient to tell us how we should approach them.

Not surprisingly then, a common theme of the essays in this festschrift is a modest profession of ignorance, a caveat persistently repeated. Professor Gneuss warns about lapsing into new hasty generalizations about the ninth century, 'a period for which we have so few written records. . . . Many questions must remain unanswered for the time being.' Roberta Frank gives a comprehensive statement of the difficulties in making subtle, refined judgments 'in a dead language like Old English, in a poetic corpus lacking almost all chronological bearings.' A certain relish in this predicament may be detected in Alain Renoir's statement about *Beowulf* that he shoud be at a loss 'to tell when, where, by whom, and under what circumstances this greatest of all early-Germanic epics was composed,' and that he has seen no reason to assume he is singular in such ignorance. John C. Pope, in an article devoted to the meaning of 'gehedde' (*Beowulf* 505), not only concedes but also emphasizes the limitations that prevent our knowing enough about that word, to say nothing of 'thyle'; much is unknown about Unferth simply because we cannot be sure what meaning 'the poet and his audience attached to the term "thyle,"' nor do we know how Unferth might have figured in other traditional tales the audience might be counted on to know. Unferth does not present the only such problem of identity to bemuse Old English readers. If Wulf and Eadwacer just may have been dogs (see Renoir n 21), what of Deor, who announces who he is? Deor may or may not have been a famous scop when the poem was first heard. 'We do not know,' warns Morton W. Bloomfield. '*Deor* invites speculation and is not easily open to definitive answers. We must rely on probableness.' It is not that Unferth, Wulf, Eadwacer, and Deor are vague or missing persons. They are sharply present in words, the words that they are represented as speaking or those spoken to or about them, hauntingly vivid words, but not conclusive ones.

Finally, no Anglo-Saxonist is to the manner born. English-speaking people have a start on the language, but for all Anglo-Saxonists, the language has the dear worth of what is acquired at some cost. That modern scholar who offers an introductory book on Anglo-Saxon vocabulary to help lighten 'the burden of learning "Old Anguish" '[3] can count on the pang or at least the smile of recognition. Even so appetent and gifted a linguist as Henry Wadsworth Longfellow cautioned that whoever undertook to read *Beowulf* in the original would find it 'no child's-play.'[4] Such effort exacts more than casual attention to words, and the habit lingers. Old because they constitute the basic stratum in our tongue and new because many are acquired late in our own ontogeny, Anglo-Saxon words seem pristine, discovered things.

By design this volume illustrates modes of interpretation of Old English literary texts, an apposite topic for honouring a critic and scholar whose writings include an influential book entitled *The Interpretation of Old English Poems*. The editors do not pretend to give examples of all approaches used in Anglo-Saxon studies today. In particular, paleography, work on manuscript contexts, on numerology, and on retrieval of the intellectual history of topoi are absent. No essay represents allegoresis, though more than one acknowledges the influence of patristic readings. Although notes to several essays are in effect bibliographical introductions to their topics, we include no separate bibliographical essay. Perhaps that omission is itself a fitting, though accidental, tribute to Professor Greenfield as a signal bibilographer.

Particularly rich in stylistics (Clemoes, Brown, Renoir, Frese, Irving, and Calder) and word studies (Frank, Pope, Rissanen, and Stanley), the volume also includes historical critics (Gneuss and Cross), work on the aesthetics of reception (Clemoes and Renoir), iconography (Mellinkoff), genre criticism (Bloomfield and Frese), source studies (Anderson, Cross, and Bloomfield), textual criticism and editorial notes (Stanley), and grammatical research (Rissanen). It includes one essay that uses interdisciplinary work in a fundamental fashion (Nelson) and one deconstructionist reading (Frese). In fact, many of these critics and scholars are eclectic in their effort to say how the works they discuss seem to them and in their care to check against too casual an impressionism. Many blend the old new criticism and the newly informed, if old, respect for history and language that has marked Anglo-Saxon studies.

Responsive to both the immediacy and the otherness of Anglo-Saxon literature, they meet the zestful example of the scholar, critic, and teacher whom this festschrift honours. His students, including those who have strayed from Old English into later medieval studies or even beyond, will remember with two of the editors that his introduction to the field when they were graduate students made Old English a new joy.

NOTES

1 H.W. and F.G. Fowler *The King's English* 3rd ed (Oxford 1931) 11
2 Quotations are from *The Anglo-Saxon Minor Poems* ASPR 6 ed E.V.K. Dobbie (New York 1942). However, we have kept ms 'wea' (13a).
3 Stephen A. Barney with Ellen Wertheimer and David Stevens, *Word-Hoard: An Introduction to Old English Vocabulary* (New Haven 1977) vii
4 'Anglo-Saxon Literature' *North American Review* 47 (1838) 102. The review

is anonymous but was reprinted by Longfellow in *Poets and Poetry of Europe*.
See Marijane Osborn 'Translations of *Beowulf* (and "The Fight at Finnsburg")'
in Chauncey B. Tinker *The Translations of Beowulf: A Critical Bibliography*
(New Haven 1903) rpt with an updated bibliography (Hamden, Conn 1974)
168

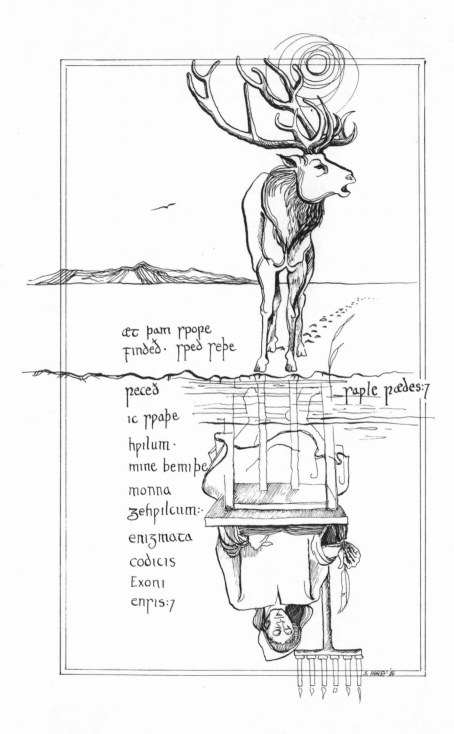

æt þam rþoþe
rindeð rþeð reþe

peceð   raþle pædes:⁊

ic rþaþe

hþilum·

mine bemiþe

monna

zehþilcum:·

enizmata

codicis

Exoni

enris:⁊

PART I

WORDS AND CULTURE

In its special fusion of Christian and pagan materials and attitudes, in its aesthetic techniques so different from those of later ages . . . [our earliest English literary heritage] reveals its particular nature as a body of literature. Though that nature is not ours, we can still understand and respond to it through the efforts of those historical, textual, and literary critics who have opened doors and windows for its illumination.

A New Critical History of Old English Literature 1986

PETER CLEMOES

'Symbolic' Language in
Old English Poetry[1]

F IFTEEN YEARS AGO, in an article entitled 'The Significance of Names in Old English Literature,' Fred C. Robinson provided a perceptive and thoughtful survey of passages in which Old English authors display a lively sense of the meanings of proper names.[2] A pursuit of etymological significance in names received from tradition, he reminds us, was a well-established practice among the Anglo-Saxons. Carried on a wave of biblical studies though it was, this mode of thinking was not confined to the Bible or to the Latin language, but was considered just as applicable to the vernacular. Hagiography furnishes a good example: a saint's name was expected to signify his special powers. Guthlac, the early-eighth-century Fenland ascetic, was given in infancy ('as though by divine plan,' his biographer, Felix, thought)[3] a name which by common consent came to be interpreted as 'reward for battle' and thus to epitomize contemporary ideas about the eremitic life. Sure enough, the meaning of his name provides a recurrent theme in celebrations of him, whether Latin or vernacular. For instance, in Robinson's words, 'the tone and events' of the Old English poem *Guthlac A* 'validate again and again the hagiographic prophecy latent in the saint's baptismal name.'[4] But a belief that a name which was customarily assigned to a person could embody that person's significance was not limited to Christian tradition. It was more widespread in Anglo-Saxon culture than that. Name-interpretation may well have been a Germanic propensity long before it was systematized by Christian learning. Robinson discusses as a case in point the name 'Hygelac' in *Beowulf*. The personage so named rules Beowulf's people, the Geats, in the poem but is said to be an early-sixth-century king of the Danes by the Frankish historian, Gregory of Tours, towards the end of that century. The name, 'Hygelac,' comprising 'hyge,' 'mind, thought,' and 'lāc,' 'play, strife, commotion' or the like, probably meant approximately 'instability of mind' to the *Beowulf* poet and his audience, Robinson concludes on two grounds – the similar meaning evidently associated with cognate forms of the name by Saxo Grammaticus and Snorri Sturluson in twelfth- to thirteenth-century Scandinavian tradition and the nature of other 'hyge-' and '-lac' compounds in Old English.[5] Frankish sources, in reporting a raid by Hygelac on the Frankish coast and his defeat and death there, offer no characterization of him; their interest is in the other side. The *Beowulf* poet, dealing with Hygelac as part of Beowulf's background, holds him directly responsible for the disastrous outcome of the raid on the Frankish coast: 'hyne wyrd fornam, // syþðan he for wlenco / wean ahsode' ('fate destroyed him, after he courted trouble out of boldness' 1205b–6).[6] Hygelac, in the poet's eyes, took an unjustified or misjudged chance. Saxo and Snorri, describing a king of Sweden so named (of Ireland, actually, in Saxo's case), who was attacked, defeated, and killed by Danes, write within a tradition consisting essentially of a king's name, a frivolous, miserly character attached to it, and the death of the name's owner at the hands of enemies. It is not unreasonable to infer therefore that a fatal flaw of intellectual unreliability was part of a traditional view of Hygelac for the *Beowulf* poet too.[7] Very probably in the raid-story as he and his contemporaries knew it a name and a congruent attribute had already formed a mutually supportive association. As Robinson rightly emphasizes, this is different from a name being invented artificially to label a certain kind of human make-up abstractly conceived;[8] nor is it a matter of a personification being invented analytically to fit a name. Instead, a name and an action have coalesced in a cultural process, the name providing a linguistic nucleus for a traditional story.

I have rehearsed this case-history at length here because I believe it represents a mode of thinking that was of much wider operation in vernacular narrative poetry and, indeed, fundamental to it. Names were not unique in acting thus on a poet's imagination: they took their place within a range of similar inherited linguistic stimuli. They were but a normal working part of the basic apparatus of Old English poetry. Epithets of relationship, for example, were a similar tool in the hands of the *Beowulf* poet. Beowulf, the hero, comes before us initially as follower of his king and member of his people – 'Higelaces þegn // god mid Geatum' (194b–5a). His name takes a further 148 lines to follow (343b). And throughout his three main actions – his fights against Grendel (736b–836), Grendel's mother (1492–1569) and the dragon (2538–95 and 2669–

711a) – Beowulf acts as representative of his kin and of his people. He is recurrently 'mæg Higelaces,' 'sunu Ecgþeowes,' 'Weder-Geata leod,' and so on. These are the epithets called into play when Beowulf exerts his mental and physical resources at critical moments, for instance when coming to grips with Grendel for the first time: 'Gemunde þa se goda, / mæg Higelaces, // æfenspræce, / uplang astod // ond him fæste wiðfeng' ('Then the good kinsman of Hygelac was mindful of his evening-speech, stood upright and seized him firmly' 758–60a). And it is with these epithets that value judgments are associated at all stages, for instance, when the hero is being contrasted to the depraved Heremod – 'He [Beowulf] þær eallum wearð // mæg Higelaces / manna cynne, // freondum gefægra ('He, kinsman of Hygelac, was in that respect more pleasing to everybody, to his friends' 913b–15a) – or when, à propos of the resolute, spirited, ambitious 'mæg Hylaces' (1530b) in his fight against Grendel's mother, throwing aside the sword which has failed him and relying on his strength alone, the narrator comments: 'Swa sceal man don, // þonne he æt guðe / gegan þenceð // longsumne lof; / na ymb his lif cearað' ('So a man does, when he means to achieve in battle long-lasting praise; he does not care at all about his life' 1534b–6). Beowulf, as 'mæg Hylaces,' is fulfilling his type. In what he does he is realizing the potential in his lineage. He is exerting his inherited powers. He is acting out the moral and martial qualities implied by the epithets of relationship repeatedly used of him.

The same goes for epithets of other kinds too. Those of personal kingship, for example. Numerous and often used terms, such as 'þeoden' ('leader of a people'), '-cyning' ('king') compounds ('eorð-,' 'folc-,' 'leod-,' 'þeod-cyning') and 'folces' or 'rices hyrde' ('guardian of a people or kingdom'), relate a king to his whole people, while others, equally plentiful and frequent, such as 'dryhten' ('leader of a troop of noble warriors') in simplex or compound form ('frea-,' 'freo-,' 'gum-,' 'mon-,' 'sige-,' 'wine-dryhten'), connect him with his troop of close followers, his 'comitatus.' With his full share of lineage terms, a king is acting out his hereditary potential within sets of functional social relationships. The business of traditional epithets is to relate his potential to these customary categories. For instance, the established expression 'hordweard hæleþa' ('guardian of the treasure of noble warriors') twins the material and military functions of royal leadership. The interest in an individual ruler – a Hrothgar, Hygelac, or Beowulf – is to observe his particular activation of the attributes of personal kingship enshrined in traditional appellations. To take a single example, when Beowulf makes the final cut that despatches the dragon (only to die himself), he does so as protector of his people: 'forwrat Wedra helm / wyrm on middan' ('The protector of the Weder-Geats cut through the dragon in the middle' 2705). Beowulf's rôle as 'Wedra helm' is no mere formality; in these circumstances to perform it is to die. The epithet represents a living principle exemplified in a particular action – in this case movingly.

Action realizes the qualities inherent in its actor. That is clearly evident, for instance, when young Wiglaf, Beowulf's nephew, aiding his hard-pressed uncle, deals the dragon a critical blow with his sword: 'Ða ic æt þearfe [gefrægn] / þeodcyninges // andlongne eorl / ellen cyðan, // cræft ond cenðu, swa him gecynde wæs' ('I heard that then, at the king of the people's time of need, the noble warrior at his side made known his fighting spirit, ability and boldness, as was natural to him' 2694-6). Information such as what training in wielding a sword Wiglaf had received is not worthy of mention: what really matters is his revelation of innate 'ellen,' 'cræft' and 'cenðu.'

Narrative is about the interaction of basic natures. 'Ecg sceal wið hellme // hilde gebidan' ('Sword-edge experiences battle against helmet'), it is declared in *Maxims II* (16b-17a),[9] and correspondingly in *Beowulf* fighting is 'þonne heoru bunden, / hamere geþruen, // sweord swate fah / swin ofer helme // ecgum dyhtig / andweard scireð' ('when the bound sword, forged with the hammer, the sword stained with blood, strong in its edges, shears the opposing boar above the helmet' 1285-7).

An actor gives outward signs of his inner nature. A horrible light like a flame shines from Grendel's eyes; the dragon emits fire. Human beings are to be judged by what they say and do: 'Æghwæþres sceal // scearp scyldwiga / gescad witan, // worda ond worca, / se þe wel þenceð' ('A sharp shield-warrior, who thinks well, is a judge of words and deeds' 287b-9), says the Danish coastguard to the newly arrived Beowulf. Interpretation of words and deeds consists of identifying the attribute they signify. The Danes react to Grendel's raiding Heorot on a successive night by giving up sleeping in the hall 'ða him gebeacnod wæs, // gesægd soðlice / sweotolan tacne // healðegnes hete' ('when the hall-thane's hate was shown to them, told unmistakably by a clear sign' 140b-2a). The reiterated raid made plain the underlying malevolence. Grendel's cast of mind was 'gebeacnod'; his patterned action was a 'tacen' of that attitude.

Material symbols sum up sequences of action evocatively. Grendel's torn off hand, arm and shoulder were such a one:

                    Hæfde East-Denum
Geatmecga leod   gilp gelæsted,
swylce oncyþõe   ealle gebette,
inwidsorge,   þe hie ær drugon
ond for þreanydum   þolian scoldon,
torn unlytel.   Þæt wæs tacen sweotol,
syþõan hildedeor   hond alegde,
earm ond eaxle   - þær wæs eal geador
Grendles grape -   under geapne hrof

The man of the Geats had fulfilled his boast to the East Danes, likewise had completely remedied distress, grief caused by malice, which they had endured and had to suffer out of sad necessity, no small affliction. That was a clear sign, after the man brave in battle laid down the hand, arm and shoulder – there all together was Grendel's grasp – under the spacious roof.   (828b-36)

Grendel's mother, panic-stricken though she was, made sure she removed this shameful symbol when she raided the hall in revenge. After his victory at the bottom of the pool Beowulf dramatically brought Grendel's head into Hrothgar's hall 'tires to tacne' ('as a token of glory' 1654a):

Þa wæs be feaxe   on flet boren
Grendles heafod,   þær guman druncon,
egeslic for eorlum   ond þære idese mid,
wliteseon wrætlic;   weras on sawon

Then Grendel's head was carried by the hair on to the floor of the hall where men were drinking, terrible in front of noble warriors and the lady with them, an amazing spectacle; men gazed at it.   (1647-50)

Beowulf's skilfully constructed memorial mound, high and broad on a cliff, a landmark for seafarers, was 'beadurofes becn' ('a sign of a man famed for battle' 3160a), an emblem of the reputation that outlived him. (Hrothgar had declared to him 'Þu þe self hafast // dædum gefremed, / þæt þin dom lyfað // awa to aldre' ['You yourself have achieved by your deeds that your glory will live for ever' 953b-5a].)
    Just so, reputation was transmitted from one generation to another through linguistic craft. For any given generation the time-honoured expressions of poetry crystallized social experience in the past. For example, to view a warrior-leader as 'beahgifa' ('ring-giver') was to codify

him according to one of the two complementary fundamental actions society had traditionally recognized in personal leadership. *Maxims II* declares, 'Geongne æþeling sceolan / gode gesiðas // byldan to beaduwe / and to beahgife' ('Good companions encourage a young prince to battle and to ring-giving' 14–15).[10] 'Beahgifu' ('ring-giving') is the acting out of a general potential of leadership as classified by conventional wisdom. And just as the general force of the maxim is evident from the verb 'sceolan,' so too the authority of the social experience enshrined in the term 'beahgifu' is guaranteed by its conventional form: 'ring-giving' stands traditionally for all bestowal of benefits by a leader, and the two-stressed compound 'beahgifu' provides the nucleus of a standard unit of Old English verse. Such expressions are conventional wisdom in conventional form. The form is the product of a cultural process. For instance, the words 'eodor' ('an enclosure, precinct'), 'helm' ('a cover'), and 'hleo' ('a shelter') are used only in poetry (accompanied by an appropriate genitive plural) to refer to a king as protector of a social group (as in *Beowulf*). Traditional poetic artifice has turned an expression such as 'eorla hleo' or 'wigendra hleo' ('protector of noble warriors') into a means of making an actor in the present event of a poem represent a fundamental capacity in human relations which has been identified by social experience in the past. In the present action it serves as a cultural token, or symbol, of standard experience.

Much modern criticism would call such an expression a 'formula.' As Milman Parry defined the 'formula,' and as F.P. Magoun, Jr, and others have applied the term to Old English poetry, it refers to 'a group of words regularly used under the same metrical conditions to express a given essential idea.'[11] Others before me have felt dissatisfied with this conception. My own sense of its inadequacy is based on my belief that a traditional thought and a traditional form were inherited by a poet, such as the *Beowulf* one, as an indivisible whole: for him and his like 'a given essential idea' was not a meaning to which some wording was regularly attached; it was no abstracted idea, defined as an item in a body of systematic thought. It was a semantic potential in a received form of wording. The meaning existed through the wording. It was an inseparable part of a cultural organism. The meaning had being when the expression was used in a narrative context, just as the significance of Grendel's severed head came to life when the grisly object was carried into the midst of the company in Hrothgar's hall. For example, when Beowulf and his men, returning triumphantly from Denmark, hurry eagerly to meet King Hygelac (this is the first time he enters the action 'in propria persona'):

> Hi sið drugon,
> elne geeodon,   to ðæs ðe eorla hleo,
> bonan Ongenþeoes   burgum in innan,
> geongne guðcynign   godne gefrunon
> hringas dælan.

They journeyed, went on spiritedly, until they learned that the protector of noble warriors, slayer of Ongentheow, brave young battle-king, was distributing rings in the palace. (1966b–70a)

The person they are hastening to greet is designated not by his name but in the first place by the epithet 'eorla hleo.' He is 'eorla hleo' indeed: young as he is, he is 'bona Ongenþeoes' – responsible for the killing of his people's 'old and terrible' (2929a) enemy – and he is caught in the act, so to speak, of dispensing largesse. Beowulf and his men, we feel, are right to want to meet such a king again. We correlate with their eagerness our response to a doughty, liberal, youthful 'eorla hleo' and there is a match. Our response, so confirmed, reinforces the age-old authority of the term 'eorla hleo' and that authority in turn validates our response. The story has effected a fusion between an ancient impulse and a contemporary reaction. The poet has not just had an old-fashioned idea and found old-fashioned words to fit it and left the result to look after itself. By activating the expression 'eorla hleo' mentally and emotionally in his story-telling he releases in his audience some of the imaginative potential of it as a token of experience which has been endorsed by society time out of mind. A new event takes place in the cultural tradition of which the linguistic symbol is a part.

When the referent of a linguistic symbol is an action, rather than an actor, the symbol necessarily becomes part of the narrative itself. For instance, this is true of 'hringas dælan' (1970a), referring to what King Hygelac was doing as Beowulf and his men pressed on to greet him. The expression is at once emblematic of Hygelac's liberality and is indistinguishable from the narrative line. 'Symbolic narrative,' this could be called. More than a single two-accent phrase can be involved in 'symbolic narrative.' For example, when Beowulf's life-and-death struggle with Grendel has reached a critical stage, 'Nolde eorla hleo / ænige þinga

// þone cwealmcuman / cwicne forlætan' ('The protector of noble warriors did not mean on any account to leave the slaughter-comer alive' 791–2). The compound agent noun 'cwealmcuma' expresses the essence of Grendel as a destructive being: in this raid on Heorot he has already been characterized as 'scynscaþa' ('phantom-injurer' 707a),[12] 'manscaða' ('crime-injurer' 712a and 737b) and 'hearmscaþa' ('harm-injurer' 766a). The social force of Beowulf as 'eorla hleo' is pitted against the anti-social one of Grendel as 'cwealmcuma.' The very existence of this creature whose nature is to enter Heorot as killer is an affront to society. He embodies an antisocial contradiction between killing and living. 'Cwealm-cuman' and its adjective 'cwicne,' close grammatically and jointly fulfilling the alliterative structure of the verse, culturally formalize this contradiction and thus epitomize the intolerable paradox the 'eorla hleo' resolves to end: the antisocial killer shall not live; society shall restore its normal relationships. The adjective shares symbolic status with the noun and the whole statement of resolve, as a narrative extension of 'eorla hleo,' acquires symbolic proportions. The formal mechanism here is not an action-symbol but verse structure making a dramatic pattern out of actor-symbols. At all events, whatever the means, in symbolic narrative, symbol and narrative setting become one. The result, at once deep and dramatic, is Old English poetry at its finest.

My sense of symbolic language in this poetry is therefore one of dramatically exploitable and evocative pieces of language which combine socially established semantic potential with culturally established conformity. The semantic potential has to do with the active essense of beings, their innate active attributes. A poem such as *Beowulf* deals with mighty beings in collaboration or conflict. Its disposition of symbolic language plots the traditional themes underlying these beings' interactions. For instance, King Beowulf and the dragon, alike enmeshed in events, inflict death on one another simultaneously. In the dragon-killing itself the close relationship between Beowulf and Wiglaf, uncle and nephew, is important. When Beowulf is mortally wounded, Wiglaf takes the initiative as 'andlongne eorl' ('the noble warrior at [the king's] side' 2695a),[13] and the two of them jointly triumph as 'sibæðelingas' ('related princes' 2708a): they destroy the dragon through mutually exerting the attributes they share by inheritance. When Wiglaf directed the blow that weakened the dragon 'sio hand gebarn // modiges mannes, / þær he his mæges healp' ('the hand of the brave man was badly burned as he helped his kinsman' 2697b–8). The alliterative link between 'modiges' ('mannes') and 'mæges'

(2698a–b) twins the courage and the kinship. The binary structure of the verse formalizes this thematic association.

The less oral and the more written Old English poetry became with increasing Christianization – in other words, the less a poem was thought of as an event and the more it became a text (*Beowulf*, I believe, lies somewhere in between)[14] – the less organic the traditional socio-cultural expressions became. More and more they were applied to imported, manuscript-based stories. They became a sort of poeticizing discourse, a kind of rhetoric. Their function as society's tokens of its own antecedents, as its means of self-renewal, was compromised: they could no longer fulfill their raison d'être. Increasingly they came to serve the concepts of a universal church.

Poets trained in the ways of Latin rhetoric prised the closed system of poetry apart. They abstracted the binary structure and made it an instrument of two-part thought. They made punchy patterns out of it, as when Cynewulf, in his poem on the Ascension, sets out every man's choice between heaven and hell:

> swa helle hienþu   swa heofones mærþu,
> swa þæt leohte leoht   swa ða laþan niht,
> swa þrymmes þræce   swa þystra wræce,
> swa mid dryhten dream   swa mid deoflum hream,
> swa wite mid wraþum   swa wuldor mid arum,
> swa lif swa deað

> either the humiliation of hell   or the glory of heaven,
> either the radiant light   or the loathsome night,
> either the throng of glory   or the misery of darkness,
> either joy with the Lord   or clamour with devils,
> either punishment with enemies   or glory with angels,
> either life or death.   (*Christ II* 591–6a)[15]

The rhymed pairs of phrases form the referential pattern hell/heaven, / heaven/hell, heaven/hell, heaven/hell, / hell/heaven, clinched by the concluding, summarizing, terse 'swa lif swa deað.' Or rhetorician-poets mounted elaborate figures, as when Christ says to the sinner on the Day of Judgment in the course of a long speech of reproach and condemnation:

> Ic wæs on worulde wædla   þæt ðu wurde welig in heofonum,

earm ic wæs on eðle þinum   þæt þu wurde eadig on minum

I was poor in the world   that you might become rich in heaven,
I was wretched in your country   that you might become fortunate in
mine.   (*Christ III* 1495-6)[16]

The contrast between unhappiness and happiness, between the 'patria'
of earth and that of heaven and between 'I' and 'you' offers more scope
for interrelationships than does Cynewulf's one-for-one antithesis. Set
out plainly twice in parallel two-member sentences conforming to the
structure of the verse, the distinctions in *Christ III* rely on expressive
form: the central opposition between wretchedness and bliss is firmly
stated in two alliterative word-pairs, 'wædla'/'welig' and 'earm'/'eadig,'
linked to each other by rhyme; chiastic word-order marks the association
between condition and place in the first statement, 'on worulde wædla'/
'welig in heofonum,' and the connection between condition and person
in the second, 'earm ic wæs'/'þæt þu wurde eadig'; inverted word-order
goes with unhappiness and normal word-order with happiness. Christ's
love is explicitly unselfish; the formality of its utterance corresponds to
its calculated operation and to the implication that it has been rejected.
Emotion and intellect combine impressively. Whether straightforwardly
as in Cynewulf's case or subtly as here, the binary verse was made to
externalize a schematic antithesis. It had become a framework for abstract
thought. Much as vernacular poetry had to offer the expression of
Christian spirituality, the future inevitably lay with prose.
    Ælfric, gifted late Old English writer of prose that he was, well
understood the inheritance he received when, as I believe, he adapted
the binary structure of poetry to his prose purposes. Take, for instance,
his description of Christ enthroned on the Day of Judgment in his sermon
In Octavis Pentecosten:

Þonne sitt se Hælend   on his heofonlican ðrymsetle,
mihtig and wuldorful,   and milde þam godum,
egeslic and andrysne   þam earmum synfullum,
and ealle men geseoð   swutollice þone Hælend
on ðære menniscnysse,   ac ne moton swaðeah
ða earman synfullan   geseon his godcundnysse;
ða godan ana   geseoð þa godcundnysse

Then the Saviour will sit   on his heavenly throne,

mighty and glorious,   and gentle to the good,
terrible and dreadful   to the wretched and sinful,
and all men will see   clearly the Saviour
in his humanity,   but yet the wretched sinful
will not be able   to see his divinity;
the good alone   will see the divinity.[17]

The first three pairs of two-accent phrases concern Christ's appearance outwards and the remaining four pairs humanity's returning vision of him. There is an emanation and a reaction. But the description is not pictorial; the process is an interaction of four attributes – divinity and humanity in Christ, goodness and sinfulness in men – and the words made prominent by alliteration in the rhythmical structure of the prose plot the interaction of these attributes. First, divinity and humanity are blended in Christ: 'Hælend' and 'heofonlican' chime together. But goodness and badness in men separate Christ's divinity from his humanity: the final, enduring coupling is between 'godan' and 'godcundnysse.' Ælfric, trained to analyse, realized that the binary principle of verse had an artistic potential for two-element thought in religious prose. In this new environment binary structure became a means of architecting regularity over a whole topic. Balance and proportion in expression could be made to corroborate analogies and contrasts in a planned sequence of thought and could thus accord aesthetically with general principles of universal validity. With this shift Old English literature had become absorbed into the Christian Middle Ages. Harmonized with the divine order at the centre of all life,[18] vernacular language now serviced a world-wide religious symbolism, prose-based and intellectually conceived. It had outgrown its pre-Christian seed-bed. The transition was complete from the poetry that was the cultural organism of an aristocratic warrior society.

NOTES

1 This study was read at the first meeting of the International Society of Anglo-Saxonists at Brussels in August 1983, a society in whose formation Stanley Greenfield played a central part. I dedicate its publication to him with affection and respect. I owe much to his friendship and to the steady illumination of his writings on Old English poetry.

2 *Anglia* 86 (1968) 14–58

3 *Felix's Life of Saint Guthlac* ed Bertram Colgrave (Cambridge 1956) x

4 'Names' 46

5 'Names' 53-7

6 My quotations of *Beowulf* are from *Beowulf and The Fight at Finnsburg* ed Fr. Klaeber, 3rd ed with supplement (Boston 1941).

7 Cf Robinson 'Names' 56n

8 'Names' 14

9 *The Anglo-Saxon Minor Poems* ed Elliott van Kirk Dobbie, ASPR 6 (New York 1942) 56

10 *Minor Poems* ed Dobbie 56

11 Milman Parry 'Studies in the Epic Technique of Oral Verse-Making. I: Homer and Homeric Style' repr in *The Making of Homeric Verse: The Collected Papers of Milman Parry* ed Adam Parry (Oxford 1971) 272.

12 Ms 'syn-'; 'scyn-' first proposed by C.W.M. Grein in his edition *Beovulf nebst den Fragmenten Finnsburg und Valdere* (Cassel and Göttingen 1867)

13 Translating with Ritchie Girvan, rev of Johannes Hoops *Beowulfstudien MLR* 28 (1933) 246

14 Cf Peter Clemoes 'Style as the Criterion for Dating the Composition of *Beowulf*' in *The Dating of 'Beowulf'* ed Colin Chase (Toronto 1981) 179-80

15 *The Exeter Book* ed George Philip Krapp and Elliott van Kirk Dobbie ASPR 3 (New York 1936) 19

16 *Exeter Book* ed Krapp and Dobbie

17 *Homilies of Ælfric: A Supplementary Collection* ed John C. Pope, 2 vols EETS 259-60 (London 1967-8) 1: 434; no 11 lines 347-53

18 See my inaugural lecture *Rhythm and Cosmic Order in Old English Christian Literature* (Cambridge 1970) esp 16-21 (Ælfric) and 21-3 (Wulfstan).

GEORGE HARDIN BROWN

Old English Verse as a Medium for Christian Theology

EVEN TODAY some readers who come to the overtly Christian poems in the Anglo-Saxon Poetic Records typically regard those poems as weakened and diluted mutations of earlier heroic pagan verses. Reacting with the same humanistic distaste that classicists often display for Christian Latin poetry, these readers by deploring the historic evolution of the poetry and fruitlessly searching for an 'urgermanischen Geist' fail to appreciate the beauty of the actual poetry.[1] Other readers, long and perhaps overly familiar with the tenets of Christian dogma, simply accept the appearance of Christian doctrine in the Old English poems as commonplace and conventional, or they leave the poem and an analysis of its inherent merits too soon in order to discover its biblical and patristic sources. Some others, with good will, simply do not see that the Christian Old English poems are as good as the secular ones. For all these and others, I would urge that we take a fresh look at the best Old English Christian poetry with an eye to how the poets express, incorporate and assimilate the religious matter. We can then perceive better the qualities of its composite art. The poem *Christ I, The Advent Lyrics*, provides an ideal subject for such a study, for, as Professor Greenfield noted years ago, '*Christ I*, clearly, shows a beautiful confluence of Christian doctrine and feeling and Old English poetic feeling and tradition.'[2] In fact, in *Christ I*, it is marvellous, even miraculous, how extraordinarily apt the Old English poetic lines are in expressing some of the most difficult and paradoxical Judaeo-Christian religious tenets.

The term 'miraculous' to describe this phenomenon would not be metaphoric or hyperbolic for the Old English poetic creator. He would share the prevalent early medieval view, propounded by Augustine in a number of his universally admired works, that a miracle is a wonderful manifestation of God's providence, not contrary to but part of nature in God's deep and mysterious design.[3] In Bede's account, Cædmon's gift of singing in 'verses which he had never heard before in praise of God the Creator' is a miracle because God wonderfully articulated what he already had imbued in Cædmon's nature and prepared for in his Anglo-Saxon monastic surrounding.[4] This miracle is akin to the signs and wonders of the Old and New Testaments that reveal God's care for his needy people at the opportune time, by supplying them with a physical gift, such as food, that symbolizes a spiritual strengthening as well. God's gift of religious song to Cædmon meant that the food of spiritual life needed to sustain the young Anglo-Saxon church with its monastic communities would not remain entirely a foreign Continental Latin commodity, unpalatable to and undigestible by the English masses. The power of the native poetry from the pagan heroic past with its enormous hold on the Anglo-Saxon spirit was miraculously redirected into a new spiritual life. Through a divine emissary, the bashful shepherd Cædmon received a power of expression like that given to the reticent Jeremiah, who cried out in his weakness, 'Ah, Lord God! Behold, I do not know how to speak, for I am only a youth,' to which the Lord responded, 'Behold, I have put my words in your mouth' (Jeremiah 1:6,9). Just as Isaiah, Jeremiah, Joel, and Amos couched their prophetic messages in traditional Hebrew verse form, the transformed Cædmon displayed great poetic talent in translating God's message into traditional Old English verse for the needs of the Anglo-Saxon church. Bede and his contemporaries, like the ancient Israelites, perceived God as dispensing his gifts through nature and man's art, and believed that the divine 'afflatus' inspires the already prepared receptor. A brief excerpt of Bede's account, familiar though it is, furnishes important data for consideration here:

After ruminating over [the sacred scripture, Cædmon] turned it into the most melodious verse: and it sounded so sweet as he recited it that his teachers became in turn his audience. He sang about the creation of the world, the origin of the human race, and the whole history of Genesis, of the departure of Israel from Egypt and the entry into the promised land and many other of the stories taken from the sacred Scriptures: of the incarnation, passion, and resurrection of the Lord, of his ascension into heaven, of the coming of the Holy Spirit and the teaching of the apostles. He also made songs about the terrors of future judgment, the horrors of the pains of hell, and the joys of the heavenly kingdom. In addition he composed many other songs about the divine mercies and judgments, in all of which he sought to turn his hearers away from delight in sin and arouse in them the love and practice of good works.[5]

This catalogue of Cædmon's works covers the biblical and catechetical essentials for instruction in the Christian faith, made available to the Anglo-Saxon audience in assimilable form. Thereby, the reluctant cowherd, late-blooming scholar, quickly amassed an impressive bibliography. Apparently none of his original songs survives, except for the little *Hymn* found in the margins of a number of manuscripts of *The Ecclesiastical History*. Brief as it is, however, that *Hymn*, so extensively analysed and admired by Old English scholars such as Wrenn, Pope, and others, attests to Cædmon's great art.[6]

Contained within this narrative of divine inspiration lies a natural wonder. For just as the prophecies and psalms are beautifully expressed in the poetic medium of ancient Near Eastern verse forms, so Cædmon, as the first of a noble line of poets to which Cynewulf belongs, expressed the Judaeo-Christian message in the naturally appropriate Germanic medium. Old English verse itself demonstrates a special native potency particularly suited to expressing the Christian doctrine. A major aspect of Cædmon's miraculous act consisted of bringing together a religion and a medium eminently suited for one another. Quite properly modern scholars explore Bede's narrative about Cædmon to discover something about oral formulaic composition, and to analyse Cædmon's *Hymn* for its typical versification. We can also examine the account and the *Hymn* for what it tells us of the assimilative process of Christian doctrine into a Germanic milieu.

The creed of Christian faith consists of paradox and an astounding resolution of opposites. It holds that the incomprehensible, transcendent, spiritual, eternally blissful God beyond history became flesh as an historical, mortal, affective, touchable, agonized man. It claims the Son preexisted his own creation and his mother. This woman is a virgin before and after being a mother, simultaneously the humble Galilean handmaid and the empress queen of the universe. Mankind, for whom the God-man dies, is a creature of God but he is likewise His enemy. Man is vicious and depraved but worthy of the sacrificial death of the Son of God; he is a disobedient, worthless servant but an adopted son and co-heir with Christ, sharing his Body. Man is a wandering exile in earth's vale of tears; he is a secure citizen in the New Jerusalem. The Church is ruled by the Holy Spirit; the Church is ruled by all too fallible

men. The Christian faith affirms these and many more naturally irre-
solvable antitheses.

Germanic verse possesses the extraordinary qualities to set forth these
tenets in a manner that no other culture can match. It can do so on
account of its own nature and basic structure. The Old English bipartite
line, with its two stressed syllables in each half of the line, sets up an
intrinsic opposition that is emphasized by the caesura but resolved by
the linking alliteration. Thus each line or combination of half-lines can
yoke both similar and disparate elements, especially by the alliterative
binding of the stressed syllables. For example, in Cædmon's *Hymn* we
find the felicitous combinations, 'Meotudes meahte / ond his modeðanc,'
with God's power and intention conjoined (line 2), and 'firum foldan,
/ Frea ælmihtig,' in which the omnipotent God is poetically united with
his world created for man (line 9). Moreover, Old English verse not only
possesses the common poetic qualities of enumeration and variation,
imagistic and figurative language, it also vaunts a diction of multiple
and augmentative statement, misleadingly termed 'synonymous.' Arthur
Brodeur's first two chapters in *The Art of Beowulf* give us a sensitive
analysis of this variation and diction in *Beowulf*. A similar analysis might
be made for the best of Old English religious verse. This would serve
to counter the many insensitive and deceptive statements made about
Old English verse, such as Colgrave's remark, in a note on Cædmon's
Hymn, that variation is 'a favourite device in which the same idea is
repeated in different words.'[7] This categorizes variation as a repetitious
filler instead of the rich, complex, nuanced poetic device it is in the
hands of a true 'scop.' To draw an analogy from another ancient verse
form to make my point: James Kugel in his recent provocative study,
The Idea of Biblical Poetry, has demonstrated that Hebrew verse is not
really composed of synonymous parallelism, as it has been understood
since Bishop Robert Lowth's classic eighteenth-century definition of
Hebrew poetry as 'parallelismus membrorum'; rather, the second half
of the two-part verse adds a further emphasis and point. The set should
be considered in terms of 'A is so, and what's more, B.' That is, the second,
B, element of a verse such as 'By day the Lord sends forth his love /
and by night his song is with me' is augmentative, retrospective (looking
back to A), and prospective (looking beyond it).[8] In its own way, Old
English variation serves the same function, not of synonymous repetition,
but of supplementation and refinement, of emphasis and point.

Using as evidence principally the first two Advent Lyrics in *Christ
I* with some reference to verses in some of the other ten, I now want

to demonstrate how Old English verse with these marvellous attributes can serve as a splendid medium for the expression and precision of Christian dogma. Of the first lyric, only sixteen and a half lines remain of a probable thirty or so, because of the damaged condition of *The Exeter Book* manuscript.

cyninge.
Ðu eart se weallstan   þe ða wyrhtan iu
wiðwurpon to weorce.   Wel þe geriseð
þæt þu heafod sie   healle mærre,
ond gesomnige   side weallas   5
fæste gefoge,   flint unbræcne,
þæt geond eorðb[yr]g eall   eagna gesihþe
wundrien to worlde   wuldres ealdor.
Gesweotula nu þurh searocræft   þin sylfes weorc,
soðfæst, sigorbeorht,   ond sona forlæt   10
weall wið wealle.   Nu is þam weorce þearf
þæt se cræftga cume   ond se cyning sylfa,
ond þonne gebete,   nu gebrosnad is,
hus under hrofe.   He þæt hra gescop,
leomo læmena;   nu sceal liffrea   15
þone wergan heap   wraþum ahreddan,
earme from egsan,   swa he oft dyde.

...to the King.
You are the wall-stone which the workmen of old
rejected from the work. Indeed it is fitting
that you be the head of the great hall,
and draw together the vast walls,
the unbroken flint, with a firm joining,
in order that throughout earth's cities all things
        with the gift of sight
may wonder eternally, O Lord of Glory.
Reveal now by your mysterious skill your own work,
O true and victorious One, and then leave standing
wall against wall. Now for your works there is need
that the Maker come, the King himself,
and thereupon repair – it is now decayed –
the house under its roof. He created the body,
the limbs of clay. Now must the Lord

save this weary multitude from wrath,
the wretched ones from terror, as He has often done.[9]

The lyric aptly commences, even in its fragmented state, with 'cyninge,' 'to the King.'[10] The first complete phrase of the poem, 'Ðu eart se weallstan/ þe ða wyrhtan iu // wiðwurpon to weorce,' furnishes a good example of the bound juxtaposition of opposites that Old English verse excels in, put to the service of Christian paradox. The poet sets up a tension between the nouns 'weallstan,' the cornerstone, and the 'wyrhtan,' the perverse workers who reject it, by placing them on each side of the caesura, tied by an alliteration on the stressed nouns, which is carried over into the next line by 'wiðwurpon to weorce,' 'rejected for the work.' The poet exploits the transferral not only with the same alliteration, but also with repetitions of certain key thematic words. Thus, he emphasizes the metaphor of construction throughout this lyric by his repetitions of some form of 'weorce': 'wyhrtan' (2), 'to weorce' (3), 'weorc' (9), 'þam weorce þearf' (11). He is also fond of unifying and echoing the individual sections by carrying over the same thematic words into the following section or sections. Thus, 'weorc' reappears in the fourth line of the next lyric (line 21 of *Christ I*) and 'cyning' in the twelfth line of this first lyric and first line of the second, 'þu riht cyning' (18), even though there is no Latin precedent for these nouns in the second antiphonal source, 'O clavis David.' In the first poem, in line 4, with 'heafod' the poet goes beyond the antiphon's 'lapis angularis,' 'weallstan,' to its referent in Psalm 118 (117 of the Vulgate), verse 22: 'The stone which the builders rejected has become the head of the corner' ('caput anguli,' a Hebraism). This verse was interpreted as Messianic by Mark (12:10) and Matthew (21:42) and quoted directly as applying to Christ in 1 Peter 2:7. 'Heafod' now becomes both the 'head stone' that joins the walls (5 and 6) and 'head of the illustrious house,' joined by alliterating *h*, and alluding to the 'domus Israel' of the antiphon.

In the second part of the fragment, lines 11b – 17, the builder, 'se cræftga,' who is the 'cyning sylfa' from line 1, is urged to come and repair, make good, 'gebete,' what has crumbled, 'gebrosnad is.' That word interestingly reappears in the fourth lyric negatively, 'no gebrosnad wearð,' to describe Mary's unsullied maidenhood (84b). In this second part of the first poem the author is surely alluding to the text from Amos 9:11-12, quoted in Acts 15:16 as a prophetic reference to the Saviour:

After this I will return,

and I will rebuild the dwelling of David, which has fallen; I will rebuild its ruins, and I will set it up.

A comparison of the Old English verse with the text in Amos (even in modern English translation, though more striking in Hebrew) affords a nice opportunity to note the similar and different verse techniques, each with its own merits and style of variation.

The metaphor of builder and artificer in the second part of the lyric allows the poet to speak of the Creator-Logos Christ in a way that echoes God's forming of man from clay in Genesis (2:7) – note the phrase in line 15, 'leomo læmena.' However, the 'liffrea' is also the restorer to life and freedom, who rescues 'þone wergan heap' from 'wraþum.'

In the first part of the second lyric the poet explores the semantic range inherent in the metaphor, 'O key of David':

O clavis David, et sceptrum domus Israel, qui aperis et nemo claudit; claudis et nemo aperit: veni et educ vinctum de domo carceris, sedentem in tenebris et umbra mortis.

O key of David, and sceptre of the House of Israel, who opens and no one closes; you close and no one opens: come and lead the bound captive, sitting in darkness and the shadow of death, from the house of prison.

His poetic exploitation of the theme runs as follows, in the damaged text recovered by Pope and discussed by Greenfield:[11]

Eala þu reccend	ond þu ryht cyning,	
se þe locan healdeð,	lif ontyneð	
eadgu[m], upwegas,	oþrum forwyrneð	20
wlitigan wilsiþes	gif his weorc ne deag,	
huru we for þearfe	þas word sprecað,	
ond myndgiað	þone þe mon gescop	
þæt he ne læte	to lose weorðan	
cearfulra þing,	þe we in carcerne	25
sittað sorgende,	sunnan wenað,	
hwonne us liffrea	leoht ontyne,	
weorðe ussum mode	to mundboran	
ond þæt tydre gewitt	tire bewinde,	
gedo usic þæs wyrðe,	þe he to wuldre forlet	30
þa we heanlice	hweorfan sceoldan	

on þis enge lond,   eðle bescyrede.
   Forþon secgan mæg,   se ðe soð spriceð,
þæt he ahredde,   þa forhwyfred wæs,
frumcyn fira.   Wæs seo fæmne geong,   35
mægð manes leas,   þe he him to meder geceas;
þæt wæs geworden   butan weres frigum,
þæt þurh bearnes gebyrd   bryd eacen wearð.
Nænig efenlic þam,   ær ne siþþan,
in worlde gewearð   wifes gearnung;   40
þæt degol wæs,   dryhtnes geryne.
Eal giofu gæstlic   grundsceat geondspreot;
þær wisna fela   wearð inlihted
lare longsume   þurh lifes fruman
þe ær under hoðman   biholen lægon,   45
witgena woðsong,   þa se waldend cwom,
se þe reorda gehwæs   ryne gemiclað
ðara þe geneahhe   noman scyppendes
þurh horscne had   hergan willað.

O thou ruler and thou just king, he that guards the locks, opens life, the heavenward ways, to the blessed one, to another denies the fair journey he desires if his work does not avail, verily we speak these words for need, and beg him who created man to be mindful lest he allow the condition of us anxious ones to come to ruin, of us who sit sorrowing, wait in hope of the sun, when the lord of life may disclose the light to us, become a protector to our spirit and envelop the feeble understanding with splendour, may make us thus worthy, whom he admitted to glory when we had had to turn away abjectly into this narrow land, bereft of home.

One may say – he who speaks truth –
that he rescued, when it was lost,
the race of men. The girl was young,
a virgin free of sin, she whom He chose for a mother.
It was accomplished without the love of a man
that the bride was magnified by the birth of a child.
Nothing approaching that, before or since,
no such merit of woman existed in the world.
Such a thing is miraculous, a mystery of God.
All spiritual gifts sprang up throughout the earth;
then many a shoot became illumined

by the Giver of Life, old knowledge
which formerly in dark soil lay planted,
the chants of the prophets, when the Ruler came,
he who enlarges the secret meaning of each speech
of those who fittingly, in a wise way,
will praise the name of the Creator.

As the key that controls existential locks, Christ can open and reveal life, 'life ontyneð' (19b).[12] The poet takes advantage of the wide meaning, both transitive and intransitive, of 'ontynan.' In line 27, we wait for the Sun of salvation, the 'liffrea,' 'to open up the light,' in the dark prison of our sin. The poet transfers the figure in the eighth lyric, where the Saviour is urged 'to unlock the golden gates, which in former days a long while ago stood locked, command them to be opened,' 'hat ontynan' (251-3). In this second lyric, 'sunnan wenað,' 'we yearn for the sun' (26), the poet leaves the obvious pun, 'sunna'/'sunu,' undeveloped; he saves that for the fifth lyric on Christ as the 'Oriens,' 'Earendel,' the radiant Beam of God.[13] There, especially in lines 106 to 114, he can make much of the pun that only Germanic allows: 'sunnan leoma' (106b), 'sunu soþan fæder' (110a),

Eala earendel,   engla beorhtast,
ofer middangeard   monnum sended,   105
ond soðfæsta   sunnan leoma,
torht ofer tunglas,   þu tida gehwane
of sylfum þe   symle inlihtes!
Swa þu, god of gode   gearo acenned,
sunu soþan fæder,   swegles in wuldre   110
butan anginne   æfre wære,
swa þec nu for þearfum   þin agen geweorc
bideð þurh byldo,   þæt þu þa beorhtan us
sunnan onsende,   ond þe sylf cymeþæt
ðu inleohte   þa þe longe ær   115
þrosme beþeahte   ond in þostrum her,
sæton sinneahtes;   synnum bifealdne
deorc deaþes sceadu   dreogan sceoldan.

O Radiance, brightest of angels
sent to men throughout the earth
and veritable splendour of the sun,

dazzling beyond the stars, you ever enlighten
of your self every era of time.
Since you, God of God, begotten of old,
son of the True Father in the glory of heaven
without beginning always existed,
so now your own works in dire need
ask confidently that you send us
the bright sun, and come yourself
that you may illumine those who long before,
covered with darkness and obscurity here,
have sat in continual night; enshrouded in sin
we had to endure the dark shadow of death.

So Emmanuel, 'God with us,' as 'sunna' without 'synnum' shines on those who had sat 'sinneahtes synnum befealdne.' Here paronomasia is put to the task of expressing Christian mystery, and alliteration unites the natures of Christ into one person, 'meotudes bearn / ond se monnes sunu.'[14]

Back in the second lyric, line 29, the Sun/Son is called upon 'to envelop ['bewinde'] the weak spirit with glory, 'tydre gewitt' with 'tire,' instead of with the chains of captivity. Next the poet introduces the theme of man's spiritual exile, a pervasive archetectonic theme 'that harmonizes the separate lyrics of the poem,' as Professor Greenfield magisterially demonstrated in an article over thirty years ago.[15] Note that in introducing this theme, the poet again uses the alliterative line for considerable effect: 'to þis enge lond, / eðle bescyrede' (32). The Lord has by his heroic leap into the world rescued the exile wandering in gloom. The poet turns to the means by which this saving Word came into our world and was made flesh: Mary. The richly complex lines 35b-38 exemplify well the facility Old English verse possesses to express Christian mystery. The young woman is 'mægð' ('maiden') and 'meder' ('mother'), conjoined by miracle and poetic structure. The virgin is 'manes leas,' without sin and spot, but she is also by implied pun, 'mannes leas,' without a man, varied in line 37b as 'butan weres frigum.'[16] We are told 'þæt þurh bearnes gebyrd / bryd eacen wearð,' 'that through the birth of the Child the bride became great.' A nice slant pun is effected by 'byrd'/'bryd,' held together by stress and alliteration, but the bolder word play lies in 'eacen,' which means 'great,' 'magnified,' 'endowed,' 'full' – as in 'full of grace' – but also 'pregnant.' The clever poet plays out this paradox by repeating it with interesting variation in the fourth lyric, lines 71a, 74–77:

Eala wifa wynn . . .
arece us þæt geryne   þæt þe of roderum cwom,
hu þu eacnunge   æfre onfenge   75
bearnes þurh bebyrde,   ond þone gebedscipe
æfter monwisan   mod ne cuðes.

O joy of women . . .
explain to us the mystery that came to you from the skies,
how you ever received a magnification
by the birth of a child, and intercourse
according to human notions never knew.

The other lyrics proffer many more examples of the way in which Old English verse serves Christian mystery. Three explores the allegorical reality of the heavenly Jerusalem – that favourite medieval exegetical theme.[17] Four and nine are dedicated to further treatment of the Virgin, and seven is the confrontation of Joseph with the pregnant Mary. The rest appeal to Christ the Savior. However, ten and eleven form a climax with particular stress on Christ as emanation of the Godhead and Second Person of the Trinity. Twelve serves as a final reflection on the meaning and obligation of the Incarnation for mankind now, and the promise of future eternal life with the 'hælend sylfa' (435). In all these parts, the Old English verse rises to the challenge and discloses mystery with art.

In recent years respected Old English scholars, well versed in patristic lore, such as J.E. Cross, Roger Lass, and Thomas Hill, have enlightened us about this poet's sophisticated use of sources in Scripture, liturgy, and the Fathers. Others, like Jackson Campbell and particularly Stanley Greenfield, have called attention to the qualities of structure and thematic development. What I have tried to do here is to present *Christ I* as an example of the special aptitude of Old English verse in the hands of a first-rate poet to express some of the most complex religious mysteries of the Creed. In a more extended treatment, I could demonstrate how other great Old English religious poems similarly use the native prosody to express Christian paradox: the *Dream of the Rood*, to cite an obvious example, unites the cross as the glorious 'sigebeam' with the sinner-narrator as 'synnum fah' (13); Christ is at once hypostatically and metrically the 'geong haeleþ' and 'God ælmihtig' (39); and the 'rod' is eternally joined to the 'ricen cyning' (44). Old English poetic structure itself in the hands of a gifted 'scop' is remarkably suited to representing

Christian mysteries in their beauty and paradox. There is good reason, inherent in the nature of the verse, why Old English poets, following the example of Cædmon, could sing the praise of the Creator so well, turning Scriptural texts 'into the most melodious verse.'

NOTES

1 In the Introduction to his important monograph, *The Search for Anglo-Saxon Paganism* (Cambridge 1975), E.G. Stanley remarks that 'a good number of books and articles, the vast majority, emphasize the fundamentally Christian nature of Old English literature as it is known to us ...' (ix). Nonetheless, the attitudes described in the text of his book remain widespread.

2 Stanley B. Greenfield *A Critical History of Old English Literature* (New York 1965) 128

3 For a summary of Augustine's doctrine on miracles with citations to the major texts, see Benedicta Ward *Miracles and the Medieval Mind* (Philadelphia 1982) 2-4.

4 See Bede, *Ecclesiastical History of the English People* ed Bertram Colgrave and R.A.B. Mynors (Oxford 1969) bk IV ch 24, 414-21.

5 Bede *EH* 419

6 See C.L. Wrenn 'The Poetry of Cædmon,' *PBA* 22 (1946) 277-95, rpt in *Essential Articles for the Study of Old English Poetry* ed Jess B. Bessinger, Jr, and Stanley J. Kahrl (Hamden 1968) 407-27; F.P. Magoun, Jr 'Bede's Story of Cædmon: The Case History of an Anglo-Saxon Oral Singer' *Speculum* 30 (1955) 49-63; Bernard F. Huppé *Doctrine and Poetry: Augustine's Influence on Old English Poetry* (New York 1959) 99-130, rpt in *Old English Literature: Twenty-two Analytical Essays* (Lincoln, Nebraska 1968) 117-38; Jeff Opland *Anglo-Saxon Oral Poetry* (New Haven 1980) 106-29; John C. Pope, ed *Seven Old English Poems*, 2nd ed (New York 1981) 45-53.

7 Bede *EH* 417 n 2

8 James L. Kugel *The Idea of Biblical Poetry: Parallelism and Its History* (New Haven 1981) ch 1. See also Joze Krasovec *Antithetic Structure in Biblical Hebrew Poetry*, Vetus Testamentum, Supplement 35 (Leiden 1984).

9 In this essay most of the Old English text is from *Christ I* of *The Exeter Book* ed George Philip Krapp and Elliott Van Kirk Dobbie, ASPR 3 (New York 1936) 1-15. However, I have substituted the recovered or plausible readings by John C. Pope in 'The text of the damaged passage in the Exeter Book: Advent (*Christ I*) 18-32' *ASE* 9 (1981) 137-56. In the main, the translation is that of Jackson J. Campbell in his edition of *The Advent Lyrics of the Exeter Book* (Princeton 1959), except that for lines 18-32 I have substituted

Professor Pope's translation in the article just cited. I have benefited from the notes in both Cook's and Campbell's editions as well as from Campbell's article, 'Structural Patterns in the Old English Advent Lyrics' *ELH* 23 (1956) 239-55, and from Robert Burlin's study, *The Old English Advent* (New Haven 1968). Edward Burgert provided and discussed the Latin O Antiphons that serve as bases for the Old English Advent Lyrics, in *The Dependence of Part I of Cynewulf's Christ upon the Antiphonary* (Washington, DC 1921), except for Lyric 10, suggested by Simon Tugwell, 'Advent Lyrics 348-77 (Lyric x)' *MÆ* 39 (1970) 34.

10 As Roberta Frank called to my attention when we were graduate students, the opening words of a number of Old English acephalous poetic fragments seem curiously appropriate in a similar way: the tragic *Battle of Maldon* begins with the ominous 'brocen wurde,' 'were crushed (or broken)' and *The Finnsburh Fragment* starts with the destructive 'nas byrnað,' 'are burning.'

11 Pope 155-6; Stanley B. Greenfield '*Þancword* for John C. Pope: *Advent* Lyric II Again' *MP* 83 (1985) 166-8. Professor Greenfield's suggestion to emend 'þas word sprecaþ,' line 22b, to 'þancword sprecaþ' is very attractive, since it gives excellent meaning to the passage, is metrically preferable, and has a formulaic precedent in *Widsið*, line 137; apparently a reader of the manuscript also found difficulty with the line and inserted an 'n' (or 'r') above the 'a' of 'þas.' However, since the reading as it stands makes sense, I have left it unemended.

12 On Christ as the divine key, see Greenfield 'Of Locks and Keys – Line 19a of the O.E. *Christ*' *MLN* 67 (1952) 238-40.

13 For the anti-Arian theological significance of the 'Eala Earendel,' see J.E. Cross 'The "Coeternal Beam" in the O.E. *Advent Poem (Christ I)* ll. 104-129' *Neophil* 48 (1964) 72-81.

14 For the Old English poetic use of sacred wordplay, see Roberta Frank 'Wordplay in Old English Poetry' diss Harvard University 1968, esp ch 1, and 'Some Uses of Paronomasia in Old English Scriptural Verse' *Speculum* 47 (1972) 207-26, and the bibliography cited therein, esp Fred C. Robinson 'The Significance of Names in Old English Literature' *Anglia* 86 (1968) 14-58.

15 Greenfield 'The Theme of Spiritual Exile in *Christ I*' *PQ* 32 (1953) 321-7

16 In this, the Old English poet anticipates the Middle English lyric, 'I syng of a myden þat is makeless,' *Religious Lyrics of the XVth Century* ed Carleton Brown (Oxford 1939) #81, where 'makeless' means 'sinless,' 'without mate,' and 'matchless.'

17 See J.E. Cross '*Halga Hyht* and Poetic Stimulus in *The Advent Poem (Christ I)*, 50-70' *Neophil* 53 (1969) 194-9. A reinforcement to Professor Cross's contention that the poet identifies 'Hierusalem' with 'Sion' may be the pun

'Sioh nu' (59) for 'Sion.' Frank points out other instances of wordplay on 'Sion' and 'seon'/'sion,' 'to see,' in *Exodus* and *Christ III*, in 'Paronomasia in Old English' 217-18.

HELMUT GNEUSS

King Alfred and the History
of Anglo-Saxon Libraries

KING ALFRED'S 'Preface' to his translation of Gregory the Great's *Cura
Pastoralis*, written in the form of a letter to be sent with this translation,
well deserves the popularity it has gained among literary historians and
editors of anthologies, for it is one of the earliest texts in original Old
English prose and a specimen of the early West Saxon dialect preserved
in a manuscript of the period; it is, above all, the most important evidence
of King Alfred's educational policy and a key to our understanding of
the beginnings of English literary prose.[1]

As we know, Alfred reminds his readers in his 'Preface' of those happy
times long past, when the Anglo-Saxon kings commanded power and
respect, when religious life, learning, and scholarship flourished in
England. He contrasts this with the grim situation at the time of his
succeeding to the throne and finally explains how he means to promote
the education of both ecclesiastics and laymen. Alfred also considers the
developments which have resulted in the lamentable decline of Anglo-
Saxon culture, but this is just what is often overlooked or even mis-
interpreted in the commentaries on the 'Preface,' in spite of the importance
of what Alfred has to say and although the evidence of Alfred's letter
is now supported and confirmed by many historians.

Let me give just a few examples from anthologies which comment
on Alfred's 'Preface':[2]

The reference to the devastation wrought by the Danes and its effect on culture
is a valuable addition to what we learn from the *Chronicle*.

... the Preface ... with its references to the decay of culture during the conflict
with the Vikings ...

Largely responsible for the subsequent retardation of learning, the Danish incursions that began in 787 were, as it happened, directed against a people who had become preeminent for education and scholarship in Western Europe.

Alfred's decision to translate the medieval classics into English grew out of the ruin of the eighth-century English renaissance by the ninth-century Danish invasions.

The following quotations are from books and articles by literary historians:[3]

The decay of learning consequent upon Danish raids made it imperative that an attempt should be made to revive the education of the clergy.

Perhaps Alfred paints the picture in too dark colors, for the Church, after all, was alive and apparently in sound health throughout the ninth century. There is little doubt, however, that the Church in England had entered into a state of quiescence in its teaching and needed a good rousing.

Die Klosterbibliotheken seien [according to Alfred's 'Preface'] in der Missionszeit mühevoll aufgebaut worden. Jetzt stünden sie, soweit sie die Wikingerplünderungen überlebt hätten, leer, da die Mönche und Priester die Folianten nicht lesen könnten.

The decline of learning originated with destructive onslaughts by Danish pirates.

And finally from recent handbooks on the history of the English language:[4]

For nearly a century [ie before 871] attack had centred on the only places from which education could proceed.

The culture of the north of England in the seventh and eighth centuries was to spread over the entire country, despite the decline that it suffered as a result of the hammering onslaughts of the Danes.

A notable decay of monastic life had set in towards the end of the ninth century, as a result of prosperity under the king's rule.

It is clear that some of these statements differ considerably and even contradict each other. The majority of the writers – and many others

– however, explain the decline in learning which Alfred laments as a result of the Viking raids and invasions. But let me stress again that many commentators on the 'Preface' do not go into the question of what caused the loss of Latin learning and culture,[5] which is perfectly understandable, as they are mainly interested in Alfred's translations and his plans for the future.

Now let Alfred speak for himself:

Ða ic ða ðis eall gemunde, ða gemunde ic eac hu ic geseah, ær ðæm ðe hit eall forhergod wære ond forbærned, hu ða ciricean giond eall Angelcynn stodon maðma ond boca gefyldæ, ond eac micel mengeo Godes ðiowa; ond ða swiðe lytle fiorme ðara boca wiston, for ðæm ðe hie hiora nanwuht ongiotan ne meahton, for ðæm ðe hie næron on hiora agen geðiode awritene. Swelce hie cwæden: 'Ure ieldran, ða ðe ðas stowa ær hioldon, hie lufodon wisdom, ond ðurh ðone hie begeaton welan ond us læfdon. Her mon mæg giet gesion hiora swæð, ac we him ne cunnon æfter spyrigean. For ðæm we habbað nu ægðer forlæten ge ðone welan ge ðone wisdom, for ðæm ðe we noldon to ðæm spore mid ure mode onlutan.'[6]

Alfred, therefore, makes a specific reference to the lack of knowledge of Latin, 'ær ðæm ðe hit eall forhergod wære ond forbærned,' that is, *before* the destruction of the churches and monasteries by the Vikings. At that time, however, the books and libraries were still there, as he had seen himself, and this can, without doubt, only refer to the decade before the invasion by the 'great army,' the fifties and early sixties of the ninth century (Alfred was born in 848). This would mean that the Vikings were certainly responsible for the later destruction of the churches and libraries in many places throughout the country, but not for the obvious indications of a lack of religious learning and knowledge of Latin on the part of the clergy, apparently still quite strong in number, who were not, therefore, in a position to pass on such knowledge either. Alfred even sees the Scandinavian invasion as a divine retribution for the clergy having neglected its duties:

Geðenc hwelc witu us ða becomon for ðisse worulde, ða ða we hit nohwæðer ne selfe ne lufedon, ne eac oðrum monnum ne lefdon; ðone naman ænne we hæfdon ðætte we Cristne wæron, ond swiðe feawa ða ðeawas.[7]

Alfred's account of the situation is confirmed by the historical sources of the ninth century – of which, unfortunately, there are not many –

and historians today seem to have come to the conclusion that at least until the middle of the ninth century the Viking raids did not seriously endanger the existence and work of the Anglo-Saxon Church.[8] The entries in the *Anglo-Saxon Chronicle* refer to raids and attacks principally along the coast for the period from the late eighth to the middle of the ninth century, and even later it is not until after the invasion by the 'micel here' in 865 that large parts of the country are occupied. Admittedly, the *Chronicle* does not provide us with a complete record of all the Scandinavian activities in Anglo-Saxon England; we know, for example, rather more by chance, from other sources, of an attack in the area of the mouth of the Tyne in the year 800, of a possible threat to the Kentish coast in 804, of King Rædwulf of Northumbria's death while fighting the Vikings in 844 and of a Scandinavian settlement in the area of the Wrekin in Shropshire in 855.[9]

Until the arrival of the 'micel here,' however, the Anglo-Saxon kingdoms and the Anglo-Saxon Church were obviously not in any serious danger. The spectacular early attacks on Lindisfarne (793) and Jarrow (794) – both unprotected and in exposed positions – had understandably caused a stir among contemporaries, as can be seen from Alcuin's letters, which are still a subject of major interest for Archbishop Wulfstan at the beginning of the eleventh century.[10] But the existence and organization of the English Church were not endangered by these early attacks. The monks and their Bishop were able to return to Lindisfarne and only had to flee from there more than 80 years later (875).[11] The attack on Jarrow ended in a defeat for the Vikings.[12] There is proof that the monastery at Whitby – in an equally exposed coastal position as that of Lindisfarne and Jarrow – was still functioning around the middle of the ninth century.[13]

As far as there are reliable documents for the ninth century they confirm what Alfred reports in the 'Preface' – obviously from his personal knowledge of at least the southern part of the country. The great centres of religion and learning were not affected by Scandinavian attacks, at least until around 850. The letter from Lupus of Ferrières to Abbot Ealdsige of York (852) containing a request for several texts, some of them rare even then, is well known and has often been quoted.[14] Professor Brooks has established that only since the fifties of the century, after the storming of Canterbury by the Vikings (851), did the quality of the script and language of the charters written in Christ Church, Canterbury clearly deteriorate.[15] Nobody will wish to doubt the fact that the increasing political and military instability in the country would naturally make itself felt in church life, but this process will have to be ascribed mainly to the second half of the ninth century[16] and cannot be used as a satisfactory explanation for the decline in learning so lamented by Alfred, the origins of which should be looked for earlier.

There must, therefore, have been other reasons, whose detailed explanation and assessment should be left to the historian. Above all we have to consider the developments in the Anglo-Saxon monasteries and among the clergy in general in the century preceding the great Scandinavian invasions. The great centres of learning in the seventh and eighth centuries were the seats of the bishops and the monasteries in particular. The reformers of the tenth century were not the first to bear witness to the fact that the monastic houses increasingly lost the character of communities living according to a rule; Asser before them and Alcuin much earlier had said the same. The difficulties facing Alfred when he, in his turn, wanted to found monasteries are well known.[17] It seems clear, at any rate, that he considered only the bishops as possible outside helpers in his educational program; it was into their care that he gave his translation of the *Cura Pastoralis*. The question of whether Anglo-Saxon monks could not be recruited for his new foundations because of the prosperity in the country – as Asser sees it – or perhaps because everybody was concerned mainly with protecting his own life against the Vikings – as Asser and William of Malmesbury hint – remains open.[18]

There are, however, definite signs of the increasing decline of monastic discipline as early as the eighth century;[19] one such sign might even be found in the Old English *Guthlac* poems.[20] Alcuin's letters to the monks of Lindisfarne, Jarrow, and Wearmouth may well contain only the usual admonitions to what were, after all, communities whose behaviour was beyond reproach, but the complaint he voices in a letter to Abbot Ethelbald (of Jarrow and Wearmouth) can scarcely be interpreted as a mere topos:

Heu, frater, heu, quia poene ubique regularis uite in hac terra cadit normula et secularis uite crescit formula.[21]

The secularization of the Anglo-Saxon monasteries has probably to be seen in connection with their ownership and property. In early times they were obviously often 'Eigenklöster,' owned and controlled by a secular overlord who frequently had no compunctions about using them to his own advantage.[22] That this is true of the first half of the eighth century can be seen from the well-known letter by Bede to Archbishop Egbert of York[23] and from the Acts of the Council of Clofesho in 747 (section 5). An Act passed by another Council at the beginning of the ninth century expressly forbids the election of a layman as the head of a monastery.[24] The 'saecularium prioratus' is forbidden as late as about 970 by the Council of Winchester, which issued the *Regularis Concordia*, the reason given being that this practice had led in the past 'ad magni ruinam detrimenti.'[25]

In addition to this there are numerous instances of secular lords obviously illegally appropriating monasteries or monastic property in the eighth and ninth centuries. As early as the middle of the eighth century Boniface complains about this fact in letters to King Æthelbald of Mercia and to Archbishop Cuthberht of Canterbury, as does Pope Paul I in a letter to King Eadberht of Northumbria and Archbishop Egbert of York.[26] There is documentary proof of quarrels and litigation in connection with this practice in which kings, bishops, and even monasteries were involved in the late eighth and in the ninth centuries.[27] Even King Alfred is in a position simply to make over two monasteries to Asser – as a Christmas present, so to speak – with the comment that even greater gifts are to follow these two ('parva illa').[28] And finally, a reference in Æthelwold's so-called 'Historical Postcript' to his translation of the Benedictine Rule must be seen in the light of this malpractice:

þæs þe ic wene sio æfæstnes þæs halgan regules on ærum tidum gewanod wearþ þurh reaflac yfelra manna 7 þurh geþafunge þara cynenga þe to Gode lytelne ege hæfdon.[29]

As I mentioned before, however, we should leave it to the historian to judge the extent to which all this did, in fact, contribute to the decline of the monasteries and the decay of Anglo-Saxon culture. Let us now see what we know about books and libraries in ninth-century England, and whether this will confirm what we can gather from other sources about the development of the monasteries and the decline of learning. Great caution is, however, called for here: the difficulty and uncertainty in the dating of Old English texts and above all the loss of a large part of the holdings of the English medieval libraries make completely reliable and exact judgments impossible.

Assessment is particularly difficult in the case of those works and texts which originated in England. The situation seems fairly clear in the case of Anglo-Latin literature. Admittedly, it would be unrealistic to believe that the development and achievements of the late seventh and the eighth centuries – represented by the works of Aldhelm, Bede, Boniface, and Alcuin – must necessarily continue in the ninth century, but it seems striking that only one piece of poetry carries on the old tradition at the beginning of this century: early Anglo-Latin literature then ends with Æthelwulf's *De Abbatibus* and only at the end of the ninth century a new beginning is made by Asser – a Welshman.[30]

There is no reliable evidence of Old English prose having existed before King Alfred's time and therefore also in the ninth century. We have no reason to doubt what Cuthberht has to say in his 'Letter on the Death of Bede,' according to which Bede was working on translations of the gospel according to St John and of excerpts from Isidore's *De natura rerum* just before his death.[31] Nothing of this has been preserved, however, and there seems to be some doubt about whether these early Old English versions were more than rough drafts.

Professor Vleeskruyer has expressly supported the theory that there was an early tradition of Mercian prose; he speaks of the

accumulating evidence that a vigorous tradition of Mercian vernacular writing preceded his [Alfred's] work and, to a large extent, rendered it possible.[32]

But there is little evidence of such prose before Alfred's time. In his edition of the *Old English Martyrology*, Günter Kotzor has shown that there are indications that this text may have been written before the late ninth century;[33] apart from this there are only the charters and the laws, and in addition, early glossaries and interlinear glosses. Recently it has even been claimed that the laws were not written down before Alfred's day,[34] and we must not forget that Alfred's and Ine's collections have only been preserved in manuscripts written since the tenth century, while the early laws of the Kentish kings are recorded in a twelfth-century manuscript. Yet we shall have to give Bede more credence in this respect when he refers specifically to Æthelberht's laws as 'conscripta Anglorum sermone.'[35] Basically, however, the picture of Old English prose before Alfred's time has not changed in the last hundred years since Sweet's *Oldest English Texts* were published; except for the *Martyrology* there do not seem to have been any 'literary' texts.

Whereas there are scarcely any original Anglo-Latin works or Old English prose texts from the ninth century before Alfred's time, the situation may be entirely different as far as Old English poetry is concerned. Ever since Dr Sisam's lecture at the British Academy fifty years ago, Cynewulf's works have been generally accepted as dating from this period[36] while other poems, too – including *Beowulf* – have repeatedly been placed in the ninth century. I leave open the question of whether such works can be considered as proof of a continuation of the monastic culture and learning of the eighth century; I hardly need to mention the fact that by now we are well able to determine quite accurately the dialectal origin of Old English poetic texts,[37] but that there are still no absolutely safe criteria for dating them[38] with the exception of works such as Cædmon's *Hymn* or the *Battle of Maldon*, which can be associated with historical events.

My main argument in confirmation of what King Alfred has to say is not, however, based on original works of English literature but on what we know about libraries and the production of books in the ninth century. For I have come to the conclusion that the books to which Alfred refers as being still available in considerable numbers were for the most part written in the eighth century or even earlier, and that the production of books from the beginning of the ninth century until Alfred's time – ie mainly *before* the great Danish invasion – must be considered as fairly insignificant. The figures I am going to quote now should, of course, be regarded with due caution.[39] We must take into consideration the enormous losses of medieval English books; we must also remember that there may, in future, be modifications in the dating of some of the surviving early manuscripts. Nevertheless, it seems to me that the picture as a whole will not substantially change as a result of such re-dating, or as a result of the possible discovery of further manuscripts or fragments.

Almost one thousand extant manuscripts and manuscript fragments have been preserved which were written before the end of the eleventh century in Anglo-Saxon England or were in the possession of Anglo-Saxon libraries (this figure does not include documents on single sheets). As might be expected, the great majority of these manuscripts date from the tenth and eleventh centuries: some 250 from the beginning of the tenth to the turn of the century, and more than 500 from the eleventh century, of which more than 200, I might add, must be attributed to the late eleventh century, ie to the beginning of the Norman period. The large number of surviving books written since the tenth century can be explained by the fact that they had a better chance of survival compared with those written earlier, but also by the effects of the great Benedictine reform.

The number of earlier manuscripts which have been preserved is much smaller: for the period from the conversion to the turn of the ninth and tenth centuries there are slightly more than 200, of which 131 were written before the beginning of the ninth century, most of them, moreover, in the eighth century (only ten can be dated earlier with any degree of certainty). On the other hand, from the ninth century up till the beginning of the tenth century, there are 77 manuscripts preserved. These figures offer a basis for comparison, for the destruction of the churches, monasteries, and libraries referred to by Alfred must, necessarily, have affected books written in the eighth *and* in the ninth century in equal measure although, admittedly, some of the earlier manuscripts may have survived under more favourable conditions because they were taken to the continent in the course of the Anglo-Saxon mission.

The figure for the ninth century (77 extant manuscripts) seems to compare favourably with that for the earlier period (131). A closer look at the places of origin of the manuscripts produces quite a different picture, however. For whereas the manuscripts written in the eighth century and earlier almost all originated in England,[40] this is not the case with the manuscripts of the ninth century: more than 60 of them were written on the continent – mostly on French territory – and there is no proof of their having come to England before the tenth century. It seems safe to assume that most of them were imported during and after the Benedictine Reform in order to supply and restore the English monastic libraries and to serve as exemplars for copying.[41]

This leaves only very few manuscripts as evidence of Anglo-Saxon book production in the ninth century, namely sixteen, which can be said with any certainty to date from this period. Of these, however, six or seven belong to the period of King Alfred (some of them to his immediate circle),[42] including the Parker Chronicle, two manuscripts of the translation of the *Cura Pastoralis*, two fragments of the *Old English Martyrology*, and a copy of Aldhelm's *De laude virginitatis*. Thus only ten manuscripts remain[43] which can be considered as products of Anglo-Saxon scriptoria in the ninth century before Alfred, and even if we add those nine which, according to the paleographers, are datable at the turn of the eighth and ninth centuries[44] the resulting figure, compared with the book production of eighth-century England, and compared with several thousand surviving ninth-century manuscripts written on the continent, confirms beyond doubt what we learn from other sources about the secularization of the Anglo-Saxon monasteries and the decline of learning in the ninth century.[45]

What Alfred has to say in his 'Preface' is, therefore, also confirmed by the history of book production and libraries in the ninth century. We should, however, take care not to lapse into over-hasty generalizations about a period for which we have so few written records, all the more so as there is no contemporary historian writing in any detail about this period. Many questions must remain unanswered for the time being. But it seems significant that there is no indication of the existence in England of any of the important texts of the Carolingian reforms before Alfred's day and even in the early tenth century. Paul the Deacon's homiliary,[46] the Rule for Canons by Bishop Chrodegang of Metz,[47] the writings of Theodulf of Orleans, Smaragdus and Benedict of Aniane – to name but a few – can none of them, unless we are completely wrong, be proved as having been in England before the tenth century.[48]

It has been maintained repeatedly that the old Anglo-Saxon tradition of learning had survived at least in West Mercia, which was not affected by Scandinavian settlement.[49] This assertion is based, above all, on chapter 77 of Asser's biography of Alfred, in which four clergymen of Mercian origin are mentioned who taught Alfred and helped him with his plans for the revitalization of learning. There is, however, scarcely any proof in the history of English libraries that Mercia was playing this role in the ninth century, for neither the number of extant manuscripts nor their origins (as far as they are localizable) support this theory, although it has to be admitted that the translations of Gregory the Great's *Dialogues* (by Bishop Wærferth of Worcester) and of Bede's *Historia ecclesiastica* seem to have originated in Mercia.

The question of where the Latin originals for the translations made by Alfred and his circle came from is also of some importance. It can only be answered very unsatisfactorily, as there are still no comprehensive critical editions of some of these Latin texts. It is certain that the translator of Bede's *History* had an English manuscript at his disposal.[50] In her edition of the Old English Orosius, Professor Bately has shown that the translator may have used a manuscript of English or Irish origin.[51] There are no similar proofs yet for the other texts, but Professor Wittig was able to demonstrate recently the problems that are involved in the search for commentaries which were used in the translation work on *Boethius*. According to him it is perfectly possible that Alfred's circle had a knowledge of classical Latin authors, but this does not mean that the manuscripts they had at their disposal came from Anglo-Saxon libraries,[52] and even if all the exemplars used for the Alfredian translations were of English origin or provenance this would not tell us anything about learning and the knowledge of Latin among the Anglo-Saxons in the ninth century in general.

It would appear, then, that Alfred's 'Preface' is a reliable historical document; yet, finally, I should like to go into the question of whether there is a limit to the credibility of the King. Is his representation of conditions in England in the ninth century perhaps exaggerated after all? Can it be that the literary topos of the decline of learning and scholarship played a role in the writing of the 'Preface'? Is it even possible that Alfred is guilty of propaganda to help his cause?

Alfred's description of the situation at the time he succeeded to the kingdom does, indeed, seem to border on exaggeration:

Swæ clæne hio [ie lar] wæs oðfeallenu on Angelcynne ðæt swiðe feawa wæron behionan Humbre ðe hiora ðeninga cuðen understondan on Englisc oððe furðum an ærendgewrit of Lædene on Englisc areccean; ond ic wene ðætte noht monige begiondan Humbre næren. Swæ feawa hiora wæron ðæt ic furðum anne anlepne ne mæg geðencean be suðan Temese ða ða ic to rice feng.[53]

But we must bear in mind that this is a reference to the worst time of crisis for the West Saxon kingdom and that Ælfric also states in the preface to his Grammar that no English priest was able to write a letter in Latin before the reforms of Dunstan and Æthelwold.[54] We should hardly be justified in considering this merely an echo of Alfred's 'Preface,' and it is also hard to believe that the meaning of Alfred's words is only 'tonal or attitudinal, not factual,' as has been suggested recently.[55]

When Alfred refers to the Viking raids as divine retribution for the neglect of Christian duties and when he laments the decline of learning in England we may regard these remarks as literary topoi; we may also assume that the king came across instances of such topoi in his reading.[56] This should not, however, lead to a misunderstanding; neither of the topoi in his 'Preface' is considered by Alfred to be an empty formula or just a literary device. He laments, as in fact others before him had done, a process of decay which he himself has witnessed and is able to link this with the attacks and raids of the Vikings. There are numerous instances of similar complaints in Alcuin's work and in his case these occasionally look like a rhetorician's devices; that is certainly not the case with Alfred.

In recent times distinguished historians have repeatedly claimed that Alfred made propaganda for himself, for his political and military undertakings as well as for his educational reforms.[57] According to them, Alfred himself was responsible for compiling the *Anglo-Saxon Chronicle*, and in this work as well as in the 'Preface' to the *Cura Pastoralis* his achievements were exaggerated and glorified, as they were, too, in Asser's biography of the king. Professor Whitelock has countered these theories with convincing arguments,[58] and these arguments do not need to be repeated here. But let me add a few remarks on Alfred's 'Preface.'[59] The most important point is, beyond doubt, the fact that everything we know about the history of scholarship and education in England in the ninth century and about the ecclesiastical institutions which were involved in teaching is in complete accord with what Alfred, his contemporaries, and the succeeding generations have to tell us. It is difficult to see what Alfred could have gained from a tendentious representation of things in the 'Preface.' Let us remember in particular that his introductory letter was, after all, a personal letter to the Anglo-Saxon bishops. These men were, moreover, familiar with the conditions in their dioceses and beyond; they knew very well what the situation in the libraries was and what possibilities for teaching there were in their sees and in the former monasteries (as far as the latter still existed in some form or other) and they had been able to observe developments over the previous decades with their own eyes. Does it seem likely that the king would send to just such men a report which did not reflect the true situation and thus rob himself of his credibility?

Finally, let me offer a general thought for consideration: it is a well-known fact that modern ideas creep into the interpretation of medieval texts again and again, and the idea of political progaganda in Alfredian literature seems to me to be just such an instance. It presupposes that news and ideas should be spread as quickly and as widely as possible to influence and sway the reader or listener, and this is just what Professor Davis assumes in the case of the *Anglo-Saxon Chronicle*:

At a time when the East Anglians, Northumbrians and Mercians had all submitted to the Danes, and even one of his own ealdormen deserted him, it must have been a matter of life and death to persuade the West Saxons that their fate could be different since they had reason to hope for victory. That seems to have been the purpose of the Anglo-Saxon Chronicle.[60]

But how many Anglo-Saxons did the message of the *Chronicle* or the 'Preface' to the *Cura Pastoralis* actually reach in the late ninth century? In his well-known essay, Dr Sisam has shown us the problems that had to be overcome if Alfred only wanted to have ten copies of his translations made.[61] Would such copies (including those of the *Anglo-Saxon Chronicle*) in fact be available to a wide public once they had reached their destination? Were they not reserved for a small circle of readers, usually members of the clergy? This is, of course, true of Asser's biography, written in Latin, to an even greater extent than it is of the other works.

I should like to end my paper with a plea in favour of the credibility of Alfred's 'Preface.' I am convinced that Alfred adds and lends precision to our knowledge of the historical developments, of learning and literature, of libraries and book production in England in the ninth century. Let us hope that future editors of the 'Preface' will stress these facts more clearly in their commentaries, and that historians in the future will continue to consider Alfred's letter an important and reliable source of information.[62]

NOTES

1 For editions and pertinent books and articles, see Stanley B. Greenfield and Fred C. Robinson *A Bibliography of Publications on Old English Literature to the End of 1972* (Toronto 1980), esp 310-13, 316-17, and 26-32 for editions in collections. Early editions are listed by Francis P. Magoun, Jr 'King Alfred's Letter on Educational Policy According to the Cambridge Manuscripts' *MS* 11 (1949) 114-15. Articles not yet included in the Greenfield-Robinson Bibliography are: Bernard F. Huppé 'Alfred and Ælfric: A Study of Two Prefaces' in *The Old English Homily and Its Backgrounds* ed Paul E. Szarmach and Bernard F. Huppé (Albany, NY 1978) 119-37; T.A. Shippey 'Wealth and Wisdom in King Alfred's Preface to the Old English *Pastoral Care*' *EHR* 94 (1979) 346-55; Paul E. Szarmach 'The Meaning of Alfred's *Preface* to the *Pastoral Care*' *Mediaevalia* 6 (1982 for 1980) 57-86; P.R. Orton 'King Alfred's Prose *Preface* to the Old English *Pastoral Care*, ll. 30-41' *Peritia* 2 (1983) 140-8. All quotations from the Old English text of the 'Preface' are from the critical edition in *Sweet's Anglo-Saxon Reader in Prose and Verse* rev Dorothy Whitelock (Oxford 1967) 4-7 [cited as 'Preface'].

2 W.J. Sedgefield *An Anglo-Saxon Book of Verse and Prose* (Manchester 1928) 288; P.S. Ardern *First Readings in Old English* (Wellington, New Zealand 1951) 12; Robert J. Kispert *Old English: An Introduction* (New York 1971) 83; W.F. Bolton *An Old English Anthology* (London 1963) 29

3 P.G. Thomas 'Alfred and the Old English Prose of his Reign' in *The Cambridge History of English Literature*, ed A.W. Ward and A.R. Waller (Cambridge 1907) 1:91; G.K. Anderson *The Literature of the Anglo-Saxons* 2nd ed (Princeton 1966) 260; Herbert Pilch, Hildegard Tristram *Altenglische Literatur* (Heidelberg 1979) 155-6; Haldeen Braddy 'England and the English before Alfred' *Costerus* 7 (1973) 39

4 Barbara Strang *A History of English* (London 1970) 321; Thomas Pyles and John Algeo *The Origin and Development of the English Language* 3rd ed

(New York 1982) 134; A.C. Partridge *A Companion to Old and Middle English Studies* (London 1982) 99

5 This is even true of the detailed notes by Fr. Klaeber 'Zu König Alfreds Vorrede zu seiner Übersetzung der Cura Pastoralis' *Anglia* 47 (1923) 53-65, and Francis P. Magoun, Jr 'Some Notes on King Alfred's Circular Letter on Educational Policy Addressed to His Bishops' *MS* 10 (1948) 93-107. Notable exceptions are Bright's *Old English Grammar and Reader* ed Frederic G. Cassidy and Richard N. Ringler 3rd ed (New York 1971) 181, note to line 23 ff, where attention is clearly drawn to the problem, and Orton 'King Alfred's Prose Preface.' See also Michael Swanton *Anglo-Saxon Prose* (London 1975) xvi-xvii. T.A. Shippey's 'Wealth and Wisdom' (cp n 1) correctly outlines the sequence of periods and events as Alfred saw them, but it seems doubtful if Alfred meant to leave a gap of about 150 years between what Professor Shippey calls periods I (the end of the seventh century) and II (AD 855-65), and his article does not discuss what caused the loss of Latin learning in England. The best historical commentary to the 'Preface' is to be found in what is now the indispensable handbook for all Alfredian studies, *Alfred the Great: Asser's Life of King Alfred and Other Contemporary Sources*, translated with an introduction and notes by Simon Keynes and Michael Lapidge, Penguin Classics (Harmondsworth 1983) 294-6. Several monographs on Alfred and his literary and educational activities are at present in preparation.

6 'Preface' lines 30-41; cp the translation by Dorothy Whitelock in *English Historical Documents c. 500–1042* 2nd ed (London 1979) 818-19 [abbreviated from now on as *EHD*].

7 'Preface' lines 25-9; cp *EHD* 889.

8 See Dorothy Whitelock *EHD* 90-1; P.H. Sawyer *The Age of the Vikings* (London 1962) 19-20, 139-42; Eric John 'The King and the Monks in the Tenth-Century Reformation' in *Orbis Britanniae and other studies* (Leicester 1966) 154-80; D.J.V. Fisher *The Anglo-Saxon Age c. 400-1042* (London 1973) 201-7, and 'The Church in England between the Death of Bede and the Danish Invasions' *TRHS* 5th series 2 (1952) 1-19; see also N.P. Brooks 'England in the Ninth Century: The Crucible of Defeat' *TRHS* 5th series 29 (1979) 14.

9 See *EHD* 281-2 (Roger of Wendover's *Flores Historiarum* sa 800 and 844) for the incidents in Northumbria; *EHD* 514 no 82 (= no 160 in P.H. Sawyer *Anglo-Saxon Charters: An Annotated List and Bibliography* [London 1968]) for the threat to Kent; *EHD* 526-7, no 90 (= Sawyer, no 206) for the Wrekin settlement. I prefer, wherever possible, references to the translations in *EHD* because this book is easily accessible and has excellent, up-to-date introductions to each item, together with bibliographical notes.

10 See especially *EHD* 842-6, nos 193 and 194, Alcuin's letters no 16 and 20 in MGH *Epistolae* IV ed Ernst Dümmler (1895). See also *Two Alcuin Letter-Books* ed Colin Chase (Toronto 1975) 5-6.

11 See *EHD* 273, 277 (the *Historia Regum*, ascribed to Simeon of Durham, sa 793 and 875) and 875-6, no 214 (a letter by Ecgred, Bishop of Lindisfarne, written between 830 and 837). For a possible, temporary evacuation of Lindisfarne in the time of Bishop Ecgred (830–46), and for a thorough analysis of the various sources for the history of the community in the ninth century, see T.J. Brown 'The Lives of the Authors and the Later History of the MS' in *Evangeliorum Quattuor Codex Lindisfarnensis* ed T.D. Kendrick et al, 2 vols (Olten 1956-60) 2: 20-1.

12 See the Anglo-Saxon Chronicle, mss D and E for 794, and the note by Charles Plummer ed *Two of the Saxon Chronicles Parallel* (Oxford 1892-9) 2: 64. Professor Rosemary Cramp, however, considers the reference to the attack on Jarrow in 794 as dubious: 'Excavations at the Saxon Monastic Sites of Wearmouth and Jarrow, co. Durham: an interim report' *Medieval Archaeology* 13 (1969) 24.

13 *EHD* 90.

14 *EHD* 877-8, no 216. On the possible existence of a monastic community under an abbot at York see now Peter Godman ed Alcuin: *The Bishops, Kings and Saints of York* (Oxford 1982) 95-7, note on line 1218, and Michael Lapidge 'Booklists from Anglo-Saxon England' in *Learning and Literature in Anglo-Saxon England. Studies presented to Peter Clemoes on the occasion of his sixty-fifth birthday* ed Michael Lapidge and Helmut Gneuss (Cambridge 1985) 40n37.

15 Nicholas Brooks *The Early History of the Church of Canterbury: Christ Church from 597 to 1066* (Leicester 1984) 167-74, and 'England in the Ninth Century' 15. But see also F.M. Stenton *The Latin Charters of the Anglo-Saxon Period* (Oxford 1955) 41, for the 'decay of Kentish scholarship' evidenced in Canterbury charters of 825 and 839.

16 See Gillian Fellows Jensen 'The Vikings in England: a review' *ASE* 4 (1975) 204-5; Patrick Wormald 'The Ninth Century' in *The Anglo-Saxons* ed James Campbell (Ithaca, NY 1982) 132, 144-5; Brooks *The Early History of the Church of Canterbury* 150-1. Evidence for the effect of a Scandinavian raid earlier in the century is provided by the well-known inscription in the Codex Aureus, *EHD* 539-40, no 98, cp Brooks 151. Unfortunately, the early ninth-century provenance of the manuscript is uncertain. For paleographical reasons, the date of the inscription suggested by Professor Whitelock appears to be too late; see J.J.G. Alexander *Insular Manuscripts: 6th to the 9th Century* (London 1978) no 30.

17 See Dom David Knowles *The Monastic Order in England* 2nd ed (Cambridge 1963) 23-4, 31-6, 695.

18 Asser's *Life of King Alfred* ed W.H. Stevenson, with article on recent work by Dorothy Whitelock (Oxford 1959) 80-1, ch 93; William of Malmesbury *De Gestis Regum Anglorum* ed William Stubbs, Rolls Series 90 (London 1887) 1: 132-3

19 See Whitelock *EHD* 85-8, and especially the Acts of the Council of Clofesho, AD 747, sections 4, 7, 19 and 20, printed by Arthur W. Haddan and William Stubbs eds *Councils and Ecclesiastical Documents Relating to Great Britain and Ireland* 3 vols (Oxford 1871) 3: 360-76. See also the discussion in H.H. Glunz *History of the Vulgate in England* (Cambridge 1933) 55-63.

20 See Jane Roberts ed *The Guthlac Poems of the Exeter Book* (Oxford 1979) 145, note on lines 412 ff; but see also Cynthia E. Cornell 'Sources of the Old English Guthlac Poems' diss University of Missouri – Columbia 1976, 53-65, for an interpretation of this passage based on earlier literary traditions.

21 Dümmler, no 67; the quotation is taken from *Two Alcuin Letter-Books* ed Chase 23. Cp also Dümmler nos 19, 20, 21, 129, 230, all translated by Stephen Allott in *Alcuin of York: His Life and Letters* (York 1974). A letter by Alcuin to Cyneberht, Bishop of Winchester, even seems to anticipate Alfred's 'Preface': Dümmler, no 189 (Haddan and Stubbs 3: 482-3).

22 See Felix Liebermann *Die Gesetze der Angelsachsen* 3 vols (Halle 1903-16) 2: 539-40, 547-8, s vv 'Kirchenherr,' 'Kloster'; Heinrich Boehmer 'Das Eigenkirchentum in England' in *Texte und Forschungen zur englischen Kulturgeschichte. Festgabe für Felix Liebermann* (Halle 1921) esp 338; Knowles *The Monastic Order in England* esp chs 32-34; John *Orbis Britanniae* 154-80; H.R. Loyn *Anglo-Saxon England and the Norman Conquest* (London 1962) 247-8. For more recent views see Patrick Wormald 'Bede, *Beowulf*, and the Conversion of the Anglo-Saxon Aristocracy' in *Bede and Anglo-Saxon England. Papers in honour of the 1300th anniversary of the birth of Bede, given at Cornell University in 1973 and 1974* ed Robert T. Farrell, British Archeological Reports 46 (Oxford 1978) 52-4, and 'The Age of Bede and Aethelbald' in *The Anglo-Saxons* ed James Campbell 87-8; Brooks *The Early History of the Church of Canterbury* ch 9.

23 *EHD* 799-810, no 170

24 For the Synod of Clofesho held in 803, see Haddan and Stubbs 3: 545, and cp 3: 516.

25 *Regularis Concordia* ed Dom Thomas Symons (London 1953) 7

26 *Die Briefe des heiligen Bonifatius und Lullus* ed Michael Tangl MGH Epistolae selectae 1 (1916) nos 73 (= *EHD* 820, no 177) and 78; *EHD* 830-1, no 184.

But cp D.J.V. Fisher *The Anglo-Saxon Age* 171-2, and 'The Church in England' 8-9.

27 See *EHD* 505-7, no 77 (Sawyer no 1257); *EHD* 508-10, no 79 (Sawyer no 1258); *EHD* 516-7, no 84 (Sawyer no 1433); Haddan and Stubbs 3: 544-5 (Sawyer no 1431). See also Wormald 'The Ninth Century' 139.

28 Asser's *Life of King Alfred* ch 81, and Stevenson's notes 320-1. See also Keynes and Lapidge *Alfred the Great* 264n192.

29 'Eadgars Establishment of Monasteries' in *Leechdoms, Wortcunning and Starcraft of Early England* ed T.O. Cockayne, Rolls Series 35 (London 1864–6) 3:442; cp *EHD* 920-3, no 238, and *Councils and Synods with other Documents relating to the English Church I. A.D. 871-1204* ed D. Whitelock, M. Brett, and C.N.L. Brooke (Oxford 1981) 1:142-54.

30 Cp Michael Lapidge 'The Present State of Anglo-Latin Studies' in *Insular Latin Studies. Papers on Latin Texts and Manuscripts of the British Isles: 550-1066* ed Michael W. Herren (Toronto 1981) 54: 'The ninth is the darkest century in the record of Latin culture in England.' For Asser's 'barbarous Latin' see C.N.L. Brooke 'Historical Writing in England between 850 and 1150' *Settimane di studio del Centro italiano di studi sull' alto medioevo* 17 (1970) 232, and W.H. Stevenson's introduction to Asser's *Life of King Alfred* lxxxix–xciv.

31 Bede's *Ecclesiastical History of the English People* ed Bertram Colgrave and R.A.B. Mynors (Oxford 1969) 582

32 R. Vleeskruyer ed *The Life of St. Chad. An Old English Homily* (Amsterdam 1953) 41 and cp 40n4.

33 *Das altenglische Martyrologium* ed Günter Kotzor, Abhandlungen der Bayer Akad der Wiss, Philos-Hist Kl, NF 88 (Munich 1981) 1:449*-54*. Professor Cross has suggested a terminus a quo somewhat before 850: J.E. Cross, '"Legimus in Ecclesiasticis Historiis": A Sermon for All Saints, and Its Use in Old English Prose' *Traditio* 33 (1977) 134-5, and 'Popes of Rome in the Old English Martyrology' *ARCA: Classical and Medieval Texts, Papers and Monographs* 3: *Papers of the Liverpool Latin Seminar* 2 (Liverpool 1979) 203-4.

34 Hanna Vollrath 'Gesetzgebung und Schriftlichkeit: Das Beispiel der angelsächsischen Gesetze' *Historisches Jahrbuch* 99 (1979) 28-54; cp also C.P. Wormald '*Lex Scripta* and *Verbum Regis*: Legislation and Germanic Kingship, from Euric to Cnut' in *Early Medieval Kingship* ed P.H. Sawyer and I.N. Wood (Leeds 1977) 105-38, and 'The Uses of Literacy in Anglo-Saxon England and Its Neighbours' *TRHS* 5th series 27 (1977) 103.

35 *Historia ecclesiastica* II.5. For the written transmission of the laws of Æthel-

berht and Ine, see Liebermann *Die Gesetze der Angelsachsen* 3:1 and 63-4.

36 Kenneth Sisam 'Cynewulf and his Poetry' *PBA* 18 (1932) 303-31, repr in the author's *Studies in the History of Old English Literature* (Oxford 1953) 1-28; for further evidence see P.O.E. Gradon ed Cynewulf's *Elene* (London 1958) 22-3. But see also Rosemary Woolf ed *Juliana* (London 1955) 19: 'Juliana clearly comes at the end of a period ... There could be no poetic progress from it ...' An earlier date for Cynewulf has been suggested by Godfrid Storms, 'The Weakening of o.e. Unstressed *i* to *e* and the Date of Cynewulf' *ES* 37 (1956) 104-10. Cp Daniel G. Calder *Cynewulf* (Boston 1981) 15-18.

37 See Franz Wenisch '*Judith* – eine westsächsische Dichtung?' *Anglia* 100 (1982) 300 and references on 279n42, n43.

38 See Ashley Crandell Amos *Linguistic Means of Determining the Dates of Old English Literary Texts* (Cambridge, Mass 1980), and *The Dating of Beowulf* ed Colin Chase, Toronto Old English Series 6 (Toronto 1981). It seems remarkable that Professor Norman Blake suggests that 'some neglected aspects of Old English poetry indicate that a respectable case can be made for the theory that the poems in the four poetic codices were composed in the Alfredian period rather than earlier,' 'The Dating of Old English Poetry' in *An English Miscellany presented to W.S. Mackie* ed Brian S. Lee (Cape Town 1977) 27.

39 These figures are based on 'A preliminary list of manuscripts written or owned in England up to 1100' *ASE* 9 (1981) 1-60. Further manuscripts or fragments that will have to be added to this list have come to my notice, and more will no doubt be found. Cp also the figures given by Patrick Wormald in *The Anglo-Saxons* ed James Campbell 254 note to 147.

40 The main sources of general information about these manuscripts are: E.A. Lowe, *CLA* 11 vols with supplement (Oxford 1934-72), the same author's *English Uncial* (Oxford 1960), and J.J.G. Alexander *Insular Manuscripts* (see n 16 above). Only ten per cent of the extant manuscripts written up to the beginning of the ninth century originated outside England: ten written in the seventh century or earlier ('Preliminary List,' nos 83, 245, 281, 297, 311, 529, 654, 834, 944, 945), and three written during the eighth century ('Preliminary List,' nos 87, 266, 299).

41 See T.A.M. Bishop *English Caroline Minuscule* (Oxford 1971) xvii–xviii, and Michael Lapidge 'The Present State of Anglo-Latin Studies' 56-8. For a number of manuscripts which may have been brought to England by Alfred's continental helpers, particularly Grimbald, see Keynes and Lapidge *Alfred the Great* 214n26. These manuscripts were written in N.E. France and Rheims and its vicinity: 'Preliminary List' nos 70, 77, 140, 263, 490, 492, 661, 939.

The figures quoted by Allen J. Frantzen 'The Age of Alfred,' in *Anglo-Latin in the Context of Old English Literature* ed Paul E. Szarmach *Old English Newsletter, Subsidia* 9 (Binghamton 1983) 11 do not take into account the continental origin of most of the ninth-century manuscripts.

42 'Preliminary List' nos 52, 282, 298, 375, 462, 626. To these might be added no 611 (Oxford, Bodleian Library, Digby 63), dated 867–92, but possibly written in a part of the country occupied by the invaders; for this manuscript see now David N. Dumville 'Motes and Beams: Two Insular Computistical Manuscripts' *Peritia* 2 (1983) 248-56.

43 'Preliminary List' nos 28, 88, 126, 327, 385, 448, 576 (611, see n 42 above), 857, 898. An authoritative study of the ninth-century English manuscripts is the recent (1982) Oxford D PHIL thesis by Jennifer Morrish, as yet unpublished, who now adds a few more manuscripts to those hitherto considered as written in England and datable in the ninth century, but this does not affect my general conclusions in this paper. Cp Dr Morrish's article 'King Alfred's Letter as a Source on Learning in England in the Ninth Century' in *Studies in Earlier Old English Prose* ed Paul E. Szarmach (Albany, NY 1986) 87-107. It will be seen that her interpretation of the manuscript evidence differs from mine and is closer to the more optimistic view of Sir Frank Stenton, *Anglo-Saxon England* 3rd ed (Oxford 1971) 190-1. See also David Dumville 'English Libraries before 1066: Use and Abuse of the Manuscript Evidence' in *Insular Latin Studies* ed Michael W. Herren 168, and 'Motes and Beams' 254-5.

44 'Preliminary List' nos 45, 432, 443, 456, 635, 646, 780, 885, 911

45 Dorothy Whitelock has suggested that ninth-century English vernacular manuscripts had little chance of survival because of subsequent changes in language, spelling and paleography: *EHD* 91-2. But this would not explain the lack of surviving Latin manuscripts of the period. For the number of extant continental ninth-century manuscripts see Bernhard Bischoff *Paläographie des römischen Altertums und des abendländischen Mittelalters* (Berlin 1979) 260, and T.J. Brown 'Latin Paleography since Traube' *Codicologica* 1 (1976) 65 and n33.

46 J.E. Cross ('The Literate Anglo-Saxon – On Sources and Disseminations' *PBA* 58 [1972] 84-5 and 85n2) thinks that 'the homiliary's content could be known in England without a considerable lapse of time' and that even Cynewulf may have used it; but there is no safe evidence for this. See also Cyril L. Smetana 'Paul the Deacon's Patristic Anthology' in *The Old English Homily* (see n1 above) 75-97.

47 It seems very doubtful to me if the knowledge of this rule in England can be inferred from the report of the papal legates to England, written in 786 (Haddan and Stubbs 3:450, ch 4, and 461; cp *EHD* no 191), or from Archbishop

Wulfred's privilege granted to the 'familia' of Christ Church, Canterbury, in 813 (Haddan and Stubbs 3:575-6; Sawyer no 1265). See J. Armitage Robinson *The Times of Saint Dunstan* (Oxford 1923) 170; D.J.V. Fisher *The Anglo-Saxon Age* 188 and 203; Brooks *The Early History of the Church of Canterbury* 155-6 and notes on pp 356-7.

48 This does not imply, of course, that there was a complete lack of contact between English and continental scriptoria during the ninth century. Dr Mildred Budny has kindly drawn my attention to what are clearly Carolingian symptoms in a ninth-century gospel-book from St Augustine's Canterbury, ms BL Royal 1.E.vi; see now her abstract in *Old English Newsletter* 17.2 (1984) A-38, and Katharina Bierbrauer *Die Ornamentik frühkarolingischer Handschriften aus Bayern* Abhandlungen der Bayer Akad der Wiss, Philos-Hist Kl, NF 84 (Munich 1979) 71 and n 252. See also Patrick Wormald 'The Ninth Century' 142-3.

49 See F.M. Stenton *Anglo-Saxon England* 271.

50 See Dorothy Whitelock 'The Old English Bede' *PBA* 48 (1962) 70 and n 123, and 'The list of chapter-headings in the Old English Bede' in *Old English Studies in Honour of John C. Pope* ed Robert B. Burlin and Edward B. Irving, Jr (Toronto 1974) 266-7. For the translation of Gregory's *Dialogues*, see the materials provided by David Yerkes *The Two Versions of Waerferth's Translation of Gregory's Dialogues: An Old English Thesaurus* Toronto Old English Series 4 (Toronto 1979).

51 Janet Bately ed *The Old English Orosius* EETS ss 6 (1980) lv–lxxii

52 Joseph S. Wittig 'King Alfred's *Boethius* and its Latin sources: a reconsideration' *ASE* 11 (1983) 157-98. For the suggestion of Welsh and continental exemplars for some or all of the Alfredian translations, see also T.J. Brown 'An Historical Introduction to the Use of Classical Latin Authors in the British Isles from the Fifth to the Eleventh Century' *Settimane di studio del Centro italiano di studi sull' alto medioevo* 22 (1975) 290. It is, however, difficult to believe with Professor Simeon Potter that scores of manuscripts of Gregory's *Cura Pastoralis* must have been available in ninth-century Wessex: 'The Old English *Pastoral Care*' *TPS* (1947) 115.

53 'Preface' lines 14-20; see *EHD* 888.

54 *Ælfrics Grammatik und Glossar* ed Julius Zupitza, 2. Aufl mit Vorwort von Helmut Gneuss (Berlin 1966) 3

55 Paul E. Szarmach 'The Meaning of Alfred's *Preface* to the *Pastoral Care*' (see above n1) 59

56 For the topos of enemy attacks as divine retribution, see Whitelock, *EHD* 26-7; for the conventional motif of the decay of learning, Josef Fleckenstein,

Die Bildungsreform Karls des Grossen als Verwirklichung der norma rectitudinis (Freiburg im Breisgau 1953) 50 and notes.

57 See J.M. Wallace-Hadrill, 'The Franks and the English in the Ninth Century; Some Common Historical Interests' *History* 35 (1950) 202-18 esp 212-13, repr with Postscript in the author's *Early Medieval History* (Oxford 1975) 201-16; P.H. Sawyer *The Age of the Vikings* 20; C.N.L. Brooke 'Historical Writing in England between 850 and 1150' (see above n 30) 232; R.H.C. Davis 'Alfred the Great: Propaganda and Truth' *History* 56 (1971) 169-82; D.P. Kirby 'Asser and his Life of King Alfred' *Studia Celtica* 6 (1971) 12-35; Antonia Gransden, *Historical Writing in England c. 550 to c. 1307* (London 1974) 34-5.

58 Dorothy Whitelock 'The Importance of the Battle of Edington A.D. 878' *Report for 1977 of the Society of the Friends of Edington Priory Church* rpt in Dorothy Whitelock *From Bede to Alfred: Studies in Early Anglo-Saxon Literature and History* (London 1980); see *EHD* 123 and 140, and Keynes and Lapidge *Alfred the Great* 40-1 and 217n62. See also Dorothy Whitelock *The Genuine Asser* (Reading 1968) 20, on the suggestion that Asser's Life of King Alfred was a later forgery, written for propaganda purposes.

59 Cp Professor Davis' criticism of the 'Preface' in 'Alfred the Great' 175.

60 'Alfred the Great' 180-1

61 Kenneth Sisam 'The Publication of Alfred's *Pastoral Care*' in *Studies in the History of Old English Literature* 140-7. See also N.R. Ker *The Pastoral Care* EEMF 6 (Copenhagen 1956) 19. For the view that the reformed tenth-century English monasteries should be regarded as centres of royalist propaganda, see Eric John *Orbis Britanniae* 179-80.

62 This is a revised version of a paper read at the first conference of the International Society of Anglo-Saxonists in Brussels on 22 August 1983.

RUTH MELLINKOFF

Serpent Imagery in the Illustrated Old English Hexateuch

SERPENTS are portrayed in unusual, sometimes unique ways in the illustrated Old English Hexateuch.[1] They are novel creations and, like so many other innovations in this eleventh-century manuscript, are attributable either to a literal rendering of the Old English text into images,[2] or to the introduction of elements or ideas not mentioned in the text but intimately bound up with the Anglo-Saxon milieu.[3] The literal illustration of text, that is, the impulse to create word-pictures, is responsible for some of the picturesque, even amusing illustrations of serpents, while Anglo-Saxon originality is disclosed both in some uncommon designs for serpents, and by a new iconographical feature – a serpent-head finial on Moses' rod. This innovative serpent imagery and its relationship, or lack of any, to the Old English text, as well as its iconographical significance, is what I propose to discuss.

Scandinavian influences which had penetrated the Anglo-Saxon world, especially from the tenth century, may be responsible for some of the distinctive portrayals of serpents, snakes, and dragons.[4] As has been noted previously, the dragon-headed Noah's ark on folios 14r, 14v, 15r, and 15v reflects Viking taste.[5] Scandinavian taste, however, is also discernible in the design of the serpents attacking the Israelites of Numbers 21:6 on folio 123v (fig 1); in the brazen serpent of Numbers 21:9 on folio 124r (fig 2); in the Garden of Eden serpent on folio 7r; and in the giant Hell serpent on folio 2r. The Hell serpent is portrayed in the apocryphal Fall of Lucifer and his rebel angels, an event not mentioned in biblical text, but described in the treatise on the Old and New Testament that precedes the paraphrase;[6] this surely accounts for its depiction in the manuscript. The serpent's open mouth and teeth hold a mandorla that is swallowing the fallen angels, but of special interest here is its huge tail, coiled in a manner that recalls the Scandinavian design known as the 'Great beast Jellinge style.'[7]

Another Scandinavian style genre is recognizable in the other folios: wound and looped around the Israelites, the serpents of Numbers 21:6 (fig 1) recall the Urnes beast-type design known as 'snake' Urnes.[8] The serpents have been transformed into a simple interlace of ribbons that coil upon themselves in graceful loops, creating the unexpected impression of serpents squeezing the Israelites to death instead of biting them. The same Urnes style is revealed in the brazen serpent wound around the pillar in undulating loops (fig 2), and again by a more realistic serpent wound in and out of the Eden tree on folio 7r. This uncustomary serpent imagery does not reflect any special interpretation of text; the serpent designs do not alter biblical meaning. This imagery does, however, divulge aesthetic preferences, and it shows how Scandinavian styles were absorbed into Anglo-Saxon art; its novelty, therefore, derives from the adaptation of Scandinavian design elements into traditional biblical imagery.

Originality of another order appears in illustrations which are responses to biblical text. This is displayed, for example, in the portrayal of the struggle for supremacy between Aaron and Pharaoh's magicians as described in Exodus 7. Directed by God to impress Pharaoh, Aaron has turned his rod into a serpent. Pharaoh has responded by calling his own magicians who also turn their rods into serpents, 'But Aaron's rod devoured their rods' (verse 12). This event is illustrated in the top scene of folio 81v (fig 3). What we see is Aaron's serpent swallowing four of the magicians' serpents. The biblical text states that rod swallowed rods, yet the artist's interpretation of that text saw serpents and rods as equivalents, a concept that is unusual but not unique, for the same idea has been similarly construed and portrayed in other artistic examples.[9]

That serpent and rod were interchangeable, or had a special affinity, is disclosed in a more informing and remarkable way by a sequence of pictures beginning in the lower scene of folio 78r (fig 4) where Moses holds a serpent by its tail – a depiction of Exodus 4:3 in which the Lord told Moses to cast down his rod and it would turn into a serpent. The transformation of the serpent back to a rod (verse 4) is not, however, illustrated; instead, something more subtle takes place. On the next folio, 78v,[10] Moses is again holding his rod, but it now has a serpent head (with small dog-like ears) at the rod's top, the same kind of head that the serpent had in the earlier event. From 78v onwards until Moses receives his horned headdress on 105v,[11] whenever Moses holds or uses his rod, and occasionally Aaron too, the rod has this distinctive serpent-head finial.

Figure 1 London, British Library ms Cotton Claudius, B.iv, folio 123 verso (photo: British Library)

Figure 3 London, British Library ms Cotton Claudius, B.iv, folio 81 verso
(photo: British Library)

Figure 4 London, British Library ms Cotton Claudius, B.iv, folio 78 recto
(photo: British Library)

acrygað egað into þinum huyum, ⁊to þinum bedde, ⁊to þinum
hoꝥd clifan · ⁊to þinpa þegna huyum · ⁊on þin folc ⁊on þine ofnaſ
⁊on þine mete lafa · ⁊cѡþe · ⁊to dinum folce · ⁊into eallum þinum
dropum · gað þaꝥ fꝛoxaꝥ · ⁊dꝛihten cѡæð to moyſe cѡeð to aa-
rone herf up þine hand ofeꝛ eal þæt flod · ⁊ofeꝛ burna ⁊ofeꝛ
moꝥaꝥ · ⁊alæd up þa fꝛoxaꝥ ofeꝛ eall egypta land.

aaꝛon ahof up hiſ hand ofeꝛ eal egypta pæteꝛu · ⁊þa fꝛoxaꝥ
aꝛugon up ofeꝛ eal egypta land · pitod lice phaꝛao clypode
moyſe · ⁊aaꝛon · ⁊cpæð to him biddaþ to þꝛyne dꝛihten þæt
he adꝛife ealle daꝥ fꝛoxaꝥ fꝛam me · ⁊fꝛam minum folce ·
⁊ic foꝛ læte þæt iꝛꝛa heliſce folc þæt hit offꝛige gode ·
þacpæð moyſeꝥ to phaꝛaone geꝛæcme andagan hѡænne ðu
pille þæt ic foꝛ þe ge bidde · ⁊to þin folc · þaꝥ þaꝥ fꝛoxaꝥ beon
adꝛifene fꝛam þe · ⁊fꝛam þinum folce · þæt hi aꝥan onpæteꝛu
Ða ⁊ꝛꝛapode phaꝛao ⁊cpæð · nuto moꝥgen · Ðacpæð moyſeꝥ
icdo ꝛtah dam þe ðu cpæð · þæt ðu pite þæt nyꝛ nan ofeꝛ
ꝛpilc god ⁊pilce uꝛe god · ⁊þa fꝛoxaꝥ faꝛaþ fꝛam þe · ⁊fꝛam
þinum þegnum ·

Figure 5   London, British Library ms Cotton Claudius, B.iv, folio 82 verso
(photo: British Library)

Figure 6 Initial I. Stuttgart Landesbibliothek ms Hist 418, folio 3 re
(photo: Stuttgart Landesbibliothek)

Some of the miniatures are very faded, yet with a magnifying glass the traces of the serpent head can easily be detected. To recognize this intention, it is enough here, however, to compare the serpent-head finial in the lower scene of folio 81v (fig 3) or the ones on folio 82v (fig 5).[12] Note too that the head is designed like the real serpent's head on 78r (fig 4).

This conflation of rod and serpent into a wonder-working wand for Moses is expressive acknowledgment of the traditional power associated with serpents. It confesses not only the kinship of rod and serpent, but also the desire to show the special magical capacities incorporated into that God-given staff. Unlike the evil connotations of the Hell or Eden serpents, the serpent atop the rod of Moses has positive connotations; the antithetical ideas about serpents here as elsewhere only mirror the ambiguous imagery of biblical text. Leviathan, the Eden serpent, and a host of apocalyptic dragons symbolize evil, yet the serpent as a symbol of wisdom and healing is also biblical. The serpent's wisdom is described as "more subtle than any beast of the field" in Genesis 3:1, and Christ himself in Matthew 10:16 urges his disciples to be "wise as serpents." Tremendous healing and protective power of the serpent, moreover, is disclosed by the brazen serpent raised by Moses (Numbers 21:6), alluded to in John 3:14 when he likens the lifting up of the brazen serpent to the lifting up of the Son of Man, an allusion traditionally interpreted as the lifting up of Christ on the cross.

This bivalent (or multivalent) symbolism for biblical serpents in turn echoes and continues the serpents' ancient and ubiquitous traditional meanings. As a representative of powerful natural forces, the serpent, not unlike other animals and birds such as the lion or eagle, has been characterized by polyvalence and ambiguity.[13] As the objects of mixed feeling, serpents have sometimes been seen as the embodiment of evil, yet in other contexts they have served as emblems of healing, protection, and wisdom.

Belief in their beneficial qualities has spanned many centuries and cultures, as the history of serpent worship can attest. A survey is not possible here,[14] but a few examples should suffice for this essay: serpents have been associated with the guardianship of wealth and treasure, as well as homes and tombs;[15] repeated evidence of the feeding of household snakes reports the belief that snakes were the reincarnation of souls of the dead;[16] and the fierce power and protective capacity of serpents has been reflected in their use as charms, devised on swords and helmets[17] and used on banners and standards from the Roman era through the Middle Ages.[18]

As possessor of wisdom and the secrets of knowledge, the serpent was believed to be beneficial, a conviction that may be responsible for the ancient legend about a 'dragon tree.'[19] Generally thought to be a long-lived palm, the dragon tree was believed to exude a red sap capable of promoting health and sometimes bestowing eternal life. Later interpreted as the Tree of Life, distinct from the Tree of Knowledge, the dragon tree was first represented by Schongauer in an engraving of the *Flight into Egypt*, complete with a reptile on the tree's trunk.[20]

The healing powers of serpents have, of course, been testified to in many other ways, as for example by the belief that the beneficial waters of certain springs and wells are due to their snakes,[21] and by the important worship of healing deities such as Asklepios.[22] It is of great interest to note that in ancient times the staff (or rod) and the serpent were interchangeable, for each incorporated the same extraordinary powers.[23] As a shorthand emblem for a branch or tree, the staff symbolized the secrets of growth and imperishability – a sign of the continuous renewal of life by the earth – and similar ideas were conveyed by the serpent through the renewal of its skin.[24] The initial separate use of serpent and staff for Asklepios, only later united in the well-known staff encircled by a serpent, demonstrates their inherent sameness.[25]

Staff or serpent or both, incorporating the primeval forces of the earth, could do wondrous things; with or without a serpent, the staff or rod because of its inherent power became the perennial magic wand. The sign of the power of Moses also lay in his magic wand – the rod so intimately tied to serpents. Bestowed by God, Moses' rod is expressed by its magical power in wonder-working performances in Exodus where Moses uses it to produce plagues, force water from rocks, and perform those other miracles. Although the context of the serpent-head on Moses' rod throughout the illustrated Old English Hexateuch establishes the serpent in that context as beneficent, the pictures do not suggest the typology so extensively elaborated in the visual arts from the twelfth century on, as represented, for example, by a folio from a twelfth-century manuscript (fig 6).[26] In the initial 'I,' just below Noah's ark at the left, Moses holds a serpent in his hand as an attribute of the miracle of his rod, while, directly opposite, a reptile symbolizing the brazen serpent is draped on a stylized branch. Both of these portrayals were meant to be understood as typological antecedents for Christ's raising up on the cross, the scene that appears directly below them. As pointed out by James

Marrow, 'medieval commentators not only recognized Christ in the brazen serpent, but also equated this serpent with the one miraculously transformed from the rod cast down by Moses.'[27]

But neither that typology nor any other complex theological Christian doctrine is suggested by the serpent-head rod of Moses in the Old English Hexateuch. Rather, these portrayals recall some of the age-old ideas associated with serpents and their magical, beneficial powers that continued to flourish, albeit sub rosa, side by side with interpretations of the serpent as evil.[28] Some of those magical powers rubbed off on Moses himself, who has been seen as one of the greatest magicians of all time.[29] Popular tradition saw several Old Testament biblical figures as magicians; as Keith Thomas suggested, it was 'an idea stimulated by the hermetic theory that Adam's knowledge of all natural things, though lost at the Fall, had been transmitted downwards through Noah, Solomon, and other select adepts. Moses, "learned in all the wisdom of the Egyptians" (Acts 7:22), was especially famous for his magical powers.'[30]

The tradition which attributes the composition of manuals of magic to Solomon, Moses, and others goes back to remote antiquity.[31] Moreover, we have continuous evidence of those magical books through the Middle Ages and later.[32] Numerous magical tracts attributed to Solomon circulated, and magical works allegedly derived from Moses travelled through the centuries under varying names such as 'The Work of Moses on the Holy Name,' 'The Crown of Moses,' the 'Eighth Book of Moses,' and 'The Sword of Moses.'[33] Although the Church officially disapproved of such magical tracts and those who insisted on using them, the heinousness of those works and practices was neither understood nor appreciated at the popular level. Not so remarkable; the slim line dividing magic and religion has repeatedly been dissolved, leaving behind an intimate tie between magic and holiness at many levels.

Evidence from the medieval mystery plays, for example, reveals that Moses was sometimes portrayed by a person adept in the tricks of legerdemain. In the Wakefield play of *Pharaoh*, Moses uses the language of conjury.[34] Accompanied by two assistants, the actor could easily have turned his rod into a serpent, then back into a rod – a trick easily accomplished by a common juggler, and one that would have been expected by an audience that looked forward to such simple entertainment.

The concept of Moses as magician has reverberated through the ages, exposed, for example, by the claim of John Thornton of Sapcote, Leicestershire, who in 1523 claimed that he had been curing animals for thirty years with a 'Moses rod.'[35] Special divining tools used to search for treasure have often been called 'Mosaical rods,' and even the clergy were not exempt from their attractions, as divulged by the Dean of Westminster who in 1634 allowed an expedition equipped with Mosaical rods and led by the King's clock-master, Davy Ramesey, to search for treasure in the Abbey.[36] Additional evidence of Mosaical rods used for mineral discoveries in the seventeenth century is reported in 1686: 'A strange kind of exploration and peculiar way of Rhabdomany is that which is used for mineral discoveries: with a forked hazel, commonly called Moses' rod, which freely held forth will stir and play if any mine be under it.'[37] These magical practices were often clothed with respectability by stressing the importance of practitioners' being in suitable spiritual condition; their manipulations were often preceded by proper fasting and prayer.

All of those practices, in whatever period, can be aptly described as divine or sanctified magic. Sacred magic also correctly describes the concept of a serpent-head for Moses' rod in this manuscript. Although it was surely not generated by ideas connected with the staff and serpent of Asklepios,[38] nor was it a precursor of late magical practices with Mosaical divining rods, yet all of these separate phenomena partake of the same ideas: the power of rods or serpents, or a combination of both, is loosened by God (or some other deity) to perform miracles beneficial to mankind.

NOTES

1 BL ms Cotton Claudius B.iv. See references for this manuscript in my *The Horned Moses in Medieval Art and Thought* (Berkeley 1970); see also the facsimile, *The Old English Illustrated Hexateuch* ed C.R. Dodwell and Peter Clemoes, EEMF 18 (Copenhagen, London, Baltimore 1974); and Elzbieta Temple *Anglo-Saxon Manuscripts 900-1066* (London 1976) 102-3.

2 The portrayal of Moses with horns, for example; see Mellinkoff *Horned Moses* 13-27; and see Dodwell's introduction to the facsimile 65-73.

3 See for example the introduction of the round, diptych design for the biblical tablets of the Law, described in my article, 'The Round-topped Tablets of the Law: Sacred Symbol and Emblem of Evil' *Journal of Jewish Art* 1 (1974) 28-43, and also 'The round, cap-shaped hats depicted on Jews in BM Cotton Claudius B.iv' *ASE* 2 (1973) 155-65, esp 160 n 4.

4 All reptiles are grouped together and treated as interchangeable in this essay because the particular type is of no significance here.

5 See, for example, Dodwell's introduction to the facsimile (n 1 above) 71.

6 *The Old English Version of the Heptateuch* ed S.J. Crawford, EETS OS 160 (1922; rpt Oxford 1969) 19-20

7 See T.D. Kendrick *Late Saxon and Viking Art* (1949; rpt London 1974) 88, 110, and 115.

8 Kendrick 110-27

9 This concept is represented in a similar fashion in some Hebrew illuminated manuscripts produced in fourteenth-century Catalonia; see Bezalel Narkiss *Hebrew Illuminated Manuscripts in the British Isles, The Spanish and Portuguese Manuscripts* (Jerusalem and London 1982) 1: part 2, plates xcii and xciii, where Aaron's serpent is swallowing serpents, but here only two. This idea is quite different from the one displayed by the Early Christian cycle of wall paintings in Old St Paul's in Rome as they are known from sixteenth-century copies; see Joseph Garber *Wirkungen der frühchristlichen Gemäldezyklen der alten Peters und Pauls-basiliken in Rom* (Berlin-Vienna 1918) plate 15, where we see four serpents but no swallowing.

10 I did not reproduce this folio because it is confusing. The folio shows Moses with horns but they are a much later addition; see *Horned Moses* 17.

11 I have no explanation for the termination of the serpent-head rod at this stage in the manuscript. Any ideas I have connected with horned Moses imagery are only speculation and not worth mentioning here.

12 Aaron seems to be holding the serpent-head rod in the lower left scene. It is difficult to decide whether or not he is holding it for Moses or if it is Aaron's own, since Aaron too had a magical rod. But it does not matter since the meaning of the rod is the same.

13 See Meyer Schapiro *Words and Pictures* (The Hague 1973) 63n102. See also the important and fascinating essay by Jacques Le Goff, 'Ecclesiastical Culture and Folklore in the Middle Ages: Saint Marcellus of Paris and the Dragon' in *Time, Work, and Culture in the Middle Ages* trans Arthur Goldhammer (1977; trans Chicago 1980) 159-88.

14 S.A. Cook's article 'Serpent-Worship' in the eleventh edition of the *Encyclopaedia Britannica* is still a good, succinct account. Also of some interest are M. Oldfield Howey *The Encircled Serpent* (New York 1955) and a more specialized study by Adolphe J. Reinach, 'Divinités Gauloises au Serpent' *Revue Archéologique* 4th series 24 (1911) 221-56.

15 See Jacob Grimm *Teutonic Mythology* 4th ed trans James E. Stallybrass, 4 vols (New York 1966) 2:688-91.

16 Grimm 684-6

17 Grimm 687-8

18 See Le Goff (n 13 above); and see Alexander Haggerty Krappe 'The Fighting Snakes in the Historia Britonum of Nennius' *Revue Celtique* 43 (1926) 124-31; and J.S.P. Tatlock 'The Dragons of Wessex and Wales' *Speculum* 8 (1933) 223-35.

19 See Laurinda S. Dixon *Alchemical Imagery in Bosch's Garden of Delights*

(Ann Arbor 1980) 18-19.

20 Robert A. Koch 'Martin Schongauer's Dragon Tree' *Print Review* no 5 (1976) 114-19

21 Grimm (n 15 above) 588n1

22 The literature is vast, but an interesting collection of material can be found in Emma J. Edelstein and Ludwig Edelstein *Asclepius* 2 vols (Baltimore 1945).

23 J. Schouten *The Rod and Serpent of Asklepios: Symbol of Medicine* trans M.E. Hollander (Amsterdam 1967) 41

24 Schouten 42

25 Schouten 41

26 Pen and ink drawing, twelfth century, Josephus' *Antiquitates Judaicae*, Stuttgart Württembergische Landesbibiliothek Cod Hist 418, fol 3, initial I

27 James H. Marrow *Passion Iconography in Northern European Art of the Late Middle Ages and Early Renaissance* (Kortrijk, Belgium 1979) 77. For a brief summary of how this typological image developed in the visual arts, see Gertrud Schiller *Iconography of Christian Art* trans Janet Seligman 2 vols (1968; trans London 1972) 2:125-6.

28 See Le Goff (n 13 above).

29 See Joshua Trachtenberg *Jewish Magic and Superstition* (1939; rpt New York 1961) 218; and see his *The Devil and the Jews* (1943; rpt New York 1961) 57-8.

30 Keith Thomas *Religion and the Decline of Magic* (New York 1971) 271

31 See *The Devil and the Jews* (n29 above) 231n16; and see Lynn Thorndike *A History of Magic and Experimental Science* 8 vols (New York 1923) 2:279-89.

32 See Thorndike (n31 above); and see Emile Grillot de Givry 'The Books of the Sorcerers' in *Picture Museum of Sorcery, Magic, and Alchemy* trans J. Courtenay Locke (1929; trans New York 1963) 95-103.

33 *The Sword of Moses* ed M. Gaster (London 1896) 22-3.

34 For a description and references to these plays, see Louis B. Wright 'Juggling Tricks and Conjury on the English Stage before 1642' *MP* 24 (1926-7) 271-2.

35 Thomas (n30 above) 185

36 Thomas 236

37 John Aubrey *Remains of Gentilisme and Judaisme* Publications of the Folk-Lore Society 4 (London 1881) 115

38 Old English medical texts, however, do demonstrate an acquaintance with Asklepios; see Linda E. Voigts 'One Anglo-Saxon view of the Classical Gods' *Studies in Iconography* 3 (1977) 3-16.

ALAIN RENOIR

Old English Formulas and Themes as Tools for Contextual Interpretation

I N A PIONEERING ESSAY, published in 1955, Stanley Greenfield presented us with a masterful study of the theme of exile in Old English poetry and pointed out that 'the association with other contexts using a similar formula will inevitably color a particular instance of a formula so that a whole host of overtones springs into action' and must accordingly affect our understanding of the passage in which the formula occurs.[1] The extent to which the statement has proved influential may be inferred from the fact that the principles underlying it have been stretched in a number of directions by eminent scholars attempting to meet the needs of rapidly expanding research into various aspects of poetry with roots in the Indo-European oral-formulaic tradition. One thinks of Adrien Bonjour's immediately subsequent inference that the overtones of oral-formulaic elements could actually enable the audience to apprehend 'in advance' certain aspects of the narrative,[2] or of the theory which John Miles Foley advanced two decades later to the effect that oral-formulaic elements could affect the impact of certain elements in a given narrative 'by locating them in relation to archetypal paradigms.'[3]

Over and above its intrinsic importance as an indispensable tool for the modern interpreter of Old English poetry, Greenfield's axiom offers the great advantage of being applicable regardless of the actual circumstances under which the poem was composed. As long as the rhetoric conforms primarily to the principles of oral-formulaic composition, it matters relatively little whether, for example, we wish to subscribe to Larry Benson's authoritative opinion that 'we should assume literate production of ... Beowulf'[4] or to Robert Creed's equally authoritative opinion that the extant text of Beowulf 'is a copy of a recording of a performance.'[5] From the point of view of Anglo-Saxonists, the extent to which this flexibility enhances the usefulness of a critical tool may be assessed by recalling Donald Fry's observation that most scholars will agree that 'Old English poetry used oral forms, but no reliable test can distinguish written from oral poems.'[6] These considerations make it clear that, whereas critical systems assuming either oral or written composition are as likely to mislead us as to help us, the associative principle formulated by Greenfield is likely to help us with almost any English poem composed before the Norman Conquest. For this reason, the adjective 'oral-formulaic' is used here to refer to a rhetorical tradition which predates literacy – in contrast to such formulaic conventions as have developed in various written genres – but does not imply that particular poems illustrative of this rhetoric were necessarily composed orally.

As the foregoing discussion may have already suggested, the term on which I should like to pick up in the quotation from Greenfield's essay is the noun 'context,' and I should further like to consider it in relation to the text. In so doing, I am aware that the most influential literary theorists of our time have won the admiration of the academic community by demonstrating that the traditional significance of both text and context is by no means so certain as it used to be and that literary theory can most readily be practised without reference to any work of literature.[7] Since my purpose here is to show how a given context can occasionally help us interpret a given text, I can only regret that I have no choice but to take a step backward within the history of literary studies.

My position does not imply the belief that the enterprise which I advocate will necessarily yield foolproof results, for the text and context of Old English poetry seems to take a mischievous delight in presenting us with insoluble problems. For the immediate purpose, I shall disregard the problems connected with the text, since they are often accidental and terminal.[8] We regret, for example, that the only extant manuscript of *Riddle* 89 has been so eaten by worms that only nineteen scattered words and a few letters remain of what would presumably have printed ten lines in a modern edition, but we can do nothing about it.[9] In contrast, the context usually presents us with problems which are built into the history of the culture and for which partial solutions may not seldom be attempted. The nature of these problems may best be understood by recalling that readers of poetry – and, indeed, of all literature ancient or modern – usually bring three separate but interacting contexts to bear upon the interpretation of the text, and the process need not necessarily be conscious.

The first – and, I believe, the most important – context is historical.

A reader coming to William Butler Yeats' *Easter 1916* without any knowledge of Irish history and of the Easter Uprising would be unlikely to interpret the poem as it was intended to be. The historical context which we bring to bear on the text may, of course, be provided by remotest antiquity as well as by the immediate present or any period in between, and it may be general (as when Yeats celebrates a national uprising) or intimate (as when he includes in his song of praise 'a drunken, vainglorious lout' [32] whom we know to have earned his bitter resentment).[10] Furthermore, it may include the reader's personal experience: a member of the English contingent which put down the Easter Uprising would probably not construe the poem exactly as would a survivor of the same Uprising. Nor, as already suggested, need we be consciously aware of the facts which influence our interpretation, since our formal or informal historical education – however broad or limited it may be – has trained us to interpret certain statements and situations without analysing the reasons for our interpretations.[11] The testimony of medieval literature, for example, leads one to suspect that mentions of Attila the Hun were not interpreted in the same manner by South Germans and by Scandinavians.

The second context is that which Fred Robinson has aptly termed the 'most immediate context,' in an essay which demonstrates that 'when we read an Old English literary text we should take care to find out what precedes it in its manuscript state and what follows it.'[12] The relevance of this 'most immediate context' is by no means limited to Old English, and a reader whose initiation to Shakespeare's sonnets came through a single sonnet examined without reference to the others would almost certainly produce an interpretation somewhat different from those of readers who see the same sonnet within the context of the entire sequence.

The third context is that of literary tradition. Whether our tradition extends all the way back to Homer or only as far as the television programs on which we were nurtured, it necessarily influences our reaction to subsequent literary experiences. The point may be illustrated by our recalling the opening lines of a well-known poem which Langston Hughes published in 1925 to express the frustration and hope of Black Americans:

I, too, sing America.

I am the darker brother.

They send me to eat in the kitchen
When company comes.
But I laugh,
And eat well,
And grow strong.

Over a half-century after the publication of the poem, readers totally unacquainted with American history and equipped with no literary tradition might well construe these lines literally as the peevish reaction of a child who thinks his family discriminates against him because of his complexion; and readers approaching the poem within the exclusive context of American social history between the two world wars might construe the message as an exasperated threat of ethnic uprising. In contrast, readers familiar not only with recent social history but with the high points of the Anglo-American literary tradition and its classical background will be cued in by the opening line and accordingly bring to the subsequent text echoes of Homer, Virgil, Milton, and the innumerable poems where Walt Whitman 'sings' of everything under the sun. In this light, the poem will no longer be an expression of childish irritation or merely an exasperated threat of uprising, but rather a celebration of the forthcoming birth of a nation; and readers acquainted with the corpus of Hughes' work will further appreciate the message within the immediate context which underscores its significance.

If the arguments presented thus far contain even the smallest speck of validity, then our attempts to interpret Old English poetry must perforce be off to an unpromising start, for it is no secret that the contexts which I have listed tend to be so elusive in respect to much early-Germanic poetry as to prove nearly useless to prospective interpreters. Notwithstanding Kevin Kiernan's meticulous investigation of the date of *Beowulf* and its manuscript,[13] as well as an impressive collection of recent essays on the same topic[14] and a major study in which John Niles tackles the same question and examines the facts of the poem,[15] I readily confess that I should be at a loss to tell when, where, by whom, and under what circumstances this greatest of all early-Germanic epics was composed; and I see no reason to assume that I stand alone in my ignorance. I feel even more helpless when I turn to the *Hildebrandslied*, since multitudes of trustworthy scholars have followed one another in arguing respectively that the ultimate original of the only extant text must have been composed in every Germanic language from Gothic to Old English,[16] and since the theological contents of the manuscript on whose front and back covers it was recorded provide us with a totally irrelevant immediate context.[17] In addition, since there are reasons to assume that such Old English poetry as has come down to us represents only a small fraction of what must have been composed orally and in writing before the Norman Conquest,[18] the surviving corpus is too limited to enable us to rely consistently on allusions or borrowings to interpret a given poem within the context of a national literary tradition as we understand it today.

This kind of contextual vacuum may possibly explain why certain Old English poems whose vocabulary and syntax are relatively clear have been subjected to radically different and mutually exclusive interpretations even at the most fundamental level. One thinks, for example, of *The Wife's Lament*, whose speaker has been identified as a thane, a dead woman, a rejected wife, a would-be sorceress, a heathen god, and a voice yearning for the union of God and the Church;[19] or of *Wulf and Eadwacer*, which has been interpreted as a riddle for the name 'Cynewulf' and various other things, a fragment of a soliloquy, a translation from an Old Norse original connected with the *Volsunga Saga*, as well as a touching story about dogs,[20] or - more recently and with very attractive logic - as 'the eloquent lament of a grieving mother reciting a formal *giedd* for her son,'[21] and it seems illustrative of the bewildering nature of the case that, whereas the oft-quoted Benjamin Thorpe admitted with scholarly integrity that he could 'make no sense' out of the poem,[22] a less candid twentieth-century epigone succeeded in milking seventeen pages of literary criticism out of the poem without ever taking its contents into account.[23]

The instances adduced thus far are of course extreme cases, but they are illustrative of a situation which deprives prospective interpreters of the context needed for a responsible critical discussion of much Old English poetry. Speaking strictly from the point of view of literary appreciation, I believe that in certain respects and under certain circumstances the formulas and themes of oral-formulaic rhetoric may serve as a partial substitute for the paucity or even the total absence of the historical contexts on which we usually rely. The fact is that formulaic elements become formulaic precisely because they are repeated - whether the repetition be word-for-word, as in the case of a great many Homeric epithets, or take the form of paradigms to be fleshed out to meet the requirements of the occasion, as in the case of Germanic formulas - and anything which is repeated often enough is bound to call to mind what we have already heard Greenfield call 'a host of overtones' which necessarily affect our interpretation and appreciation. For motion-picture buffs, the mere mention or sight of a little man walking away on a lonely

road will automatically call to mind familiar situations because Charlie
Chaplin has used it in so many films that it has become a formula.

For students of Old English, any poem or section thereof which opens
with the exclamation 'hwæt' followed by a brief statement of facts which
have been learned by the plural speaking voice immediately calls up
echoes of *Beowulf*, and our reaction must almost necessarily be coloured
by the degree to which that opening and whatever comes thereafter
conform to the Beowulfian model in our mind. By this kind of standard,
the *Hildebrandslied* has some serious explaining to do, since its opening
statement – 'Ik gihorta ðat seggen'[24] – is clearly reminiscent of *Beowulf*
but nevertheless speaks in the first person singular, hears what has been
said instead of learning of events, and omits the initial exclamation. In
contrast, *Andreas* moves to the head of the class with the appropriate
exclamation followed by a statement to the effect that we learned of twelve
glorious men in days of old: 'Hwæt! we gefrunan / on fyrndagum //
twelfe under tunglum / tireadige hæleð, // þeodnes þegnas' (1a–3a).
Nor are our expectations disappointed by what follows, since the next
few lines (3b–11b) are reminiscent of the account of Scield Sceafing and
the remainder of the narrative tells the story of a hero who crossed the
sea to fight evil in a foreign land and reveals so many Beowulfian
techniques that Charles Kennedy has argued that the *Andreas*-poet 'has
frequently given evidence of knowledge, and here and there of conscious
imitation, of the *Beowulf*.'[25]

What I have been doing here with Old Germanic poetry is in effect
the same thing which I did with the opening lines of Langston Hughes'
poem, but the same method which works with modern literature may
prove utterly misleading with Old Germanic poetry. Obviously, the fact
that recent scholarship has shaken our assumptions about the date of
composition of *Beowulf* raises unavoidable questions about influence
and imitation: perhaps as a result of my own limited experience, I can
think of very few poets who have been influenced by their successors.
Even if we could demonstrate that the *Andreas*-poet had actually read
Beowulf or listened to an oral performance thereof, we still could not
dismiss the validity of Greenfield's observation that 'the nature of
composition by theme and formula is such' that the poet may quite simply
have composed 'under the influence of his poetic heritage.'[26] As for the
nature of that poetic heritage, it is quite clear – though not necessarily
exclusively – the tradition of oral-formulaic rhetoric. Space will not permit
a detailed examination of the extent to which *Andreas* belongs to the

oral-formulaic tradition, but two typical instances should suffice to illustrate the point.

The first instance is the opening statement. As we have seen, it is very similar to the opening statement of *Beowulf* and bears a close family resemblance to that of the *Hildebrandslied*. In addition, we may recall that it was the first oral formula to be identified as such by Francis Peabody Magoun in his seminal essay on the subject[27] and that, depending on the mode of analysis, it happens to be either the most common or the second most common opening formula in the surviving corpus of Old English poetry,[28] where it is attested to in texts whose respective chronologies remain uncertain. *Beowulf* aside, the poems in which it occurs do not immediately come to the modern reader's mind, and we may be tempted to blame their failure to serve our need on the fact that their public-relations department has been relatively inactive in recent years. Yet I doubt that they would normally have come to the mind of Old English audiences any sooner than to our own. Regardless of the actual mode of composition, vernacular poetry in the early Middle Ages was commonly performed orally,[29] and I suspect that the audiences of the time were fundamentally similar to modern movie-goers, who attend the performance but have no opportunity to peruse the script, so that they almost always remember the outline of the plot, an occasional scene if it happens to be especially arresting, and the principal performers, but would usually be at a loss if asked anything about the techniques of the text. Yet it would be hard to imagine that Russian audiences between the 1920s and the early 1940s could have remained emotionally unaffected by the film techniques of Sergei Eisenstein, although the chances are that very few among them realised consciously the nature or provenance of these techniques; and it would be equally hard to imagine that Old English audiences could have remained impervious to the cumulative impact of formulaic elements constantly reiterated under similar narrative circumstances.

The second instance is the occurrence of a much-studied oral-formulaic theme which is known as 'the hero on the beach' even when there is no beach in sight and in which a hero at the outset or conclusion of a journey, in the vicinity of some of his own people, stands at the juncture between two elements in the presence of something which shines. It was originally identified in *Andreas* by David Crowne in 1960[30] and has since been found in *Beowulf*, where it occurs several times, as well as in other Old and Middle English poems and in Old German, Middle High

German, and Old Norse texts.[31] As in the case of the opening formula, it would be futile to interpret the pervasiveness of this theme as an indication of imitation or influence as long as we have not established for certain the chronological relationship between the poems involved; and any critical interpretation or evaluation based on groundless assumptions is likely to prove as shaky as the assumptions themselves. In other words, our only choice is between interpreting the text in a vacuum or returning to Greenfield's point about the importance of the 'poetic heritage' represented by the oral-formulaic context.

The mechanics whereby the oral-formulaic context affects us may be illustrated with a brief example. Within the surviving corpus of Old Germanic literature, the theme of the hero on the beach normally occurs before a scene of slaughter or the mention of a scene of slaughter,[32] so that the most elementary logic suggests that some kind of association between the theme and approaching danger must have existed for both the poet and the audience, whether consciously or otherwise, and anticipation must have taken place accordingly. It certainly does take place for those modern readers who have become aware of the connection. In *Beowulf,* for example, we are told almost at the outset that the hero sets out on an overseas expedition to tackle a monster (194a–209b) whose irascibility and formidable strength have been impressed upon us throughout most of the preceding narrative (86a–193b). Nobody, of course, would expect the encounter between Grendel and Beowulf to be anything except slaughterous, but the emotional impact of the anticipation is intensified by the brilliant manipulation of the theme of the hero on the beach, which tells us that the yet unlocalized but fully expected slaughter is near at hand rather than safely scheduled for a vague and distant future. As Beowulf and his companions approach the end of their sea journey, thus reaching the juncture between the world of the waters and that of the land, the very first thing which they notice is something shining:

> ... ða liðende   land gesawon,
> brimclifu blican ...   (221a–222a)

For the properly trained audience, the tension is thus intensified by the presence of the theme; and the original audience must have been much better trained in this respect – though perhaps unconsciously so – than modern scholars can ever hope to be.

Nor are we permitted to forget the theme and its suggestive function, since the next five hundred lines (222a–727b) keep the idea going in our

mind with twelve different mentions of various shining objects, ranging
from shiny shields ('beorhte randas' [231b]) to the sun rising in the East
('leoht eastan com, // beorht beacen godes' [569b-70a]).[33] The final
mention is one which no reader of the poem can ever forget and which
appropriately occurs at the very point when the expected slaughter is
about to begin: as Grendel has finally made his way from the outside
world of the wild into the civilized world of Heorot, the only thing which
we are permitted to see is the ugly light of his eyes glowing ominously
through the opaque darkness:

> ... him of eagum stood
> ligge gelicost   leoht unfæger.   (726b-727b)

Al Capp is said to have claimed that his *Li'l Abner* could be enjoyed
at one level by readers who merely followed the action and at a much
more rewarding level by those initiates who construed the narrative in
the light of the social and political allusions therein.[34] By a similar
principle, the five-hundred-line progression (221a-725b) between the
landfall and Grendel's attack on Heorot would be very effective by any
standards and for any audience; but, for initiates attuned to the implications of oral-formulaic devices, it becomes one of the most successfully
and excruciatingly suspense-laden sequences in the history of mimetic
literature. Yet our response to this masterful performance will be fully
satisfactory only if we skip the indirect process of recalling where we
have encountered the theme before and if we react to the theme itself
without having to analyse its provenance – in other words, if we let the
theme inform the occasion rather than the other way around as our literate
education has taught us to do. For this purpose, incidentally, it is only
of secondary importance whether the poem was composed orally or in
writing, but it is of primary importance that it should be the work of
a poet steeped in the oral-formulaic tradition and composing with the
expectation that the audience will appreciate the mechanics of that
tradition.

   As I have already mentioned, not enough Old English poetry survived
to enable us to establish a truly satisfactory interpretative context, be
it oral-formulaic or not. In contrast to the history of literary influence
and imitation, however, the oral-formulaic context at times enables us
to break through the linguistic, geographic, and chronological limitations
of the surviving corpus. When we find the same theme occurring under
similar circumstances in Old English, Old German, and Archaic Greek,[35]

for example, we have occasion to suspect that we are dealing with an oral-formulaic element of Indo-European origin which must have been pervasive in the literature of the languages which have preserved it. Even if the vicissitudes of time have preserved only one instance thereof in a given literature, we are thus in a position to turn to other times and literatures in order to guess something of its function and affective impact, and we thereby have a partial substitute for other contexts which may no longer be available to us. If there is a lesson in the foregoing observations it is simply that, when we approach the task of interpreting Old English poems with roots in the oral-formulaic tradition, we should do well to remember Greenfield's statements that formulas can activate 'a whole host of overtones' and that certain kinds of similarities between such poems may simply indicate that each poet composed 'under the influence of his poetic heritage.' As we do so, however, we should also remember Greenfield's own warning that 'the interpretation of poems is at best a precarious business.'[36]

NOTES

1 Stanley B. Greenfield 'The Formulaic Expression of the Theme of "Exile" in Anglo-Saxon Poetry' *Speculum* 30 (1955) 205

2 Adrien Bonjour '*Beowulf* and the Beasts of Battle' *PMLA* 72 (1957) 556

3 John Miles Foley 'Formula and Theme in Old English Poetry' in *Oral Literature and the Formula* ed Benjamin A. Stolz and Richard S. Shannon (Ann Arbor 1976) 218. Foley's extremely influential contribution in emphasizing the importance of shifting our attention from specific associations to 'archetypal paradigms' has been further developed in his '*Beowulf* and the Psychohistory of Anglo-Saxon Culture' *American Imago* 34 (1977), where he argues that 'the traditional society educates its members – that is, it provides them with necessary information – through the repeated and collective experience of performed epic poetry, by presenting them time and again with a verbal montage of the group's poetic models and thereby with the data which these models encode' (134), and again that 'the psychohistorical matrix which underlies and generates the epic narrative remains available to all members of the society through repeated oral performances' (153).

4 Larry D. Benson 'The Literary Character of Anglo-Saxon Formulaic Poetry' *PMLA* 81 (1966) 340

5 Robert P. Creed 'The *Beowulf*-Poet: Master of Sound-Patterning' in *Oral Traditional Literature: A Festschrift for Albert Bates Lord* ed John Miles Foley (Columbus, Ohio 1981) 194

6 Donald K. Fry 'Cædmon as a Formulaic Poet' *Forum for Modern Language Studies* 10 (1974) 227

7 See, eg, Stanley E. Fish's famous statement that 'the objectivity of the text is an illusion' in his extremely influential 'Literature in the Reader: Affective Stylistics' *NLH* 2 (1970) 140; or Geoffrey H. Hartman's argument that literary interpretation 'implies ... that a work has become detached from its original context or that criticism helps detach (decontextualize) it,' in his 'War in Heaven: A Review of Harold Bloom's *The Anxiety of Influence: a Theory of Poetry*' in Hartman *The Fate of Reading and Other Essays* (Chicago 1975) 41. Robert De Maria examines these and other fashionable trends in literary theory and believes that they are practised 'to the exclusion, and even to the avowed extinction, of authors and literary subjects,' in his 'The Ideal Reader: A Critical Fiction' *PMLA* 93 (1978) 463

8 My statement is emphatically not intended to imply the notion that textual problems are by nature insoluble or that the facts of oral-formulaic composition are always irrelevant to textual and related scholarship. Quite on the contrary, one recalls how these facts have helped Joseph J. Duggan propose a convincing solution for the well-known puzzle presented by the presence of the so-called Baligant episode in the *Chanson de Roland*, in his *The Song of Roland: Formulaic Style and Poetic Art* (Berkeley 1973) 63-104; or how they help John D. Niles explain the fact that a character who is killed in a medieval epic reappears alive and well in a subsequent episode of the same epic, in his 'Narrative Anomalies in "La Chançun de Willame"' *Viator* 9 (1978) 251-64; or how they help Robert P. Creed propose a reconsideration of the lineation of *Beowulf*, in his 'The Basis of the Meter of *Beowulf*' in *Approaches to Beowulfian Scansion* ed Alain Renoir and Ann Hernandez, University of California Old English Colloquium Series 1 (Berkeley 1982) 27-35

9 All these citations and quotations from Old English poetry are from the texts printed in ASPR ed George P. Krapp and Elliott V.K. Dobbie.

10 The allusion is to John MacBride, who had married and then divorced the woman with whom Yeats had been in love for years.

11 Norman N. Holland, *The Dynamics of Literary Response* (1968; rpt New York 1975), argues that 'clearly, meaning is not simply "there" in the text; rather it is something we construct from the text within the limits of the text' (25) so that we 'perceive the text as things we know in life. ... Unconsciously, however, we bring quite other things to the text ...' (62).

12 Fred C. Robinson 'Old English Literature in Its Most Immediate Context' in *Old English Literature in Context* ed John D. Niles (Cambridge 1980) 11

13 Kevin S. Kiernan, *Beowulf and the Beowulf Manuscript* (New Brunswick

1981), sees the extant poem as the 'fusion of two originally distinct *Beowulf* narratives' (271) and dates it in the eleventh century (277), thus explicitly (13n1) going to the opposite extreme from Jane Weightman, *The Language and Dialect of Later Old English Poetry* (Liverpool 1907), who would date the original poem in the seventh century (v); and one recalls that Ritchie Girvan, *Beowulf and the Seventh Century* (1935; London 1971), has more recently than Weightman argued 'for 680–700' (25).

14 *The Dating of Beowulf* ed Colin Chase (Toronto 1981), with Chase's fine survey of the problem ('Opinions on the Date of *Beowulf*' [3-8] and essays in which Kevin Kiernan ('The Eleventh-Century Origin of *Beowulf* and the *Beowulf* Manuscript') argues, as in his book (n13 above), in favour of the eleventh century (eg, 20-1), John C. Pope ('On the Date of Composition of *Beowulf*') seems satisfied with 'almost any time in the eighth century' (195), Peter Clemoes ('Style as the Criterion for Dating the Composition of *Beowulf*') regards the 'composition of *Beowulf* during the second half of the eighth century as much the most likely' (185), Walter Goffart ('Hetware and Hugas: Datable Anachronisms in *Beowulf*') suggests that a *'terminus a quo* would have to be fixed ... near the year 923' (100), and Thomas Cable ('Metrical style as Evidence for the Date of *Beowulf*') can find 'no metrical reason why all the poems on our list from *Daniel* to *The Metres of Boethius*, including *Beowulf*, should not be assigned dates of composition in the ninth century' (82). We may accordingly say that recent scholarship would place the date of *Beowulf* in the eighth, ninth, tenth, and eleventh centuries.

15 John D. Niles, *Beowulf: The Poem and Its Tradition* (Cambridge, Mass, 1983), raises serious doubts about the reasons for assigning an early date to *Beowulf* and concludes that 'until additional facts are discovered, one is wiser to admit one's ignorance of when, where, and how the poem was written down than to pretend to have knowledge that is beyond our grasp' (117), even though he cautiously admits that 'if guess comes to guess, the second quarter of the tenth century provides a plausible historical setting for the composition of *Beowulf*' (116).

16 Eg, Richard H. Lawson, *'The Hildebrandslied* Originally Gothic?' *NM* 74 (1973), urges us 'not to repudiate out of hand the proposal of a Gothic origin' (339), and Moritz Trautmann, 'Finn und Hildebrand' *Bonner Beiträge zur Anglistik* 7 (1903), argues for an Old English original, which he proceeds to reconstruct (121-3). A.T. Hatto, 'On the Excellence of the *Hildebrandslied*: A Comparative Study in Dynamics' *MLR* 68 (1973), expresses what seems to be the prevalent opinion when he writes that the extant text is a ' "Saxonized" version of a (scribal) Bavarian version of an original (oral) Longobardic lay' (820n).

17 The extant text of the *Hildebrandslied* is copied on the first and last folio sides (1r and 76v) of theol fol 54 in the Kassel Landesbibliothek. Satisfactory unbound photocopies of both pages are provided in *Das Hildebrandslied* ed George Baesecke (Halle 1945); smaller and somewhat less clear reproductions are likewise provided in Willy Krogmann *Das Hildebrandslied in der langobardischen Urfassung hergestellt* (Berlin 1959) 49.

18 If we accept Donald K. Fry's very plausible theory in his 'The Memory of Cædmon' in *Oral Traditional Literature: A Festschrift for Albert Bates Lord* ed John Miles Foley that Old English manuscripts 'were not very many in the first place. Indeed the manuscript of a traditional society ... was memory' (292), and, if we keep in mind that the most elementary common sense tells us that the oral poems which were never recorded *were nevertheless composed*, we must logically conclude that the surviving corpus necessarily represents an even smaller fraction of the total production than was supposed when the diminutive size of that corpus was attributed exclusively to the depredations of time, invasions, and Reformation.

19 Rudolph C. Bambas, 'Another View of the Old English "Wife's Lament"' *JEGP* 62 (1963) 303-9, sees the speaker as a thane; Thomas M. Davis, 'Another View of *"The Wife's Lament"*' *PELL* 1 (1965) 291-305, sees the speaker as a person accused of 'perhaps sorcery' (303); Stanley B. Greenfield, '*The Wife's Lament* Reconsidered' *PMLA* 68 (1953) 907-12, convincingly sees the speaker as an imprisoned wife; A.N. Doane, 'Heathen Form and Christian Function in "The Wife's Lament"' *MS* 28 (1966) 77-91, sees the speaker as a minor heathen deity; M.J. Swanton, '*The Wife's Lament* and *The Husband's Message*: A Reconsideration' *Anglia* 82 (1964), sees the speaker as a voice yearning for the union of 'God with the Church' (276). These and other theories are outlined in Eleanor Lench '*The Wife's Lament*: A Poem of the Living Dead' *Comitatus* 1 (1970) 3-23.

20 Eg, Frederick Tupper, 'The Cynewulfian Runes of the First Riddle' *MLN* 25 (1910) 235-41, proposed 'Cynewulf' as a solution for the would-be riddle, as Heinrich Leo had already suggested in the Halle Program for 1857, while 'millstone' has been proposed by H. Pätzig 'Zum ersten Rätsel des Exeterbuchs' *Archiv* 145 (1923) 204-7; Ferdinand Holthausen, 'Zu alt- und mittelenglischen Denkmälern iv. 34: Klage um Wulf' *Anglia* 15 (1893) 188-9, sees the poem as a fragment of a monologue, as have several other scholars; Henry Schofield, 'Signy's Lament' *PMLA* 17 (1902) 262-95, sees the poem as an adaptation from Old Norse connected with the *Volsunga Saga*; Walter J. Sedgefield, 'Old English Notes' *MLR* 26 (1931) 74-5, makes a case for the canine theory.

21 Dolores Warwick Frese 'Wulf and Eadwacer: The Adulterous Woman Reconsidered' *Notre Dame English Journal* 15 (1983) 1

22 Benjamin Thorpe ed *Codex Exoniensis* (London 1842) 527 n to 380

23 My own '*Wulf and Eadwacer*: A Noninterpretation' in *Franciplegius: Medieval and Linguistic Studies in Honor of Francis Peabody Magoun, Jr.* ed Jess B. Bessinger, Jr, and Robert P. Creed (New York 1965) 147-63, with comments on salient interpretations to 1963 (147-8)

24 *Das Hildebrandslied* in Wilhelm Braune *Althochdeutsches Lesebuch* rev Karl Helm 11th ed (Halle 1949) 72-3

25 Charles W. Kennedy *The Earliest English Poetry* (London 1943) 279, with a discussion of the similarities between *Andreas* and *Beowulf* 267-79. For a detailed study of the parallels between the two poems, see Leonard J. Peters 'The Relationship of the Old English *Andreas* to *Beowulf*' *PMLA* 66 (1951) 844-62.

26 Stanley B. Greenfield *A Critical History of Old English Literature* (New York 1965) 104. Greenfield, who 'cannot altogether discount the possibility that the *Andreas* poet knew the *Beowulf* and was attracted to the story of Andreas because of the resemblance' (104), discusses similarities between the two poems on 103-4.

27 Francis P. Magoun, Jr 'Oral-Formulaic Character of Anglo-Saxon Narrative Poetry' *Speculum* 28 (1953) 446-67

28 The form under which the formulaic opening occurs in the *Hildebrands-lied*, with the verb 'to hear,' is the most common; if we decide that the use of the alternative verb 'to learn' in *Beowulf, Andreas*, and other poems warrants a different classification, then the latter would be the second most common, as pointed out by Magoun 'Oral-Formulaic Character' 453. With either verb, the formula is used to introduce either whole poems or sections thereof.

29 One thinks, eg, of Alcuin's letter of 797, urging the Bishop of Lindisfarne to stop banqueting clerics from listening to the singing of vernacular poems instead of the reading of sermons: 'Ibi decet lectorem audiri, non citharistam; sermones patrum, non carmina gentilium,' in 'Letter 81' in *Monumenta Alcuiniana* ed Wilhelm Wattenbach and Ernst Dümmler (Berlin 1873).

30 David K. Crowne 'The Hero on the Beach: An Example of Composition by Theme in Anglo-Saxon Poetry' *NM* 61 (1960) 362-72. Crowne's analysis specifically noted the juncture between land and water, hence the title, but subsequent analysts have expanded the image to include the juncture between any two elements.

31 See, eg, Donald K. Fry 'The Hero on the Beach in Finnsburh' *NM* 67 (1966) 27-31, 'The Heroine on the Beach in *Judith*' *NM* 68 (1967) 168-84, and 'Themes and Type-Scenes in *Elene* 1-113' *Speculum* 44 (1969) 35-45; Janet Thormann 'Variations on the Theme of "The Hero on the Beach" in *The Phoenix*' *NM* 71 (1970) 187-90; Carol Jean Wolf 'Christ as Hero on the Beach in *The*

Dream of the Rood' NM 71 (1970) 202-10; James D. Johnson 'The Hero on the Beach in the *Alliterative Morte Darthure' NM* 76 (1975) 271-81; Alexandra Hennessey Olsen 'Guthlac on the Beach' *Neophil* 64 (1980) 290-6. I have discussed occurrences of the theme in Old and Middle High German in my 'Oral-Formulaic Theme Survival: A Possible Instance in the *Nibelungenlied' NM* 65 (1964) 70-5, and 'The Armor of the *Hildebrandslied*: An Oral-Formulaic Point of View' *NM* 78 (1977) 389-95, as well as in other essays; and Michael D. Cherniss identifies the same theme in Old Norse in an essay in progress based on a paper delivered at the 1981 MLA Convention.

32 Crowne 'Hero on the Beach' 372

33 The other references to various shining things occur in lines 303a, 311a, 321b, 322b, 405b, 413b, 496a, 604b–606b, and 648b.

34 E.J. Kahn, Jr 'Ooff!! (Sob!) Eep!! (Gulp!) Zowie!!!' in Louis G. Locke et al *Toward Liberal Education* rev ed (New York 1952) esp 322-3 (rpt from the *New Yorker* 23 [29 Nov 1947] 45-57)

35 Robert P. Creed, 'The Singer Looks at His Sources' in *Studies in Old English Literature in Honor of Arthur G. Brodeur* ed Stanley B. Greenfield (Eugene, Or 1963) 44-52, identifies the same oral-formulaic theme in both *Beowulf* and the *Odyssey*, and I have identified that same theme in the *Hildebrands-lied* in my 'Oral-Formulaic Context: Implications for the Comparative Crit-icism of Mediaeval Texts' in *Oral Traditional Literature* ed Foley, 416-39.

36 Stanley B. Greenfield *The Interpretation of Old English Poems* (London 1972) 159

PART II

WORDS AND THE WORK

Can we have it both ways, then? I would argue so. .. Relevance can and must be both historical and modern, focusing upon that aspect of text and context which has a special resonance in our own moral and aesthetic consciousness without, at the same time, falsifying or distorting historical probability.

The Interpretation of Old English Poems 1972

DOLORES WARWICK FRESE

Poetic Prowess in *Brunanburh* and *Maldon*: Winning, Losing, and Literary Outcome

ḢISTORY, so one truism has it, is written by the winners, poetry by the losers. Implicit in this whimsical and somewhat overtidy observation there are certain generic assumptions that have informed the morphology of criticism on *The Battle of Brunanburh* and *The Battle of Maldon*. Assuming these two modes of human inscription to be mutually exclusive, critics have typically perceived the annalistic text of *Brunanburh*, preserved as the historical entry for 937 in four manuscripts of the *Anglo-Saxon Chronicle*,[1] as the work of a 'gifted and well trained publicist,' to use Klaeber's faintly damning phrase.[2] In recording the politically significant events of 937, patriotic 'feelings of exultation at the victory over a foreign foe' are assumed to have inspired the versified dilations of some Wessex historian who, according to Elliott Van Kirk Dobbie, 'took the opportunity to commemorate Æthelstan's victory in a more vigorous and striking way than would be possible in a prose annal.'[3] The record of events 'ymbe Brunanburh' has thus come to be thought of as a kind of secular *Biblia Versificata* – the casting of history into verse being a pedagogical device to underscore the importance of the content.

The Battle of Brunanburh has invariably been compared to *The Battle of Maldon* and it has suffered by comparison. *Maldon*, with its dazzling varieties of impersonated consciousness, has always been understood and admired as poetry, while *Brunanburh* is typically assigned secondary status as commemorative battle verse whose enthusiastic maker produced, in place of an annal entry, what Dobbie called 'an unrestrained song of triumph, in which the poet seems to know little, and care less, of the actual course of events.'[4] Typical of this nearly formulaic comparison is Fred C. Robinson's obervation that '*The Battle of Maldon* is not a glossy and relatively uncomplicated occasional poem like *The Battle of Brunanburh*.'[5] Even Stanley Greenfield, whose critical prowess has come to the rescue of many an Old English poem in distress, at one point reduces *The Battle of Brunanburh* to 'a tissue of heroic formulaic clichés, themes, and stylistic variation' although he concedes, more generously, that 'the conventional heroic epithets and stylistic mannerisms are nevertheless infused with a vitality and spirit that is hard to analyze.'[6]

Faced with so formidable a shield-wall of opinion upon the minor merits of *The Battle of Brunanburh*, one feels a certain degree of critical 'ofermod' in undertaking to argue that *Brunanburh* is, indeed, an accomplished poem. The first part of this essay will venture a provisional literary analysis that attempts to account for that poetic 'vitality' correctly perceived by Greenfield, suggesting that the animate centre of the poem has been equipped by its maker with a number of mechanisms that deliberately defend it from premature understanding. The poem does this by constructing, in the fashion of consciousness, an alternate, relatively complete, but more superficial and hence less threatening version of its own perceptions.

There are a number of surface features that authorize this simpler version of *Brunanburh* as mere historical or pseudo-historical partisan record. The documentary 'Her' with which the text begins,[7] its closing reference to the written record – 'þæs þe us secgað bec' (68b) – the naming of the combatants, the numbering of the dead, the brief, compact narrative organization into categories of winners and losers, the English exulting in the win – 'wiges hremige' (59b) – the whipped and woeful intruders shamed in spirit – 'æwiscmode' (56b) – as they head home to Dublin, all contribute to the annalistic surface.

Brunanburh can be, and so often has been, read this way simply because the poem has been cunningly constructed to resemble a superficial chronicle account of who – what – when and where, describing how the victors 'ahton wælstowe geweald.' Its radical poetic centre, however, inducts us into sympathy for the invaders, even as it values military protagonists and antagonists as equal and almost interchangeable human presences. So successful is the protective chronicle colouration which the poet has afforded this centre that it is the historical annals themselves and not any poetic codex that account for the textual survival of *Brunanburh*.

Not all readers, to be sure, have taken so narrowly constrained a view of *Brunanburh*. Neil Isaacs sensitively observes the metaphoric connection of men and weapons that operates on several levels throughout the poem,[8] as does W.F. Bolton, whose essay traces the single device of variation through prosodic, lexical, and syntactic patterns.[9] Ann Johnson provides another attentive account of various elaborate rhetorical schema that appear as 'the instrument of conscious artistry,'[10] and Frances Lipp, in her fine essay on 'Contrast and Point of View in *The Battle of Brunanburh*,'[11] notes a peculiar emotional effect produced by the focus on suffering inflicted on the invaders by the English, although her conclusion about the 'ultimate insignificance of the enemy' established by portraying their entrapment in 'the perennial sufferings of man, caught in a moment of this transitory life' seems to me to be an exactly wrong observation. Traugott Lawlor, whose relatively unknown essay is by far the most extended and refined excursion into the literary texture of the poem, traces explicit and implicit notions of craft and art that abound in *The Battle of Brunanburh*, linking the art of war and weapon-making to the craft of making books and poems, all of it joined on the intersection of words and weapons that produce a carving of history. But even Lawlor reduces the ultimate experience of the poem to a 'deep sense of pattern' seen as some sort of appropriate regimental format for a panegyric celebration of military control. Lawlor concludes by observing that this 'notably successful example of its genre' is 'by its nature not capable of powerful emotion or deep human insight.'[12]

Each of these essayists finds occasion to praise the trope of the sun shining brightly over the bloodstained battlefield; each notes certain aspects of structure and form that announce an intention towards conscious artifice. All value the poem's terminal connection of these events at Brunanburh with those marking the first arrival of the Angles and Saxons in the early history of Britain. But it is primarily history, not poetry, that is typically invoked to substantiate the text of *Brunanburh*, even among those commentators who mean to value it. Its efflorescence into meaning is assumed to be historical, not literary, and its authenticated poetic devices, like the sun itself, are assessed and praised as luminous, surprisingly realized and pleasurable poetic ruptures of an essentially historical narrative, even as *Brunanburh* itself ruptures the historical narrativity of those four prose chronicles responsible for its preservation.

Despite this virtual unanimity about the poem's status as mere historical panegyric I wish to argue that *The Battle of Brunanburh* is not primarily an 'exultavit' performed upon the corpse of a vanquished enemy so much as it is a deeply incanted experience of the purification of enmity. In the passage from verbal non-meaning to meaning which is the experience of the poem,[13] the phantasm of historical antagonism is gradually replaced by an intricate poetic contra-diction which expresses unanimity and fraternity between victors and vanquished. The explicitly stated nobility of 'Æþelstan cyning' (1a) and 'Eadmund æþeling' (3a) in their pugilistic winning of 'hord and hamas' (10a) constitutes a naturalized claim to the soil of Britain when that same vocabulary of nobility and settlement is attached, immediately thereafter, to the sun itself. But the equivalence is not a simple one, for that poetically noble creation, God's 'æþele gesceaft' (16b), is made to shine here on the just and the unjust, on living and dead, equally illuminating both winners and losers:

> Hettend crungun,
> Sceotta leoda   and scipflotan
> fæge feollan,   feld dænnede
> secga swate,   siðþan sunne up
> on morgentid,   mære tungol,
> glad ofer grundas,   godes condel beorht,
> eces drihtnes,   oð sio æþele gesceaft
> sah to setle. (10b–17a)

The poet's single sentence reproduced the morning-noon-night comprehensiveness of a day, a lifetime, a history. But here verbal process, like the sun's process, at once so resplendent and so fatal in its rising and falling, signals the nobly ascendant Æthelstan and Eadmund even as it simultaneously accords funereal dignity to their vanquished enemy as an equally noble creature 'sah to setle.'

This initial incanting of fraternity between brother and brother, between man and nature, and most subtly between friend and foe is repeated at the conclusion of the poem when the original Anglo-Saxon invaders, Hengist and Horsa, are invoked by the poetically brilliant device that represents them as an earlier version of the sun itself through the words that show them in their own rising-from-the-east: 'siþþan eastan hider // Engle and Seaxe / up becoman' (69b–70b). Here at the end, replicating the poem's opening movement, the overtone of solar triumphalism identifying Æthelstan and Eadmund with their ancestral forebears is richly qualified by the fact that those original 'Engle and Seaxe' came up by sea, arriving 'ofer brad brimu' (71a) in all their barbaric glory. They thus become in this poem verbal and iconic correlatives of Constantine and Anlaf, the only other 'scipflotan' named in the world of the text, but seafarers whose landseeking in Britain was not fated to such a productive outcome. As we verbally experience this poetic encroachment of one situation upon the other, the specifics of successive historical encroachment become neutralized, dissolved and finally replaced by a sense of sympathetic inclusiveness which the poem communicates through suggestive verbal arrangements that consistently feature identity and equivalence, even as they detail the bellicose encounter. Through the inclusion of interchangeable versions of history that were, and were not, fated to be, *The Battle of Brunanburh* engenders a profound feeling of detachment from time, from the specifics of history and from enmity itself. It is the subtly cognate fates of men, not the experience of hostility, that constitutes the poem's final deposit of meaning. The sense of all life as a puissant flick preoccupies poet and reader, while the dismemberment of consciousness inherent in such reflection translates into an italicized sympathy for the mutilated dead of the poem.

The fact is that while the imagined writer of chronicle here is seen to relish his recording of defeat as he meticulously numbers the more signal casualties of battle – five kings and seven earls on that battlefield, we are told – nevertheless, the poet does not really wish to take the lives of the enemy. The five young kings and seven earls of Anlaf are not really dead, but only sleeping – 'sweordum aswefede' (30a) the poet says, laying hostility to rest. The mortal combat of their gray-haired elders becomes an exchange of weapons, a game played on the battlefield with the sons of Edward: 'wæpengewrixles, / þæs hi on wælfelda // wiþ Eadweardes / afaran plegodan' (51a–52b). One can almost imagine here an early, poetic attestation to the famed English sense of 'fair play' and the almost apothegmic connection between the playing fields and the battlefields of Britain. The entire invading army is domesticated to a 'litle weorode' (34b) and a single ship crowding a small sea becomes the frail vessel wherein all awareness momentarily survives. Confronted with this series of emotionally powerful images of the reversibility and fragility of human consciousness, we cannot remain untouched by a certain covert sense of relief and affirmative release when told that the old king did save his life. Indeed, I sense little scorn and a certain elegant sympathy attaching to this poetic account of his perilous survival.

In fact, the severity of form, the poem's charged reduction of itself to utter essentials, becomes part of the intensified – nearly amphibolic – experience that *Brunanburh* begets everywhere upon its materials. Æthelstan and Eadmund oppose Constantine and Anlaf. The fact that the historical coalition of invaders involved a third party in the reported person of Owen, King of the Strathclyde Britons,[14] does not enter the poem, for the artist's concern here is to formulate the experienced sense of interchangeable equivalence that has something psychologically palindromic at its base. Thus Wessex and Mercia meet Scottish and Irish; the named city of Brunanburh engenders the explicit naming of the counter city of Dublin. When the Northmen depart, 'Difelin secan, // eft Iraland' (55b–56a), they are subtly brothered to Æthelstan and Eadmund who are actually made to follow in the verbal footsteps of the men they have defeated: 'Swilce þa gebroþer / begen ætsamne, // cyning and æþeling, / cyþþe sohton, // Wesseaxena land' (57a–59a). Winners and losers are situated in great equivalence here by poetic outcome, even as they are radically differentiated by historical outcome.

It is worth noting, too, that the poem's next sentence, following directly upon this antiphonal account of victor and vanquished, reiterates and confirms the sense of identity and fraternal survival by implying that the ultimate combat is not between man and man but rather involves that larger engagement where 'mors et vita duello conflixere mirando,' a contest in which the beasts of battle, who now make their formulaic appearance, are defeated by the poet's inclusive act of memorial inscription:

Letan him behindan   hræw bryttian
saluwigpadan,   þone sweartan hræfn,
hyrnednebban,   and þane hasewanpadan,
earn æften hwit,   æses brucan,
grædigne guðhafoc   and þæt græge deor,
wulf on wealde.   (60a–65a)

The pronomial and verbal plurals are most immediately referential to the Wessex kinsmen but they are inclusive enough to be extended to all the human survivors, winners and losers alike, who have been granted the territory of survival in the poet's claimed territory. It is mortality, signalled by the animal predators, who 'ahton wealstowe geweald,' constructing one version of victory at Brunanburh; historical enemies leave this territory of death together and reenter the land of the living via their various human geographies, equally immortal survivors in the presence of this poem.

This reduction of superficial historical opposition to a received experience of human fraternity is the poem's compressed achievement. Even the verse pairs communicate this urgent sense of equivalence by their nearly unanimous two-word structures. In fact, when prepositions, pronouns, articles, conjunctions, enclitics and positional adverbs like 'her' and 'þær' are assimilated into narrative consciousness, what remains in all but seven of the 146 verse pairs of this poem are half-lines consisting of just two words. The convention of enmity is severely challenged by such an exhibition of dependent closeness. Furthermore, when the poem is read as a set of sixteen sentences of rhythmically varying length[15] – as the manuscript facts invite us to do – we find that the entire poem consists of four quartets of interlocking thought, and that each fourth sentence contributes to this incrementally expanded meaning by explicitly challenging its own prior content of articulated enmity through the presentation of some subtle, even startling, device of implied sympathy. Thus we have the diurnally beneficent sun trope, the young sleeping lords, the elder warriors at play on the battlefield, and finally the poetically invoked appearance of the patronymic invaders, themselves now living presences in the book of history and the book of poetry alike. Each of these ritualistically located poetic inventions finds a way to spare the life of the historically dead, and something like melodic fulfilment emerges.

I would suggest then, though I have only touched briefly on a few of the possible arguments for such a suggestion, that *The Battle of Brunanburh* is only accidentally a chronicle account of versified local events at Brunanburh – wherever that may be – in 937 or thereabouts.[16] Its true prestige accrues from its rather distinguished achievement as poetry, not from the fact of its anomolous preservation in the *Anglo-Saxon Chronicle*, along with five other truly undistinguished, and accordingly unremembered, verse texts.[17] The author's intention to write poetry rather than mere historical record becomes more apparent as the husk of history in all its finished estrangement is discarded and the quickened poem still lies before us, richly inviting in its image of that peculiar transcendence that comes with the accomplished loving of one's enemy. But such access out of history into poetry was imaginatively available to the battle poet only in the historical situation of winning, for that fundamental Christian imperative to love your enemy is itself based on certain retrospectively triumphal assumptions.

It seems worth noting in this connection that the 'speaking voice' in *Brunanburh* is intensely imagined as the 'text-voice' of written historical record, and it is that imaginative intensity which produces this uncannily silent battle poem. For in fact, *The Battle of Brunanburh* is an entirely soundless imagined experience; the act of human utterance has been completely subsumed here into the silence of written record.

Here, as in all artful poetry, verbal behaviour reproduces in some analogous way the activity of the poet who does not foresee or rehearse the exact literary shape, but discovers it in the act of composing the poem, finding in the very process of composition those verbal arrangements that appear adequate to the inner sense of perception.[18]

I do not mean to raise shades of Milman Parry in this reference to the-poet-in-the-act-of-composition, but simply to point to a fact characteristic of all poetry with expressive content. In the case of the *Brunanburh* poet, that inner perception took shape under the aegis of an imagined subsequent text of history and he composed his poem accordingly. That so many readers have chanced or chosen to approach *Brunanburh* as versified history rather than as genuine poetry in spite of its accomplished literarity is really not so surprising, for, as Suzanne Langer has noted, 'the affliction of literature is its relation to fact.'[19] The formal decisions of the *Brunanburh* poet were guided by his own deep apprehensions of just that historical affliction attending his literary subject matter. In choosing to utter his poem as if he were a chronicler he is authorized to record certain truths beyond mere historical partisan account. This constitutes a record intended for the 'inward ear,' that aesthetic organ that corresponds to Wordsworth's 'inward eye which is the bliss of solitude.' Hence, there are no reported speech acts in *The Battle of Brunanburh*; there are no activated sounds. In fact, the absolute and aggressive negation of external audition is a significant subtlety of the text. No 'hlaford maðelode'; no birds sing. Even the obligatory beasts of battle previously mentioned appear quite soundlessly, in contrast to their clamorous appearance in the richly voiced text of *Maldon*. An insistent poetic point is made of this aesthetic fact: King Constantine had no need to exult – 'hreman ne þorfte' (39b). Five lines later the gray-haired man had no need to boast – 'gelpan ne þorfte' (44b); a mere two lines later we are told that he and Anlaf had no need to laugh – 'hlehhan ne þorftun' (47b). Beneath the overt denotation of defeated intruders litotically recorded we experience an extraordinary serial negation of the only verbs of utterance allowed into the *Brunanburh* poem thus far, serving here as a preparation for the utterly arresting voice-of-the-book which comes at the end of the poem – 'þæs þe us secgað bec' (68b) – which so stunningly returns us to those silent beginnings of the written records of the Anglo-Saxons which the silent word 'her' in this poem has invoked in principio.

In view of this absolute soundlessness of *The Battle of Brunanburh* perhaps we should return yet again to that question of whether the

Brunanburh poet committed an aesthetically anachronistic act of syn-aesthesia in his phrase 'feld dænnede // sæcga swate' (12b–13a). The phrase has been variously translated as 'the field grew dark,' 'grew slippery,' or 'resounded' with the blood of men – the last auditory rendering tentatively adopted by Fred C. Robinson and Stanley Greenfield among others, following the suggestion of Carl T. Berkhout,[20] who argues an underlying 'vox sanguinis' scriptural tradition in defence of his reading, an interpretation quite consonant with the poem's otherwise unbroken silence that mirrors the rarity of reported speech in the *Anglo-Saxon Chronicle*.

The textual silence of *Brunanburh* is dramatically different from the dictional plenitude of *Maldon*. Here utterance abounds, and in that fact of mimetically imagined live utterance we can begin to approach the meaning of *The Battle of Maldon*. The unmistakable controlling intention towards artifice rather than annal is inscribed in this chain of mimetic speech acts. Byrhtnoth speaks, Ælfwine speaks; then Offa and Leofsunu and Dunnere and Byrhtwold speak, all in response to the provocative words of the Viking messenger whose own theatrically imagined verbal provocation Fred C. Robinson has acutely identified as perhaps 'the first literary use of dialect in English.'[21] Together, these imagined speeches account for far more than a quarter of the surviving text of *Maldon*. Even the fact that the manuscript itself, like the fallen force it memorializes, has beeen maimed at head and heel – 'fragmentum ... capite et calce mutilum' in the words of Wanley, its seventeenth-century paleographic observer – this heavy presence of unmediated individual utterance provides a telling aesthetic descriptor of the poem-as-a-whole. The dramatised centre of *The Battle of Maldon* yields crucial information about poetic intention, for the impulse behind all mimetic impersonation is the projection into the experiential moment of the real presence of moral crisis. And if the affliction of literature is its relation to fact, then the affliction of drama – again according to Suzanne Langer – is 'its nearness to moral questions.'[22]

Clearly, what is being dramatized, celebrated, inscribed at the heart of *The Battle of Maldon* is individual moral choice, and this fact has been granted peculiar literary efficacy by the poet's construction of a text where utterance is surrounded by utterance surrounded by utterance. The imaginative vivification of speech, explicitly viewed as an act of moral distinction, becomes fraught with literary excitement as man after man refers, in turn, to present, past, and future speech acts, viewing them, as the poet at his composing stand views them, as semiological substitutes for what Jean Starobinski has called the body's 'superlative power of persuasion.'[23]

When the Viking messenger announces to Byrhtnoth that his superiors have *commanded* him to *tell* the English about the insulting proposal that the invaders be bought off with tribute – 'heton ðe secgan' (30a) – and when Byrhtnoth replies, in a critically much discussed line, 'Gehyrst þu, sælida, / hwæt þis folc secgeð?' (45), the literal question of whether or not voices could carry across a causeway at high or low tide, or whether the English may have communicated contempt with a rousing Bronx cheer or some four-letter gesture towards the invaders,[24] is far less significant than the fact that the poetry here, as everywhere in *Maldon*, insists on being perceived as utterance, consciously heard and spoken. Indeed, when Byrhtnoth finally tells the Vikings that the way is open to them and that 'god ana wat // hwa þære wælstowe / wealdan mote' (94b–95b) the reader's mind is all but bidden to complete the nearly colloquial 'god ana wat' with its colloquially ironic pendant, 'and God isn't saying.'

For indeed, the unspeakable knowledge of the Divine Mind is what generates the promethean human posture of individual heroic utterance which must always be made in ignorance of ultimate outcome. This raid on the inarticulate, this insistence on heroic articulatory performance with its signalling of present, active choice, has always been a conventional literary sign of pathos denied and it serves powerfully here in the poem whose occasion is the losing battle.[25]

Ælfwine remembers the speeches made over mead, the boasts raised from the bench; Offa follows with a specific exhortation to memorialize those acts of utterance: 'Hwæt þu, Ælfwine, hafast / ealle gemanode' (231). Byrhtnoth himself is remembered in this poem as a wordsmith rather than as a warsmith: in the course of the poem he 'commands,' 'speaks,' 'exhorts,' 'instructs,' 'calls out over cold water,' his words as protagonistically real as the antagonistic arrows that follow upon them. He 'laughs,' 'lauds God,' 'thanks his retainer,' Eadward the Tall, for a particularly skilful kill. The etymological entering of almost every Anglo-Saxon word for utterance into the text of *The Battle of Maldon* finally achieves a superfluity of specification that becomes poetically meaningful. What we have here is not some display of rhetorical 'ofermod,' attempting to include in one relatively compressed heroic lay the entire gamut of Aristotelian modes of utterance named under the topic of Diction: 'a command, a prayer, a statement, a threat, a question, an answer and so forth,' says Aristotle.[26] Rather, the spoken word becomes the very image of life in which this poem lives and creates its heroic ethos. The traitorous triplets, Godric, Godwine, and Godwig, flee wordlessly from the battle and from the text. The image of their cowardice, aside from the wordless impersonation of Byrthnoth by which so many are misled when Godric steals his fallen leader's horse and flees to the woods, is given shapely reinforcement by the ironic recollection of the poet who joins his heroes when he recalls, in his own voice, that Offa had earlier uttered a prophetic pre-diction of this present heroic contra-diction:

> Swa him Offa on dæg   ær asæde
> on þam meþelstede,   þa he gemot hæfde,
> þæt þær modiglice   manega spræcon
> þe eft æt þearfe   þolian noldon.   (198-201)

The poet's 'remembrance of words past' engenders similar remembrance in the mimetically representational present of the text. Offa's ironic prophecy, here ostensibly recalled by the poet, is an interesting literary invention which would seem to underscore the idea that the poet, in performing his poem, sees himself, in fact, as performing *his* boast. The alliterative lines, like the heroic people they represent, operate under a single stern imperative: advance and die. Immediately prior to the inscribing of Offa's utterance about the many whose words and deeds would *not* prove to be morally coterminous, the poet has proffered a plausible justification for his own survival and hence a justification for his text as well. But now, choosing to record Offa's words, he signals awareness of the fact that his status as a survivor might nonetheless still be construed as evidence of possible cowardice. This plenum of consciousness, so poignantly represented, immeasurably heightens the risk of the poetic performance, and forces attention onto the moral crux of the heroic situation which requires that words and deeds must be inexorably interchangeable to be valorizing.

Utterance as performance is deeply involved with the poetic outcome of *The Battle of Maldon*. Imagined utterance as the chief descriptor of this poem conveys most tellingly the tragic implications of a battle whose outcome is signally affected by verbal performance. Even with the missing lines at the end of the poem, there is no mistaking the coalescence of literary and military description in the final words of Byrhtwold: 'Hige sceal þe heardra, / heorte þe cenre, // mod sceal þe mare, / þe ure mægen lytlað' (312-13). Neither can the missing lines at the outset of the poem obscure the intentionally dramatic imaginative shape of *Maldon* whereby the opening scene prophesies its own ending, serving the destinal needs of the action to come. The horses driven off into the woods, the hawk let to fly there, are the theatrical as well as the moral signals of irreversible action underway. This reversion of the animal order to the fastness of the woods does indeed anticipate the subsequent, less-than-humanly-heroic flight of the cowards.[27] I would like to suggest, as well, that here we may have an early version of what later came to be a conventional stage utterance of determination that there would be no quarter given, no quarry or prisoners taken from one's own ranks. We are told of Offa's kinsman that 'he let him þa of handon / leofne fleogan // hafoc wið þæs holtes' (7–8a) and that this was done explicitly as a sign to the witnessing audience before the first words are spoken. 'Let ... fleogan ... hafoc' may survive in the familiar 'Cry havoc! and let slip the dogs of war'; indeed 'cry havoc' occurs in a number of Shakespeare's plays and it is glossed 'let no prisoners be taken.'[28]

In venturing this possible connection of *Maldon* with early theatrical tradition of a non-liturgical sort, we are reminded again of the often noted fact that 'ofermod' – that crucial lexical item on which hangs the moral judgment of Byrhtnoth as hero or grandstander – is a word that is entered in an eleventh-century Anglo-Saxon glossary as a synonym for 'cot(h)urnus,' the thick-soled boot worn by tragic actors.[29] Whether one wishes to assign Byrthnoth to the company of Lucifer, the only other figure of Old English poetry accused of 'ofermod,' or to assign him status as a secular saint whose commemorative poem connects him to the tradition of hagiographical texts, as more than one scholar has done,[30] it is impossible to deny the peculiar efficacy of Tolkien's deservedly famous 'Ofermod' essay.[31] The deep potency of this essay derives from Tolkien's generically inspired act of sympathetic response to the essentially dramatic text of *Maldon* which caused the poet-as-critic to generate his own *dramatized* text as a necessary imaginative prolegomenon to the subsequent act of academic criticism. This dramatic and mimetic centre of *The Battle of Maldon* supplies the major artifactual aspect of the poem. The morally crucial present, with its valorizing act of individual heroic utterance in the face of irreversible and imminent closure, was central to the poetic conception that redeems and reverses the already accomplished negative outcome of the historical encounter.

This last observation aligns this interpretation with those challenging the common observation that the poem was certainly composed not long after the historical engagement,[32] an argument based on the appearance of exact detail and word still seeming to be fresh in the mind of the poet. What emerges, however, in any close comparison of literary and historical account, is the disparity and readjustment of historical and poetic versions dealing with the events at Maldon, 991: 'Her wæs Gypeswic gehergod. & æfter þæm swyðe raþe wæs Byrihtnoð ealdorman ofslagan æt Meldune. & on þam geare man gerædde þæt man geald ærest gafol Daniscum mannum. for þam myclan brogan þe hi worhton be þam sæ riman. þæt wæs ærest x. þusend punda. þæne ræd gerædde ærest Syric arcebisceop.'[33]

All extant chronicle accounts are in substantial agreement about the painful historical facts that confronted the *Maldon* poet: the Danes wrought great terror; this was the first time that tribute *was* advised and consented to. It is hard to imagine a more inventive employment of poetic licence than that which remembers the heroes as we 'see' and 'hear' them in *The Battle of Maldon*. Furthermore, the following entries for 992, a time presumabaly near enough to the miseries of Maldon to have refreshed a poet's already smarting store of memories, records the Falstaffian courage of one ealdorman Ælfric, commissioned Æthelred to assemble all the ships that 'were worth anything' – 'ealle þa scipu þe ahtes wæron' – and the army as well, in order that they might discover whether they could entrap the Danish army anywhere thereabouts – 'cunnian meahton hi þone here ahwær utan betræppan.' Ealdorman Ælfric's approach to ambush was to send a warning to the army the night before they were supposed to fight: 'Ða sende se ealdorman Ælfric & het warnian þone here'; as for the local hero himself, he snuck away from the army during the night, though the chronicler does record that this was 'to his own great shame': 'þa sceoc he on niht fram ðære fyrde, him sylfum to myclum bysmore.' In a later battle, this one in 1003, where, incredibly enough, this same Ælfric was commissioned again to lead the army, he drew forth his old tricks – 'he teah þa forð his ealdan wrencas' – and as soon as the troops were within each other's line of vision – 'þæt ægþer here on oðer hawede' – Ealdorman Ælfric pretended that he was sick, and began to heave and vomit and said that he was sick and in that way he tricked that folk that he was supposed to have led, 'so it is said.' The annalist concludes this inglorious portion of the entry for 1003: 'þa bebræd he hine seocne & ongan he hine brecan to spiwenne & cwæð þæt he gesycled wære & swa þeah þæt folc becyrde þæt he læden scolde, swa hit gecweden is.'

It is not necessary to claim that the Anglo-Saxon chronicler was the *Maldon* poet's Holinshed – though neither is it necessary to exclude such a possibility – in noting that the historical materials of military cowardice, manipulative negotiating, flight from combative encounter, and visceral gracelessness under pressure that culminates in the deceiving of a people who should have been given leadership are all raw materials from the historical record which appear in the *Maldon* poet's imaginatively reclaimed subject matter. The fact that these items all occur in *Chronicle* entries near enough to the spare record of 991 to have been immediately and suggestively available to the *Maldon* poet lends credibility to the possibility that his inspiration was the creation of valorized poetry out of historical loss.

In a recent essay on 'Keats and the Historical Method in Literary Criticism,' Jerome McGann invites us all to a more rigorously observed analysis of contextualized language in our literary criticism, and suggests that we must define more particularly 'the sociology of poetic utterance' if we are ever to escape 'the mare's nest of pseudo-problems created by those several generations of critics who agreed to enter the prison house of language.'[34] The comparative consideration of historical and poetic text in *The Battle of Brunanburh* and *The Battle of Maldon* provides one interesting exercise in elucidating those psychological and sociological networks generated by winning and losing, and it deepens our understanding and appreciation of imaginative enterprise and its informative effect on literary outcome.

NOTES

1 Benjamin Thorpe ed *The Anglo-Saxon Chronicle, According to the Several Original Authorities* (London 1861) 1:200-8
2 Quoted in *The Anglo-Saxon Minor Poems* ed Elliott Van Kirk Dobbie ASPR 6 (New York 1942) xl. All quotations from *The Battle of Maldon* and *The Battle of Brunanburh* are taken from this edition 7-20.
3 Dobbie xl
4 Dobbie xl
5 Fred C. Robinson 'Some Aspects of the *Maldon* Poet's Artistry' *JEGP* 75 (Jan–April 1976) 31
6 Stanley B. Greenfield *A Critical History of Old English Literature* (New York 1965) 98
7 Peter Hunter Blair *An Introduction to Anglo-Saxon England* 2nd ed (Cambridge 1977) 88 observes, 'It should be noted that the word *Her* is the regular introduction to a new annal and that the poem properly begins with the word *Æþelstan.*'
8 Neil Isaacs 'Battlefield Tour: *Brunanburg*' *NM* 63 (1962) 236-44

9 W.F. Bolton '"Variation" in *The Battle of Burnanburh*' *RES* ns 19 (1968) 363-72

10 Ann S. Johnson 'The Rhetoric of Brunanburh' *PQ* 47 (1968) 487-93. Johnson's essay is built around Bede's *De schematibus et tropis* and argues a high degree of self-conscious artistic patterning of classical tropes and schema in the making of the poetry.

11 Frances Lipp *PQ* 48 (1969) 166-77; Lipp's conclusions are found on 177.

12 Traugott Lawlor 'Brunanburh: Craft and Art' in *Literary Studies: Essays in Memory of Francis A. Drumm* ed John H. Dorenkamp (Wetteren, Belgium 1973) 52-67, at 67.

13 Jean Starobinski, writing on Rousseau, 'Rousseau's Happy Days' *NLH* 11 (Autumn 1979) 154, notes how 'The passage from non-meaning to meaning' in literary as in cognitive process typically utilizes the functional significance of natural phenomena – in Rousseau, the iterative visual and auditory movement of waves.

14 See Dobbie's 'Introduction' xxxvii

15 Here I follow the punctuation adopted by John Collins Pope; see *Seven Old English Poems* ed John C. Pope (Indianapolis 1966) 5-8.

16 See Dobbie's 'Introduction' xxxviii–xl for the problems connected with secure identification of the locale of the battle.

17 See Dobbie 20-6

18 For a refined discussion of the subtleties involved in the construction of poetic 'voice' appropriate to various forms of poems see Ralph Rader 'The Dramatic Monologue and Related Lyric Forms' *Crit I* 3 (Autumn 1976) 131-51. I am particularly indebted here to Rader's account of the unforeseen discovery of specific poetic 'shape' (150), an especially acute portion of his essay.

19 Suzanne Langer *Feeling and Form* (New York 1953) xi

20 Carl T. Berkhout 'Feld Dennade – Again' *ELN* 11 (1974) 161-2, gives a succinct résumé of the range of views that have been proposed in translating this slippery verb. The 'vox sanguinis' eloquence suggested by Berkhout would have to be translated/understood as some version of 'the field cried out with the blood of men' to maintain the auditory integrity of the text: with such a clearly soundless cry the poet would be understood to be making a 'silent comment' of his own. I am indebted to Lewis E. Nicholson for some vigorous exchange on this point.

21 Robinson 'Aspects of Artistry' 26; Robinson's ingenious suggestion immediately calls to mind that somewhat later and clearly performative humour of the Wakefield *Second Sheperds' Pageant*, where not Northern but Southern dialect is the butt of the joke: 'Now take outt that Sothren tothe, / And sett in a torde!' (215-16) *Medieval Drama* ed David Bevington (Boston 1975) 391

22 Langer *Feeling* xi

23 Starobinski 'Rousseau' 163

24 George Clark in '*The Battle of Maldon*: A Heroic Poem' *Speculum* 43 (1968) 52-71 provides a careful discrimination between the literary and geo-historical possibilities of the poetic situation, corroborating with his own eyewitness (earwitness?) account of his 9 August 1966 visit to the site of the battle J.B. Bessinger's earlier caveat against historically over-confined interpretations: '*Maldon* and the *Olafsdrapa*: An Historical Caveat' in *Studies in Old English Literature* ed Stanley B. Greenfield (Eugene 1963) 23-5. Clark's essay, in analysing the poetic importance of inexorable movement of the 'natural clock' of the tides in the course of *Maldon*, notes, significantly, that 'the poem has no irrelevant realism' (67). Throughout this essay, and in a later brief pendant study, 'The Battle of *The Battle of Maldon*' *NM* 69 (1968) 374-9, where he notes that 'every member of the English army chooses to flee and live or advance and die' (378), Clark is particularly acute in selecting out those situational data that are peculiarly coefficient with poetic process itself. Professor Clark has also graciously shared with me the text of an address he delivered at the 1982 Annual Meeting of the Modern Language Association on 'Time and Tide at Maldon.' Earl R. Anderson, in 'Flyting in *The Battle of Maldon*' *NM* 71 (1970) 197-202, concludes his essay with what he calls 'one flight of exegetical fancy' (202), supplying a reading of the gestural symbolism of Byrhtnoth's shield and spear movement as a correlative to the verbal hostilities. In fact, the language of gesture, here and everywhere so abundantly present in the poetry of *Maldon*, is deeply connected to the dramatic imagination and to the mimesis of theatrical enactment that I believe are fundamental to the *Maldon* poet's literary performance.

25 Morton W. Bloomfield 'Beowulf, Byrthnoth, and the Judgment of God: Trial by Combat in Anglo-Saxon England' *Speculum* 44 (October 1969) 545-59; Bloomfield notes the 'God ana wat' phrase (547) in discussing the 'judicium Dei' mentality that operates in shaping poetic event and outcome in *The Battle of Maldon*. Bloomfield's suggestion that Byrhtnoth's behaviour may have constituted a virtual 'tempting of God' by requiring premature judgment by Him is a most provocative correlate of classical tragedy's 'treading on the purple.' Fred C. Robinson 'God, Death and Loyalty in *The Battle of Maldon*' in *J.R.R. Tolkien, Scholar and Storyteller, Essays in Memoriam* ed Mary Salu and Robert T. Farrell (Ithaca 1979) 76-98 notes (86) the frequent occurrence of the phrase 'God ana wat' in gnomic utterances.

26 Aristotle *On Poetry and Music* ed Milton C. Nahm, trans S.H. Butcher, The Library of Liberal Arts no 6 (New York 1948) 25

27 Clark '*Maldon*, Heroic Poem' 55-7 discusses the 'delicate question' of the

loyalty credentials of the implied informant and/or speaker of the poem, and supplies a useful 'catalogue of warriors' for the scholarly combatants on this question. See my prior reference (n 24) to Clark's 'advance and die' observation on the battle itself.

28 See, for example, *King John* II.i.357; *Julius Caesar* III.i.273; *Corialanus* III.i.275; and *Hamlet* v.ii.375. I am indebted to my colleague, Lewis Soens, for his informed conversations on hawking that have shaped this suggestion.

29 For a careful tracing of the complex problems and the history of criticism on the etymology, lexicography, and semantics involved in this textual crux see Helmut Gneuss' magisterial essay, '*The Battle of Maldon* 89: Byrthnoth's *ofermod* Once Again' *SP* 73 (April 1976) 117-39. See also Bosworth-Toller 736. It is worth noting here that the Bosworth-Toller highly qualified translation for 'ofermod coturnus' as 'a high style (?)' must surely connect at some prior point in the history of the term with the sublimities associated with tragic performance in antiquity.

30 See, for example, N.F. Blake 'The Battle of Maldon' *Neophil* 69 (1965) 332-45; W.F. Bolton 'Byrhtnoth in the Wilderness' *MLR* 64 (July 1969) 481-90; J.E. Cross 'Oswald and Bryhtnoth: A Christian Saint and a Hero Who Is Christian' *ES* 46 (1965) 93-109.

31 See J.R.R. Tolkien 'The Homecoming of Beorhtnoth, Beorhthelm's Son,' and especially the section 'Ofermod' in *Essays and Studies* 6 (1953) 3-18.

32 See Michael J. Swanton, 'The Battle of Maldon: A Literary Caveat' *JEGP* 67 (1968) 441-50, for a vigorous challenge to the 'recent military history' interpretations. Edward B. Irving, Jr, in 'The Heroic Style in *The Battle of Maldon*' *SP* 58 (July 1961) 457-67 is typical of those commentators who, while bringing great literary sensitivity to the critical task of explication, still shape their interpretation around the 'very recent memory' premise of poetic recall. This traditional view has been intelligently reassessed by Robinson 'Aspects of Artistry' with particularly felicitous attention to hitherto unnoted ironic poignancies in the poetry that are available only at a somewhat later, retrospective moment of hypothesized composition. See Robinson 28-32.

33 Here and in subsequent chronicle entries I am following Cott Tiber B iv as printed in Thorpe *Chronicle* 238, 40 and 52.

34 Jerome McGann *MLN* 94 (1979) 988-1032

EDWARD B. IRVING, JR

Crucifixion Witnessed, or Dramatic Interaction in *The Dream of the Rood*

VERY FEW of the countless artistic representations of the Crucifixion in the Middle Ages have the capacity to seize our imaginations like the Old English poem we call *The Dream of the Rood*.[1] Probably it is rivalled only in the visual arts. Other literary attempts in English to express the complex experience of suffering and witnessing that dominates the event seem to fall short of *The Dream of the Rood*'s special intensity. I think specifically of the later religious lyrics where the listener or reader is urged to meditate on the catalogued afflictions of Christ; or the more dramatic renditions where the listener or reader, taken into the scene as spectator or passer-by, is movingly addressed directly by a reproachful Christ from the cross (particularly in the 'O vos omnes' theme),[2] or where pain is inflicted on Christ's passive body by a squad of irritable soldiers (York Crucifixion play) or (a close analogue) literary or dramatic works where the listener or reader is invited to share the helpless agony of Mary on Golgotha – this last often a dialogue between Christ's two natures, with Mary representing the suffering human and the majestic son on the cross the divine.[3]

This essay will explore the process of dramatization and the psychology of the two main characters in the poem, especially in the first half of it, trying to isolate more clearly what, despite many excellent critical attempts, have never yet been quite satisfactorily defined: the operative elements in *The Dream of the Rood*'s massive emotional power. This attempt will not be quite satisfactory either, it goes without saying, but I hope it may advance our understanding and appreciation a small way by taking a slightly different approach; in any encounter with such a masterpiece, that may be worth doing.

From the very beginning of the poem and all the way on to its ending, we can see a clear process under way, a development away from confusion, or even from downright befuddlement, towards clarity, confidence, and certainty. A poem of progressive enlightenment must begin in the dark. It should be noted that this vision-poem starts with total non-vision, the blackness of sleep and midnight, though the enthusiastic tone of the opening lines in itself hints strongly at the prospect of ultimate success.

> Hwæt! Ic swefna cyst   secgan wylle
> h[w]æt me gemætte   to midre nihte,
> syðþan reordberend   reste wunedon.   (1-3)[4]

Listen to me, I wish to tell the very best of visions, what I dreamed at midnight, when speech-bearers dwelt in their beds.

At once this darkness becomes semi-darkness, the dubious and impeded vision of the subjunctive: 'Þuhte me þæt ic gesawe / syllicre treow' ('it seemed to me that I might have seen a very strange tree'). This subjunctive form of the verb 'to see' later clarifies itself, as the features of the objects seen become more distinct, into the firmer indicatives of lines 14 and 21: 'geseah ic' ('I clearly saw') (giving the perfective prefix 'ge-' full value). There is still much paradox here, of course, since the more plainly the object is seen, the more details are made out, the less its nature seems to be understood.

It is a very strange Tree that the character I will henceforth call simply Dreamer thinks he might have seen, a Tree first perceived as an almost formless upward surge of light and power into the air, becoming some kind of signalling object, a 'beacon,' covered with brightly radiant gold and gems. That Dreamer does not yet know himself what this object is is implied by the very fact that he is at once contrasted with, and feels himself inferior to, certain others who do know – who identify it and show their reverence towards it. Hosts of angels behold it and know it, angels we see only after his (and our) eyes have been steadily guided upward to the cross-beam and then above. The angels thus seem to appear in that 'heavenly' space above the cross-bar where we see them depicted in early Christian art, bending towards or cradling Christ's serene and divine head, while below the cross-beam, in the mortal or 'earthly' space, blood flows from Christ's wounds or his legs may be twisted in pain.[5]

This tree is then a public sight, drawing the attentive gaze of many. Yet it is not the most common kind of public sight that it might at first superficially resemble, the gallows of an ordinary criminal. Like Anglo-Saxon poets elsewhere, Dreamer proceeds in his definition of what he is looking at by first eliminating what the thing is *not*. If it were a mere gallows, it could never be the cynosure of the admiring gaze of the fair and the holy, and of all men and all nature.

But repetition of the word 'syllic' ('strange') in line 13 recalls us to the state of mind of the puzzled Dreamer who cannot view the tree as the rest of the universe apparently does; they know something he does not yet know. The tree's uncomfortable strangeness takes on new meaning through the way it now makes impact on Dreamer (an impact reinforced effectively by the alliteration of 'syllic' and 'synnum'):

Syllic wæs se sigebeam,   ond ic synnum fah,
forwundod mid wommum.   (13–14a)

Strange was that potent tree and I stained with sins, desperately wounded with corruptions.

All that we have so far been told is that Dreamer sees the glorious beauty of the tree. Why then, from where, does he get this sudden overwhelming sense of sin? One might call it an abrupt and startling sense of self, as if the object of his vision had turned without warning into a mirror of blinding clarity. It would be much too rational to say flatly that he thinks along such lines as these: 'Because I'm not able to *see* what those angels are obviously looking at, since I don't know what it can be, I must be stained and sick with sin.' But that connection of ideas must be some part of it. Part of it too is his apparent intuition that beneath all that gold and glory is hidden something uglier, blood and wounds like his own, an ugliness he seems to sense the presence of even before we are told that he actually sees it. I am fumbling without much success after something important here. Perhaps Dreamer's puzzlement, and insight, and the flickering ambivalence of what he is straining so hard to see clearly (yet perhaps also resisting the implications of) are all better reflected in strictly poetic form resistant to paraphrase: for example, in pun-like turns on words and paradoxical echoes that bring out both positive and negative meanings, in 'fah' ('bright-coloured') and 'fag' ('marked with evil'), or in 'bewunden' ('wound about, adorned') and 'forwundod' ('desperately wounded').[6] Despite the difficulties of vision, or because of the effort they demand, or because of Dreamer's new self-knowledge, it is at this point, as I remarked earlier, that he shifts fully into the indicative and can analyse with more assurance the mysteries before him, or at least take them more firmly into his range of vision.

He looks hard at the object. He sees a tree of glory, covered with *clothing* (can it then be a human figure, somehow?), shining with joys (emotionally electrifying and positive), drenched in the light and jewels of honour and reverence. Words wrenched slightly askew from their expected meanings (like 'wædum,' 'clothing') keep telling us that this is a riddle-object before us, and that there are rules to the guessing-game one must play in identifying it. One rule is that the object is not to be called by its proper name, Rood, until the Rood itself, in lofty heroic style, names itself proudly, at the very moment when it ceases entirely to be a forest-tree and rises symbolically to become a cross, The Cross: 'Rod wæs ic aræred' ('Rood was I raised up'44). It reminds us of how, at the appropriate stage in his advance into Denmark to take on the task of fighting the monster Grendel, another riddling heroic figure proclaims his identity: 'Beowulf is min nama' (*Beowulf* 343).

Now, though still far from being able to guess the riddle, Dreamer peers and scrutinizes anxiously, and not altogether in vain. His vision penetrates some distance.

> Gimmas hæfdon
> bewrigene weorðlice   weald[end]es treow.[7]
> Hwæðre ic þurh þæt gold   ongytan meahte
> earmra ærgewin,   þæt hit ærest ongan
> swætan on þa swiðran healfe.   (16b–20a)

Jewels had covered beautifully the tree of the ruler. But still I could perceive *through* that gold the ancient agony of wretched men, could perceive that it first began to bleed on the right side.

Dreamer speaks almost as if he had solved the riddle, breaking through a deceptive façade (jewels) to the bitter and ugly truth within. Not only does he seem to see through this mask of outward beauty in space, he seems also to peer back through time to some past history of suffering, as if the very past began to betray itself by bleeding, at the very moment when he saw it. The intense effort of perception has its immediate effect. His intuition forces him to confront himself in this glimpse of blood and agony. He is now, as he must be, paradoxically terrified of the beautiful sight: 'forht ic wæs for þære fægran gesyhðe' (21a).

Yet at this point he must stop. Without other help, he can see no more and can go no further in understanding either what is in front of him or the obscure emotions seething inside him. He can only lie passively watching the glimmering rapid transmutations of the lovely/hideous riddle-object before him: its changing of clothes and colours (hinting, though Dreamer does not yet know this, at Christ's garments, bruised skin, streaming blood); its abrupt shift from being soaked in blood-wetness to gleaming with treasure (with perhaps some constant quality of shininess as a common visual ground); its state of being 'fus,' restlessly unstable and always ready to be converted into something else at any moment.

To have the Rood itself (or, to name and personify our second character, Rood himself) furnish the needed help by explaining his own meaning to Dreamer seems to require, theologically speaking, that Dreamer first be in a state of repentance, as Robert Burlin has pointed out, citing the word 'hreowcearig' in line 25 as meaning 'repentant.'[8] Such repentance involves complex feelings: Dreamer's bafflement, and his anxiety about his lack of understanding; his admiration for the Tree's remote and dazzling beauty; his flinching back from what he does partly discover about what is in front of him and what is within him; his silent child-like waiting in hope of some further guidance.

There is a clear and important transition from Dreamer's confused state to the beginning of Rood's autobiographical narrative, one that links the two characters. Rood seems at the outset of his story more than a little like Dreamer, unable to make full sense of the ironies and paradoxes of his own experience – or at least telling his story in a way to give that impression, for Rood always speaks in the present dramatic moment and without retrospective and authoritative understanding of the full meaning of the events in which he participates.

The first lines of Rood's speech place him in a somewhat misleading context:

> Ðæt wæs geara iu,   (ic þæt gyta geman),
> þæt ic wæs aheawen   holtes on ende,
> astyred of stefne minum.   (28–30a)

That was very long ago – I still remember it – that I was hewn down at the forest's edge, moved from my trunk.

The first line is formulaic in an old tradition of heroic poetry. It is reminiscent, for example, of the opening of Beowulf's long speech before his doomed fight with the dragon, where the hero falls back on his early memories to strengthen himself for present action:

Fela ic giogoðe   guðræsa genæs,
orleghwila;   ic þæt eall gemon.   (2426-7)[9]

I survived many warlike encounters in youth, times of fighting. I remember all that.

The associations of such a formula might prepare us to think of Rood as a heroic figure but, as he tells what happened to him, we wonder whether he indeed plays any heroic role at all, for he seems disturbingly passive for a hero, allowing others to cut him down (warriors are 'hewn down' in Old English poetry just as trees are), carry him, make evil use of him. His history thus is a close parallel to the preceding vision, where the glorious (heroic) Tree as Dreamer sees it is half the time scarred and blurred by marks of defeat and bloody agony. The placing of verbs at the crucial beginnings of verses in lines 30-3 ('astyred,' 'genamon,' 'geworhton,' 'heton,' 'bæron,' 'gefæstnodon') relentlessly stresses the series of brutal actions carried out *on* him, ironically reminding us of the many actions this hero is *not* carrying out himself. When Rood at last sees Christ approaching him to be crucified, the exertion of heroic will is largely transferred from the passive Rood to Christ ('he me wolde on gestigan,' 'he wanted to climb up on me' 34).

But it is important to see that, if Rood begins in some sense from where Dreamer is, there is almost immediately a movement in his case from merely inert passivity towards a tense and deliberate willing of such inaction, a willing so strong as to be a kind of action, as Rood comes to understand the incredible situation in which he has been placed. To the extent (a large extent) that he partakes of the role of hero, he must now endure the hardest fate a hero can suffer: to be blocked completely from taking any action. Action is the natural mode of the hero's being and his essential definition. To be thus blocked from it is to feel great pain. Familiar examples from *Beowulf* are King Hrothgar seething with helpless anger under Grendel's unrelenting attacks on his hall, or Hengest enduring the long winter in a foreign hall, prevented for a time by complex circumstances from avenging his king's death. Rood can neither defend his king nor avenge his death. Worse yet, unimaginably terrible, God his king has ordered him to be an accomplice, chief agent even, in the very torture and murder of God: Rood is given the technical term 'bana' ('bane,' or 'slayer') in line 66. Though Rood now feels this pain, he does not yet fully understand that what he now suffers is the new Christian heroism of the martyr rather than the old Germanic heroism. Literally uprooted Tree – a hero not allowed to be a hero – and figuratively uprooted Dreamer thus share a sense of disorientation.

Such a parallel between Rood and Dreamer seems a compelling one. The way Rood speaks at first shows full sympathy with Dreamer's confusion, as if he were implying something like: 'Even though I myself actually went through this experience, at first I couldn't understand it.' In Dreamer's original vision, the same paradox of blood and glory was laid out in spatial terms, side by side, or so nearly simultaneous as to seem to overlap in time; this is now matched by the more clearly temporal, step-by-step experience of Rood himself. Possibly there is a further parallel to Dreamer's humiliating sense of being stained by sins in Rood's compulsive returning to the topic of what he feels as his 'heroic sin,' that is, his failure to act to protect or avenge his lord. One might imagine Rood saying: 'I too have felt miserably guilty, just as you are feeling now.' Though Rood's narrative now moves rapidly into the heart of mystery, it must not move so rapidly that the merely human Dreamer cannot follow.

Although up till now I have been doggedly insisting on viewing the interaction between these two fictional characters on the level of literal drama and assuming that this level is of primary importance in the poem's effect on its audience, this artificially limited way of looking at the poem is bound to become intolerably strained, for obviously we cannot go on pretending that we really do not know anything about the symbolic (that is, 'real') meaning of the text. This is only to say, to put it in theatrical terms, that the dramatic irony of the scene is too highly developed to be ignored. If Dreamer and Rood do not know – or do not know clearly and fully at this point in the narrative time-line of the poem – we know, although it is not easy to state discursively and explicitly all that we know when we begin to lay out all the complexities the dramatic situation implies within a new and 'proper' framework of theological meaning. What does the Rood stand for?[10] We can enumerate some things: Christ as man, a human sufferer pierced by dark nails and racked by conflicts and doubts; as son (an Isaac type dumbly obedient to the inexplicable demands of a father who seems to have forsaken him); as the innocent Paradisal world of non-human nature (the Tree as Peaceable Kingdom), violated and appalled by man's cruelty and forced, against nature, to torture nature's own creator; as a dignified and proud participant and witness/martyr; as an apostle-preacher giving us the most literally 'inside' version of the Crucifixion we could imagine; as an object-lesson in how this pride and this new kind of heroic achievement can grow precisely out of the enduring of abasement and humiliation. As has come to be generally recognized, making the figure of the Rood represent chiefly the passively suffering human dimension of Christ allows the actual character of Christ who appears in the poem to be one of pure heroic will, in part human courage but chiefly God's intense will to save mankind. Yet the theological information the poem provides is nothing Christians do not already know. In that sense they hardly need the poem. What makes the poem needed is the way it leads to understanding not through ideas but through feelings about ideas as they are acted out in dramatic time. The knowledge we gain must be experiential: like Dreamer and Rood, we come to know through sharing in suffering and suspense.

One chief way the nature, duration, and intensity of Rood's suffering is brought out is by the stylistic feature that is most striking in the first part of Rood's speech (28-73): extraordinarily heavy repetitions of certain words and phrases. Use of so rigorously limited a set of words in itself creates a feeling of psychological entrapment. As part of a spoken utterance, the repetitions vividly imitate the obsessive and reiterative mumblings of a shock-victim. 'I saw ... but I didn't dare ... I could have ... but I didn't ... I trembled ... but I couldn't ... they hurt me ... but I couldn't hurt them.' Four times in only 13 lines the phrase 'ic ne dorste' (with minor variations) appears; each time it does, we are brought back from some new detail of horror and outrage to the small prison of paralysed action, Rood's tormented inability to take vengeance. Rood's every wish to act is blocked by the stern adversatives of necessity, 'hwæðre,' 'ac,' in a way at least vaguely analogous to the frustration of Dreamer's attempts to seize on the security of a single meaning for his vision of the Tree. However Rood feels, whatever occurs, he must remain fixed in his standing position. He cannot bow, or break, or use his strength to crush the insolent 'enemies' who torment him and his beloved king. He must always stand fast, his only movement an anguished trembling in resonance with the anguished trembling of the earth itself convulsed in earthquake. The movements that surround Rood emphasize his immobility: Christ hurries to climb up and embrace him; dark nails are driven into him; blood streams down. Only at the end he moves just a little, bowing forward to let the disciples lift Christ's body down from the remorseful clutch of its wretched murderer and most faithful retainer.

Enduring physical and emotional pain is only part of Rood's role in this scene. He must also play the important role of eyewitness. Here again the repetitions are many: not only the 'geseah ic' of lines 33 and 51 and the 'ic þæt eall beheold' of 58, but Rood's showing forth of his deep wounds, still there to be inspected as evidence by Dreamer (here briefly playing the part of doubting Thomas to the resurrected Christ); the witnessing crowd of 'many' who observe Christ's courage in mounting the 'high gallows'; the watch or wake of the mourning disciples over Christ's cooling body; Rood's own witnessing (and this is surely an original detail) of the carving of the sepulchre from 'bright stone.' At all points, the event of the Crucifixion experience must be fully attested and publicly authenticated.

And its implications must be understood. Like Dreamer (as I have been arguing), Rood seems to move gradually towards such understanding, first from frightened passivity to violent conflict and horror, which reaches a climax in lines 46–9 describing the nailing, wounding, mocking, bleeding of Rood and King together, and then on towards summary statement, a stage that may begin in line 50:

> Feala ic on þam beorge   gebiden hæbbe
> wraðra wyrda.   Geseah ic weruda God
> þearle þenian.   (50–52a)

I have experienced many angry fates on that hill. I saw the God of Hosts stretched out in agony.

Such verses suggest at least some small measure of distance from the immediate pain, and a clearer and calmer view of what has been happening. As Rood looks about him in the lines that follow – is now *able* to look about him and beyond his own pain – he sees that darkness has fallen and that all Creation weeps, lamenting the King's fall. We recognize the 'cosmic' setting in which Rood first appeared in Dreamer's vision. Now Rood is able to name Christ for the first time in the poem, seeing and naming this scene as we ourselves see it: 'Crist wæs on rode' ('Christ was on the cross' 56). This same phrase is, incidentally, given special prominence in the runic verses from the poem selected to be carved on the Ruthwell Cross: it appears at the top of the west face. We should recall that that great stone cross is personified; all the passages on it come from Rood's speech.

Now the narrative slows down markedly in pace and intensity. Rood watches gravely as the disciples come to remove, mourn over, and bury Christ's body. Since they fill our field of vision while this goes on, they shift our attention away from Rood's vivid experiences towards what he is watching. After singing their own sorrow-song, the three personified crosses stand alone in a weeping group reminiscent of the three Marys of many pictures of the Crucifixion scene and of the later religious drama. Like Christ, the crosses are then brought to ground and buried; like Christ, Rood undergoes later resurrection and receives great honour. The actions here are spaced out and fewer; feelings are given more leisure for expression. We are moving towards Rood's calm interpretation of his own passionate story and his application of it to Dreamer, as the poem shifts down very noticeably from the intense narrative mode to the discursive and hortatory. Both modes would certainly have seemed equally important to the original poet and audience, but for many modern readers the interesting part of the poem is over at this point. Older editors often tried to jettison the last half as inept later addition or interpolation. But the poem cannot truly be over until Dreamer's questions are concretely answered, the dialogue is completed, and Dreamer's own response to the explanation made to him is registered. And so, point by point, the mysteries of the initial vision are explicitly made clear.

The experience undergone by Rood himself in being first lowered (humiliated, wounded, buried) and then raised to glory is first summarized for Dreamer as a 'personal' experience before it is explicitly extended to the experience of Christ and combined with it:

>   On me Bearn Godes
> þrowode hwile.   Forþan ic þrymfæst nu
> hlifige under heofenum,   ond ic hælan mæg
> æghwylcne anra   þara þe him bið egesa to me.   (83b-86)

On me God's son suffered for a time, and so now glorious I tower under the heavens, and I can heal everyone who is in awe of me.

Here the Tree we saw in the earlier vision towering towards heaven and worshipped by all Creation reappears, but now we can see and understand why it soars so high – because God's son went so low. The suffering

is exactly what brings the glory; there is no way pain can be separated
from the splendour that inheres in the Incarnation. The rhythms of the
pattern are compelling. I fell, I rose; I was tormented, I am worshipped,
with the alliteration strongly marking this contrast of pain and glory
in 'þrowode'/'þrymfæst' (84) and in 'leodum laðost'/'lifes weg' (88). The
wounded and bewildered Rood has now become, despite and because
of his own suffering, a healer and a guide for all men who seek him,
enlightened and able to give enlightenment through his own ordeal. He
makes his final reference to his natural origin in the forest in a crucial
identification of himself with Mary, the natural member of the race of
women who was, like him, elected by God to be 'theotokos,' God-bearer.
Three strong epithets for God ('wuldres, Ealdor,' 'heofonrices Weard,'
'ælmihtig God') are massed in the sentence to emphasize the divine power
that fused itself with these two earthly beings, woman and tree, in the
Incarnation and in the Crucifixion.

The parallel with Mary seems to bring the Rood down closer to the
world of men. Certainly for the rest of his speech his attention is entirely
human-directed. Dreamer is instructed to describe the vision he has had
to men and to identify to them the object of his vision ('þæt hit is wuldres
beam,' 'that it is the tree of glory' 97) in explicit terms. God suffered
on the rood expressly for the many sins of 'manncyn' and of Adam (98-
100). God rose from death to help men, and he will return on Dooms-
day to seek mankind. He will search out and he will find each individual
man on that day. Then the normal response of each person will be fear,
exactly like – now we understand it! – the fear felt by Dreamer in the
vision as he became conscious that his sins were exposed to God's view.
In the new context we see such anxiety as an experience all must go
through. Yet the scene of Judgment is put in consoling terms. Such fear
is not to be feared. There will be no person there who will not be afraid,
because every man was afraid to volunteer to die on the Cross. Against
this background, the Rood's courage stands out absolutely. He has
managed to transcend and vanquish the fear inherent in all ordinary
beings, and has thus now become the true source of courage for all,
worn as a crucifix on each man's breast at Judgment Day. Every soul
can seek heaven through that symbol. The whole immense story, as in
Paradise Lost, has now been internalized. Cosmic narrative and myth
are contracted into one small but all-powerful talisman, the Rood as
the Key to the Kingdom.

Dreamer's final lines can best be seen, in contrast with his profound
disorientation at the opening, as a new orientation, a repointing and

redirection of himself. As God's (and the Rood's) full attention is now blazingly directed upon the Dreamer, he is at once pulled magnetically towards the Rood, and continues to point towards it:

> Gebæd ic me þa to þan beame   bliðe mode,
> elne mycle,   þær ic ana wæs
> mæte werede.   Wæs modsefa
> afysed on forðwege;   feala ealra gebad
> langunghwila.   (122–126a)

I prayed earnestly towards that tree with happy heart and great zeal, where I was alone with a tiny band. My mind was ready for the journey outward; I had lived through a great many times of misery.

It should be noted that Dreamer not only prays to and towards Rood but he is also 'imitating,' that is, he is using language that recalls Rood's story. The body of Christ was also abandoned by its friends, as Dreamer says he is, and left 'with a tiny band' (69); Rood too told us what he had lived through ('gebiden' 79). Dreamer is now intent on seeking the fulfilment of his life's hope in the 'sigebeam' and realizes that his protection depends entirely on the Rood ('geriht to þære rode' 131). His friends having already passed on to heaven, Dreamer waits for the time his friend Rood will return in reality, not merely in the mists of dream as before, and will bring him back to the great feast in God's hall. By viewing the Rood as rescuer, the Dreamer can place himself appropriately among those fabled waiters-in-hell, the Old Testament patriarchs who expect the arrival of Christ on the great day of the Harrowing of Hell. To those so long in burning and darkness (and Dreamer's painful experience during his vision may include him among these), the heroic Son appears to open up hell and lead them all in triumph back to his native land. That same young hero Rood once saw hastening fearlessly towards his execution is now the young king assuming his birthright in his own kingdom and sharing that birthright in glory with his ecstatic followers. All the elements of the initial vision are now in place and fully lighted. The poem ends here on a satisfactorily resolving chord.

I have tried to show that *The Dream of the Rood* differs from the common medieval lecture-dialogue of Platonic ancestry (Lady Philosophy explaining the universe to the prisoner Boethius, or Beatrice instructing Dante, or – in parody – the Eagle suffocating the hapless Chaucer in verbiage in *The House of Fame*) in that the lecturer is entitled to speak with ultimate authority only when he has first shared with his listener similar acute bewilderment and pain. In this poem the essential experience, the Crucifixion, is thus seen from two angles that meet in a single image of unparalleled spiritual and psychological richness.

NOTES

1 Since the critical literature on the poem is so voluminous, I mention here only a few key essays. Introduction to the two recent separate editions should be consulted: that of Bruce Dickins and Alan S.C. Ross, *The Dream of the Rood* 4th ed, (London 1954, rpt 1963; New York 1966), and that of Michael Swanton, *The Dream of the Rood* (Manchester 1970). A brief but thoughtful critical essay is J.A. Burrow 'An Approach to *The Dream of the Rood*' *Neophil* 43 (1959) 123-33. On the poem's doctrinal content especially, see H.R. Patch 'Liturgical Influence on *The Dream of the Rood*' *PMLA* 24 (1919) 233-57; J.V. Fleming '*The Dream of the Rood* and Anglo-Saxon Monasticism' *Traditio* 22 (1960) 43-72; Faith H. Patten 'Structure and Meaning in *The Dream of the Rood*' *ES* 49 (1968) 394-401; Robert B. Burlin 'The Ruthwell Cross, *The Dream of the Rood* and the Vita Contemplativa' *SP* 65 (1968) 23-43; N.A. Lee 'The Unity of *The Dream of the Rood*' *Neophil* 56 (1972) 469-86.

2 See Rosemary Woolf *The English Religious Lyric in the Middle Ages* (Oxford 1968) 42-5 and elsewhere, for discussion of the use of this theme, derived ultimately from Lamentations 1:12, 'O vos omnes qui transitis per viam, attendite et videte si est dolor sicut dolor meus,' always taken to be a speech of Christ, usually from the Cross.

3 See Woolf's *English Religious Lyric* and also her study *The English Mystery Plays* (London 1972), esp 238-68.

4 Quotations from the text are taken from Swanton's edition; macrons are omitted.

5 See Swanton 52-5, and Adolf Katzenellenbogen 'The Image of Christ in the Early Middle Ages' in *Life and Thought in the Early Middle Ages* ed Robert S. Hoyt (Minneapolis 1967) 66-84.

6 Swanton 64

7 Probably the usual emendation of 'wealdes' to 'wealdendes' ('of the Ruler') should be made here for the sake of the metre; yet 'wealdes treow' might possibly stand in contrast to 'wuldres treow' (14), anticipating the clarifying 'Haelendes treow' (25).

8 See the article by Burlin cited above, esp 30.

9 Quoted from Fr Klaeber *Beowulf and the Fight at Finnsburg* 3rd ed (Boston 1951)

10 See the works listed in note 1.

DANIEL G. CALDER

Figurative Language and Its Contexts in *Andreas*: A Study in Medieval Expressionism

I CONTEXTS

IN THE PRACTICE of literary criticism, it should be axiomatic that a poet is assumed competent until proved inept. Such consideration, however, is not always granted; in Anglo-Saxon studies the contrary has too frequently prevailed. But of one critic this cannot be said. Stanley B. Greenfield's many writings – his own sympathetic analyses and his careful assessments of the criticism of others – create a model for the critical act. To one of Greenfield's dicta we might pay special attention. It comes from the 'Preface' to his book, *The Interpretation of Old English Poems*:

The interpretation of Old English *poems* – not *poetry*. One of my basic tenets is that some of the main streams of modern Old English criticism tend to detract from the special nature, the unique identity, of particular poems. This is not to deny a poem's participation in the community and commonality of its Anglo-Saxon poetical and cultural heritage, but rather to draw attention, in crucial matters of interpretation, small and large, to the convergence of various kinds of poetic and extra-poetic elements in the immediate text, and to make that text speak to us across the years with the dignity and self-assurance of its individuality.[1]

Still, many an Anglo-Saxon poem has been deprived of this 'dignity' by a scholar or community of scholars working at the remove of some one thousand years.

Before sweeping any item of our sparsely populated Anglo-Saxon corpus into the poetical dustbin, we must strive – heroically, I think – to love it. I am always dismayed by the utter casualness with which any number of Anglo-Saxon poems get sentenced to oblivion on the grounds that they are demonstrably inferior, that they do not do what we all agree poetry should do. To honour Stanley Greenfield, who has rescued so much of Anglo-Saxon literature, I offer this partial attempt to save one relic – *Andreas* – from condescension.

The criticism of *Andreas* has proceeded with a strange and often unclear sense of context. Much of the commentary has deflected attention from *Andreas* itself by insisting that the Beowulfian 'echoes' that resound throughout the poem define its proper context. For within less than forty years after its first modern edition, *Andreas* was linked to *Beowulf*,[2] and the bond thus forged has proved unbreakable. The two poems do indeed share many words, compounds, and images – even whole lines – and the assumption instantly arose that the *Andreas* poet must have consciously used *Beowulf* as a quarry for the construction of his own work. But, so it goes, in the transferring of diction from the Germanic epic to his Christian saint's life, this poet created a bizarre and embarrassing hybrid. He has paid for his sin; few poets have received the kind and intensity of scorn that has been heaped upon the hapless author of *Andreas*. A small sampling must suffice: Rosemary Woolf thinks that 'compared with *Beowulf*, *Andreas* seems light-weight, mechanical, even occasionally ludicrous';[3] E.G. Stanley labels the composer of *Andreas* 'a poetical dunderhead';[4] the poem's most recent editor, Kenneth R. Brooks, finds the terms 'ludicrous,' 'clumsy,' 'incongruous,' 'tasteless and inappropriate,' and 'lacking in invention' reasonable epithets to apply;[5] and even the latest commentator, Edward B. Irving, Jr, who seems sincere in his intent to view the work approvingly, cannot resist the occasional lament that some of the poet's effects are 'risible.'[6] Given these descriptions, a stranger to *Andreas* would think the poem odd indeed. But *Andreas* has attracted some commendation: Arthur G. Brodeur grants that the poet had 'a real flair for vivid and forceful, and sometimes beautiful phrase and image';[7] Alvin A. Lee claims that 'the fabric of the highly wrought, associative imagery characteristic of *Andreas* raises it to the level of a complex and rich symbolic poem, where many of the apparent absurdities disappear.'[8]

Let us begin with a two-sided premise: *Beowulf* takes place in a real world, *Andreas* does not. David Hamilton has argued this point, though he has not drawn it out to its logical conclusion. In two provocative, though somewhat undeveloped, essays, he asks us to abandon our requirement that *Andreas* be like *Beowulf* and concentrate instead on the metaphorical nature of the language and the 'separation of genres and also of styles.'[9] Further, he writes: 'The actions in *Beowulf* are larger than life, but not radically different from it. The action of *Andreas*, however, is supernatural, and we accept it only in a controlled, didactic frame of reference.'[10] This frame of reference is a sophisticated allegorical (and Christian) construct. A whole cadre of very recent interpreters has brilliantly demonstrated that behind the 'unrealistic' plot of *Andreas* lies a network of Christian images and typological identifications which can account for the incongruities of action.

I will turn to these shortly, but we can now see that the problem of context is indeed at the very centre of all the critical arguments. For the unwary, the formulaic quality of Old English poetry can cast a pall of sameness over every poem. Yet simple logic demands that we acknowledge that shifts in context can fundamentally alter the semantic and metaphoric function of those formulas; total meaning does not inhere in the half-line itself, but in the grid of associations the entire text provides.[11] A particular image (or nexus) rooted in the 'real,' historical world of *Beowulf* can hardly convey the same signification in the 'symbolic,' typological world of *Andreas*. To assume it does – or should – is to reduce the two contexts to one. So long as the diction of *Andreas* continues to be explored – and judged – exclusively with reference to *Beowulf*, then the poem is doomed to being infelicitously construed. Any reclamation, therefore, must distance these two poems from each other. I do not wish to recount here the long history of the scholarship on the assumed indebtedness of the one to the other.[12] However, I hope I may be permitted the assertion that *Andreas* is a unique creation – *even if* the poet did, consciously or not, echo *Beowulf* throughout.

Beowulf and *Andreas* present two views of history, views which are not so much in opposition as they are unrelated. And the consequences of this difference in historical perspective for an understanding of figurative language in each work are great. While the 'reality' of *Beowulf* does not imply an aesthetic 'realism,' it does entail a circumscribed perspective on human events. In *Beowulf* the supernatural may impinge on the characters' lives, but it does so within the realm of the knowable. Eternity is a concept vaguely present at best, and for the most part mere history prevails. Sequence may be disrupted in *Beowulf*, but the reader can refashion it. The absence of a clear pattern caused by such fragmentation becomes the poet's vehicle for considering the possibility of a plan in the affairs of men. Heaven and hell are ideas which govern how men will be judged, yet they do not actually intrude. This epic poem presents a tragic, retrospective meditation on human frailty and the evanescence of time. The poet says that Beowulf departs to seek 'the judgment of the righteous'; in so saying he essentially dismisses his hero with a comforting moralization, and thereby refuses to yoke eternity with time.

In *Andreas*, narrative sequence is more or less preserved, but time and eternity collide in ways that shatter a sense of linear movement. The typological perspective thus elicited from the poem's acts and events conforms (potentially) to the many lists of biblical types that the fathers had constructed. *Andreas* enjoys an ever-growing number of such commentaries, not all of which need be described here.[13] Perhaps the most comprehensive statement is that by James W. Earl. Seeing *Andreas* as a poem about conversion, he believes

that the unity of the poem depends upon the various traditional images of conversion in the early Church, especially the imagery of baptism, the Harrowing of Hell, and the Last Judgment. By analyzing these traditional images in the poem, we will see that the early episodes, Andrew's voyage and Matthew's liberation from prison, are very much part of the central conversion theme, serving as prophecy and figure for the ultimate conversion of the cannibals.[14]

In other words, *Andreas*, typologically speaking, reflects the process of biblical exegesis in both content and form. Just as the flood in *Exodus* prefigures the Harrowing of Hell and both prefigure the Last Judgment, as well as the sacrament of baptism, so Andreas' voyage and Matthew's liberation not only draw to themselves these biblical (and apocryphal) meanings but also create a similar structure through parallels within the confines of the poem. All typology is based upon the idea of the intersection of eternity with time, of Christ with the world. And so, however discrete (and incongruous) the events in *Andreas* may seem, they are but shadows of an eternal reality which is always shining through each earthly manifestation.

I have no quarrel with this approach to the poem. The explosion of typological commentary has added immensely to our knowledge of Anglo-Saxon Christian poetry; the method has made what was once dark now bright. I can even agree that the *Andreas* poet made a special effort to expand the typological implications of his source so as to reinforce the pattern he found already there. But that is just the point – the basic typological equivalences in *Andreas* (and in most of the other Anglo-Saxon Saints' Lives) may also exist in the source. Indeed, they exist, strictly speaking, in all eternity. While the current research points to what is there, it does not truly *interpret* the poem. Identification of a typological system, however necessary, however applicable, should not be equated with analysis; discovery is not the same as understanding. This becomes more than obvious when one compares the Anglo-Saxon poem with its Latin source.[15] With some minor, though important, exceptions, the typological structure of source and poem can be made to align. But there is no relation at all between the functionally bland language of the source, which M.R. James characterizes as a 'tale of wonder,'[16] and the extravagant diction of this complex religious poem.

And this returns us, once again, to *Beowulf*, a poem with some resemblances in figurative language to *Andreas*, though not as many or as significant as the sheer weight of the scholarship would seem to suggest. Before making some summary comments on the extensive differences between *Beowulf* and *Andreas*, it may serve us well to recall T.A. Shippey's comments on the description of two dawn scenes, one from each poem. He remarks that 'the really destructive point for the theory of borrowing [from *Beowulf*] is that the *Andreas*-passage overlaps with at least eight other Old English poems to only a lesser degree.'[17] At times *Andreas* almost seems like an anthology of formulas culled from other Anglo-Saxon poems. Thus to concentrate on its supposed affinities with the language of *Beowulf* is to ignore these many other echoes. It is also to disregard the more than 160 hapax legomena in *Andreas* itself. In fact, the pleasure the *Andreas* poet so exuberantly takes in the creation of a new poetic diction indicates the intensity of his desire to speak with an individual voice while still practising a communal art.[18]

Beowulf is an epic tragedy, depicting the loss of a hero and a world;[19] *Andreas*, a Christian Romance (Saint's Life) portraying the final perfecting of an apostle and the redemption of a world (*the* world, if we acknowledge the typology). The tone of *Beowulf* is solemn, measured, elegiac; that of *Andreas*, excited, syncopated, joyful. However vast the historical sweep presented in *Beowulf*, it is more than overmatched by the interpenetration of history by eternity in *Andreas*. *Beowulf* takes a retrospective view of time and history; *Andreas* projects a typological scheme onto a series of events. The reality of *Beowulf* is essentially metonymic, that of *Andreas* metaphoric.[20] So while *Beowulf* resists an allegorical interpretation, *Andreas* embraces one. *Beowulf* concerns itself with an attempt to find a meaning in conflicting historical patterns, while *Andreas* exults in eternal paradigms. Finally, I repeat that *Beowulf* takes place in something which strongly resembles a world we know, a world where chance and human error too frequently triumph; it is mimetic. *Andreas* plays out its action on a cosmic stage where the end is known even as the narrative unfolds under the protective eye of divine providence; it is abstract, ritualistic, and symbolic.

Andreas, then, demands a reading on its own terms, one which allows these many differences to define the poem's separateness from all sources – both actual and assumed, both narrative and dictional. The success of this reading will consist in grasping the dynamics of the extraordinary (and often disturbing) figurative language in *Andreas*, noting how that language works within the most important context – the poem proper.

II   'SCENE ONE': THE EXPRESSIONISTIC MODE

Lines 1–121 of *Andreas* constitute the first completed movement of the poem. We may call it 'Scene one,' because the poem is – in style and structure – so much more 'dramatized' than the nearest Latin analogue. As in most of the scenes of his poem, the poet has marked off this section with a definite coda, a signal that the movement has ended. Compare source and poem: 'After the Lord had spoken to him, He returned to heaven.'

> Gewat him þa se halga   helm ælwihta,
> engla scyppend,   to þam uplican
> eðelrice;   he is onriht cyning,
> staðolfæst styrend,   in stowa gehwam.   (118a–121b)

Then the holy Guardian of all creatures, the Creator of angels, departed to the celestial noble kingdom; He is King by right, a firm Steersman, in every place.

When narrative details permit, scenes are often brought to a close with God's return to heaven, a description or characterization of paradise, and a narrational distancing effected by some generalizing comments – here about God's protective power. Nothing resembling this device or practice is found in the source, which plods dully along to the next piece of business. The larger effect of this pointed creation of 'scenes' in *Andreas* is to underscore the highly ritual quality of the narrative. Rhythmic units replace simple consecutiveness, and, in many instances, the ritual allows the reality of paradise, the truth of eternity, to be immediately present. Thus ritual narrative in *Andreas* can enact the basic proposition of typology – that eternity has penetrated time, as it constantly still does.

Within this first unit appear all the features which give *Andreas* its special, yet problematic, quality. At the core of the scene is the depiction of relationships of power, both appropriate and perverted. Christ's presence as a royal dispenser creates the oft-noted apostolic comitatus, with the twelve companions serving as 'þeodnes þegnas' ('thanes of the prince,' 3a); as King he determines the apostles' 'lot' (6b, 14b). On these matters the source is silent. Christ's power expressed through action and image ('wundorcræfte,' 'marvellous craft' 13b) forcefully confronts and opposes another 'authority' represented by the devil and his host ('dwolcræft,' 'sorcery' 34a, 'feondes cræft,' 'the enemy's craft' 49b, 'searocræft,' 'cunning' 109a). The nearly dualistic view that all power in the universe clusters around these two poles – the Mermedonians are 'deofles þegnas' ('thanes of the devil' 43b) – is more than casually important. From it derives the central idea that history everywhere demonstrates the clash between the two; it is an ancient, archetypal vision, reenacting the mythic struggle of Christ and Satan which began in heaven, continued in biblical history, and then lodged itself in the souls of individual Christians, a vision captured most compellingly in the theology of baptism.[21] Temporal history is the record of this great encounter, the apostles a military vanguard in the initial skirmishes of the concluding phase. Human action is thus seen to parallel and to reflect the archetype, a perspective absent from the source.

The present setting is created in a highly abstract way. Whereas the source depicts Mermedonia as a possible locale inhabited by wicked men with dreadful, though precisely described, customs, the site – at first unnamed – in the poem is an abstract projection of its citizens' evil: 'Eal wæs þaet mearcland / morðre bewunden' ('That border-land was completely bewound with murder' 19). This half-line – 'morðre bewunden' – occurs in no other surviving Anglo-Saxon text; it is an absolute statement countered only by the firmness with which Christ's praise is 'wound' in Matthew's heart ('fæste bewunden' 58b). The apostle's state of being responds to the moralized setting and so demonstrates that the world shown us here is unitary. Perhaps we should also note that the poet later describes the minds of the unbelieving Jews as 'morðre bewunden' (770b–72b).

Compared to the Latin text, and compared to most other Anglo-Saxon poems, *Andreas* reaches an especially intense level of energy. The Meremedonians do not just 'pluck out [Matthew's] eyes'; instead

swylc wæs þæs folces   freoðoleas tacen,

unlædra eafoð,   þæt hie eagena gesihð,
hettend heorogrimme,   heafodgimmas,
agetton gealgmode   gara ordum.   (29a–32b)

such was the savage trait of that people, the violence of the wretched ones, that they, fierce enemies, destroyed with cruel intent, with the points of spears, the sight of the eyes, the gems of the head.

Violence is heightened and increased at every turn. Like the 'character-ization' of the setting, the qualification of the action is extreme, and massive hordes move against Matthew like a cosmic swarm:

Þær wæs cirm micel
geond Mermedonia,   manfulra hloð,
fordenera gedræg,   syþþan deofles þegn
geascodon   æðelinges sið.   (41a–44b)

There was a great outcry throughout Mermedonia, a throng of wicked ones, a crown of the damned, when the devil's thanes heard of the hero's journey.

The actors in this universal drama speak with a predictably singular voice, a sound that echoes without modulation straight through the poem: God talks only with a holy, clear, beautiful, or harmonious voice (the examples are too numerous to cite); his Christian warriors speak either in a sad or sorrowful tone, or else they mirror his brightness and harmony. The Mermedonians and their hellish leaders mimic chaos, ugliness, and disharmony ('cirm micel') in words of malice, scorn, insult, and mocking – reiterated motifs and weapons as well. In *Andreas* the requirement that Matthew and Andrew endure the 'hearmcwide' (79a) of the cannibals etches the more sharply their roles as imitators of Christ.

Twenty-one hapax legomena occur in this first scene, giving the modern reader some sense of the poet's fascination with the play of language itself. Rhetorical dilation replaces the short, merely functional dialogue of the source; the extent of elaborate variation confirms that at times the poet concentrates on the flexibility of his medium and the display of his own brilliance. He is not one to exercise restraint, but the energy his pyrotechnics release becomes an integral part of his vision. As I shall try to show, he makes language not only create a reality, but also be changed by it in turn. His delight in games pushes language to its breaking point. It seems as if the poet would ask more of his received formulaic

wordhoard that it can reasonably do. Certainly that is how many scholars
have branded the 'excesses' of the battle imagery. To many, the description
of the twelve apostles as 'rofe rincas' ('brave chieftains' 8a), or 'tireadige
hæleð' ('glorious heroes' 2b), whose 'glory did not fail in the battle when
banners clashed together' (3b–4b), is both a historical *and* a metaphorical
absurdity. Limits have here been reached, but the question remains open
whether they have been transgressed.

The hapax legomena group themselves around key concepts, compounds which in their novelty dramatize the severity and importance
of the two saints' missions: an 'evil chain' ('inwitwrasen' 63b) holds
Matthew in 'leoðubendum' ('limb-bonds' 100b), in 'nearonedum' ('cruel
bondage' 102a). And extreme contrast in the language lets us know that
the poet's descriptions of violence are not empty phantasms: 'on nearonedum. / Þe is neorxnawang' (102). Here Matthew's release from 'cruel
bondage' is literally the promised 'paradise.' It is a propitious accident
of language that the one can be so easily changed into the other, although
this may be an accident of the poet's making. (Similar verbal play occurs
when Andrew and Matthew are reunited in the prison: 'Geseh þa under
swegle / swæsne geferan, // halig haligne; / hyht wæs geniwad,' 'then
he saw under heaven his dear companion, one saint the other; hope was
renewed' 1009a–1010b. Matthew and Andrew are united, indeed given
one identity, by this abrupt juxtaposition; language once again actualizes
the characters' drama and reveals a theological truth.)[22]

The world in scene one is on the brink of chaos and the poem's language
both describes and embodies this turmoil. This used to be called, with
some implicit warning, the fallacy of imitative form. The phrase assumes
a rationalist poetic, one basically at odds with the dominant emotionalism
of *Andreas*, and I think that the poet intended, consciously or not, to
let such interplay between style and content support, rather than under-
mine, his meaning. In all of its aspects, the language of *Andreas* expresses
the poet's multi-layered Christian thoughts.

There is, in fact, an aesthetic mode which characterizes what goes
on in *Andreas*: expressionism. (One might even posit that much of the
Anglo-Saxon aesthetic could be characterized in this way.) I realize that
by using this term, one applied principally to a movement in modern
art and literature, I risk accusation of impertinent ahistoricism. But I
mean the term in its most general sense, as 'a quality of expressive emphasis
and distortion which may be found in works of art of any people or
period.'[23] Herbert Read writes that expressionism is 'one of the basic
modes of perceiving and representing the world around us,'[24] and it is

that mode of perception and representation which enables us to comprehend the seemingly bizarre metaphoric strategies of *Andreas*.

The common stylistic qualities of expressionism are easily identifiable: tension, energy, deliberate distortion, a telescoping of narrative sequence, a disintegration into scenes or 'stations' in dramatic or semi-dramatic forms, an abstraction that is purposively anti-mimetic. Expressionism is also pugnaciously dialectical, but expressionistic works do not conclude with a new synthesis emerging from the confrontation between thesis and antithesis; instead, as Krispyn notes, 'the antithesis [in expressionism] moreover, is not static, but dynamic in the sense that the tension between the poles must inevitably lead to the destruction of one, while the other becomes absolute.'[25]

All this to express a strong emotion, or, as is more appropriate with *Andreas*, an ideology or world view. Further, literary expressionism is usually rhetorical, adopting 'a fervent declamatory tone.' It is 'passionate and shrill,' and shows 'a predilection for ecstasy and despair and hence a tendency towards the inflated and the grotesque; a mystical, even religious element with frequent apocalyptic overtones.'[26] Exaggeration plays a major stylistic role in all forms of expressionism. Another prime feature is 'simultaneity,'[27] a particularly important aspect with regard to *Andreas*, where eternity overlays all the historical actions on several levels.

A 'close reading' of the commentary on *Andreas* suggests that it too has responded to the poem's 'expressionistic mode.' The critics' choices of (usually pejorative) terms reveal a definite, though certainly unintended, image cluster. It has been called, and rightly so, 'unrealistic,' 'grotesque,' 'extreme,' 'intense,' 'artificial,' 'violent,' 'strikingly imaginative,' full of 'violations of narrative logic,' 'forced,' and 'extravagant' – clearly not a poem that fails to make an impression. For many that impression has been decidedly negative; but whether one is attracted to or repulsed by *Andreas*, a sense of its extremely emotional and forceful quality emerges as a constant.

The characteristics of expressionism readily pertain to the opening section of *Andreas*, and they also extend to define the entire work. But more important than general resemblances, however emphatically they may describe this poem, is the status of figurative language in an expressionistic work. For it is the problem of metaphor in *Andreas* which has been the largest – and the most long-lasting – of all the critical stumbling blocks placed in the way of understanding this most idiosyncratic of the Anglo-Saxon Saints' Lives.

III   DECORUM AND THE ABSOLUTE METAPHOR

With few intervals, the history of Western aesthetics discloses an unbroken allegiance to the mimetic principles first enunciated by Aristotle; his views of metaphor were consistent with these principles. Metaphor was the highest of the poetic figures and should always be constructed according to the rules of a proper decorum. There should be a fitting and appropriate relation between the two items compared in any metaphorical expression.[28] The far-fetched metaphor was considered monstrous. Reviewing, as I have, the criticism of *Andreas*, we see how tenaciously this notion still holds scholarly minds. Joyce Hill's is the latest, and in some ways the most sophisticated, version of the argument, one that rejects the dominant metaphor of battle in *Andreas*. She grants that the topos of the 'miles Christi' was a possible and paradoxical metaphor for writers of Saints' Lives to use. While we *might* explain the application of Germanic heroic and military images to Christian themes through this standard image, she concludes that

the [*Andreas*] poet does not make reference to the wider perspective of the *miles Christi* tradition in which the hero's struggles may be seen as a pattern and model of the Christian life. The saint's acts conform to those of the *miles Christi* only because the nature of his actions and experiences are predetermined in the given narrative, which the poet does not alter. If he was aware of the implication of his narrative, that spiritual warfare is one of obedience to God and calls for a different relationship between God and man than that between lord and retainer, he does not articulate it. The notions of military service suggested by the language of the poem are not modified by concepts of [divine] service . . .[29]

A rather rigid sense of decorum inspires these lines: one can use battle metaphors in Christian contexts, but only if battle implies its opposite, a quiescent service, as defined in the Benedictine Rule. That such a topos was widely used in medieval texts cannot be disputed; that every instance of a battle mataphor must conform to this prescription seems severe. But the *Andreas* poet's failure to observe this decorum brings upon him the judgment that his use of language is, consequently, injudicious.

The aim of expressionism is to project, and then to create, a metaphorical world where all objects are defined in accordance with the poet's vision, without validating reference to a 'real' world, or to specific topoi. Expressionism is one version of an ultimate metaphoricity, and it requires the acceptance of the autonomous or absolute figure. R.S. Furness comments on this aspect: 'the problem of metaphor is central to expressionism ... [there is a] tendency for the metaphor to become more and more independent and increasingly "absolute" ... The metaphor (or image) becomes *expressive* rather than imitative, existing as a powerful autonomous figure of speech from which radiate a host of evocative meanings.'[30] A cause for the battle imagery in *Andreas* is not hard to locate: the 'miles Christi' topos and the archetypal myth of the war between Christ and Satan, working separately or in conjunction, both provide a possible source. The poet then develops his materials into an independent metaphorical complex that is indeed absolute. It stands by itself, and coheres as an integrated system; it has an internal consistency in logic, yet one which does not necessarily correspond to any external logic. Like other expressionistic poems, *Andreas* evokes and brings into being a state of ecstasy. In *Andreas* this process helps create an emotional equivalence of the apocalpyse that the typological symbolism insists is both imminent and omnipresent. Those who have explained *Andreas* by reference to typology all begin their case by noting that the poem's flouting of 'realism' requires, thereby, a 'metaphorical,' 'allegorical,' or 'typological' (the terms are used almost interchangeably) account. They are quite right to insist upon this. What I suggest is that the expressionistic mode of *Andreas* is the vehicle for this tenor, that here style both equals and enables meaning. The typological critics almost entirely ignore the poem's language, but they should not. The metaphorical language here pushed to extremity mirrors, not the real world, but the vision of the world that yearns – indeed cries out for – the apocalypse. Nothing is more absolute than the Last Judgment and the eternity which comes 'after.'

In the projected world that the *Andreas* poet fashions, events and metaphors become logical when viewed as existing on this 'stage' – an imagined space where eternity coexists with time. Struggle is the defining characteristic of this world (structurally, the necessary dialectic of the expressionistic mode) and ugliness the prime aspect of the devil's horde. Despite his attempt to paint his thanes as glorious ('þegnum þryðfullum' 1329a), the description of the devil as 'wan ond wliteleas' ('dark and beauty-less,' 1169a) remains unalterable. God's protection is a refuge from conflict, and beauty, the physical counterpart to his harmonious voice. Thus Andrew's companions become a ship's 'noble treasures' ('æfre ic ne hyrde // þon cymlicor / ceol gehladenne // heahgestreonum,' 'never have I heard of a ship more splendidly laden with noble treasures' 360b-62a), and by logical extension heroes ('hæleð') turn into 'þegnas wlitige' ('beautiful thanes' 363b). This last phrase is more than an empty tag:

the adjective 'wlitige' never appears elsewhere in conjunction with 'þegnas' or any other military form. They are 'beautiful' not only because they are God's champions and thus akin to his angels and past heroes (713ff, 870), but also because as treasures they take on the beauty of gems. This motif runs uninterruptedly throughout. We may note, too, that after Andrew's torment, the poet adds 'Næs him gewemmed wlite' ('Nor was his beauty disfigured' 1471a). Andrew's beauty partakes of that radiance which shines forever in glory (1720a–21b).

An even more striking example of a seeming disparity between action and image occurs later in the poem when Andrew goes to the prison to release Matthew. Andrew arrives before the prison door and the guards – seven of them – die upon his mere approach. In the source Andrew makes the sign of the Cross and 'Immediately all the prison guards died and fell down.'[31] The action in both texts is similar: the poem omits the sign of the Cross, but surely we accept that it is God's power working through Andrew which causes their deaths. The significant difference, however, is the poem's description of the dead men as 'blood-stained' ('deaðræs forfeng // hæleð heorodreorige,' 'sudden-death seized the blood-stained men' 995b–96a). A critic with a realistic cast of mind could find much to rail against here. Since not a single weapon has been drawn, nor even one blow exchanged, how could the guards be 'blood-stained'? We can accept the workings of God's miraculous, invisible power, but what do we do with this lapse in taste and logic? We understand it within the poem's mode of development: the blood-stained men are examples of a supremely heightened, transformed reality that permits metaphors to be actualized. All meetings between God's party and the devil's (the Mermedonians) are understood to be battles in an unending (temporal) war. Here the blood becomes a concrete emblem of Andrew's 'victory.' In this expressionistic context metaphors are literalized in order to convey symbolic meaning; in a realistic context the process is exactly the opposite, that is, literal details are made into metaphors in order to convey their symbolic import.

Related to this example is the fairly extensive description of the Mermedonians gathering the host, arraying their troops under banners with all the paraphernalia of war (1201a–28b). More than one critic has snidely remarked that here the poet reaches a kind of peak of absurdity – a Germanic army in full regalia draws up on a battlefield where there is neither field nor battle. But while a literal battle may not take place, certainly a violent struggle does; for it is at this point that the Mermedonians drag Andrew through the caves, rocky slopes, and cobbled streets. To remain consistent with his overarching vision, the poet calls up an armed mass. This is how, we have come to learn, the Mermedonians inevitably appear; it also reinforces the sense that this world is totally defined by vectors of power.

All the problematic metaphors can be interpreted in this manner. Irving's remarks, for example, that it is 'risible' to imagine 'slaughter-wolves' writing ('swa hit wælwulfas / awriten haefdon' 149) are based on the realistic notion that *wolves* cannot *write*. Of course in the real world, this is true. But the world of *Andreas*, as I have been at some pains to shows, is a far different thing. The Mermedonians' cannibalism is treated as an evil habit in the source, but they go about their grisly business in a meticulous, efficient way. They construct tanks in which to collect the blood and ovens in which to roast the flesh – distasteful, perhaps, but carefully planned. The Anglo-Saxon *Andreas* contains no such 'civilized' process:

> þæt hie banhringas   abrecan þohton,
> lungre tolysan   lic ond sawle,
> ond þonne todælan   duguðe on geogoðe,
> werum to wiste   ond to wilþege,
> fæges flæschoman;   feorh ne bemurndan
> grædige guðrincas,   he þæs gastes sið
> æfter swyltcwale   geseted wurde.
> Swa hie symble ymb þritig   þing gehedon
> nihtgerimes;   wæs him neod micel
> þæt hie tobrugdon   blodigum ceaflum
> fira flæschoman   him to foddorþege.   (150a–160b)

when they thought to break the bone-rings, quickly to separate body and soul, and then to divide to the duguth and the company of young men, as food for men and as a pleasant feast, the body of the doomed one; they did not care for his life, the greedy men of war, how the spirit's journey after the torment of death should be appointed. So always after thirty nights they held a thing; they had a great need that they tear to pieces with bloody jaws the flesh of men as food for themselves.

Here the Mermedonians do indeed act like wolves; having created that metaphorical identification, the poet is only being literal when he calls them 'wælwulfas.' Real wolf/people on a symbolic stage, their behaviour now becomes comprehensible.

Throughout *Andreas* the poet misses no opportunity to qualify his descriptions emotionally and morally. In contrast to the bare and naïve realism of his source, the poet evokes another world where ecstasy prevails. Where the source reads, 'May God bless you,' *Andreas* has:

Wes ðu gebledsod,   brego mancynnes,
dryhten hælend!   A þin dom lyfað
ge neh ge feor;   is þin nama halif,
wuldre gewlitegad   ofer werþeoda,
miltsum gemæsod.   Nænig manna is
under heofonhwealfe   hæleða cynnes,
ðætte areccan mæge   oððe rim wite
hu ðrymlice,   þeoda baldor,
gasta geocend,   þine gife dælest.   (540a–48b)

Be you blessed, Prince of mankind, Lord Saviour! Ever your glory lives both near and far; your name is holy, adorned with glory throughout the nations, celebrated for mercy. There is no man of the race of men, under the vault of the sky, who can relate or recount how gloriously, Prince of peoples, Comforter of souls, you apportion your grace.

Hatred of the devil provides the antithesis to this praise of God. The devil can only offer the Mermedonians the 'laðspell' ('bad news' 1079b) and the 'færspell' ('calamitous news' 1086a) that their imprisoned 'food' is gone. Although it is never explicitly stated, it seems obvious that such 'laðspell' is meant to contrast directly with the 'godspell' (12b) God offered man when Christ was also found missing (because resurrected) from his tomb/prison. Such primal emotions as are depicted in the poem transcend simple human response and their force pervades every character, act, and object. The descriptions of violent storms at sea contrast vividly with their unembellished source. 'For a great tempest of sea and surge had risen against them' becomes an extended cataclysm, one so extreme in its rendering that it approaches a literal version of the apocalypse. The pressure eternity and Judgment exert on the action in *Andreas* results in passages that imitate, and therefore conjure up, these final things. The first sea storm also parallels the great drowning at the end which destroys and then converts the Mermedonians; both scenes contain implicit typological allusions to Baptism and Judgment:

Þa gedrefed wearð,

onhrered hwælmere;   hornfisc plegode,
glad geond garsecg,   ond se græga mæw
wælgifre wand.   Wedercandel swearc,
windas weoxon,   wægas grundon,
streamas styredon,   strengas gurron,
wædo gewætte;   wæteregsa stod
þreata þryðum.   (369b-76a)

Then the whale-mere became troubled, stirred up; the whale played, glided through the ocean, and the grey gull, greedy for slaughter, circled round. The candle of the sky grew dark, the winds rose, the waves dashed, the [ocean] streams were in an uproar. The cordage rattled, the sheets were soaked; the water-terror stood up with the might of hosts.

And the calming of the tempest (449b-60b) specifically anticipates the later retreat of the deluge into the abyss, thus tying the two episodes together as the source does not. The final effect, however, is more than a structural tightness; it is importantly the conception of a universe where metaphysical forces are always present and where God's power always prevails. Curiously, the realism of the source turns the same possibility into a lesser display of magical command.

Perhaps the most obvious instance of the expressive use of absolute metaphor is the well known 'winter episode.' Following his first ordeal, Andrew, in prison, spends the night 'searoþancum beseted' ('beset by wise thoughts' 1255a). Outside winter rages and not even the wintry images of *The Wanderer* or *The Seafarer* can match this scene in *Andreas*:

              Snaw eorðan band
    wintergeworpum;   weder coledon
    heardum hægelscurum,   swylce hrim ond forst,
    hare hildstapan,   hæleða eðel
    lucon, leoda gesetu.   Land wæron freorig;
    cealdum cylegicelum   clang wæteres þrym,
    ofer eastreamas   is brycgade,
    blæce brimrade.   (1255b-62a)

Snow bound the earth with winter-bands [snow drifts]; the sky grew cold with hard hail-showers, likewise rime and frost, grey marching-warriors, locked the lands of men, the habitations of people. The land was freezing; with cold icicles became hard and motionless the strength of the water, over the rivers ice bridged, dark [shining?] expanse of water.

While Thomas Hill calls our attention to the general tropological meaning of cold as 'damned,'[32] he makes no comment on this frigid passage. The scene illustrates the expressionistic mode of *Andreas* particularly well: it is a separate 'station,' almost an inset within the larger sequence. The snow and hail are appliquéd onto the action; there is not the slightest hint of them in the source. They are imported, so to speak, to express and symbolize the hostile forces without, but they have no *organic* relation to anything in their immediate context. Within the larger context of Anglo-Saxon poetic culture, they most frequently express (or give the occasion for) the despair of exile. But now the emotions they traditionally evoke contrast boldly with Andrew's state of mind. This 'eorl ellenheard' ('valiant nobleman' 1254a) has become the perfect model of the loyal Christian/thane and his resoluteness a quality anchored in his 'coming' martyrdom.

Finally, a series of images at the end of *Andreas* takes us to another level of comprehension. It also represents the culmination of an important complex of motifs related to eating and drinking and their theological implications.[33] Two items are of special note. The first is the much disputed passage in which the pouring of water from the columns is ironically compared to a great serving of mead after a feast:

> Meoduscerwen wearð
> æfter symbeldæge;   slæpe tobrugdon
> searuhæbbende.   Sund grunde onfeng,
> deope gedrefed;   duguð wearð afyrhted
> þurh þæs flodes fær.   Fæge swulton,
> geonge on geofone   guðræs fornam
> þurh sealtes swelg;   þæt wæs sorgbyrþen,
> biter beorþegu.   Byrlas ne gældon,
> ombehtþegnas;   þær wæs ælcum genog
> fram dæges orde   drync sona gearu.   (1526b–35b)

There was a serving of mead [disaster] after a day of feasting; the armed men started from sleep. The flood covered the ground, deeply stirred; the duguth became terrified at the sudden attack of the flood. The doomed ones died, the rush of battle took the young men in the ocean through the abyss of salt water; that

was a burden of sorrow, bitter beer-drinking. Cupbearers, servants, did not delay.
There was enough for each, a drink soon ready, from the beginning of day.

Brooks comments that 'just as the Danes are overwhelmed by *ealuscerwen*
after the revelry consequent upon Beowulf's arrival, so the Mermedonians
are engulfed by "a generous serving of mead," and this metaphor is
elaborated to the point of absurdity in 1533ff.'[34] Yet the 'feasting' of these
cannibals is quite appropriately brought to an end by an unexpected
deluge which is likened to an orgy of drunkeness. That this flood destroys
and also is the agent of their conversion only completes the irony. So
much is clear. But if we do not grant the poem's potential to turn all
metaphors into curious and ironic realities within its own highly symbolic
contexts, we must continue to miss the way figurative language actually
functions here.

After the conversion, a change occurs. Mermedonia is no longer the
city of cannibals where a deluge depicted as a 'bitter beer-drinking'
becomes an inevitable punishment. Now the poet sees Mermedonia in
a triple image: it is the 'winburg' ('wine-city' 1637a, 1672a), the 'goldburg'
('gold-city' 1655), and the 'wederburg' ('weather-city' 1697a, that is, the
city of fair weather). Not only have the Mermedonians been converted
from cannibals to Christians – and Andrew ecstatically strengthened in
the process – but the setting itself has undergone a complete metamor-
phosis from the place 'morðre bewunden' to the island which combines
attributes of a Christian civilization reflecting paradise; the wine replaces
the blood, the gold reflects God's beauty in an earthly nobility, and the
fair-weather stands as the counterpart to and resolution of all the poem's
violent storms.

We have no doubt that *Andreas* is about conversion. But if we limit
our vision to just the 'actual' conversions that take place in the poem
and the typological reverberations these set off, then we may fail to notice
that this extravagant figurative language is an important vehicle for
expressing this very theme. The specific conversions in the imagery, such
as those just noted, fit into a system that radically alters the entire repertory
of Germanic heroic diction. By forcing this received vocabulary into
service for an alien cause, the poet succeeds – through the very violence
of his style – in converting those old epic formulas into new Christian
metaphors. He makes them work as Christian absolutes by using them
absolutely, and we must acknowledge that we can perceive the poet's
success only if we can envision the universe of *Andreas* as a projected,
symbolic stage, where metaphors express rather than imitate. Paul Ricoeur

has written that 'the power of metaphor is to project and reveal a world.'[35] Certainly the *Andreas* poet has done that to an extreme degree. Yet I would maintain that the poet knew what he was about and that it is our task to view his effort from a vantage point which will reveal its own metaphorical truths.

Andreas is the most demanding Anglo-Saxon example of the expressionistic mode. But much of Anglo-Saxon poetry – and all of the Saints Lives – shows a similar tendency. The dual vision of history which results from seeing a narrative as taking place and also having eternally taken place puts this kind of pressure on the Saints' Lives. This perspective, however, is universally Christian; it is not restricted to the Anglo-Saxons. Still it is most significantly present in the poetic hagiography which has survived from Anglo-Saxon England. None of the Latin sources has anything that remotely corresponds. One cannot explain why the Anglo-Saxons, apparently alone in their time, incorporated this dual vision into the fabric of their devotional poems on the lives of saints, but it is this way of looking at time and eternity, I suggest, which allowed them to create such powerfully symbolic works. To expect that the heroic diction as it works in a metonymic piece like *Beowulf* can be transferred unchanged to a metaphoric poem like *Andreas* is to invite disappointment. Those who have so expected have indeed been disappointed. They may also have lost much of the point, and certainly most of the sacred poetic delight.

NOTES

1 Stanley B. Greenfield *The Interpretation of Old English Poems* (London and Boston 1972) ix
2 See Arthur Fritzsche 'Das angelsächsische Gedichte Andreas und Cynewulf' (Halle 1879); also rpt in *Anglia* 2 (1879) 441-96.
3 Rosemary Woolf 'Saints' Lives' in *Continuations and Beginnings: Studies in Old English Literature* ed E.G. Stanley (London 1966) 53
4 E.G. Stanley *'Beowulf'* in *Continuations and Beginnings* 114
5 Kenneth R. Brooks ed *Andreas and the Fates of the Apostles* (Oxford 1961) passim. All quotations are taken from this edition.
6 Edward B. Irving, Jr 'A reading of *Andreas*: the poem as poem' *ASE* 12 (1983) 214
7 Arthur G. Brodeur 'A Study of Diction and Style in Three Anglo-Saxon Narrative Poems' in *Nordica et Anglica: Studies in Honor of Stefan Einarsson* ed Allan H. Orrick (The Hague 1968) 105

8 Alvin A. Lee *The Guest-Hall of Eden: Four Essays on the Design of Old English Poetry* (New Haven 1972) 90

9 David Hamilton '*Andreas* and *Beowulf*: Placing the Hero' in *Anglo-Saxon Poetry: Essays in Appreciation* ed Lewis E. Nicholson and Dolores Warwick Frese (Notre Dame 1975) 97; see also his 'The diet and digestion of allegory in *Andreas*' *ASE* 1 (1972) 147-58.

10 Hamilton 'Diet and digestion' 152; see also John D. Niles *Beowulf: The Poem and Its Tradition* (Cambridge, Mass 1983) 3: 'the magic of *Beowulf* is bound securely to the ordinary world. The setting of the main part of the poem is no make-believe landscape where anything goes ... we are still situated in the real world.'

11 See Marcus B. Hester *The Meaning of Poetic Metaphor* (The Hague and Paris 1967).

12 All the works cited above discuss the relationship of *Andreas* to *Beowulf*. To this list may be added the long introduction by George Phillip Krapp to his edition, *Andreas and the Fates of the Apostles* (Boston 1906); L. J. Peters 'The Relationship of the Old English *Andreas* to *Beowulf*' *PMLA* 64 (1951) 844-63 (who argues strongly against any such connection); and Arthur G. Brodeur *The Art of Beowulf* (Berkeley 1960) esp 1-38.

13 These are some of the important typological studies of *Andreas*: Thomas D. Hill 'The Tropological Context of Heat and Cold Imagery in Anglo-Saxon Poetry' *NM* 69 (1968) 522-32; Hill 'Figural Narrative in *Andreas*: The Conversion of the Mermedonians' *NM* 70 (1969) 261-73; Hill 'Two Notes on Patristic Allusion in *Andreas*' *Anglia* 84 (1966) 156-62; Penn Szittya 'The Living Stone and the Patriarchs: Typological Imagery in *Andreas*, lines 706-810' *JEGP* 77 (1973) 167-74; Hamilton 'Diet and digestion'; Joseph B. Trahern 'Joshua and Tobias in the Old English *Andreas*,' *SN* 42 (1970) 330-2; Constance B. Hieatt 'The Harrowing of Mermedonia: Typological Patterns in the Old English *Andreas*' *NM* 77 (1976) 49-62; Marie Michelle Walsh 'The Baptismal Flood in the Old English *Andreas*: Liturgical and Typological Depths' *Traditio* 33 (1977) 137-58; Alvin A. Lee *The Guest-Hall of Eden* 87-95.

14 James W. Earl 'The Typological Structure of *Andreas*' in *Old English Literature in Context* ed John D. Niles (Cambridge, and Totowa, NJ 1980) 66-89. Quotation on 67.

15 I hereby finesse the complicated question of the source of *Andreas*; a reasonably detailed examination can be found in the edition of Brooks, xv-xviii. The nearest we can now come to the Latin source (and that seems to be fairly near indeed) is the so-called *Casanatensis* version. For the sake of simplicity, I will refer to this work as the source; see Franz Blatt ed *Die lateinischen Bearbeitungen der Acta Andreae et Matthiae apud anthropophagos* (Giessen

and Copenhagen 1930). An English translation is available in Michael J.B. Allen and Daniel G. Calder trans *Sources and Analogues of Old English Poetry: The Major Latin Texts in Translation* (Cambridge, and Totowa, NJ 1976) 15-34; quotations from *Casanatensis* are taken from this translation.

16 M.R. James *The Apocryphal New Testament* (Oxford 1924; rpt 1972) 453

17 T.A. Shippey *Old English Verse* (London 1972) 94

18 No hapax can be taken as the creation of one author, but the high occurrence of such items strongly suggests that the poet was probably experimenting with his received language. In Old English the flexible and fecund nature of the Germanic compound would provide the ground on which the poet could 'play.' The hapax legomena are indicated by a special mark in the Glossary of the Brooks edition.

19 See Stanley B. Greenfield '*Beowulf* and Epic Tragedy' in *Studies in Old English Literature in Honor of Arthur G. Brodeur* ed Greenfield (Eugene, Or 1963) 91-105.

20 On this distinction, see Roman Jakobson and Morris Halle *Fundamentals of Language* 4th ed (The Hague and Paris 1980) 72-6; and David Lodge *The Modes of Modern Writing: Metaphor, Metonymy, and the Typology of Modern Literature* (London 1977) 73-124.

21 See Jean Daniélou *The Bible and the Liturgy* (Notre Dame, Ind 1956); and Henry Ansgar Kelly *The Devil at Baptism: Ritual, Theology, and Drama* (Ithaca 1985).

22 See Margaret Enid Bridges *Generic Contrast in Old English Hagiographical Poetry* (Copenhagen 1984) 179-211, for a different kind of commentary on the diction in *Andreas*.

23 John Willett *Expressionism* (New York 1970) 8

24 Quoted in Willett 240

25 Egbert Krispyn *Style and Society in German Literary Expressionism*, Univ of Florida Monographs, Humanities Series 15 (Gainesville, Fla 1964) 44. In addition to Willett and Krispyn, general studies of expressionism are Roy F. Allen *German Expressionistic Poetry* (Boston 1979); R.S. Furness *Expressionism* (London 1973); Hermann Friedmann and Otto Mann eds *Expressionismus: Gestalten einer literarischen Bewegung* (Heidelberg 1956); Geoffrey Perkins *Contemporary Theory of Expressionism* (Bern and Frankfurt 1974); Paul Raabe ed *Expressionismus: Aufzeichnungen und Erinnerungen der Zeitgenossen* (Olten 1965); Walter H. Sokel *The Writer in Extremis: Expressionism in Twentieth-Century German Literature* (Stanford 1959).

26 Furness 1 and 21

27 Perkins 14

28 For a detailed examination of Aristotle on metaphor, see Paul Ricoeur *The*

Rule of Metaphor trans Robert Czerny, with Kathleen McLaughlin and John Costello, sj (Toronto 1977) 9-43.

29 Joyce Hill 'The Soldier of Christ in Old English Prose and Poetry' *Leeds SE* 12 (1981) 71-2

30 Furness 18-19

31 See Thomas D. Hill 'The *Sphragis* as Apotropaic Sign: *Andreas* 1334-44' *Anglia* 101 (1983) 147-51.

32 See Hill 'Tropological Context of Heat and Cold.' But in his original edition of *A Critical History of Old English Literature*, Stanley B. Greenfield noted that the scene 'may be out of keeping with the literal situation in Mermedonia but is nevertheless a fitting *metaphoric* depiction of mood and atmosphere' (New York 1965) 106.

33 See Hamilton 'Diet and digestion' for an examination of most of these images.

34 Brooks ed 114

35 Ricoeur 93

MARIE NELSON

The Battle of Maldon and *Juliana*: The Language of Confrontation

WITH HIS TERM 'speech act,' John L. Austin introduced the concept that a speaker actually *does* something when he utters words.[1] Austin's idea that certain conditions must be present for a speech act to be successfully performed, especially as it was further developed by John Searle,[2] makes the term particularly applicable to the interpretation of confrontation, as I hope the following discussion of *The Battle of Maldon* and *Juliana* will demonstrate.

The *Maldon* poet reports that speech acts have been performed, and presents them as being performed. With 'Het' (the preterite of 'hatan,' 'to command'), the first word of the first complete sentence of the poem,[3] he reports that Byrhtnoth *commanded*[4] his young warriors to leave their horses, drive them far away, direct their thoughts to their hands, and think good thoughts. The conditions necessary for the performance of an act of *commanding* are clearly present: Byrhtnoth is in a position of authority; he has confidence in the capability of his men to obey; it is not completely obvious that they will do what he tells them in the normal course of events; and what he says counts as an attempt to tell them to get ready to fight.[5] Byrhtnoth's men recognize his speech act as a *command*, so it succeeds as 'illocution.'[6]

Byrhtnoth's *command* also succeeds as 'perlocution.'[7] His warriors do what he orders them to do. Offa's young kinsman releases his hawk;[8] Eadric begins to bear his sword to battle; and, judging from the poet's report that Eadric carried out his 'beot,' he also obeys Byrhtnoth's general command to exercise physical and mental strength.

The poet gives further attention to Byrhtnoth's acts of leadership. Byrhtnoth *encourages* his men ('trymian' 17b); he *instructs* them on how to stand and hold their place ('tæhte' 18b); and he *orders* them to hold their shields firmly and not be afraid ('bæd' 20a). 'Tæhte' and 'bæd' are clearly verbs of *commanding*; and 'trymian,' since what Byrhtnoth is asking is that his men fight with strength and courage, takes on aspects of *commanding* in this context. And thus the *Maldon* poet reports the series of speech acts by means of which Byrhtnoth prepares for the confrontation that results in his death.

The next speech act of the poem, the Viking's *demand*[9] that Byrhtnoth pay tribute, is presented as an act that is being performed. Since the *demand* is obliquely made, it will be well to have the speech before us.

'Me sendon to þe   sæmen snelle,
heton ðe secgan   þæt þu most sendan raðe
beagas wið geborge,   and eow betere is
þæt ge þisne garræs   mid gafole forgyldon
þonne we swa hearde   hilde dælon.
Ne þurfe we us spillan,   gif ge spedaþ to þam;
we willað wið þam golde   grið fæstnian.
Gif þu þæt gerædest   þe her ricost eart,
þæt þu þine leoda   lysan wille,
syllan sæmannum   on hyra sylfra dom
feoh wið freode   and niman frið æt us,
we willaþ mid þam sceattum   us to scype gangan,
on flot feran   and eow friþes healdan.'   (29-41)

'Bold seamen sent me to you,
ordered [me]   to say to you that you must quickly send
things of value for defense, and it is better for you
that you buy off this spear-conflict with tribute
than that we join in bitter conflict.
We do not need to slaughter each other, if you are rich enough;
we wish to confirm peace with the gold.
If you who have the highest rank here decide
that you wish to ransom your people,
pay money for peace to the seamen
according to their judgment and take peace from us,
we wish to go to ship with the tribute money,
to go on the deep water and hold peace with you.'

The Viking has been *ordered* to perform speech acts, and he performs them. Addressing Byrhtnoth – and apparently Byrhtnoth's men as well

- the messenger *demands* money and backs his demand with a *threat*.[10]
The demand is carried by what seems at first to be a simple *assertion*:
'"It is better for you that you buy off this spear-conflict."' But the implicit
threat of 'garræs' becomes overt with the Viking's statement of the
alternative possibility: the two forces can '"join in bitter conflict."'

In addition to *demanding*, *threatening*, and *asserting*, the Viking also
seems to be *promising*. His '"we do not need to slaughter each other"'
prepares the way for what he wishes his audience to believe is a more
desirable outcome. With his *claims* that the Vikings '"wish to confirm
peace"' and '"wish to go to ship,"' their messenger *asserts* that they
want to see a peaceful outcome. More important, however, at least as
far as his performance of an act of *promising* is concerned, the Viking
offers a course of action that he hopes Byrhtnoth will prefer to slaughtering
and being slaughtered.

The messenger predicates his own future acts and those of the '"bold
seamen"' who sent him. He apparently intends to do what he says he
will do (or at least claims that those who sent him will be satisfied with
the tribute requested); he places himself and the other Vikings under
obligation to do what he says they will do; and, finally, he expects his
words to be understood as his acceptance of that obligation. All the
conditions for *promising*, then, as Searle presents them, would seem to
be present.

Byrhtnoth's reply suggests that the Viking's speech acts are illocutionary successes; that is, that he is understood to have performed acts
of *asserting*, *demanding*, *threatening*, and, perhaps, *promising*. But
again, since Byrhtnoth's reply is as oblique as the Viking's initiation
of the dialogue, it will be well to have that reply before us.

'Gehyrst þu, sælida,   hwæt þis folc segeð?
Hi willað eow to gafole   garas syllan,
ættryne ord   and ealde swurd,
þa heregeatu   þe eow æt hilde ne deah.'   (45-8)

Byrhtnoth's response takes the form of a grammatically positive statement.
He *asserts*, having first made certain that the messenger is listening, that
his people wish to pay tribute. However, since the tribute he says they
wish to pay consists of '"spears,"' '"poisoned points,"' '"ancient
swords,"' and '"battle-gear"' of a special kind (the kind that is awarded
after death),[11] his response is actually a rejection of the Viking's proposition, and functions as a counter *threat*. Byrhtnoth's '"They wish to

pay"' speech, nevertheless, shows his understanding that a *promise*, conditional as it is, has been made.

Byrhtnoth's reply to the Viking's proposition shows that he recognizes it as precisely what it was intended to be. As perlocution, however, the Viking's speech is an utter failure, for Byrhtnoth follows his rejection of the terms offered by the Vikings with a bold *assertion* that he and his men stand ready to defend their homeland.

Byrhtnoth's *assertion* more than satisfies Searle's conditions for the performance of assertions. Byrhtnoth definitely has evidence for the truth of his statement. He knows his men and has himself just instructed them. He fully believes in the truth of what he says. And his statement counts as an undertaking to the effect that what he says represents an actual state of affairs. Indeed, description of Byrhtnoth's ringing statement of confidence in terms of speech act theory seems rather too mild for the force with which the 'hæleða hleo' ('protector of heroes') chooses to play the game of war.

As the battle begins, the actions of Byrhtnoth's men give further evidence of the truth of his *assertion* that they are ready to fight for their homeland. Wulfstan, Ælfere, and Maccus, prepared to fight ' "as long as they can wield weapons," ' successfully defend the causeway that provides the only access to the territory they are defending, and it seems that there is a good chance that they can continue to do so. Seeing this, the 'laðe gystas' ('hated strangers' 86b) now begin to 'lytegian' ('use guile') and to 'biddan' ('entreat,' 'implore,' 'strongly request') that they be permitted to cross the tidal stream that separates the two armies. And Byrhtnoth, for his 'ofermod' ('overconfidence,' 'pride'),[12] the poet says, permits them to cross.

What his men hear him do is actually *invite* (request) the Vikings to come across. These are his words as the poet presents them,

> 'Nu eow is gerymed: gað ricene to us
> guman to guþe.   God ana wat
> hwa þære wælstowe   wealdan mote.'   (93-5)

> 'Now the way is open to you: come quickly to us
> men to battle. God alone knows
> who is permitted to hold the battlefield.'

In effect, this response – Yes, you may cross – is equivalent to Byrhtnoth's earlier No, we won't pay. Both responses to challenge constitute expressions of decisions to fight, that is, to perform acts of defensive aggression that are in accordance with the rules of Anglo-Saxon society. And Byrhtnoth's speech acts, all of which require a high degree of confidence in his own ability to command and in the capability of his men to follow orders, are absolutely consistent through the challenge exchanges, the battle sequence, and his own physical defeat. Mortally wounded, he *thanks* God for the day's work he has given him and continues to lead his men, *commanding* and *encouraging* them as long as he can stand. With his dying words he *asserts* his soul's need of God's protection, but as long as he lives he defends his own land and people.

With Byrhtnoth's death, a possibility of flight that has been present from the beginning is allowed to surface. What Offa had told Byrhtnoth earlier – that not everyone who spoke bold words would support them with bold deeds – is shown to be true. But for those who remain on the battlefield there are only two possible outcomes, and, as the poet reports, '"They all wished then one of two things – to relinquish life or avenge the dear one"' (207-8).

The events that follow the death of Byrhtnoth show that his confidence in his men was fully justified. The cowardly sons of Odda may have fled, but the second part of the poem shows Byrhtnoth's men taking on the responsibility to encourage and strengthen that he formerly bore. Ælfwine recalls his earlier promises, *announces* his lineage, and *asserts* that his people will never have cause to reproach him that he would flee when his lord lay dead. Offa *cites* the need for men to encourage each other and *curses*[13] the wretched sons of Odda who caused other men to flee from battle. Leofsunu follows with an explicit *promise*,

'Ic þæt gehate,   þæt ic heonon nelle
fleon fotes trym,   ac wille furðor gan,
wrecan on gewinne   minne winedrihten.'   (246-8)

'I promise that I will not flee from here
the space of one foot, but intend to go further,
to avenge my lord in battle.'

The lower-born Dunnere also speaks bold words and *vows* to avenge his lord. Edward the tall *vows* that he will not flee one step. We are told that even a hostage fights valiantly and that Offa keeps his promise that he and his lord would either ride home together or both fall in battle. Old Byrhtwold's ringing words are the last we hear spoken, but they are followed by an account of the performance of a Godric who encourages his fellows and fights until he falls.

I have given almost my whole attention to speech acts here, feeling that such an emphasis is justified by their prominence in the narrative, but it should be pointed out that, with the exceptions already noted, the physical actions the poet records are totally congruent with the speech acts of Byrhtnoth and his men. Byrhtnoth reassures those closest to him with his physical presence, and he stands steadfast when the Vikings cross the locked tidal streams. He shakes his spear to give force to his defiant reply to the Viking demand for tribute, and he breaks off the shaft of the spear that pierces him and turns upon the Viking who threw it.

Those who take on the responsibilities of leadership after Byrhtnoth's death are equally consistent in their performance of speech acts and physical acts. Ælfwine *encourages* his fellows, then fatally wounds an invader. Offa emphasizes his bold words by shaking his ash spear, then fights to the death. Leofsunu speaks boldly, raising his shield, then advances full of anger, fights boldly, and scorns flight. Dunnere shakes his spear as he speaks, then goes forth with no concern for his life. The litany of praiseworthy actions – brave words, brave deeds, and bold gestures that both emphasize spoken messages and carry meanings of their own – continues until the poem breaks off.

Requests and *promises* are the two basic speech acts that seem to have generated the confrontational structure of *The Battle of Maldon*. The *requests* include *commands, orders, instructions, encouragements, demands*, an *entreaty*, an *invitation*, and a *curse*. The *promises* include *threats* (promises that something hearers do not want to happen will happen) and *vows* (particularly binding promises). Demands based on assumption of authority and commands based on its lawful possession, attempts to intimidate and efforts to encourage, proud assertions and an humble act of thanksgiving – all are part of a host of demonstrations that to say something can be to *do* something. And all work together in the *Maldon* poet's highly dramatic presentation of a confrontation of determined invaders and heroic defenders.

In *Juliana*, as in *The Battle of Maldon, requests* and *promises* develop a confrontational structure. Cynewulf introduces the conflict between Juliana and Heliseus, a merciless persecutor of Christians, with admirable economy. By line 46 of the 731-line poem, Heliseus has *requested* that

Juliana be his bride, her father has *pledged* that he will give Juliana to Heliseus, and Juliana is responding to Heliseus's request. The ambiguity of her speech makes it advisable to have her words before us.

'Ic þe mæg gesecgan   þæt þu þec sylfne ne þearft
swiþor swencan;   gif þu soðne God
lufast and gelyfest,   and his lof rærest,
ongietest gæsta Hleo,   ic beo gearo sona
unwaclice   willan þines.
Swylce ic þe secge,   gif þu to sæmran gode
þurh deofolgield   dæde beþencest,
hætsð hæþenfeoh,   ne meaht þu habban mec,
ne geþreatian   þe to sinhigan;
næfre þu þæs swiðlic   sar gegearwast,
þurh hæstne nið,   heardra wita,
þæt þu mec onwende   worda þissa.'[14]

'I can say to you that you need not
trouble yourself more; if you love
and believe in the true God, and lift up his praise,
recognize the Protector of souls, I am ready
at once enthusiastically to be of your purpose.
Likewise I say to you, if you entrust your actions
to inferior gods through idolatry,
violent heathen sacrifice, you can not have me
as your wife by threatening;
you can never prepare so strong a torment
through violent hostility of hard punishments
that you turn me from these words.'

Though Heliseus may have intended to *request* Juliana's hand, it is clear that she does not perceive his act as a simple request. A genuine request would permit one of at least two answers: Yes or No. Juliana's father has already said Yes, so it would seem that she has little choice but to say Yes also. Nevertheless, she says Maybe, and the form of her answer suggests that she already sees the latent *threat* in the 'request' of the man of power.

In the ordinary course of events, the person who threatens makes the conditions (the form is often 'If you don't ＿＿, then I will ＿＿'). Here Juliana's freedom of choice has been threatened, but – and this is evidence of her strength of mind – she makes the conditions under which she will marry Heliseus. She will become his bride only if he will serve her God.

The fact that Juliana is offering alternatives is emphasized by the clauses with which she draws attention to her own performance of speech acts ('"I can say to you,"' and '"Likewise I say to you"'); by the loosely parallel 'if' clauses ('"If you love and believe in the true God,"' and '"If you entrust your actions to inferior gods"'); and by the *assertion* with which she concludes her answer to Heliseus, which could be paraphrased, Nothing you can do, no matter how much you hurt me, will make me take back what I say.

It would be possible, assuming that Juliana knew about the persecutions of her time,[15] to interpret the speech just cited as a request to be made to suffer, but it seems wiser to focus on Heliseus' interpretation of her response. Heliseus orders Affricanus, Juliana's father, brought before him. 'Daraðhæbbende' ('carrying a spear' 68a – and thus showing a potentiality for the violent action suggested by Juliana's 'hætsð hæðenfeoh,' 'swiðlic sar,' 'hæstne nið,' and 'heardra wita'), he reports Juliana's words to her father. Heliseus feels that Juliana has dishonoured him. She has shamed him before his people by *ordering* him (the verb is 'het,' 74b) to pay homage to a strange god. It is more than apparent that the effect of Juliana's speech, in which she set forth the conditions under which she would marry Heliseus, whether she intended it or not, is that of an *insult*.

After Heliseus' angry display, Juliana's father *reaffirms* his intention to give his daughter to Heliseus. Originally he *pledged* ('biweddad' 33a) his daughter's hand. Now he *swears* that she will be Heliseus' wife. Cynewulf reports,

Geswearc þa swiðferð   sweor æfter worde
þære fæmnan fæder,   ferðlocan onspeon   (78-9)

The woman's father, violent in mind, swore then after
[Heliseus'] words, opened the locked place of his mind.

Drawing attention to his own speech act with '"Ic þæt geswerge"' ('"I swear that"' 80a), Affricanus performs an irrevocable act of *promising*. His *promise* concludes with this grant of his permission to Heliseus to do with Juliana as he pleases:

'Dem þu hi to deaþe   gif þe gedafen þince,
swa to life læt,   swa þe leofre sy'   (87-8)

'Condemn her to death, if you consider it suitable,
just as you permit life, should that be more pleasing to you,'

and the balanced clauses show how complete he fully expects Heliseus'
power over Juliana to be.

The scene shifts. Juliana, having taken an apparent request as a threat
to her integrity, and having had her conditions for acquiescence taken
as an insult to her suitor's honour, meets with her father. Affricanus
begins a meeting that will quickly become a confrontation with *assertions*
that the dearest, sweetest Juliana is the light of his eyes, but then *rebukes*
her for rejecting a man more nobly born and richer than she. Juliana
responds by *restating* her conditions for marriage. Angered, Affricanus
tells Juliana precisely what her situation is. He has sworn that she will
marry Heliseus and given him the power of life and death over her.

Juliana draws attention to her speech act with ' "Ic þe to soðe / secgan
wille" ' (' "I wish to say to you in truth" ' 132). Then, with the word 'man-
fremmende' 'evildoing' 137a), she *accuses* her father of having sinned
in promising her to Heliseus. Further angered, Affricanus *commands*
her to change her mind and take back the words she ' "foolishly spoke
before." ' Cynewulf uses five adjectives – 'ellenwod,' 'yrre,' 'reþe,' 'frecne,'
and 'ferðgrim' – to show the extent to which Affricanus is possessed
by anger, but Juliana remains resolute. And thus Juliana is given over
to Heliseus.

The pattern of the preceding confrontation repeats itself. Heliseus calls
Juliana the sweetest light of the sun (166) as, assuming a protector's
role, he *promises* that the punishments that await her will be turned
aside if she accepts his idols as her gods. ' "þu þreatest" ' (' "you threaten" '
176a), a phrase embedded in Juliana's response,[16] shows that she recognizes
the nature of his promise, and she *asserts* once again that she will never
give herself to Heliseus unless he turns from his false gods.

Heliseus' behaviour now becomes undeniably sadistic. Giving full rein
to his passion for unrestricted power, he orders Juliana stripped naked,
stretched out, and beaten. He speaks with threats ('beotwordum' 185a)
and with abusive words ('hospwordum' 189b). Abusive language is just
as surely intended to inflict mental pain as torture is intended to inflict
physical pain; and Heliseus takes pleasure in both, as Cynewulf's

placement of 'Ahlog þa se hererinc' ('Then the warrior exulted' 189a) between the details of beating and the utterance of abusive words indicates.

Heliseus' offer to let Juliana live if she will submit to his will (even though she earlier spoke many heedless words) shows that he is now fully taken up with the exercise of his power over life and death. He *orders* the former light of her father's eyes and his own sweetest radiance of the sun hung by the hair on a high cross where the sun can strike her (inflict injury upon her), and even the power of the sun seems to serve his own wilful purpose. And finally, as this confrontation scene ends, Heliseus has Juliana cast in prison, the suggestion being that he has assumed the power of light and darkness, and can deny light to Juliana if he wishes.

In prison, with the confrontation of Juliana and the devil, a new kind of exchange begins. The devil's first question, ' "What do you suffer?" ' is more a *greeting* than a request for information. The devil already knows what Juliana has endured. Juliana's question about the devil's identity is a genuine question, however.[17] He has appeared to her in the guise of an angel, and she needs to know his true nature. Almost as if in affirmation of her right to seek this knowledge, an *order* to seize the devil and hold him until he tells the truth comes from above. Juliana seizes the devil and the manuscript breaks off at this point.

When it picks up again, we find ourselves in the middle of what seems to be a chronicle of a dark Widsith, with the devil *boasting* about his historical triumphs. Juliana, nevertheless, is in firm control. Her questions take the form of *assertions*. With

'þu scealt furþor gen,   feond moncynnes,
siþfæt secgan,   hwa þec sende to me'   (317-18)

'You shall further still, enemy of mankind,
tell your journey, who sends you to me'

she has assumed the right to *demand* answers to her questions. The next *assertion* of her right to know forces the devil to tell her how he injures those who are dedicated to truth and fastens them to evil.

With a long account of his methods, the devil tells Juliana about his acts of aggression. He presents his account of assaults on the good with metaphors of war. The devil says he engages in battle ('guð,' 'beadu'), shooting storms and flights of arrows ('flanþracu,' 'eargfaru') against a warrior of God ('Metodes cempa') and then against a weaker warrior (sænra cempa'). When one warrior's shield ('bord'), holy shield ('halig scyld'), and armour ('guðreaf') prevent his success, he simply tries again, hoping to penetrate the defences ('wiþersteall') of war hedge ('cumbolhaga') and tower ('torr').

Juliana's next request for information takes the grammatical form of a question: how does the devil insinuate himself into the company of pure souls? The devil *demands* to know before he answers how Juliana bound him in fetters; but then, appropriately enough (bound in fetters, he is not in a position to make demands), he answers both Juliana's question and his own. Juliana's belief in the true God is the source of her power over the devil, and the king of hell is the source of the devil's power. The superiority of Juliana's power is further demonstrated when she forces the devil to *confess* his sins. He does this with a 'sum' series that leads all the way back to the temptation of Adam and Eve, then *implores* (requests from an inferior and weaker position) Juliana to release him, which she does. And so the confrontation between Juliana and the devil ends, with Juliana the obvious and complete victor.

There is another break in the manuscript, but we next find Juliana just saved from a bath of hot lead by an angel, and Heliseus so overcome by wrath that he tears his clothes, gnashes his teeth, and becomes as enraged as a wild animal (594b–600a), with all these actions showing the intensity of the passion for power that has been thwarted, and suggesting the degree to which Juliana has triumphed over her adversary. Heliseus even, for a moment, loses the power of speech. When he regains it, he *orders* Juliana to be beheaded.

With this *order*, which from her point of view is a confession of failure, Juliana rejoices. Her closing words are words of *instruction, encouragement*, and *promise* to the people who surround her. And thus the story of Juliana's heroic self-defence ends. She has triumphed over the devil, and she has triumphed over her human adversary. Her father may have given permission to Heliseus to sentence her to death or allow her to live, and it may please Heliseus to exercise that power; but all his attacks, which Juliana rightly interprets as attempts to deny her the right to protect her soul from the forces of evil, are doomed to failure.

Foreign to our general experience as it at first seems, *Juliana*'s basic structure grows from such ordinary questions as these: May I have your daughter's hand in marriage? Will you marry me? Will you accept my religion as your own? Will you tell me what I want to know? To the first question, Heliseus' *request* for permission to marry Juliana, Affricanus replies in the affirmative; so the second question, addressed by

Heliseus to Juliana, is not a request in the sense in which we ordinarily use the word. Here, since the requester has a higher position than the person to whom he presents his suit, and since her father has already answered for her, the 'proposal' assumes many of the aspects of the *demand*.

Juliana's response takes the form of a counter request. Making her own conditions for acquiescence, she presents as her single requirement Heliseus' abandonment of his religion (the worship of devils) for hers (the worship of God). At this point, both Juliana and Heliseus perceive themselves as having been threatened. Juliana's spiritual integrity has been threatened (she cannot retain it married to a worshipper of devils), and Heliseus' honour has been impugned (he has been asked by a woman to abandon his religion).

As the poem moves through a series of confrontations, Affricanus' *promises* become *vows*, and Heliseus' *requests*, which already have the force of *demands*, are accompanied by *threats*. Heliseus *asserts* his right to have Juliana on his own terms, and Juliana, speaking in her own defence from her prison cell, *asserts* her right to know about the ways of evil in the world. Her efforts succeed; indeed, she so completely triumphs over the devil that he is reduced to pitiful *requests* that he be allowed to escape.

Further *threats*, then verbal and physical assaults follow as Heliseus continues to pursue his objective. As Heliseus' anger at his lack of success in gaining power over Juliana increases, his acts become ever more recognizable as those of a determined sadist. At the same time, as Juliana continues to face his threats to her physical well-being (and those threats increase in seriousness only from Heliseus' point of view), her power to resist them becomes all the more apparent. When the series of confrontations ends, Heliseus' power to inflict death is seen to be useless. Juliana has steadfastly refused to surrender, just as she said she would at the beginning of the poem.

In this paper I have tried, aside from a comment or two on Byrhtnoth's obligation to abide by the Anglo-Saxon code of courage and Juliana's possible foreknowledge of the consequences of her initial act of self-defence, to work within the contexts of the poems under consideration. An approach of this kind does not lead to answers to the question of Byrhtnoth's 'ofermod' or to the question of the relation of Juliana's virginity to her spiritual integrity. Speech act theory may, however, provide a useful interpretive perspective, and it is my hope that the approach used here may be found to have some relevance to our efforts to understand the literature of the Anglo-Saxon period.

NOTES

1 John L. Austin *How To Do Things with Words* ed J.O. Urmson and Marina Sbisà (Cambridge 1962)
2 John Searle *Speech Acts: An Essay in the Philosophy of Language* (New York 1969)
3 Citations will be to *The Battle of Maldon* ed E.V. Gordon (New York 1966). The OE character wynn has been silently changed to its modern equivalent, 'w.'
4 Words referring to speech acts that are the focus of attention will be italicized.
5 Searle 66-7 provides rules for *requesting*, adding as an additional rule for *ordering* and *commanding* that the speaker must be in a position of authority over the hearer.
6 'Illocution' refers to the performance of such acts as *promising, requesting,* and *asserting.* A speaker may say 'I promise ____,' 'I request ____,' or 'I assert ____,' and in doing so actually perform the act of *promising, requesting,* or *asserting.* He may also perform an act of illocution without the use of a 'performative' verb like those just cited. An illocutionary act is said to be successful if the act the speaker intends to perform is perceived by the hearer as having been performed.
7 'Perlocution' refers to a speaker's success in getting a hearer to do what he wants him to do.
8 Robin S. Oggins 'Falconry in Anglo-Saxon England' *Mediaevalia* 7 (1981) 184 says that releasing the hawk would have been understood as a gesture of defiance and a declaration of readiness to die in battle.
9 Kent Bach and Robert M. Harnish, *Linguistic Communication and Speech Acts* (Cambridge 1979) 47, include *demand* in the category they call 'Requirements,' along with *bid, charge, command, dictate, direct, enjoin, instruct, order, prescribe,* and *require.*
10 Searle 58 explains that 'a promise is a pledge to do something for you, not to you, but a threat is a pledge to do something to you, not for you.'
11 Gordon cites Cyril Brett *MLR* 22 (1927) 260 on the legal use of 'heregeatu.'
12 Fred C. Robinson, 'God, Death, and Loyalty in "The Battle of Maldon"' *J.R.R. Tolkien: Scholar and Storyteller* ed Mary Salu and Robert T. Farrell (Ithaca 1979) 76-98, agrees with Helmut Gneuss ('"The Battle of Maldon" 89: Byrhtnoð's *ofermod* Once Again' *SP* 73 (1976) 117-37) that 'ofermod' implies criticism of Byrhtnoth's decision to permit the Vikings to cross the Panta.
13 Offa's words are '"Abreoðe his angin"' (242b, '"May his action fail"'), or,

as Gordon translates, '"May his conduct have an evil end."' For an interpretation of a similar form as *curse* see Barrie Ruth Straus 'Women's Words as Weapons: Speech as Action in "The Wife's Lament"' *TSLL* 23 (1981) 268-85.

14 *Juliana* ed Rosemary Woolf (New York 1966) 11. 46-57. Further citations will be to this edition. The OE character wynn has been silently changed to its modern equivalent, *w*.

15 Woolf places the original *Life* during the time of the Diocletian persecution.

16 The word also appears, as 'geþreatian' (54a), in her original response.

17 Searle 69 sees asking questions as a special case of *requesting* and (66) says that in real questions the speaker wants to find out the answer to his question.

PART III
THE WORDS:
PHILOLOGICAL STUDIES

... cruces of interpretation haunt individual words and lines ...

'*Gifstol* and goldhoard in *Beowulf*' 1974

ROBERTA FRANK

'Mere' and 'Sund': Two Sea-Changes in *Beowulf*

I T IS A TRUTH widely acknowledged, if often ignored, that the meaning
of a word in Old English prose is a fallible guide to its meaning in
poetry; there is, as Stanley Greenfield has had to remind us, no 'monolithic
semantic field for the whole province of Old English diction.'[1] Anglo-
Saxon authors seem to have had two distinct lexicons at their disposal,
separated from each other by a semantic shift as far-reaching as any
sound change. The divergence between the meaning of a word in verse
and its meaning in prose can sometimes be attributed to differing political
or ideological perspectives, the way 'mundus' meant 'the universe' to
secular Latin authors but 'this sinful world' to their Christian contemporaries, and 'salus' 'health' to the heathen and 'salvation' to the baptized.
Thus the notorious 'lofgeornost,' which in *Beowulf* and Old Norse verse
appears to mean 'most eager for praise,' has the sense 'too eager for
praise' in Old English prose, while 'dollic,' which in *Beowulf* and Old
Norse verse seems to mean 'bold, ready to risk,' deteriorates to 'foolish'
in homiletic contexts.[2]

Other shifts seem more profound, perhaps reflecting the influence of
the 'new immortality' of writing, the divorcement that gradually set in
as the logic of continuous prose replaced the flexible formulas of oral
poetry. Combining the two discourses, as each Old English poet between
the seventh and eleventh centuries did to some extent, recuperated poetry
for a different kind of mental process. The language of poetry was
generalizing, universalistic, and metaphorical ('this is that'), without
reference to spatial or visual shape; that of prose was particularistic,
allusive, and intimate, treating local variations in size, altitude, dampness,
hue, and material as distinct entities; the prose word was also more abstract,
tending towards metonymic expression ('this is put for that').[3] Thus the

noun 'feorh,' which means '(abstract principle of) life' in Old English prose, has in *Beowulf* and other Old English and Old Norse poems a physical concreteness, encompassing anything essential to life (eg, 'life-blood'); and 'ford,' which means 'a shallow crossing, ford' in Anglo-Saxon charter after charter, seems to designate 'sea' in *Beowulf*.[4] A similar synecdochic shift is found in Latin verse, but there the change in meaning is signalled by a change in number: 'vadum' in the singular means 'ford,' in the plural, 'sea.' The late West-Saxon scribes who used two different spelling conventions for certain words in their copy-texts, one for poetry and another for prose, may have been signalling something similar.[5] It is as if every Anglo-Saxon author were bilingual, 'utriusque linguae peritus,' competent in the separate dictions of poetry and prose.[6]

Such bilingualism brought with it a choice, not only of words (poetic 'mearh' against prose 'hors') but of registers; if the *Beowulf* poet could shift when he wanted to from 'mearh' to 'hors,' he could also, when it seemed useful, move back and forth between the two semantic worlds of poetry and prose, between the general/concrete and the particular/abstract meanings of a single word. In Old English poetry, the word 'mere' signified terrestrial water, elemental, corporeal, and churning; in prose, 'mere' stood for specific, real-life or literary, pools or lakes, whose locations, dimensions, and qualities were known. In a similar way, 'sund' in poetry signified 'sea,' but in prose it stood for the abstract act or power of 'swimming,' a mental construct separate from the physical world of nature. The one apparent exception to both rules is *Beowulf*, whose editors and translators are unanimous in giving a prose sense to certain occurrences of 'mere' and 'sund,' thereby providing the *Oxford English Dictionary* with its earliest citations for the meanings 'pool, lake' and 'swimming' respectively. Something strange is going on, even if a century and a half of serious *Beowulf* scholarship has tried discreetly to look the other way.

I   'MERE'

It is not far – a Mile from here –
Where stands the Monster's sluggish Meer.[7]

Not that scholars have ignored the 'mere': the haunt of the monsters in *Beowulf* has spawned a literature of its own. Contributions to the discussion fall into two camps: a saltwater school (poetic meaning) and a freshwater school (prose meaning). Stopford Brooke saw the 'mere' as an arm of the sea, and was convinced the poet did too: 'Indeed, so clearly is it drawn that I believe the describer has seen the very spot.'[8] Gregor Sarrazin agreed: 'Noch heutigen Tages kann jeder der sich die Mühe nimmt, dorthin zu reisen, die wesentlichen Züge der Lokalschilderung am Roeskilder Fjord wiedererkennen.'[9] W.S. Mackie opted for a deep inlet of the sea, although he cautiously stressed the imprecision of the poet's description.[10] Kemp Malone made a strong case for 'sea' but few converts, among whom may be counted E.B. Irving, Jr, who writes 'mere' but means 'sea,' and J.D.A. Ogilvy and Donald Baker, who rather matter-of-factly describe Grendel's lair as 'an estuary or sea-loch.'[11]

The first translation of *Beowulf* into a vernacular, N.F.S. Grundtvig's wonderful version of 1820 in rhyming Danish stanzas, defined the monsters' 'mere' with more hesitation: 'Der er et Kiær, en Søe kanskee' ('there is a pool, a lake perhaps').[12] J.J. Conybeare's 'mere' of 1826 is a swamp: 'Non est ille (locus) procul abhinc mille passuum, ubi palus sita est.'[13] Early translations into English gave 'mere' its meaning in Scott's Waverley novels ('the sluggish waters of the deadest meer') and Tennyson's Arthurian poetry ('on lonely mountain-meres'): 'a marsh, a lake, an area covered with pools of standing water.'[14] William Lawrence agreed with them against Brooke, and campaigned for over a quarter of a century on behalf of an inland pond complete with waterfall: 'This is a vivid picture of what may be seen in Norway at the present day – a waterfall breaking over beetling cliffs, which seem to overhang it, into a pool below.'[15] The notes to Frederick Klaeber's influential edition confirmed the 'mere' to be a pool 'situated in a dreary fen-district ... That Grendel lives in the sea, or in a pool connected with the sea, or in an "almost land-locked arm of the sea" ... cannot be conceded.'[16] Klaeber's opinion carried weight; he was followed by C.L. Wrenn, R.W. Chambers, and H.D. Chickering, whose much-used commentaries have contributed to making 'pool, lake' the orthodox position today.[17] Typological exegetes happily accept the 'mere' as an inland pool or lake with scriptural associations.[18] Oral-formulaists, while stressing the unnatural conjoining of elements in the poet's description, still affirm that 'the pool is always a pool.'[19] The landscape may be unreal, but a pool is part of its unreality: 'Factually the scenery could hardly exist. The combination of fenland and mountains, of windswept headlands and woods overhanging the pool is not possible: it is a gallimaufry of devices each of which is horrific in its associations.'[20] Even John Gardner's Grendel ruminates beside 'the old lake hissing and gurgling.'[21] Most of those who use the noncommittal term 'mere' (thereby winning for themselves a special sub-entry in the *Second Supplement* to the *Oxford English Dictionary*), when pushed, come down firmly on the side of 'inland lake' or 'pool'.[22] Scholars like poets discover truth through an exploration of words; the meaning of 'mere' in current English, from 'small lake, marsh' to 'barely what it is said to be,' has probably encouraged us to view Grendel's watery haunt through the wrong end of our binoculars.

The only reason we think of Grendel's dwelling as a 'mere' – rather than as a 'brim,' 'holm,' 'sund,' 'yð,' 'wæter,' 'flod,' 'stream,' or 'lagu,' the other sea-words used in the poem to describe the same location – is because the poet forces us to: by careful positioning, he associates 'mere' so intimately with the spot that the noun acquires some of the status of a proper name. 'Mere' is the first term used by the poet to denote the strange water (845), and it is from the 'mere' that the warriors ride home only ten lines later. 'Mere' is the first sea-term used by Hrothgar to pinpoint Grendel's refuge (1362);[23] 'mere' is what the heartsick Geats are left staring at, bereft of their lord (1603); and 'mere,' in the compound 'meregrund,' is what Beowulf in his report to Hygelac (2100) first calls the pool- or sea-bottom on which he wrestled with Grendel's mother, the 'merewif' (1519). All other 'mere'-compounds in *Beowulf* denote the open sea. Only once in the poem does the simplex 'mere' not refer to Grendel's haunt, and that is in the Finnsburh episode, where the word signifies the water over which a Dane, Hengest, is to sail, presumably to England (1130). Here and only here in *Beowulf* is it certain that 'mere' has the sense of its Old Norse cognate, 'marr' ('the sea'), a strictly poetic word with no prose counterpart. 'Mere,' however, does occur in prose – some two hundred and fifty times.[24]

A word like 'mere' that meant one thing in verse and something else in prose could satisfy the Old English appetite for double statement that Fred Robinson has recently described, the 'repetition of identical facts in contrasting words.'[25] For once the *Beowulf* poet got his audience to associate Grendel's abode with a 'mere,' the word would start sparkling, flashing this way and that. The facet of 'mere' most likely to gleam early and often was its topographical side, for meres, standing pools, and swamps, haunted or otherwise, were a dominant feature of the Anglo-Saxon landscape. The word is very frequent in charter bounds, often as the second element in a place-name, where it seems to be applied to any pool or pond, however small; two of these charters, from Worcestershire and Wiltshire respectively and dating probably from the tenth century, mention a 'grendles mere,' a pool named after someone or something called a grendel.[26] By featuring the haunt of his Grendel as a 'mere,' the *Beowulf* poet could summon up, at least in parts of Wessex and West Mercia, a reservoir of local belief. None of the other poetic sea-terms available to him would have had the same inland resonances; and none of the other prose words for pool – 'pol,' 'pull,' 'luh,' 'stæg,' 'wætersteall' – would have been acceptable to a poet who avoided the ordinary when describing the extraordinary to the extent of calling the dragon's teeth 'fierce bones' (2692). No Old English poet outraged stylistic decorum to the extent of mingling poetic diction and statutory prose as T.S. Eliot did in 'The nymphs are departed . . . Departed, have left no addresses.'[27] 'Mere' permitted the *Beowulf* poet to sustain his epic dignity while letting other, more familiar associations do their work. By putting the two meanings of 'mere' in apposition he gave his monsters a contemporary reality and urgency that they would not otherwise possess. The effect of blending the poetic word with its common homonym in daily life was to bring the monstrous home: 'de te fabula narratur.'

Meres were not only local landmarks, however. There were literary meres in Old English narrative prose, ranging in magnitude from a cistern or well to the Sea of Galilee, a 'rift' lake; the latter usage worried Ælfric enough to add an explanatory gloss.[28] 'Mere' translates Latin 'stagnum' ('pool, standing water') in the glossed psalters (Psalms 106, 113), in several collections of Latin–Old English glosses, in the West-Saxon Gospels of Luke and John, and in the *Letter of Alexander to Aristotle* in the *Beowulf* manuscript.[29] 'Mere' also translates 'stagnum' in the Book of Revelation, the 'lake which burneth with fire and brimstone' (Rev 21:8), the bottomless waters into which the Beast and his cohorts – the devil, death, and hell – sink. In Ælfric's *Sermo ad Populum, in Octavis Pentecosten Dicendus*, in the section that describes the torments in store for men after death, the Apocalyptic 'mere' is mentioned three times.[30] 'You shall know a word by the company it keeps': even the river Styx can, following Virgil, be glossed 'helle mere' ('pool of hell').[31] The author of the seventeenth Blickling homily, though he did not use the term 'mere,' identified an uncanny water resembling Grendel's as the entry to hell. When the *Beowulf* poet gave the name 'mere' to his monsters' burning and bottomless haunt, he forced his hearers to take an active part in the narrative, using their own knowledge to abstract from the physical 'mere' ('unbounded sea') of poetry its polar opposite, the metaphysical 'mere' ('confined and confining water') of prose. If Grendel himself was a riddle, a crosser of categories, no less could be expected of his dwelling place.[32]

By calling Grendel's dwelling-place a 'mere,' the *Beowulf* poet inevitably brought a touch of the Christian marvellous, the new eschatology, to bear on his reconstruction of a northern heroic age. He did something similar when he put a biblical word for giants, 'gigantas' (Latin 'gigantes'), alongside the poetic word 'eotenas' (ON 'jǫtnar'), placing the earth-born hulks of Genesis 6:1-4 and Job 25:5 in apposition to the 'eaters' of Norse myth.[33] This pairing of an allusive Christian term with a semantically charged poetic counter, a word common in Old Norse but found in Old English only in *Beowulf* and the mid-twelfth-century gloss to the Canterbury Psalter,[34] is characteristic of the poet's art, his sophisticated balancing of the roles and registers of Christian homilist and northern scop. The two 'meres' build an equally sophisticated set that permits the poet to hint at a congruence between secular and Christian wisdom without ever forging an overt theological equation. What was just a horrifying sea to the Danes in Heorot was a foretaste of hell to the poet's audience.

II   'SUND'

'Art thou Beo-wulf,' then he cry'd,
'With Brecca on the Ocean wide
That didst in Swimming erst contend?'[35]

Of the eleven occurrences of 'sund' ('sea') and its declensional forms in *Beowulf*, it is universally agreed that seven have that meaning; the remaining four instances (507, 517, 1436, 1618) are said to have the prose meaning 'swimming,' although this sense is found elsewhere in poetry only in *Solomon and Saturn*, a late, apparently West-Saxon composition with a high incidence of prosaic words.[36] 'Sund' is often said to be a common word for 'swimming' in Old Norse, but there is no evidence for this usage before the late twelfth century, and then chiefly in prose.[37] In skaldic and eddic verse of the tenth, eleventh, and early twelfth century, 'sund,' usually accompanied by the prepositions 'í,' 'at,' 'á,' 'fyr,' 'of,' and 'yfir,' means 'sea, sound' as it still does in modern Danish, Swedish, and Norwegian; only in Icelandic did the meaning 'swimming' become dominant.[38] Yet the first editor of *Beowulf*, the Icelander Grímur Jónsson Thorkelin, who got much else wrong, somehow resisted translating phrases like 'ymb sund' and 'æt sunde' as if they were 'um (of) sund' and 'at sundi' in eighteenth-century Icelandic speech.[39] Not even the numerous aquatic wrestling and endurance contests in late medieval Icelandic prose romance induced him to choose 'swimming' over 'sea.'[40]

Two of the four instances of 'sund' ('swimming') in *Beowulf* are almost certainly ghost-meanings, examples of 'literary interpretation masquerading as lexicographical fact.'[41] When, in line 1618, the poet relates that Beowulf, after leaving Grendel's underwater hall, was quickly 'on sunde' ('in the water'), context makes it fairly clear that he was not about to deploy a fishing rod; to define 'sund' in terms of his eventual emergence from the 'mere' – whether by swimming, gliding, plunging, darting, or whatever – is to give the word an unwarranted and overdetermined sense. And when, in line 1436, the poet gloats that a dead sea-monster was 'sundes þe sænra' ('the slower with respect to [the course over] the water'), it is as unacceptable to equate 'sund' with an abstract 'swimming' as it is to equate 'siðfæt' with 'sailing' in the parallel half-line 'siðfates sæne' ('slow with respect to the course [over water]'), used of a prospective journey by ship in *Andreas* and *Elene*.[42] Such translations, of course, fit in a literal way the passages in question, but do so at the cost of dissolving both the concreteness and the figurative colouration of the original.

The two remaining instances in *Beowulf* of 'sund' ('swimming') seem different, in part because they occur not in the narrative present but in an account of something that happened years earlier, and in part because they are spoken not by an authenticating narrator but by a character in the poem who has every reason to want to muddy the waters. They occur close together in Unferth's version of Beowulf's adventure with Breca: 'ymb sund flite' ('you competed at swimming' 507) and 'he þe æt sunde oferflat' ('he defeated you at swimming' 517). Midway between these verses, Unferth refers to the 'sea' on which Beowulf and Breca 'rowed' ('on sund reon,' 512), a half-line repeated by Beowulf in his reply to Unferth (539). 'Sund,' whether 'sea' or 'swimming,' is not a common word in Old English: it occurs uncompounded only six times in prose and twenty-six times in verse, a frequency of less than once every thousand lines of poetry.[43] Unferth, in his opening twelve lines, uses the term three times, a concentration without parallel in the corpus.

The notion that Beowulf and Breca were contenders in a swimming match got started early. Although Thorkelin retained a manuscript reading that allowed for a vessel in the neighbourhood of his hero, Grundtvig's translation of *Beowulf* kept the two boys in the water for a week, 'swimming like two fish, and soon like dead herring,' a view that understandably won the day.[44] A seven-day swimming match between a corsleted, sword-girt youth and an opponent named Breca (ON 'breki' 'breaker, surf') appealed not only to nineteenth-century mythologizing critics but also to our own century, desperate to mix some solid facts with the hypotheses of *Beowulf* scholarship.[45] The hero's acknowledgment that he had, indeed, been in the water with Breca has seemed precious evidence for the existence of an earlier lay about a heroic swimming contest known to the audience of *Beowulf*.[46] The danger, of course, is that all problems – textual or lexical – connected with Beowulf's exploit will be dismissed as 'an inheritance from the older legends which had come down from a ruder age.'[47]

The poet's account of the swimming match has often struck readers as 'exaggerated,' 'fantastic,' and 'quite preposterous';[48] but the perception of absurdity is notoriously relative and the *Beowulf* poet is rather good at making the impossible seem real; scholars are too. Not until the 1960s and 1970s was the textual evidence for Beowulf's long-distance swimming reexamined and found wanting;[49] the two studies concerned solely with the Unferth episode concluded that the thyle's twin references to a swimming match should be translated as 'you competed at rowing' and 'he defeated you at rowing' respectively.[50] The quarrelsome thyle would have been delighted at the controversy he initiated, especially if he had deliberately created a 'gap' of indeterminacy by employing 'sund' in both its poetic and prose senses simultaneously, keeping a handle on the truth while insinuating something quite different.

Swimming and rowing, floating and sailing, even flying and jogging, are such closely related notions, sharing the same 'ground,' that conceptual interchanges between them are easy to grasp: boats move on limbs and swim; swimmers fling their oars and skim the waves.[51] There is universal agreement that one of these two metaphoric equations is present in Unferth's opening lines, but which of the two and where is disputed. The traditional view takes Unferth's single reference to rowing metaphorically (= swim), and the five ornate half-lines that follow literally, as a description of arms at swim. But it is at least as likely that this passage contains the figurative meaning 'rowing,' as do the comparable expressions 'hreran mid handum' ('stirring [the sea] with hands' *Wanderer* 4) and 'mere hrerendum mundum' ('with hands stirring the sea' *Andreas* 491); the humble prose word 'to row,' which never has the sense 'to swim' outside of *Beowulf*, is more likely to be a clarifying element, resolving the ambiguity initiated five lines earlier by 'ymb sund flite' ('contended around the sea'):[52]

> þa git on sund reon;
> þær git eagorstream   earmum þehton,

mæton merestræta,   mundum brugdon,
glidon ofer garsecg;   (512b–515a)

    ... when you rowed to sea;
there you covered the flowing tide with arms,
spanned the sea-paths, flung hands,
glided over the ocean.

Unferth's speech is dripping with irony, oblique and mocking, a
rhetorical bow-wow designed 'to stress and ridicule the vehement efforts
in the sea of two young men frantically striving to make good a foolish
boast.'[53] To lend dignity to the swimming of juveniles by presenting
it as rowing would not have been in his best interests; but a description
of adolescent exertion at the oars in terms suitable to poodles paddling
furiously in a pond might have the necessary derisory cast. Like his initial
and final 'sund' (507, 517), the four verbs used by Unferth to depict the
action are double-valenced, appropriate to swimming as well as rowing.
Swimmers conceivably 'glide' in Old English; ships definitely do. Arms
without oars can 'thatch' the sea almost as well as arms with them. And
the expression 'mundum brugdon,' which has the boys hauling themselves
along with their hands, may allude to swimming (at least a dog-paddle)
but can also, and perhaps more easily, refer to the wielding of oars,
as in 'arum bregdað' ('they ply oars' *Gifts of Men* 57). The poet could
have distinguished between swimming and rowing in these lines simply
by substituting feet ('fotum brugdon' = kicked) or oars ('arum brugdon'
= rowed) for hands; but he didn't care to. The progression in Unferth's
speech from rowing to covering with arms, spanning, flinging hands,
and gliding is a movement from specificity to ambiguity, from the real
to the disguised.

Hamlet – in Saxo and in Shakespeare – always speaks the truth, but
in such a way that his answers, which depend on a literal interpretation
of metaphor or familiar poetic imagery, are misconstrued by his hearers.
The Old Norse skald was skilled in this kind of duplicity, turning praise
into blame and vice versa. On a more elementary level, Unferth seems
to be playing the same game of disguises, riddling in such a way as
to make his meaning clear to the initiated and misleading to the naïve.
Beowulf shows what a consummate solver he is by 'reading' Unferth's
verses correctly and by inserting as answer in his reply the thyle's one
unambiguous reference to rowing: 'on sund reon' (512, 539). And when
Beowulf adds that he and Breca rowed to sea with, not oars, but 'bare

swords firm in hand' (539), he may be repaying Unferth in skaldic coin, for in the inverse world of the kenning 'oars of wounds' and 'oars of battle' cleave skulls as well as waves.[54] The association of oar and sword is only slightly less oblique in the *Chronicle of Æthelweard*, whose Vikings in quick succession 'plied their oars; dropped their rowing gear; interlocked arms shone on the waves.'[55]

Towards the end of his defence, Beowulf almost outdoes the thyle in fantasy when he recounts how lumbering sea-monsters went to their places around the table to dine – off him. Just as Unferth may have exploited the different meanings of 'sund' in poetry and prose, Beowulf shows that he can play on the concrete and abstract senses of the verb 'þegnian': 'I served up food to them with a precious sword' and 'I struck them down' (560). Both flyting combatants wear their aristocratic accents like a coat of arms, exchanging passwords and pointed allusions in a duel in which words, like the tongue of Pope's celebrated jackdaw, 'speak twice as much for being split.'[56]

That the Unferth episode is a set piece, related in an immediate and exact way to the Old Norse flyting, has been established;[57] it is also clear that the kind of verbal wit vented by Beowulf and Unferth has numerous parallels in the Scandinavian material. In Saxo's *History of the Danes*, for example, an adventurer named Eric the Eloquent sails to a decadent and demoralized Scylding court, where he is greeted not with the gratitude owed a redeemer but with versified slurs; an Unferth-like official calls him a silly fool, weakling, detestable scoundrel, and stray.[58] Eric's reply, as recorded in Latin hexameters, is restrained, if oblique:

> A blockhead, unrestrained and unseemly in his emotions,
>   cannot conduct his affairs with due moderation.
> Sailing tackle outstrips the pull of rowers; gales
>   ruffle the seas, but a drearier breeze the earth.
> Oars cleave the waves; falsehood the land; the latter
>   is vexed by men's mouths, but hands weigh hard on the other.[59]

The idea of self-control, the governing of turbulent emotions, leads into the image of a ship sailing on tempestuous seas, whose gales are paired with the windy speech of landlubbers: oars on the sound match falsehood ashore, the former worked by hand, the latter by mouth. The verbal ambiguities almost certainly present in the Norse original, binding together the nautical and moral spheres, are quite lost in Saxo's rendition;[60] but the junctures between the separate clauses pose a silent riddle: how can mouths lying on land be compared to hands rowing at sea? The solution, the missing term in the equation, is an insult traditional in skaldic verse: while Eric was boldly cutting the seas with his oars, his opponent sat at home and plied his tongue, a kenning for which is 'oar of words.'[61]

The disjunctions and silences characteristic of the northern flyting must have been challengingly meaningful to audiences raised on such fare, but outsiders – from Saxo on – have found them impenetrable and unprofitable: 'kennings increase no man's virtue but darken joy.'[62] Darkness was not the *Beowulf* poet's way, and he concentrated most of his energies on the communicated product, on clarity and explicitness. His 'mere' and 'sund,' although visually unspecific, were semantically clear: each term, representing a concrete category of varying dimensions, could mean one thing while simultaneously signifying something else. In the case of 'mere,' the *Beowulf* poet renovated a poetic counter minted long ago into a medium of current exchange, one relevant to contemporary supernaturalism, both popular and Christian. The message, the goal, was inclusion and mutual comprehension, a kind of linguistic exogamy that reached out to reattach prose and poetic meanings, sensing that under each lay the lineaments of a common language. In the case of 'sund,' the poet had Unferth use his skill with words to suggest the colloquial, prose meaning 'swimming,' while employing the term in its strictly poetic sense: the artless among his listeners might understand 'in swimming' and 'at swimming,' but they would be wrong. The thyle's game was illusion and exclusion, for he shows the two senses of 'sund' to be ultimately incompatible; his goal was a kind of linguistic endogamy that kept his own clever diction apart from the language in everyday spoken use.

The *Beowulf* poet was as clear as he could be about the nature of Unferth's rhetoric. The fragile underpinnings of the thyle's verbal play are revealed when both Beowulf and Unferth affirm that the two youths 'on sund reon' ('rowed to sea'), a recognizable second half-line formula (ON 'á vág róa, á sió róa') in which 'sund' has to mean 'sea.'[63] But, not expecting this kind of subtlety in a traditional poem, we miss the cue: we take Unferth's 'ymb sund' and 'æt sunde' in a prose sense, convert 'rowed' to 'swam,' and attribute the consequent 'strained use of words' to the poet's unthinking dependence on a preexisting heroic lay.[64] Obfuscation is taken as elucidation; what was straight is made crooked; and we conclude finally that the poet did not know what he was doing.

The diction of *Beowulf* 'gives the impression that it is new of the poet's age.'[65] Although his reconstruction of ancient days in Denmark is chronologically sophisticated, rich in local colour and fitting speeches, his language, like that of all writers, expresses the values of his own time, establishing a bond between himself, his audience, and other poets. It has been estimated that 'as half of the chief material of major agreed-upon language remains steady over a generation or two, so the other two quarters are respectively discarded as outworn and artificial and, on the other hand, brought in with enthusiasm by many writers all at once as the newly expressive material to be agreed upon.'[66] Detecting these quarters in a dead language like Old English, in a poetic corpus lacking almost all chronological bearings, is probably impossible; for without local guides, even the stalker of a subtle overtone, of lexical fission and fusion, of the newly expressive, tends to lose himself in a night in which all cats are grey.

But not invariably, at least not when the cats come in pairs. The *Beowulf* poet's fondness for double statement, for artful variations of the kind that Stanley Greenfield and Fred Robinson have explored with notable skill, gives us one handle for grasping his modernity;[67] for it is largely through such repetition that the poet provides an implicit commentary on the events he narrates. Other shifts in perspective are achieved through the poet's use of 'new' words, whether taken over from contemporary Latin-Christian culture (the mythologically charged 'candel,' 'gigant,' and 'non') or from contemporary Scandinavian society (the mythologically charged 'eoton'; the culturally charged 'eodor' and 'þengel'; the colloquial archaism 'bront').[68] Yet a third way for the poet to 'make it new,' a method whose obviousness has probably disguised its importance, was to jux-tapose the different meanings in poetry and prose of words like 'mere' and 'sund.' The resonant poetic word, from a diction mysterious and powerful, would appear to its hearers to be reaching back to the middle region that separates what has perished from what is current; the same word in prose or normal speech could look to the future.

Such pairings, whether centripetal ('mere') or centrifugal ('sund') in force, are probably related to the *Beowulf* poet's concern to underline the temporal and cultural distance between a pagan Scandinavian past and the England of his day. His tactics on the lexical level seem analogous to his strategy on the level of narrative: his auguries, sacrifices, and exotic cremations stress the pastness of the past, yet he projects onto his northern heroic age the moral and political values of the present.[69] In the same way, the poetic meanings of 'mere' and 'sund' contribute a sense of alterity, of distance, of a time when Dane, Geat, and Anglo-Saxon all spoke one tongue; the contemporizing prose meanings promote continuity. The *Beowulf* poet plotted his words to conquer a remoteness, the space between himself and the sixth-century world he wanted to portray. A similar conquest of distance, between us and the past to which the text belongs, is among the achievements of the interpreter of Old English poetry to whom this piece is dedicated. Stanley Greenfield's sensitive readings and translations never fail to make 'the special nature, the unique identity of particular poems ... speak to us across the years with the dignity and self-assurance of its individuality.'[70]

NOTES

1 Stanley B. Greenfield *The Interpretation of Old English Poems* (London and Boston 1972) 43. Levin L. Schücking, *Untersuchung zur Bedeutungslehre der angelsächsichen Dichtersprache* (Heidelberg 1915) 7, early warned: 'Kommen Worte in der Umgangssprache wie in der dichterischen vor, so muss man untersuchen, ob sie wirklich dieselbe Bedeutung hier wie dort haben. ...'

2 On 'lofgeornost,' see J.R.R. Tolkien's section 'Ofermod' in 'The Homecoming of Beorhtnoth Beorhthelm's Son' *E&S* 6 (1953) 13-18; E.G. Stanley 'Hæthenra Hyht in *Beowulf*' in *Studies in Old English Literature in Honor of Arthur G. Brodeur* ed Stanley B. Greenfield (Eugene, Ore 1963) 148; Greenfield *The Interpretation of Old English Poems* 39-43; Mary P. Richards 'A Reexamination of *Beowulf*, ll. 3180-3182' *ELN* 10 (1973) 163-7; and John D. Niles *'Beowulf': The Poem and Its Tradition* (Cambridge, Mass 1983) 207. For a full listing of scholarly opinion, see *Old English Word Studies: A Preliminary Author and Word Index* ed Angus Cameron, Allison Kingsmill, and Ashley Crandell Amos, Toronto Old English Series 8 (Toronto 1983) sv. The Old English lexicographical information in this paper comes from *A Microfiche Concordance to Old English* ed Antonette diPaolo Healey and Richard L. Venezky (Toronto 1980). 'Lofgjarn' occurs just once in Old Norse poetry: see Gustav Neckel ed *Edda: Die Lieder des Codex Regius nebst verwandten Denkmälern*, I, *Text* 4th ed rev Hans Kuhn (Heidelberg 1962) 332 (*Vǫlsunga saga* ch 27). On Old Norse 'dul' ('audacity, pride') see Finnur Jónsson *Lexicon poeticum antiquae linguae septentrionalis ... af Sveinbjörn Egilsson* 2nd ed (Copenhagen 1931); Johan Fritzner *Ordbog over det gamle norske Sprog* I-III (Oslo 1883-96) IV (supplement by Finn Hødnebø, Oslo 1972); and Richard Cleasby and Gudbrand Vigfússon *An Icelandic-English Dictionary* 2nd ed with supplement by Sir William A. Craigie (Oxford 1957) sv. The father who advises his son to shun 'dollic word' ('rash words') in the Old English poem *Precepts*, line 34, has the homiletic sense in mind

(ASPR 3:141). On 'dollice' in *Beowulf* 2646a, see now S.B. Greenfield 'Beowulf and the judgement of the righteous' in *Learning and Literature in Anglo-Saxon England* ed Michael Lapidge and Helmut Gneuss (Cambridge 1985) 400.

3 On this distinction between the metaphorical and the metonymic, see Roman Jakobson and Morris Halle *Fundamentals of Language* (The Hague 1956) pt II. Also Northrop Frye *The Great Code: The Bible and Literature* (New York 1981) pt I ch 1, esp 6-12.

4 On 'feorh,' see Fred C. Robinson 'Lexicography and Literary Criticism: A Caveat' in *Philological Essays: Studies in Old and Middle English Language and Literature in Honor of Herbert Dean Meritt* (The Hague 1970) 104; on Old Norse 'fjör,' see Finnur Jónsson's note in *Lexicon Poeticum* sv: 'In many of these examples *fjör* is treated as something substantial ... possibly the blood is thought of as identical with life.' Alistair Campbell, 'The Use in *Beowulf* of Earlier Heroic Verse' in *England before the Conquest: Studies in Primary Sources Presented to Dorothy Whitelock* ed Peter Clemoes and Kathleen Hughes (Cambridge 1971) 284, notes the exceptional meaning of 'ford' in *Beowulf*.

5 E.G. Stanley 'Spellings of the *Waldend* Group' in *Studies in Language, Literature, and Culture of the Middle Ages and Later* ed E.B. Atwood and A.A. Hill (Austin 1969) 38-69; Angelika Lutz 'Spellings of the *waldend* group – again' *ASE* 13 (1984) 51-63

6 In classical usage, the phrase 'utriusque linguae peritus' signified a knowledge of Latin and Greek; in Anglo-Saxon England, it meant a knowledge of Latin and Old English: see Donald A. Bullough 'The Educational Tradition in England from Alfred to Ælfric: Teaching *Utriusque Linguae*' *Settimane di studio del Centro italiano di studi sull'alto medioevo* 19 (1972) 453-94.

7 A. Diedrich Wackerbarth *Beowulf, an Epic Poem* (London 1849) 53

8 Stopford Brooke *The History of Early English Literature* (London 1892) 1: 42-3

9 Gregor Sarrazin 'Neue *Beowulf*-Studien: VIII, Der Grendel-see' *E Stn* 42 (1910) 6

10 W.S. Mackie 'The Demons' Home in *Beowulf*' *JEGP* 37 (1938) 461

11 Kemp Malone 'Grendel and His Abode' in *Studia philologica et litteraria in honorem L. Spitzer* ed A.G. Hatcher and K.-L. Selig (Bern 1958) 297-308; E.B. Irving, Jr *A Reading of Beowulf* (New Haven 1968) 121: 'Grendel's sea-bottom hall'; J.D.A. Ogilvy and Donald C. Baker *Reading Beowulf: An Introduction to the Poem, Its Background, and Its Style* (Norman, Okla 1983) 61. See also Richard J. Schrader 'Sacred Groves, Marvellous Waters, and Grendel's Abode' *Florilegium* 5 (1983) 77.

12 N.F.S. Grundtvig *Bjowulfs Drape. Et Gothisk Helte-Digt fra forrige Aar-Tusinde af Angel-Saxisk paa Danske Riim* (Copenhagen 1820) 126

13 John J. Conybeare *Illustrations of Anglo-Saxon Poetry* ed William D. Conybeare (London 1826) 107

14 Sir Walter Scott *Peveril of the Peak* (1823) in *The Works of Sir Walter Scott, Bart*, 25 vols New Century Library (London 1905) 15:3; ch 1. Alfred Tennyson 'Sir Galahad' (1842) in *A Collection of Poems by Alfred Tennyson* ed Christopher Ricks (New York 1972) 220; stanza 4

15 William W. Lawrence *Beowulf and Epic Tradition* (Cambridge, Mass 1928) 184. See also Lawrence 'The Haunted Mere in *Beowulf*' *PMLA* 27 (1912) 208-45, and 'Grendel's Lair' *JEGP* 38 (1939) 477-80.

16 Frederick Klaeber ed *Beowulf and the Fight at Finnsburg* 3rd ed with first and second supplement (Boston 1950) 182

17 C.L. Wrenn *Beowulf with the Finnesburg Fragment* (London 1953) 210; R.W. Chambers *Beowulf: An Introduction to the Study of the Poem with a Discussion of the Stories of Offa and Finn* 2nd ed (Cambridge 1932) 3rd ed with supplement by C.L. Wrenn (Cambridge 1959) 450-67; H.D. Chickering, Jr *Beowulf: A Dual-Language Edition* (New York 1977) 334-5

18 D.W. Robertson, Jr 'The Doctrine of Charity in Medieval Literary Gardens: A Topical Approach through Symbolism and Allegory' *Speculum* 26 (1951) 32-6; Margaret E. Goldsmith *The Mode and Meaning of Beowulf* (London 1970) 112-23; Alvin A. Lee *The Guest-Hall of Eden: Four Essays on the Design of Old English Poetry* (New Haven 1972) 202-7

19 Niles *Beowulf: The Poem and Its Tradition* 17

20 E.G. Stanley 'Old English Poetic Diction and the Interpretation of *The Wanderer, The Seafarer*, and *The Penitent's Prayer*' *Anglia* 73 (1956) 441

21 John Gardner *Grendel* (New York 1971) 9

22 *Supplement* sv 'mere': 'Add: 2. "Frequently used of Grendel's abode in the Old English poem *Beowulf*".' Some examples: D.W. Robertson, Jr 'The Doctrine of Charity' 33: 'Grendel's mere has other attributes . . . the hart pursued by hounds chooses rather to give up its life than to hide its head in the grove surrounding the pool'; Stanley B. Greenfield *A Readable Beowulf: The Old English Epic Newly Translated* (Carbondale, Ill 1982) 64n34: 'mere/Lake.'

23 The poet mentions a 'fyrgenstream' ('mighty stream' 1359) in the vicinity of the mere, but never identifies the two.

24 See *Microfiche Concordance* sv 'mere,' where the 'pool' word must be distinguished from the 'boundary' word ('mære').

25 Fred C. Robinson 'Two Aspects of Variation in Old English Poetry' in *Old English Poetry: Essays on Style* ed Daniel G. Calder (Berkeley 1979) 137-8. Robinson's splendid *'Beowulf' and the Appositive Style* (Knoxville 1985)

appeared too late to be ransacked for this essay. See esp ch 2 ('Apposed Word Meanings and Religious Perspectives') where he shows how 'dual semantic layers' in words like 'mægen,' 'synn,' 'firen,' and 'bealu' 'are activated by the dual perspectives in the poem' (55).

26 On the dating and localization of these charters, see Michael Lapidge 'Beowulf, Adlhelm, the Liber Monstrorum, and Wessex' S Med 3 Serie 23/1 (1982) 179-84.

27 T.S. Eliot The Waste Land III lines 179-81

28 Ælfric 'Dominica VI post Pentecosten' in Homilies of Ælfric: A Supplementary Collection ed John C. Pope 2 vols EETS 259, 260 (London 1967-8) 2:517, (lines 45-8): 'þæt wæter flewð ... into ðam mere ... and men hit heton sæ, for ðære micelnysse þæs micclan flodes' ('the river flows into that lake, which is called "sea" because of the magnitude of that great water'). Ælfric is here adapting Bede's commentary on Luke, which notes that in Hebrew all waters, sweet or salt, are called 'mare,' and that Lake Gennesareth is the same as the Sea of Galilee (Pope 517).

29 See Microfiche Concordance sv 'mere.'

30 Homilies of Ælfric ed Pope 1:441 (lines 459, 466, 473). An anonymous homily, partially ed Rudolph Willard Two Apocrypha in Old English Homilies Beiträge zur englischen Philologie 30 (Leipzig 1935), has as a place of evil a very deep and fiery 'mere' (line 398).

31 J.R. Firth in Selected Papers of J.R. Firth, 1952-1959 ed F.R. Palmer (London 1968) 179. The Styx is described as a 'palus' ('fen, swamp, area covered with pools of standing water') in Aeneid 6:323.

32 Nigel F. Barley, 'Structural Aspects of the Anglo-Saxon Riddle' Semiotica 10 (1974) 157, finds Grendel 'little more than a totally individuated riddle image'; see also Craig Williamson trans A Feast of Creatures: Anglo-Saxon Riddle-Songs (Philadelphia and London 1982) 39-41.

33 E.G. Stanley, 'The Date of Beowulf: Some Doubts and No Conclusions' in The Dating of Beowulf ed Colin Chase, Toronto Old English Series 6 (Toronto 1981) 197, notes the poet's sophisticated integration of the two vocabularies; also Robinson 'Beowulf' and the Appositive Style 31-2.

34 Eadwine's Canterbury Psalter ed Fred Harsley EETS os 92 (London 1889) 18.6 ('etenæs'), 32.16 ('eten') glossing 'gigas.' Frank-Günter Berghaus, Die Verwandtschaftsverhältnisse der altenglischen Interlinearversionen des Psalters und der Cantica Palaestra 272 (Göttingen 1979) 63, 134, has concluded that the Old English gloss in the Canterbury Psalter was revised shortly after 900 by an Anglian corrector.

35 Wackerbarth Beowulf, An Epic Poem 21

36 E.G. Stanley 'Studies in the Prosaic Vocabulary of Old English Verse' NM

72 (1971) 391-2; Hans Schabram *Superbia: Studien zum altenglischen Wortschatz I* (Munich 1965) 126-7. The 'sund' ('swimming') of fish is twice paired with the 'flyht' of birds in Ælfric's prose: 'De initio creaturae' in *The Sermones Catholici or Homilies of Ælfric* ed Benjamin Thorpe 2 vols, Ælfric Society (London 1844-6) 1:16, line 6; *Exameron Anglice, or The Old English Hexameron* ed Samuel J. Crawford, Bibliothek der angelsächsischen Prosa 10 (Hamburg 1921) line 239. Only in Ælfric's homily on Cuthbert, which is a rhythmical composition, can 'sund' mean 'sea': 'Þa Cuðberhtus ða sælican nytenu on sund asende' ('then Cuthbert sent those marine creatures [seals] to sea'). See *Ælfric's Catholic Homilies: The Second Series, Text* ed Malcolm Godden EETS ss 5 (London 1979) 83, line 86. In the Old English *Apollonius of Tyre*, *Orosius*, and *Alexander's Letter to Aristotle*, 'sund' seems to mean either 'with the current' or 'swimming.'

37 On 'sund' usually meaning 'swimming' in Icelandic, see James Earl 'Beowulf's Rowing-Match' *Neophil* 63 (1979) 287.

38 Old Norse 'sund' ('swimming') occurs twice in the eddic *Rígsþúla* ('nema sund,' 'fremja sund') and once in a skaldic stanza attributed to Haraldr harðráði ('nema sund'). The former poem is notoriously difficult to date, with critical opinion ranging from the ninth to thirteenth century; for an attempt to pinpoint its composition between 1247 and 1257, see Klaus von See 'Der Alter der *Rígsþúla' Acta Philogica Scandinavica* 24 (1957) 1-12. Although King Haraldr died at the battle of Stamford Bridge, his 'lausavísa,' like so many of the royal stanzas, was probably not composed until the second half of the twelfth century.

39 G.J. Thorkelin *De Danorum rebus gestis secul. III et IV. Poëma Danicum dialecto Anglo-Saxonica* (Copenhagen 1815) 40-3, 110, 122. Thorkelin's many misunderstandings of the text include the elimination of Breca (his name is taken as a common noun 'booty, plunder'); the flinging of arms over the sea in lines 513-14 ('þær git eagorstream earmum þehton ... mundum brugdon') is read as the storming of fortresses ('ibi fluctus sanguinis rivis miseri texistis ... castella terruistis' 41).

40 For more on these contests, see Martin Puhvel 'The Swimming Prowess of *Beowulf' Folklore* 82 (1971) 276-80, and Peter A. Jorgensen 'Beowulf's Swimming Contest with Breca: Some Old Norse Parallels' *Folklore* 89 (1978) 52-9; on swimming feats a little further afield (Armenia), see Earl R. Anderson 'Beowulf's Retreat from Frisia: Analogues from the Fifth and Eighth Centuries' *ELN* 19 (1981) 89-93.

41 Robinson 'Lexicography and Literary Criticism' 100

42 *Andreas* 204, 211; *Elene* 220. Citations of Old English poetry are from the ASPR. The one possible 'sund' ('swimming') compound in *Beowulf* ('sundnytt')

has been admirably dispatched by Karl Wentersdorf 'Beowulf's Withdrawal from Frisia: A Reconsideration' *SP* 68 (1971) 402-3, and Fred C. Robinson 'Elements of the Marvellous in the Characterization of Beowulf: A Reconsideration of Textual Evidence' in *Old English Studies in Honour of John C. Pope* ed Robert B. Burlin and E.B. Irving, Jr (Toronto 1974) 134n17. 'Sundnytt,' whether 'swimming office' or 'use of the sea,' is a hapax legomenon; however, 'sundornytt' ('special duty') is found elsewhere in Old English, including *Beowulf* 667, and fits the context at least as well as 'sundnytt.'

43 The *Beowulf* poet uses the simplex eleven times or 42 per cent of all poetic occurrences; he and the poet of *Andreas* together account for over 60 per cent of the uses in poetry.

44 Grundtvig *Bjowulfs Drape* 48: 'I svømmed, som to Fiske / Ja snart som døde Sild.' In Danish, 'dead as a herring' = dead as a doornail. Robinson, 'Elements of the Marvellous' 135n24, observes that Thorkelin, *De Danorum rebus gestis* ..., 46, kept the manuscript reading 'wudu weallendu' (581), rather than emending to 'wadu weallendu' in conformity with *Beowulf* 546.

45 On mythologizing critics, see Robinson 'Elements of the Marvellous' 132, and Klaeber *Beowulf* 147n2.

46 See Campbell 'The Use in *Beowulf* of Earlier Heroic Verse' 284; Larry D. Benson 'The Originality of *Beowulf*' in *The Interpretation of Narrative: Theory and Practice* ed Morton W. Bloomfield, Harvard English Studies 1 (Cambridge, Mass 1970) esp 20-2.

47 Lawrence *Beowulf and Epic Tradition* 153

48 Klaeber 147; Johannes Hoops *Kommentar zum Beowulf* (Heidelberg 1932) 78; Norman E. Eliason 'The Þyle and Scop in *Beowulf*' *Speculum* 38 (1963) 271

49 Fred C. Robinson 'Beowulf's Retreat from Frisia: Some Textual Problems in ll. 2361-62' *SP* 62 (1965) 1-16; Wentersdorf, 'Beowulf's Withdrawal from Frisia' (1971); and Robinson 'Elements of the Marvellous' (1974). Stanley B. Greenfield has recently asked that some of the marvellous be returned: 'A Touch of the Monstrous in the Hero, or Beowulf Re-Marvellized' *ES* 63 (1982) 294-300.

50 Karl P. Wentersdorf 'Beowulf's Adventure with Breca' *SP* 72 (1975) 140-66; Earl 'Beowulf's Rowing Match' (1979)

51 Riddle 36 in the Exeter Book collection (ASPR 3:198), for example, describes a four-oared boat, with one man at each oar, as having four feet below (ie, the oars in the water) and eight above (ie, those of the four rowers). On limbs as oars, cf Statius *Thebais* 9.250, where 'remigium' ('outfit of oars') is used of legs.

52 Outside of *Beowulf*, 'rowan' ('to row') occurs only twice in poetry, in the

Exeter Book *Maxims*, line 185 ('roweþ'), and in *Andreas*, line 473 ('rowend'), unless Cnut's song is counted ('Roweþ cnites / noer the lant and here we þes muneches sæng'): *Liber Eliensis* ed E.O. Blake, Royal Historical Society, Camden Society 3rd series 92 (London 1962) 153. The Old Norse verb 'róa' is far more frequent in poetry, especially in eddic verse.

53 Arthur G. Brodeur *The Art of Beowulf* (Berkeley 1959) 146

54 See Rudolf Meissner *Die Kenningar der Skalden: Ein Beitrag zur skaldischen Poetik* Rheinische Beiträge und Hülfsbücher zur germanischen Philologie und Volkskunde 1 (Bonn and Leipzig 1921) 153: 'Von der Form kann die Vergleichung kaum ausgehen, vielmehr hat man daran zu denken, dass die Handhabung des Remens wie des Schwertes Kraft und Geschicklichkeit erfordert.'

55 *The Chronicle of Æthelweard* ed Alistair Campbell (London 1962) 45: 'insistunt remis, deponunt scarmos; unda coacta rutilant arma.'

56 *Art of Sinking* 97. *Martinus Scriblerus' The Art of Sinking in Poetry* ed Edna L. Steeves (New York 1932)

57 Carol Clover 'The Germanic Context of the Unferþ Episode' *Speculum* 55 (1980) 444-68

58 *Gesta Danorum*, book 5, in *Saxonis Gesta Danorum* ed Carl Knabe and Paul Herrmann rev Jørgen Olrik and Hans Ræder 2 vols (Copenhagen 1931-57) 1:112-13

59 English trans by Peter Fisher *Saxo Grammaticus: History of the Danes* 2 vols (Totowa, NJ 1979-80) 1:126-7:

> In rebus mens stulta modum deprendere nescit,
> turpis et affectus immoderata sui.
> Remorum ductus velorum vincitur usu,
> æquora ventus agit, tristior aura solum:
> Nam freta remigium penetrat, mendacia terras;
> istas ore premi constat, at illa manu.

60 I am thinking of puns like that on 'ar' ('oar' and 'honour') in the Exeter Book *Maxims*, lines 185-6: 'Weary the man who rows against the wind; very often he is accused of cowardice, of losing his valour ('ellen'); his oar (or honour) dries on board' (cf the alliterative collocations 'ellen mid arum' *Guthlac* 450; 'elne:are,' *Wanderer* 114).

61 Meissner *Die Kenningar* 133, on oar-kennings for tongue: 'Das Bild eines Werkzeuges, das an einem Punkte festliegt und sich sonst bewegt, liegt bei Ruder vor.' There is at least one skaldic stanza in which a description of the poet bending his oar at the ship's side is juxtaposed to the motion of the landlubber with his woman: Finnur Jónsson ed *Den norsk-islandske skjaldedigtning* (Copenhagen 1912-15) IB, 330, 9, 1-4.

62 Árni Jónsson *Guðmundardrápa* in *Den norsk-islandske skjaldedigtning* IIB, 461, 78, 7-8. Eric's riddling account of how he got from Norway to Denmark and his exchange of obscene verses with a woman famed for her flyting prowess (*Gesta Danorum* 1:115, 118) seem not fully understood by Saxo.

63 *Lexicon poeticum* sv 'róa'

64 Campbell 'The Use in *Beowulf* of Earlier Heroic Verse' 284

65 E.G. Stanley 'The Date of *Beowulf*' 197

66 Josephine Miles 'Values in Language; or, Where Have *Goodness, Truth*, and *Beauty* Gone?' *Crit I* 3 (Autumn 1976) 1-13 rpt in *The State of the Language* ed Leonard Michaels and Christopher Ricks (Berkeley 1980) 363

67 Robinson 'Two Aspects of Variation' 127-145; Greenfield *The Interpretation of Old English Poems* 68-72

68 The adjective 'bront' (ON 'brattr') 'steep, high' is used in Old English poetry of ships (*Beowulf* 238, *Elene* 238, *Andreas* 273) and of the sea (*Beowulf* 568); in Old Norse it is used of land and of sea-billows: eddic examples include 'brattr breki' ('steep breaker,' *Sigrdrífumál* 10) and 'brattr breki brǫndum hæri' ('steep breaker, higher than the prow,' *Reginsmál* 17), the latter verse evocative of Breca of the Brondings.

69 Roberta Frank 'The *Beowulf* Poet's Sense of History' in *The Wisdom of Poetry: Essays in Early English Literature in Honor of Morton W. Bloomfield* ed Larry D. Benson and Siegfried Wenzel (Kalamazoo 1982) 53-65

70 Greenfield *The Interpretation of Old English Poems* ix

JOHN C. POPE

Beowulf 505, 'gehedde,' and the Pretensions of Unferth

WHETHER OR NOT Unferth's name is meant to suggest 'un-friŏ' ('mar-peace'), there is no doubt that he enters the poem in a quarrelsome mood as he tries to discredit Beowulf with his (and Breca's) version of the swimming adventure, and that he has provoked among modern critics wide disagreement about his character, his status in Hrothgar's court, and his future participation, if any, in the supposed machinations of Hrothulf against the sons of Hrothgar. The various interpretations of his name and the disputes about his character and his position as 'þyle' were sensibly surveyed by the man we honour in this volume as recently as 1972,[1] but exploration and debate continue, not without profit, especially in attempts to relate Unferth's status and role to Germanic traditions that may have been familiar to the poet and his audience, yet would no doubt have been locally modified in ways we can only dimly surmise.[2]

Until recently, however, there has been substantial agreement about the purport of the passage, lines 499–505, with which the present essay is concerned, in spite of early uncertainties, almost forgotten, about the lexical identity and meaning of a word in line 505 that stands in the manuscript as 'gehedde.' It is the passage in which the poet first brings Unferth to our attention, introducing him with an abrupt 'Unferŏ maþelode' and preparing us for his carefully slanted disparagement of Beowulf by assigning a motive for it. Klaeber prints the passage as follows:

*Un*ferŏ maþelode,   Ecgláfes bearn,
þē æt fótum sæt   fréan Scyldinga,
onband beadurúne –   wæs him Béowulfes síŏ,
mōdges merefaran,   micel æfþunca,

forþon þe hē ne ūþe,   þæt ǣnig ōðer man
ǣfre mǣrða þon mā   middangeardes
gehēde under heofenum   þonne hē sylfa - :[3]

In line 505, Klaeber altered the spelling of ms 'gehedde' to 'gehēde,' since he accepted Holthausen's explanation of 'gehedde' as a corrupt spelling of the preterite third singular subjunctive of 'gehēgan,' which was thought to mean, in this context, 'perform, carry out, achieve.' Holthausen had printed 'gehēdde' (ie 'gehēde') in his first edition of the poem (Heidelberg 1905-6) and 'gehēgde' in later editions. Other editors (eg Dobbie, von Schaubert, Wrenn) retained the manuscript spelling on the chance that it was not an error but a late variant involving, as some thought, both a lengthening of the consonant and a shortening of the preceding vowel; but prior to 1973 all major editions since Klaeber's of 1922 had treated the ms 'gehedde' as preterite of 'gehēgan,' which appears unmistakably as an infinitive in *Beowulf* 425 and as the preterite 'gehēde' in *Andreas* 1496. Accordingly, although every translation I have consulted differs in some shade of interpretation from every other, the following version, with its parenthesized alternatives, may serve as the general sense of the passage during the greater part of the twentieth century:

Unferth spoke, son of Ecglaf, who sat at the feet of the lord of the Scyldings, unbound words of strife. The undertaking of Beowulf, the brave seafarer, was a great vexation to him, for he would not allow (*or* grant) that any other man on earth should (*or* could) ever achieve more glory (*or* perform more glorious deeds) under the heavens than he himself.[4]

But this peaceable agreement among editors and translators was challenged by Fred C. Robinson, first briefly in 1970, in an article entitled 'Personal Names in Medieval Narrative and the Name of Unferth in *Beowulf*,'[5] then with fuller explanation in 1974, in 'Elements of the Marvellous in the Characterization of Beowulf.'[6] In the latter article, as part of an argument (inspired in some degree by the articles of Rosier and Eliason to which I refer in note 2) that Unferth's name can be interpreted as 'unintelligence' or 'folly' rather than 'discord' and his official title as 'þyle' can point to a position something like that of the later court jester,[7] Robinson turns to the traditional text of lines 501-5, saying,

Surely this clear statement justifies Bonjour's inference that Unferth is 'jealous of his own glory' and that only a man 'of his prominent position,' 'a distinguished and glorious thane,' would harbour such concern for his martial reputation?[8] So it would seem, but the cited passage will bear scrutiny before the point is granted. As quoted, the passage says that Unferth was unwilling to admit that 'any other man on earth should perform glorious deeds.' But this meaning is achieved only by means of an emendation of the verb 'gehedde' to 'gehede,' which is then interpreted as preterite subjunctive of 'gehegan' and assigned the meaning 'to perform (deeds).' Elsewhere in Old English the verb always occurs with 'þing,' 'seonoð,' 'spræc,' or 'mæðel' as its direct object and means 'to hold (a meeting).' Left in its original manuscript form, 'gehedde' would be preterite of 'gehedan' ('heed, care for') (see Klaeber's glossary s.v. 'hedan'). If the sentence is read this way, then Unferth emerges as a character with a most unheroic, Falstaffian attitude toward heroic deeds: he did not want to grant that other men cared for glory or for deeds of glory ('mærða') any more than he himself did. This is not an inappropriate sentiment for a man who, the poet later tells us, willingly 'forleas ellenmærðum' (1470-1). Perhaps there is more than a little of the swaggering coward in Unferth, and the speech reminding Beowulf of a past failure is motivated by a desire to scare the hero out of his commitment to face Grendel. If the speech is successful, then Unferth will have shown the Danes that he is not alone in his distaste for derring-do.[9]

I have quoted this passage in extenso, because I wish to distinguish between my willingness to accept 'gehedde' as the preterite of 'gehēdan' ('heed, care for'), and my uneasiness at the interpretation Robinson has placed upon the clause, lines 503-5. For this interpretation, as it seems to me, is only one of two grammatically possible interpretations, and not, in the immediate context or the wider context, the likelier of the two.

But first, the word itself. It has been a problem to editors from the beginning, though they have made little noise about it, and a brief survey of its various interpretations may be useful. Robinson's interpretation will, I think, emerge as the most probable, but we shall see that there are complications that have rendered that interpretation less than obvious and may still allow dissent.

Before Holthausen declared for 'gehēgan,' 'gehēdan' had been the leading candidate; but the early editors were not satisfied to attribute to it the same meaning as that which was clearly present in the unprefixed 'hēdde' of *Beowulf* 2697: 'ne hēdde hē þæs heafolan,' which Klaeber explains as 'he [Wiglaf] did not care for (i.e. aim at) the head.' Actually, the only other occurrence of 'hēdan' in the poetry is in *Exodus* 584, 'hēddon herereafes,' where it has been interpreted as meaning more than 'heeded,' namely 'took charge or possession of,' and this sense is partially supported by examples in the prose of Ælfric and the laws, though the prose also has examples of simple 'heed, care for.'[10] As for the prefixed 'gehēdan,' the only recorded instance (and that a disputed one) in Old English verse or prose, apart from 'gehedde' 505, is the present subjunctive 'gehede' in the *Meters of Boethius* 27.15. It occurs in the passage describing Death as a hunter who will not leave any trail 'ær he gehede / þæt he hwile ær // æfter spyrede' ('before he "gehede" what a little earlier he was tracking'). The general if not the exact meaning of 'gehede' ('catches, seizes, possesses, obtains'?) is evident not only from the context but by its correspondence to 'gefehð' ('seizes') in the prose version. Unfortunately, scribal error has been suspected because of the unusual meaning, and error plus dialectical substitution of Kentish 'e' for 'y' is possible, since the manuscript has traces of Kentish spellings elsewhere in the *Meters*. Emendations range from 'gehende' to 'gehȳðe.'[11]

But right or wrong, this lonely 'gehede' undoubtedly had a part to play in early interpretations of 'gehedde,' certainly by Grein's time if not before. Kemble, in the second volume of his enlarged second edition of *Beowulf*, though he referred 'gehedde' 505 (= 1004 in his lineation) to 'gehēdan' and defined it in his glossary as 'observare,' added a question mark, and preferred the notion of possession in this translation of the clause: 'because he granted not that any other man should ever have beneath the skies, more reputation in the world than he himself.'[12] Grein's verse translation in 1857 gave a similar interpretation of 'gehedde' and its clause:

da er durchaus nicht gönnste, dass ein anderer Mann
je mehr das Ruhmen in dem Mittelkreise
besässe unterm Himmel, denn er selber hatte.[13]

Grein was clearly influenced by the 'gehede' of the *Meters*, for in the *Sprachschatz* accompanying his *Bibliothek der angelsächsischen Poesie*,[14] under 'gehēdan, gehȳdan,' he listed as the sole examples of sense 4, 'asciscere' (here evidently meaning 'to take or appropriate to oneself, take possession of'), 'gehede' of *Meters* 27.15 and 'gehedde' of *Beowulf* 505. Again, in his separate edition of *Beowulf* in 1867, Grein defined 'gehēdan' as 'sich einen Sache bemächtigen, erwerben,' quoting lines 503-5 and proposing 'Ruhm erwübe' for 'mærða ... gehêdde.'[15] Moritz Heyne's third edition (Paderborn 1873) gives 'erwerben' alone. Whether in part by Grein's example, or Heyne's, or entirely from *Meters* 27.15 and some of the prose uses of 'hēdan' to which I have referred above, 'gehēdan' (as infinitive of 'gehedde' 505) was defined as 'obtain' in the glossaries of A.J. Wyatt's first two editions (Cambridge 1894 and 1898) and in the first two editions of W.J. Sedgefield (Manchester 1910 and 1913). In short, then, for a considerable period in German and English editions, 'gehēdan' was assumed to be the infinitive of 'gehedde,' but was given such meanings as 'erwerben,' 'take possession of,' 'obtain,' rather than the simple 'heed, care for' or 'hüten' that was recognized by all editors for the 'hēdan' (pret 'hēdde') of *Beowulf* 2697. The potentially perfective sense of the prefix 'ge-' may have had some influence on the preference for 'obtain,' but the combined influence of *Meters* 27.15 and the context, *Beowulf* 501-5, were probably of greater importance.

Nevertheless there may always have been an uneasiness about 'gehēdan.' Grein, in the very glossary of his 1867 edition I have quoted for his definition of 'gehēdan,' adds as an alternative interpretation, 'wenn nicht etwa *gehêdde* für *gehêde* von *gehêgan* steht ("Ruhmthaten vollbrächte").' For the 'gehêgan' of line 425, where it certainly occurs, he gives the definition 'vollbringen, ausführen,' more or less corresponding to 'perform, bring about.' We are already on the way to Holthausen's settling for 'gehēgan' and its subsequent almost universal adoption as the infinitive of 'gehedde.' The last faint protest came from R.W. Chambers, in whose revision of Wyatt's edition (Cambridge 1914) we find a footnote on 505 'gehēdde': 'This is usually interpreted "obtain" or "achieve," and is explained either as a compound of *hȳdan*, "to hide" (Bosworth-Toller; cf. 2235, 3059), or of *hēdan*, "to heed" (so Sedgefield). But it may be, as Holthausen (who reads *gehēgde*) and Schücking suppose, ... from *gehēgan* (line 425), "to carry out," in which case *mærða* = "deeds of glory."' Grein adopted all three interpretations in turn.' Chambers, mercifully, does not favour 'gehȳdan,' but his glossary offers a free choice between 'gehēdan' and 'gehēgan.' After Chambers, 'gehēgan' prevails and seems not to have been challenged until Robinson's protest against it.

The main trouble with 'gehēgan,' as we have seen, is not the spelling but the question whether it has any right to such meanings as 'perform,' 'achieve.' Looking only at *Beowulf* 425-6, '[ic sceal] āna gehēgan // ðing wið þyrse,' and at 'gehedde' 505, one might translate the first, 'I shall bring about, or carry out, alone a meeting with the giant,' and decide that 'bring about' and 'carry out' were not dangerously far from 'perform' or even 'achieve.'[16] But when one adds twelve occurrences of 'gehēgan' in other poems,[17] all agreeing with *Beowulf* 425 in governing an accusative (or, in 'mæðelhegende,' the first member of a compound) signifying a meeting or conference or a formal address, where 'hold' or 'convoke' or 'attend' or even 'bring about' might fit one of these instances or another but 'perform' or 'achieve' are hardly possible for any of them, the 'gehedde' of 505 looks very lonely as a would-be member of the 'gehēgan' family. There is, to be sure, an infinitive 'hegan' in *Daniel* 207 that has been associated by two editors of the poem with 'gehēgan' and defined by them as 'perform, do.'[18] But both the Grein-Köhler *Sprachschatz* and the Bosworth-Toller *Supplement* assign this word with great probability to 'hēgan,' 'exalt,' a weak verb formed on 'hēah,' cognate with Gothic 'hauhjan' and appearing in Old English also as 'hēan.' The participle 'geheged,' clearly meaning 'exalted,' appears in *Early English Homilies from the Twelfth Century MS Vesp. D.XIV.* ed Rubie D.N. Warner, EETS os 152 (London 1917) 99; line 13. Some scholars may feel that such a meaning as 'perform' for 'gehēgan' cannot be ruled out, since the basic etymological meaning of prehistoric Germanic '*haujan' has not been determined; but a definition of 'mæðelhēgende' in Bosworth-Toller ('Attending, holding, or addressing an assembly or council, consulting, conversing'), with a pertinent reference to Icelandic 'þing-heyjandi,' helps to suggest the usual range of meanings of 'gehēgan' and makes it very difficult to deduce such a meaning as 'perform (deeds)' or 'achieve (glory).'[19]

It seems advisable, therefore, in the present state of our understanding of the two verbs, 'gehēdan' and 'gehēgan,' to refer 'gehedde' to 'gehēdan,' and since we cannot be sure of the validity of such a meaning for 'gehēdan' as 'obtain,' which might otherwise seem attractive, to rest content with the meaning 'care for,' 'be concerned about,' as Robinson has recommended. This interpretation has two advantages besides the spelling. First, the word can bear in this context (though the early editors did not seem to think so) an easily substantiated meaning, rather than an unsubstantiated modification of its normal meaning as the supposed preterite of 'gehēgan.' Secondly, though this is perhaps a very minor consideration, it clarifies the grammar of the clause, since 'hēdan' (and therefore presumably 'gehēdan') normally takes a genitive object. Thus 'mærða,' as a genitive plural governed by 'gehedde,' is clearly separated from the adverbial 'þon mā,' whereas the translators of what has become the standard version, whether they regarded 'mā' or 'mærða' as the direct accusative object of 'gehēde,' were virtually compelled by modern usage to write 'more glory' or 'more deeds,' as if 'mā' were the object with 'mærða' a partitive genitive.

Thus I am glad to observe that Robinson's interpretation of 'gehedde' has been accepted by at least two editors. W.F. Bolton, in revising the glossary for the third, posthumous edition of Wrenn's *Beowulf*, has listed 'gehēdde' as preterite subjunctive singular of 'gehēdan,' with genitive, stating the change of identity and meaning, though without giving any authority for it or including any comment on the passage.[20] A second editor, Howell D. Chickering, Jr, has printed 'gehēdde' in his text, with the translation 'care . . . for' on the opposite page and a partially approving reference to Robinson's 1974 article in the Commentary.[21]

But alas, as we have learned,

'Tis with our Judgments as our Watches, none
Go just alike, yet each believes his own.

As I have already said, I am uneasy about Robinson's interpretation of the clause, 503-5, in which 'gehedde' occurs, and I should be reluctant to accept his interpretation of the word if I did not think it at least equally consonant with a different, less revolutionary interpretation of the clause. Robinson has given us a paraphrase rather than an exact translation of the clause, and his paraphrase is weighted towards a negative view of Unferth's concern for glory, partly by the disparaging comments that precede it, and partly by the run of the sentence itself: 'he did not want to grant that other men cared for glory any more than he himself did.' Our modern 'any more than,' though it does not have to be deflating, is frequently used to reduce the importance of what precedes it by comparison with something already known to be small or commonplace. This kind of effect can be achieved in Old English when the second term of the comparison is familair and known to be slighter in some way than the first would normally be. For example, the normal value of fire is reduced to that of sunshine by the poet of *Daniel* in order to describe the miraculous protection of the three children from the blazing furnace into which they have been thrown: 'Næs him se sweg to sorge / ðon ma þe sunnan scima' ('The roaring flame was no more painful to them than sunshine').[22] Indeed the formula 'þon ma þe' or 'þe ma þe,' though it occurs only a few times, and with varied effect, in verse, occurs frequently in prose and has much the same colloquial tone as 'any more than,' but neither the modern expression nor the Old English need be reductive.[23] It is mainly the nature of the two terms rather than the formula of comparison that matters. When the first term is more easily evaluated than the second, it is the second that is freshly defined and may be magnified. In *Genesis* B, for example, Eve beautifully expresses the bitterness of her own, previously unstated, grief at what she has done by denying that Adam's, which he has made all too plain in the course of his denunciation of her, is any greater:

> 'Þu meaht hit me witan,   wine min Adam,
> wordum þinum;   hit þe þeah wyrs ne mæg
> on þinum hyge hreowan   þonne hit me æt heortan deð.'[24]

'You may blame me for it, my friend, Adam, with your words; but it cannot grieve you worse in your mind than it does me at my heart.'

Here what precedes 'þonne' serves to increase the magnitude of what follows it.

If now we look again at *Beowulf* 503-5,

> forþon þe hē ne ūþe,   þæt ænig ōðer man
> æfre mærða þon mā   middangeardes
> gehēdde under heofenum   þonne hē sylfa

for he would not grant that any other man on earth could ever, under the heavens, care more for glorious deeds than he himself did,[25]

we shall see that the comparison differs a little from both of the examples just given, since both terms are somewhat uncertain, but resembles the second example, from *Genesis* B, more than the first, from *Daniel*, in that we should suppose that Unferth knew as well as we do that there have been a number of men in the world who cared a good deal for glorious deeds, whereas nothing at all has yet been established about how much Unferth cared. The normal assumption, therefore, since Unferth is said not to grant that anyone could surpass him in caring, is that he himself cared a great deal. This assumption is strengthened, it seems to me, by the poet's hyperbole, the piling up of 'ænig,' 'æfre,' 'middangeardes,' and 'under heofenum.' Such exaggeration is mere nonsense if Unferth did not care at all. It becomes a mildly satirical anticipation of Unferth's discomfiture if it suggests that he not only cared a great deal but had deluded himself into supposing that nobody on earth could ever have cared more.

Thus, if my interpretation of the clause is correct, the acceptance of 'gehedde' as preterite third singular (probably subjunctive because hypothetical) of 'gehēdan' rather than 'gehēgan' need not alter the usual view, that Unferth was upset out of jealousy for his own reputation. The emphasis merely shifts from actual performance of glorious deeds to a concern for such performance. What most immediately troubled Unferth was Beowulf's professed daring to undertake what no one in Hrothgar's comitatus, since the unhappy demise of a few overbold thegns some time ago, had thought of attempting. If Unferth could show, as he tried to do, that Beowulf had been foolhardy in the past, that another man had beaten him, and that he was now promising more than he could reasonably expect to perform, Unferth would not lose face by his own prudent unwillingness to encounter Grendel. Nobody, in fact, could have blamed Unferth any more than the other Danes for not wanting to be killed and eaten, if only he had not tried to downgrade a rival. It is the jealousy born of his own excessive pretensions, made reckless no doubt by drink and an incautious reliance on hearsay, that exposes him to Beowulf's scornful rejoinder and to the poet's later reminders of his loss of glory.

Much as we should like to know exactly what the poet meant by 'gehedde,' it is far more important to agree on the general purport of the passage in which the word occurs, and this turns out, I believe, to have been adequately understood long ago. Stanley Greenfield, in his new translation of the poem,[26] has not made an issue of the word. His version of lines 499 to 505 runs as follows:

> Then Unferth, son of Ecglaf, who sat
> at the feet of the Scyldings' lord, spoke
> and stirred up strife; the bold seafarer
> Beowulf's venture made him envious,
> for he would not grant that anyone
> on earth could ever gain more glory
> under the heavens than he himself.

Here, although the rendering is deliberately free, the use of 'could gain' for 'gehedde' suggests the sense 'achieve' questionably attributed to 'gehegan,' certainly not 'care for,' though it is not far from the sense 'obtain' formerly attributed to 'gehedan.' There is a clear difference between gaining glory and caring for it, but in either case Unferth's resentment is attributed to the same fundamental cause, what I have called jealousy and Greenfield envy. Critics have differed at this point, but where self-love and vainglory are concerned, envy of another's achievements and jealousy for one's own reputation are blood brothers. It seems to me, therefore, that Greenfield, who is aiming at a 'readable' style in syllabically measured verses, has successfully conveyed what is essential to the meaning of the original, though not of course its own inimitable nuances.

There is much that we can never know for certain about Unferth, not only because we cannot tell precisely what meaning the poet and his audience attached to the term 'þyle,' but still more because we do not know whether or not Unferth had any part to play in stories the poet knew, and expected his audience to know, outside the limits of this particular poem. Was there a well-known tale involving the fratricide with which Unferth was charged by Beowulf and by the poet himself? Or was this charge invented for the occasion of the flyting and, though treated by the poet as true (at line 1167), never elaborated? That the poet knew a story about Hrothulf's dealings with the sons of Hrothgar after the latter's death, and that it probably involved what could have been called treachery on Hrothulf's part, seems to me the most reasonable explanation of the poet's emphasis, during his description of the banquet scene (1017-19 and 1164-5), on the absence, for the present, of discord or treachery between uncle and nephew, and on Wealhtheow's anxieties for her sons (1169-87). It seems less clear but altogether possible that Unferth had a sinister part to play in that story. Scandinavian tales partially corroborate such a story about Hrothulf, though they say nothing of anyone corresponding to Unferth. Readers of *Beowulf* will never cease to speculate about these matters, and a novelist might well invent a tale that would incorporate what little the poem actually says about either Unferth or Hrothulf into a complicated tragedy. What is important for the poem about the poet's comments on the relations of Hrothgar, Wealhtheow, and Hrothulf is the sense that appears elsewhere too, that life cannot long escape tragic conflicts and betrayals, whatever interludes there may be of joy and good fellowship. Whether or not Unferth was included in these forebodings matters very little to our appraisal of the poem. Within the poem he is mainly, and expertly, used as a foil to Beowulf, helping primarily to allow Beowulf, in the flyting, to reveal his astonishing powers in anticipation of his defeat of Grendel, and secondarily, in the lending and failure of the sword Hrunting, to allow a tacit acknowledgment on Unferth's part of Beowulf's superiority, and at the same time to enforce that superiority by contrasting the best of man-made swords with the great sword of the giants, which alone could overcome the magic spells of the monsters and which only Beowulf could have wielded.

I agree, therefore, with those who have seen in the poet's and Beowulf's comments on Unferth later in the poem, especially in the banquet scene (1165-8) and in the passages dealing with the loan and return of Hrunting (1455-72, 1488-91, 1807-12) a clear indication that Unferth was in fact a warrior of some standing, deservedly a 'widcuð man,' as Beowulf calls him (1489), though one at least of his exploits had been morally reprehensible and nothing he had done could match the least of Beowulf's achievements. Nobody has ever ventured to find Unferth a lovable character, so far as I know, but in the matter of his being a respected fighter among the Danes as well as a privileged spokesman, I tend to agree with Bonjour's carefully reconsidered estimate in his *Twelve Beowulf Papers*[27] and with the more recent paper of Geoffrey Hughes.[28] He is certainly no professional entertainer, and though he thinks too well of himself, not a man to be despised. Those who have deduced from Hrothgar's failure to reproach him for his discourteous attack on Beowulf that he was not only a privileged character but one whose sallies, like those of later professional fools, were not taken seriously, will find much to ponder in Carol J. Clover's study, 'The Germanic Context of the Unferth Episode.'[29] By showing how many features of this flyting are well-recognized conventions in traditional heroic fiction, she suggests that the poet's audience would have been much less shocked by Unferth's behaviour than some modern critics have been. There are several reasons besides these conventions (which do not of course render less remarkable the specific relevance and individuality of the whole episode) that can be offered for Hrothgar's failure to scold Unferth. One is that Beowulf has put his adversary so firmly in his place. Another, somehow overlooked in the excitement of debate, is that the poet has chosen to emphasize what is vastly more important for the progress of the narrative than a royal rebuke to Unferth, namely the joy that Hrothgar feels at hearing in Beowulf's reply so unexpected and so persuasive a confirmation of the hope that at last a champion has been found who can defeat Grendel.

I have allowed myself to digress a little from the limits of my narrow theme. It is my hope, however, that most of what I have said about Unferth's character and behaviour in the poem as it unfolds will appear consonant with what I believe to be the tenor of lines 499-505, with or without the new interpretation of 'gehedde.'

NOTES

1 Stanley B. Greenfield *The Interpretation of Old English Poems* (London and Boston 1972) 101-7. Among the many suggested interpretations of Unferth's

name mentioned by Greenfield, that which combines a negative 'un-' with 'friŏ' ('peace') rather than 'fer(h)ŏ' ('spirit') seems clearly preferable, both for its possible application to the character and for Old English usage, since, as a second element in proper names, West Saxon '-ferŏ' regularly corresponds to Anglian '-friŏ,' and 'friŏ,' not 'ferhŏ,' is a common Germanic name-element. But I have recently received from Professor R.D. Fulk the draft of an essay (soon to be published in *Modern Philology*) in which he advances reasons that seem to me of considerable weight for supposing that Unferth's name is a Germanic inheritance having nothing to do with etymological characterization on the part of the poet. In any case, it is clearly dangerous to use a doubtful etymology of the name as a guide to the characterization in preference to what Unferth says and does in the poem and what the poet tells us (though too meagrely) about him and about what other characters think of him.

2 Among numerous recent articles on problems connected with Unferth, the following are particularly relevant as background to the present much more limited discussion: James L. Rosier 'Design for Treachery: The Unferth Intrigue' *PMLA* 77 (1962) 1-7 (as certain glosses suggest but do not prove, Unferth as 'þyle' may have been little more than a scurrilous jester, but one destined to conspire with Hrothulf in plotting the overthrow of Hrothgar's sons); Norman E. Eliason, 'The Þyle and Scop in *Beowulf*' *Speculum* 38 (1963) 267-84 (Unferth a harmless though scurrilous and cowardly fool, possibly identical with the scop[!]); J.D.A. Ogilvy 'Unferth: Foil to Beowulf?' *PMLA* 79 (1964) 370-5 (cautionary observations on Rosier's speculations and, in a final note, on Eliason's); Ida Masters Hollowell 'Unferŏ the þyle in *Beowulf*' *SP* 73 (1976) 239-65 (Germanic tradition supports the possibility that Unferth as 'þyle' held a dignified and privileged position, one distantly associated perhaps with pagan wizards or priests); Geoffrey Hughes, 'Beowulf, Unferth and Hrunting: an Interpretation' *ES* 58 (1977) 385-95 (a defence and extension of the views of older critics: Unferth a warrior of some importance, not a jester; a foil to Beowulf, whose superiority he grudgingly recognizes; yet a treacherous fratricide and an ominous figure of discord); Carol J. Clover 'The Germanic Context of the Unferth Episode' *Speculum* 55 (1980) 444-68 (brings the widespread Germanic conventions of flyting to bear on the poet's treatment of the Unferth-Beowulf exchange, establishing the extent and importance of its conventional features).

3 Fr. Klaeber ed *Beowulf and the Fight at Finnsburg* 3rd ed with First and Second Supplements (Boston 1950) lines 499-505

4 Johannes Hoops *Kommentar zum Beowulf* (Heidelberg 1932) 77, observed that 'þon mā' should mean 'noch mehr,' modern English 'the more' (thus being an adverbial expression modifying the verb and correlative with 'þonne'

in the next line), and 'mærða' should be accusative plural, object of 'gehedde,' which he did not emend but accepted as preterite of 'gehēgan' ('vollbringen, vollführen'). A grammatically close translation (though modern 'the more' doesn't quite fit) would thus give the rather awkward 'should (*or* could) ever perform glorious deeds (*or* achieve glory) in greater measure than he himself.' Klaeber's glossary offers an alternative between the construction advocated by Hoops and 'mā' as substantive object of the verb, governing 'mærða,' genitive plural, a partitive construction not possible with the new interpretation of 'gehedde' discussed below.

5 *Essays in Honor of Richebourg Gaillard McWilliams* ed Howard Creed, *Birmingham-Southern College Bulletin* 43:2 (Birmingham, Ala 1970) 43-8. On 'gehedde,' see 48n1.

6 *Old English Studies in Honour of John C. Pope* ed Robert B. Burlin and Edward B. Irving, Jr (Toronto 1974) 119-37

7 This conception of the character, developed in an extreme form by Eliason (above n2), was partially suggested by W.J. Sedgefield *An Anglo-Saxon Verse-Book* (Manchester 1922) 164: 'Unferth was the king's *þyle*, o.n. *þulr*, *i.e.* an orator clever at repartee, whose function was to amuse the company in the hall. He may have been the earlier stage of the king's jester of later times.'

8 Adrien Bonjour *The Digressions in Beowulf* (Oxford 1950) 17-22. Robinson does Bonjour the justice to refer the reader to his more temperate but still not completely derogatory view of Unferth in his *Twelve Beowulf Papers* (Neuchatel 1962) 129-33.

9 'Elements of the Marvellous' (as above, n6) 128-9

10 See 'hédan' in Bosworth-Toller, both *Dictionary* and *Supplement*; also the glossaries in the editions of *Exodus* by E.B. Irving, Jr (New Haven 1953): '*hēdan*, take care of (here virtually "seize")'; and Peter J. Lucas (London 1977): 'hēdan, HEED, take charge of.'

11 W.J. Sedgefield ed *King Alfred's Old English Version of Boethius De Consolatione Philosophiae* (Oxford 1899) 197, Met xxvii. 15 and 124, line 9, the corresponding prose. For the uncertainty of 'gehede' in such a sense and some proposed emendations, see E.A. Kock 'Interpretations and Emendations of Early English Texts. xi' *Anglia* 47 (1923) 268, no 332, and G.P. Krapp's note on *Meters* 27.15 ASPR 5 (New York 1932) 236. I agree with Sedgefield that 'geheded' in *Meters* 20.151 is probably a Kentish spelling of 'gehyded' ('hidden'), though Toller in the Bosworth-Toller *Supplement* thinks it belongs properly to 'gehēdan' with the sense 'keep, store up,' and compares 'hēddærn' ('storehouse'). A. Campbell in his *Enlarged Addenda and Corrigenda* to Toller's *Supplement* (Oxford 1972) has made confusion worse confounded by referring both 'gehede' in *Meters* 27.15 and 'gehedde' in *Beowulf* 505 to

'gehēgan,' as if 'gehede' in the *Meters* were not a present but a preterite subjunctive! (In my pronouncements here and elsewhere about recorded forms in both verse and prose I have depended on Antonette diPaolo Healey and Richard L. Venezky *A Microfiche Concordance to Old English* Toronto 1980.)

12 John M. Kemble *A Translation of the Anglo-Saxon Poem of Beowulf, with a Copious Glossary Preface and Philological Notes* (London 1837) 21. This is the second volume of Kemble's second edition. The first volume was entitled *The Anglo-Saxon Poems of Beowulf, The Travellers Song and the Battle of Finnesburh* (London 1835). Kemble's first edition (London 1833) was limited to a single volume.

13 C.W.M. Grein *Dichtungen der Angelsachsen, stabreimend übersetzt* 2 vols (Göttingen 1857-9) 1:236

14 4 vols Göttingen 1857-8 (text); 1861-4, *Sprachschatz*

15 C.W.M. Grein ed *Beovulf nebst den Fragmenten Finnsburg und Valdere* (Cassel and Göttingen 1867). Grein's first edition was in the *Bibliothek* vol 1 (1857).

16 W.J. Sedgefield in the glossary of his *Anglo-Saxon Verse-Book* (Manchester 1922) refers 'gehēdde' of *Beowulf* 505 (49; line 7 of his Selection 14) to 'gehēgan' ('venture on, risk'), an erratic definition seemingly without a past or future.

17 *Andreas* 157, 262, 609, 930, 1049, 1096, 1496; *Elene* 279 (ms 'meðel hengende'); *Phoenix* 493; *Vainglory* 13 (ms 'mæþel hergendra'); *Maxims I* 18; *Judgment Day I* 9.

18 F.A. Blackburn ed *Exodus and Daniel* (Boston and London 1907); R.T. Farrell ed *Daniel and Azarias* (London 1974)

19 The Cleasby-Vigfusson *Icelandic-English Dictionary* (Oxford 1874) gives, as the first definition of 'heyja,' 'hold, perform,' but although this may have encouraged the assignment of 'gehedde' to 'gehēgan' in the sense 'perform,' the examples that follow in the dictionary do not seem to support 'perform' in the sense of performing deeds. On the uncertainty of our understanding of 'gehēgan,' see E.G. Stanley 'Two Old English Poetic Phrases Insufficiently Understood for Literary Criticism: *þing gehegan* and *seonoþ gehegan*' in *Old English Poetry: Essays on Style* ed Daniel G. Calder (Berkeley 1979) 67-90. This includes a fully documented account of the connection with Old Frisian use of the cognate 'heia.'

20 C.L. Wrenn ed *Beowulf* 3rd ed revised by W.F. Bolton (London 1973). It seems likely that Bolton's attention was directed to the problem by Robinson's interpretation of 'gehedde' in the 1970 article (above, n5). Bolton refers to the article in the glossary of proper names sv 'Unferð.'

21 Howell D. Chickering, Jr ed and trans *Beowulf: A Dual-Language Edition* (Anchor Books, Garden City, New York 1977). Two other recent editions,

Gerhard Nickel's (Heidelberg 1976) and Michael Swanton's (Manchester 1978), take no notice of Robinson's interpretation of 'gehedde.'

22 *Daniel* 264, ed R.T. Farrell (as above, n 18); numbered 263 in Krapp's edition ASPR 1:118

23 For examples, see G.W. Small 'The syntax of *the* with the comparative' *MLN* 41 (1926) 300-13. The author distinguishes between 'þon (þe) ma' alone and 'þon (þe) ma þe.' He denies (questionably) that 'þon ma þe' is equivalent to 'þon ma ðonne' (of which he gives no examples) and does not even mention *Beowulf* 504-5, 'þon ma ... ðonne,' which appears to be a unique variant. At least I can find no exact parallel to this combination in either verse or prose, and the peculiar word order, obviously dependent in part on the poet's unusual emphasis combined with the metrical requirements, helps to set the clause apart.

24 *Genesis* 824-6 ed Krapp ASPR 1:28

25 Chickering's translation in his edition (above, n21) is a little less literal than mine since it leaves out 'middangeardes,' thus reducing the poet's emphasis:

for he would not grant   that any other man
under the heavens   might ever care more
for famous deeds   than he himself.

Chickering may have meant this to be taken in Robinson's sense, but I think it could as easily be taken in mine.

26 *A Readable Beowulf: The Old English Epic Newly Translated* by Stanley B. Greenfield, with an Introduction by Alain Renoir (Carbondale, Ill 1982)

27 Above, n 8

28 'Beowulf, Unferth, and Hrunting' above, n 2

29 Above, n 2

E.G. STANLEY

Notes on the Text of the Old English *Genesis*

UCH IN THE SPIRIT of that section in Stanley B. Greenfield and Fred C. Robinson, *A Bibliography of Publications on Old English Literature to the End of 1972* (Toronto and Buffalo 1980), to which they give the heading 'Old English Poetry: Textual Criticism' I venture to contribute these notes. The *Bibliography* makes it unnecessary to give bibliographical details (other than for items too recent to be included), and I content myself with giving references in the form of name of author, date of publication and *Bibliography* reference number, eg 'Klaeber (1931, 3693), 11' stands for 'Frederick Klaeber [ed] *The Later Genesis and Other Old English and Old Saxon Texts Relating to the Fall of Man* new ed: with supplement, Englische Textbibliothek (ed Johannes Hoops), 15 (Heidelberg: Carl Winter 1931), p 11.' Line references are to Krapp's *Junius Manuscript*, ASPR (1931, 3-87; 161-97) from the texts of which I quote, sometimes with minor changes especially of punctuation. I have made use throughout of two indispensable works of reference, R.L. Venezky and A. diPaolo Healey, *A Microfiche Concordance to Old English* (Toronto 1980), and A. Cameron, A. Kingsmill, and A.C. Amos, *Old English Word Studies: A Preliminary Author and Word Index* (Toronto 1983). I have used A.N. Doane, ed, *Genesis A, A New Edition* (Madison, Wis 1978); but not (except via Doane) the unpublished edition by David M. Wells (PH D dissertation, University of North Carolina 1969). I assume throughout that my notes will be read in conjunction with the editions by Krapp (1931, 161) Doane, and B.J. Timmer, rev ed (1954, 3695), and the material provided in them; ie I do not attempt to give a history of each textual point and its solutions.

22-3a. Emend ms 'engla weard' to 'englum wearð.' Translate, 'before on account of their pride a share in error came to the angels.' That

two words have to be emended for this interpretation is no great matter
– the emendations are far slighter than emending ms 'dæl' to 'dwæl'
– and if omission of the 'm' contraction above 'u' led to confusion with
(open) 'a' it is an easy step to the scribal introduction of the formula
'engla weard' (which occurs at *Elene* 1100, 1316, and cf *Menologium*
210).

85. It may be that 'herewosan' is a deliberate perversion of 'herewisan,'
to be compared with 'ealowosan' (*Fortunes of Men* 49); the relevant
information is assembled in Doane's note, but not the metrical evidence
on the length of '-wōsan'; and the sense advanced seems less than satisfying.
The half-line 'yrrum ealowosan' would be satisfactory with long or short
'o' (see Pope [1966, 3155], 309 Type D 33 and 312 Type D 45a), but the
half-line 'siððan herewosan' requires long 'ō' (Pope [1966, 3155], 292 Type
C 11c). The element '-wōsa' is probably to be derived from 'wōs, wēsan'
(as has been suggested), and the sense of 'herewōsa' might be 'army-
exudation, military sot,' presumably used as a general term of abuse,
but at *Daniel* 628 Nabuchodonosor is so described strictly in line with
his characterization at 116 as 'wingal.'

221-4a. Ms 'þære hatað' is best emended to 'Þæra anne hatað,' as
most editors do; '-a' and '-e' are among the grammatical endings most
commonly confused in the manuscript and 'nomen uni Phison' (Genesis
2:11) justifies 'anne.' Alliteration in this poem is not as exact as in, for
example, *Beowulf*, and 'sæ foldan dæl' (222b) probably has 'sæ' ('sea'),
ie not, as the editors think, as a form of 'se' pronoun ('which'), with
antecedent 'anne' (introduced by emendation). For an example of a half-
line in the poem with a required stave falling on the second element
of a compound, see 2298a (cf Graz [1894, 3220], 94). The lines may be
translated, 'People, dwellers on earth, men of nations, call one of them
Phison; the sea far and wide encompasses all around the stretch of land,
Evilath, with clear streams.'

401-2a. The verb 'niotan' takes the reflexive dative of the person
enjoying and the genitive of the thing enjoyed, here 'me' dat and 'þæs
leohtes' gen. Translate, 'I do not believe ... that I shall enjoy that way
of life ... which he thinks that he will enjoy ...'; cf the opening words
(235) of *Genesis* B. E. Sievers first suggested translating 'leoht' according
to the Old Saxon sense 'way of life' (*Der Heliand und die angelsächsische
Genesis* [Halle 1875] 258n25).

460-6a. For 'ceosan on' cf Ælfric *Hirtenbrief* II, ed Fehr (1966, 5291),
116 lines 23-4, 'to choose between'; 'þær ... on' (464) is best taken together
'between them.' Translate, 'And by them stood two trees which were

covered with fruit, clad with growth, as mighty God, high King of Heaven, had planted them with his hands, so that the children of men might choose between them, each one of mankind, between good and evil, between happiness and woe.'

475. Ms 'geþing' followed by 'þ' on erasure and 'o' intercalated by the corrector. The editors accept the uncorrected reading (see the apparatus and notes in Timmer [1954, 3695]), but Krapp accepts the correction, and reads 'witode geþingþo'; and elsewhere in *Genesis* B (726-31) 'witod' is in collocation with the abstracts 'hyldo' and 'unhyldo,' supporting to some extent the corrected 'geþingþo' ('honour'). Translate, 'to have his honour truly appointed there.'

618. OE 'cræft' is always masculine, though feminine cognates are known in Old Saxon and Old High German, and this, in a text derived from Old Saxon (cf Timmer [1954, 3695], 25), has led to some editorial acceptance of 'cræfta' as a fem acc pl (instead of OE masc acc pl 'cræftas') parallel with 'gesihðe' acc sg. In view of *Andreas* 1460 'cræfta gehygd' ('mighty thoughts') (and to avoid having to depart from the normal gender), 'cræfta' is better taken as gen pl dependent on 'gesihðe.' Translate 617-18a, 'Say to Adam what mighty vision you have through my coming.'

636. The gender of 'æppel,' ie masculine, is not known till the noun is used at line 637, and 'sum' 636a and again 636b is neuter accusative. Translate 636-7a, 'A certain thing she bore in her hands, a certain thing lay at her heart: the pernicious apple ...' Krapp, and Timmer (1954, 3695), 25, suggest that 'sumne' would have been more correct; and Timmer (in his note) makes the Fall a matter of two apples by translating 'sum ... sum' as 'one ... another'. Genesis 3:6 'et tulit de fructu illius et comedit deditque viro suo qui commedit' gives no warrant for that.

876b-7a. The two half-lines present a contrast and perhaps, as if to accentuate it, the verbs rhyme: 'wrihst' ('you conceal'), 'gesyhst' ('you see'). Translate 876-7a, 'Why do you feel misery, and, seeing trouble, cover shame...?'

888-90a. 'Hwæt' governs a succession of genitives, 'What did you accomplish by way of ...' Cf *Soul and Body* 17 (where the editors take 'Hwæt' as an exclamation and 'druh' as a noun ('dust') – but see Grein (1857, 259), 199, Grein (1861, 68) and again Grein-Köhler (1912, 68), sv 'druh'), *Juliana* 247, *Seafarer* 56, *Judgement Day II* 176b, in all of which 'hwæt' goes with 'dreogan,' and in none of which 'dreogan' takes a genitive object.

959. The problem whether to print such collocations as 'tuddor teondra' as compounds is well discussed by Cook (1909, 3265) in his note on

'æ bringend' at *Christ* 140 treated as two words by the editors. In some editions of Psalter glosses 9:21, however, 'ælændend' for Latin 'legislator' (treated, of course, by modern Latinists as a compound – but see P.G.W. Glare, *Oxford Latin Dictionary* IV (1973) sv) is treated inconsistently. The matter is made more complicated by forms with genitival endings of 'æ,' including 'æs lædend' in the Regius and the Tiberius Psalters and in Eadwine's Psalter; cf Gneuss (1955, 5947), 114 § 142. Taking 'tuddor teondra' as two words, translate 958–60, 'He commanded the oceans and the land to bring forth fruits of every species producing increase for the enjoyment in this world of that married pair.' When such collocations are used attributively and precede the noun they qualify it may be more convenient to print the two words as elements of a compound, eg 'þæt deað-berende deofol' 'Wulfstan' XL, ed Napier (1883, 6501) 185 line 13, 'þæs deað-berendan dracan' 'Wulfstan' XL 188 line 10, and 'deað-berende smíc' 'Wulfstan' XXII 201 line 1. The problem is one of modern printing conventions.

971 'will-gebroðor' 2003 'will-gesiðða,' 2026 'will-geðoftan,' 2147 'will-gesteallum,' and 2608 'will-gesweostor.' In *Genesis* A when 'will-' is compounded with a noun prefixed by 'ge-' and referring to a human relationship, whether of kin or sodality, the implications may be evil. At 971 the relationship between the two brothers is to be seen in the light of the first murder; at 2003 the comrades are the soldiery of Sodom and Gomorrah; at 2147 the companions are the Sodomites; and at 2608 the sisters are Lot's daughters pregnant through incest. On the other hand, at 2026 the companions are the three Amorite brothers (of Genesis 14:13-24) confederate with Abram as he frees Lot from Sodomite captivity, and no stain of sin is on them; and elsewhere in Old English 'will' has favourable connotations only, whereas 'willa' has favourable as well as unfavourable connotations, the latter 'lust of the flesh,' see Bosworth-Toller (1882–98, 75), sv 'will,' and sv 'willa' especially senses Va and (the first quotations under) VI. Doane's glossary rightly suggests that there may be wordplay on 'willflod' 1412, at once 'wiell' (> 'will,' 'wyll') ('source, surge') and 'will.' Doane thinks 'purposed' ie by God. But in view of the other compounds it could also be like 'willa' with evil implications. The distinctions in sense and form apply only to uncompounded 'will' and 'willa'; when compounded, weak nouns shed their ending, thus 'broga' but 'brohþrea' (*Genesis* 1813), 'gealga' but 'gealgmod' and 'gealgtreow,' 'sceanca' but 'sc(e)anc-' in various compounds in prose, 'scucca' but 'scuccgyldum' (*Paris Psalter* 105:26,5), 'steorra' but 'steor(r)-' in a few compounds in prose connected with astrology, etc. It is, therefore,

not improper to interpret some of the compounds as having evil overtones. I do not think that such overtones are demonstrable. While I am willing to seek and find connotations of evil in 'willflod,' I think it would be morphologically improper to do so for 'wylleburne' at *Genesis* 212 even if the reference were not to the waters of Paradise, and where in any case 'y' in the stem may have been chosen by a scribe to make that clear. Similarly, I do not think that the Deluge called 'willeburnan' (acc pl) at *Genesis* 1373 (as Doane's glossary points out, 'fontes abyssi' *Genesis* 7:11) has any connotations of 'will-' or 'willa' ('sinful desire'). Metrical considerations may be relevant here. The half-line 'willfrod ongan' (1412b) is a common and regular Type E found often in the second half of the line; with dissyllabic 'wille-' the line would be regular only if it were a first half-line and had double alliteration. At 212 dissyllabic 'wylle-' is essential, and similarly at 1373.

1056b–7a. As Doane says in his note on 1056, 'The problem goes deeper than a missing word.' In the manuscript, lines 1055-7 are faulty in alliteration of 1056 and in the same line there is no subject for 'ongon.' As a desperate solution a subject 'fæder Enoses' might be added after 'ongon,' (except that it would be metrically unsatisfactory, and if the half-line were emended to Siððan fæder ongon,' though the metre would be correct, the sudden switch from 'child of Cain' to 'father' would be bad stylistically; the emendation 'Siððan his fæder ongon' would be even more interference and it would be even more difficult to explain how the loss might have arisen. The following attempt at a solution might be found the least impossible: perhaps the original read

Caines frumbearn.   Siððan Cain ongon

and, because the repetition of the name confused the scribe, he inverted the order of the words in the first half-line and then either he or a later scribe omitted the second Cain. Translate 1055-7, 'The first was called Enoch, eldest son of Cain. Thereafter Cain did build a city with his kinfolk.'

1155–66. Genesis 5:12-14 explains the arithmetic cumbrously fitted into these lines of verse: Cainan, the son of Enos, was seventy when he begot his firstborn Mahalaleel; Cainan remained prolific for 840 more years, dying at 910. Lines 1155-66 present no difficulty: 'After Enos Cainan continued to be lord and judge, guardian and chief of the family. He was seventy years old before a son was brought to life for him. Then a son was brought forth in the land, Cainan's son, and Mahalaleel was he called. Thereafter for eight hundred and also forty years the son of Enos increased the number of nobles with souls. He had in total number of winters nine hundred, and ten more, when he left the world, when at his time under the space of the heavens his number of days was fulfilled.' The syntactical point that at 1162 the dat pl 'feowertigum' cannot go with acc pl 'eahta hund' makes emendation to 'feowertig' essential.

1405. Ms 'ed monne' has been defended as for 'ead monna' ('happiness of men'), with confusion of '-e' and '-a' common in the manuscript. Emendation is, however, more usual. I presume that 'monne' is a bad form for dat sg weak 'monnan,' and that 'ed' is a corruption of 'eðe' adj: 'eðe monnan' ('easy for the man'). The manuscript is too early for late OE dat sg 'monne, manne' (replacing 'menn') to be likely, but 'monne' instead of the rare weak form is possible. It has been suggested that at 2869a 'men' should be emended to 'mannan' to make it more like other hypermetric lines as analysed by Sievers (1887, 1277), 476; but the scansion of such lines is not sufficiently secure for any but the boldest to emend to regularize. The weak form 'mannan' acc sg is found at 2589. Translate 1404b–6, 'when holy God, the eternal one, the strong-minded King, allowed it ['egorhere' the Deluge] to rise up in currents unharmful for the man [Noah].'

1428. Ms 'þære' has been regarded as having '-e' for '-a,' as is common in the manuscript, thus 'þæra' gen pl, but it is better emended to 'þær' ('where') (it being possible that '-e' is elided before 'he,' and that therefore 'þære he' is homophonous with 'þær he'). Intransitive uses of 'dreogan' are recorded, 'to act, to busy oneself.' Translate, 'a resting place ... where he busied himself far and wide ...'

1448. 'secan nolde' echoes 'secan wolde' 1445, and the object of the earlier use of 'secan,' ie 'hine' 1443 referring to Noah, is to be understood for the second use. Translate 1443–8, 'Noah reckoned that if it [the raven] would not find land on that journey that it would eagerly seek him across the wide water in the Ark [literally, on the wave-plank]. That hope deceived him then; but the rejoicing one [accepting the emendation 'feonde'] perched on a floating corpse; the dark-feathered bird did not wish to seek him.'

1693. 'tohlodon' (inf 'tohladan') used intransitively seems to mean 'demolish, unbuild': 'but wretchedly in droves they unbuilt, linguistically cut off'; ie in this context the verb must mean 'to cease to be engaged on building [the Tower of Babel]' (Genesis 11:8), not 'to misbuild, to pile on, to build aimlessly,' as has been suggested with 'heapum' taken as 'with piles of building materials.'

1711. If ms 'freod 7 aldor' is not to be emended to the easier 'freond 7 aldor' (cf 'winedryhten') 'friend and prince,' it may perhaps be taken as recalling by way of 'peace and prince' the familiar '*Princeps Pacis*' (Isaias 9:6) rather than abstract equivalents of the Lord as 'peace and life.'

1842-3. The double-use of 'fremu̧' (gen pl dependent on 'friclan' and acc sg dependent on 'secan') is strange rhetoric. Translate, 'that we must sue for mercy, for benefits, from the Egyptians, and seek benefit for ourselves.'

1953. 'hleor-lora' may be a term of abuse, and '-lora' could be related to ME 'lorel' (and 'losel'), see *MED* svv. The first element, 'hleor,' is 'face, forehead,' and the compound seems to mean something like 'one who has lost all sense of shame' (cf *OED* sv 'Effronted'). A suitable translation might be 'brazen-faced scoundrel.'

2058. Ms 'eað mihte' has been defended, though emendation seems better since the half-line is both metrically short and unidiomatic. The common use of 'magan' with 'þe eað' gives 'þe eað mihte' to which the half-line should be emended. Translate 2057b-9, 'said that the holy one, the eternal Lord, could the better grant success to him.'

2080b. Ms 'fleonde' emended to 'Fleonde wæron,' an expanded form, a construction rare in verse (but cf ambiguous structures like *Genesis* 1437-8 'sincende wære,' quoted without consideration of the syntactical ambiguity, by G. Nickel *Die Expanded Form im Altenglischen* Kieler Beiträge zur Anglistik und Amerikanistik 3 [Neumünster 1966] 87, who lists other verse uses of expanded form). In prose the emendation would be unexceptionable. The half-line is short and the sentence lacks a finite verb. Perhaps, rather than create an expanded form by emendation, we should emend to 'Fleonde eodon' ('Fleeing they went').

2148. The sense of 'ærgestreonum' seems not merely 'ancient treasure' – with 'ær-' giving a specially favourable connotation on which see Hoops (1932, 2508), 20-4, but may derive more force from the sexual implications of 'streonan' (cf *OED* svv 'Strain' sb[1] and 'Strene'). Translate 2146b-9a, with the sense of 'willgesteallum' as interpreted above, note on line 971, 'so that you shall not reply that I have become happy on earth with comrades in pleasure, with the rich old indulgences, with the kingdom of the Sodomites.'

2252b. Ms 'þæt agan sceal,' variously, and often violently, emended, seems to contain a use of 'agan' similar to that given from early modern English onwards in *OED* sv '*Have*' 14.c, d, and 15, ie as in Modern colloquial English 'to have it coming to one.' Translate 2252b-5 (without emending ms 'ælmihtig drihten'), 'That one (ie 'þæt mennen' neuter) has it coming to her if I am in charge of what is my own, because of you, dear Abram; may the Almighty Lord be judge between us (ie between me and Hagar).'

2559. Doane's suggestion to take 'for' of ms 'swogende for sealh' as pret sg of 'faran' is good, but perhaps we are dealing with a scribal attempt to correct (or with mere haplography of) an original 'for forswealh.' Translate 2558-9, 'The ravaging fire travelled roaringly, swallowed up together all that was steep and spacious.'

2725b. An easy emendation of 'þe ic agan sceal' in the first person would be to change it to the second person, 'þe þu agan scealt' ('which you are to possess'). Translate 2723-5, 'Dwell with us and choose for yourself a home in this land where it pleases you best, a dwelling-place which you are to have.'

2730b. Ms 'flett waðas' is to be defended as a compound with the second element cognate with OIcel 'vaði,' cf OED sv 'Wothe' of which the word here might be an etymon. The emendation 'flettpaðas' involves regarding Sarah's walking on Abimelech's hall-paths as a major disgrace: the danger of being alone with him in his hall is a more likely source of outrage to her honour. (OIcel 'vaði' ['danger'] is masculine; no masculine forms of OIcel 'veiðr, veiði' or OE 'wāþ, *wæþe' [see A.H. Smith *English Place-Name Elements* II, English Place Name Society XXVI (Cambridge 1956) sv '*wæðe'] are recorded.) Translate 2729-31, 'Abraham, thy lord, has no cause to blame you because you, most beautiful kinswoman, enter the perils of my hall.'

2733b. Ms 'incit' perhaps to be emended to 'inc,' with 'ceara' as a reduced imperative, plural before the dual pronoun, though I can find no parallel for that use. See Doane's glossary sv 'cearian.' No easy emendation can improve the alliteration of the line, a Type A3 in the second half-line. Translate 2733b-5, 'Do not, the two of you, trouble to seek good men away from this homeland, friends unknown, but stay here.'

2813-14. 'scufeð ... forð' is best taken together, and without inserting 'on,' as 'move forward, advance,' transitive. Translate, 'The Almighty, the Lord, advances the ways with his hands according to your wish.'

MATTI RISSANEN
'Sum' in Old English Poetry

INTRODUCTORY

N HIS MANY BOOKS and articles, over the decades, Professor Greenfield has emphasized the importance of a close study of the language for the interpretation of Old English poetry. In this paper, I hope to show how even the most prosaic structural elements, the determiners and quantifiers, form an important part of Old English poetical grammar and how their investigation may, on a modest scale, contribute to the better understanding of certain Old English poetic passages.[1]

'Sum' can be defined as a pronoun of indefinite reference, either specific or non-specific. In the former case it refers to a particular individual, known to the speaker or writer but not yet to the hearer or reader; in the latter, it refers to any individual, either from a restricted group or from among all of the same kind.[2] 'Sum' with specific reference can be most naturally translated as 'a certain,' 'one'; with non-specific reference its best translation is 'some,' 'some one (or other).'

The distinction between specific and non-specific reference is not, however, ideal for the discussion of the uses of 'sum' and its equivalents in Old English. A division into individualizing and non-individualizing functions seems more appropriate; this division is closely related to, but not quite identical with, the specific/non-specific one. We could say that the distinction made in terms of specificity is grammatical, whereas that based on the degree of individualization pertains to discourse. Non-specific reference is always non-individualizing but specific reference does not necessarily serve the purpose of individualization. The use of 'sum' should be called individualizing only when the referent specified is of relevance to the discourse that follows.[3]

There are, of course, no absolute criteria for estimating the importance of the referent to the discourse; some inferences can, however, be drawn from the amount of information given about the individual later in the context and from the role played by the references to this individual in the thematic structure of the text. Thus, the use of 'sum' in examples 1, 2, and 3 below is regarded as individualizing. In example 4 'sum' refers to a specific apple and in 5 to a specific period of time, but the referent is not singled out for its individual importance to the narration.

In the plural, 'sum' refers to a number of individuals, specific or non-specific, either from a restricted group or from among all of the same kind (examples 6 and 10 below). For obvious reasons, its individualizing force is often non-existent or of secondary importance even when the referents are individually definable.[4] For this reason, the discussion in this article mainly concentrates on the singular uses of 'sum.'

The following examples illustrate the different types of reference for 'sum':[5]

Specific reference

1   Hie on weg hruron
   bitere ond gebolgne;   bearhtm ongeaton,
   guðhorn galan.   Sumne Geata leod
   of flanbogan   feores getwæfde,
   yðgewinnes,   þæt him on aldre stod
   herestræl hearda;   he on holme wæs
   sundes þe sænra,   ðe hyne swylt fornam.   (*Beowulf* 1430b-6)

2 Eac we þæt gefrugnon,   þæt gefyrn bi þe
  soðfæst sægde   sum woðbora
  in ealddagum,   Esaias,   (*Christ I* 301-3)

3 To raþe hine gelette   lidmanna sum,
  þa he þæs eorles   earm amyrde.   (*The Battle of Maldon* 164-5)

4 Sum heo hire on handum bær,   sum hire æt heortan læg,
  æppel unsælga,   þone hire ær forbead
  drihtna drihten,   deaðbeames ofet,   (*Genesis* B 636-8)

5 Eac hit gesælde   æt sumum cierre
  ðæt se ilca het   ealle acwellan

þa ricostan   Romana witan   (*Meters of Boethius* 9.23-5)

6 Aras þa se rica,   ymb hine rinc manig,
þryðlic þegna heap;   sume þær bidon,
heaðoreaf heoldon,   swa him se hearda bebead.   (*Beowulf* 399-401)

Non-specific reference

7   Swa beoþ modsefan
dalum gedæled,   sindon dryhtguman
ungelice.   Sum on oferhygdo
þrumme þringeð,   þrinteð him in innan
ungemedemad mod;   sindan to monige þæt!   (*Vainglory* 21-5)

8 siððan bið him se wela onwended   and wyrð him wite gegarwod,
sum heard hearmscearu.   (*Genesis* B 431-2)

9   Me þæt þuhte
wrætlicu wyrd,   þa ic þæt wundor gefrægn,
þæt se wyrm forswealg   wera gied sumes, . . .   (*Riddle* 47.1-3)

10 Sume þa wuniað   on westennum,
secað ond gesittað   sylfra willum
hamas on heolstrum.   (*Guthlac I* 81-3)

In Old English the noun itself, without a determiner or quantifier, could denote a particular individual. For this reason, the addition of the individualizing 'sum' to the noun phrase was likely to make the expression more emphatic, and it has been generally accepted that 'sum' can also have a mainly intensifying function in Old English poetical texts.[6] Some older scholars have even suggested that 'sum' could be used with a definite reference, roughly as an equivalent of a demonstrative pronoun.[7]

'SUM' AND OTHER INDEFINITE PRONOUNS

The present-day distinction between indefinite pronouns used in assertions (ie positive declarative clauses) and non-assertions can be found as early as the Old English period. 'Sum' is infrequent in non-assertions; conversely, 'ænig' and 'awiht' are not normally used in assertions. Similarly, 'sum' and the indefinite pronouns of the 'hw-' paradigm are not, in general, interchangeable. The only exceptions are the compound pronouns formed with 'nat-': 'nathwilc,' 'nathwæt.'[8] But these pronouns are very infrequent: there are only four instances of 'nathwæt' in Old English poetry, all occurring in the *Riddles* (45.1; 54.5; 61.9; 93.27), and seven of 'nathwilc' (*Beowulf* 1513; 2053; 2215; 2223; 2233; *Elene* 73; *Christ I* 189). Not a single instance is recorded in the prose texts.

11   Ða se eorl ongeat,
þæt he [in] niðsele   nathwylcum wæs,
þær him nænig wæter   wihte ne scepede,   (*Beowulf* 1512b–14)

12   Is þæt wide cuð
þæt ic of þam torhtan   temple drytnes
onfeng freolice   fæmnan clæne,
womma lease,   ond nu gehwyrfed is
þurh nathwylces.   (*Christ I* 185b–9a)

13 Þuhte him wlitescyne   on weres hade
hwit ond hiwbeorht   hæleða nathwylc
geywed ænlicra   · þonne he ær oððe sið
gesege under swegle.   (*Elene* 72b–5a)

'Sum' had one real competitor, the numeral 'an.' Throughout the Old English period these two words occur side by side with specific or non-specific indefinite reference, and towards the end of the period they develop a dependent use which very much resembles that of the present-day indefinite article. This use is amply exemplified in prose texts, and there are also instances in poetry which may be included in this category. It is only in the Middle English period that the article-like use of 'sum' completely gives way to the indefinite article derived from 'an.'[9]

This does not mean that 'sum' and 'an' would have been fully interchangeable as words of indefinite reference in Old English poetry. The meaning of 'an' is influenced by its numerical origin; for this reason, the independent individualizing 'an' always refers to a member of a restricted group, either expressed or implied in the context.[10] The uses of 'sum,' on the other hand, are characterized by its pronominal qualities. When it is used independently, the implication of a restricted group is not always present: the meaning of 'sum' can be truly pronominal 'some one,' 'a person,' etc. 'One' develops a pronominal use of this kind only in the Middle English period.

Because of the basic numerical meaning of 'an,' its individualizing force is probably stronger than that of 'sum.' It can also be more naturally used for emphasis and intensification; the frequent uses of 'an' to indicate exclusiveness ('only,' 'alone') or identity ('one and the same') no doubt contributed to its intensifying capacity.[11]

SYNTACTIC USES OF 'SUM'

As can be seen from examples 1 to 10 above, 'sum' can be used either dependently or independently. The dependent 'sum' can be placed either before or after the noun; it can also be separated from the noun by one or more words.[12] Like all Old English quantifiers, the independent 'sum' is often preceded or followed by a partitive genitive indicating the group from which an individual is singled out. This group can be restricted or it can consist of all persons or things belonging to the class or species in question. In the last-mentioned case, the construction has roughly the same meaning as the phrase formed by the dependent 'sum' and a noun.

Table 1: Occurrence of 'sum' (singular forms only) in Old English poetry and in certain prose texts

	Indep with part gen	Independent	Dependent	Total
Beowulf	18	3	2	23
Other poetical texts	44	90	29	163
Anglo-Saxon Chronicle	8	9	27	44
Trans of Orosius	4	9	36	49
Trans of Bede (sample)	4	–	46	50
Ælfric's *Homilies* and *Lives* of Saints samples	1	1	98	100

There is a distinct difference between the frequencies of occurrence of the various syntactic constructions with 'sum' in poetry and prose, as can be seen from table 1.[13] Poetical texts favour the construction with the partitive genitive; on the whole, the independent singular 'sum' is less common in prose texts, particularly in the later ones. It mainly occurs in parallel constructions: 'on þysum gere tofor se here, sum on East Engle, sum on Norþhymbre' (*Anglo-Saxon Chronicle* A 897); 'and se wulf sum gelæcð, and þa oðre tostencð' (Ælfric *Cath Hom* I 238).

The popularity of the construction with the genitive plural in OE poetry is probably, to some extent, due to the demands of metre. 'Sum' belongs to the class of words called 'Satzteilpartikeln' by Kuhn and 'proclitics' by Bliss; these words are normally unstressed when they precede the stressed element and stressed when they follow it (displacement).[14] The construction partitive genitive + 'sum' conveniently provides both stresses while leaving room for the finite verb and/or other unstressed elements at the beginning of the half-line.

The dependent uninflected 'sum' occurs only five times before the noun in OE poetry. In two instances it is unstressed (*Genesis* B 317, example 39 below, and *Genesis* B 432, example 8 above). In three examples 'sum' alliterates and is thus obviously stressed. One of the three is *Christ I* 302 (example 2 above); the other two come from *Meters of Boethius*: 'þeah bið sum corn / sædes gehealden' (22.37); 'Him siððan onginð // sum tohopa swiðe leogan' (25.49b–50).

When 'sum' is inflected, it occurs more frequently before a noun: twenty times in the singular. In sixteen examples, 'sum' alliterates: 'snotra fengel;/ sume worde het' (*Beowulf* 2156); 'We ðe gesawon / æt sumum cyrre' (*Christ and Satan* 536); 'sarum settan, / þeah he sume hwile' (*Elene* 479); 'þæt sumes goodes / sidra gesceafta' (*Meters of Boethius* 25.55). Also *Partridge* 1; *Solomon and Saturn* 427 and *Meters of Boethius* 9.15; 9.23; 15.10; 16.7; 19.10; 20.96; 22.6; 24.64; 26.4; 26.87. The inflected 'sum' does not alliterate and is obviously unstressed only in *Christ I* 318 (example 41 below); *Solomon and Saturn* 230 and *Meters of Boethius* 7.28; 28.21. As can be seen from this list, and from the examples quoted above, the dependent antepositive 'sum' is particularly common in *The Meters of Boethius*, a late text which was strongly influenced by the prose translation of the same text. (Yet none of the corresponding prose passages have an equivalent structure with 'sum' + noun.) Even if the *Meters of Boethius* examples are not given full value as evidence of Old English metrical patterns, the other instances of the stressed inflected 'sum' imply that the traditional concept of unstressed proclitics may need modification.[15]

Displacement is also possible through postposition of the dependent 'sum,' but this position is not common in Old English poetry. There are five examples: 'þær bið egsa sum // ældum geywed' (*Riddle* 3.33b–4a); *Beowulf* 271; *Whale* 12 (examples 43 and 37 below); *Paris Psalter* 52.1; 57.4 (example 44 below).

In a single example 'sum' (unstressed) is separated from the following noun (*Juliana* 18-19, example 47 below).[16]

The influence of the demands of the metre on the preference of the partitive genitive construction is proved by the fact that in most instances 'sum' follows the partitive genitive. The only exceptions are 'Wæs Seon efne / sum þara kynincga' (*Paris Psalter* 134.11); *Judith* 275 (example 51 below); *Resignation* 77; *Panther* 8; *Meters of Boethius* 25.27. 'Sum' is separated from the preceding partitive genitive in four instances: 'Wæs hira Matheus sum' (*Andreas* 11b); *Riddle* 47.3; *Beowulf* 1266; *Meters of Boethius* 28.26 (examples 9, 56, and 52).

It is somewhat surprising that the independent 'sum,' without a partitive genitive, is unstressed in the great majority of instances, even in inflected forms. The following example shows the typical metrical arrangement:

14   duguþ eal gecrong,
    wlonc bi wealle.   Sume wig fornom,
    ferede in forðwege,   sumne fugel oþbær
    ofer heanne holm,   sumne se hara wulf
    deaðe gedælde,   sumne dreorighleor
    in eorðscræfe   eorl gehydde.   (*Wanderer* 79-84)

The number of the stressed instances of the independent 'sum' is difficult to estimate accurately because it only seldom alliterates,[17] but the figure is very low, around 10 per cent of all the instances in the singular. In expressions of the following type 'sum' is probably stressed:

15 Sumum þæt gegongeð   on geoguðfeore   (*Fortunes of Men* 10)

16 ac he missenlice   monna cynne
    gielpes styreð   on his giefe bryttað,
    sumum on cystum,   sumum on cræftum,
    sumum on wlite,   sumum on wige,   (*Gifts of Men* 104-7)

Table 2: Occurrence of 'an' (the individualizing use only) in Old English poetry

	Indep with part gen	Independent	Dependent	Total
Beowulf	4	8	10	22
Other poetical texts	9	9	60	78

The syntactic structures of 'an' are, of course, the same as those of 'sum,' but there are some interesting differences in the frequencies of the constructions, as can be seen from table 2.[18] The most conspicuous difference is the prevalence of the dependent use of 'an.' Out of the 70 instances, 'an' precedes the noun in 56 and follows in 14. It is separated from the following noun in seventeen instances and from the preceding one in two (for a discussion and examples, see Rissanen 200-12; 295-9). With a partitive genitive 'an' occurs less frequently than 'sum': it follows the genitive in eight instances (*Beowulf* 1037; 1294; 2599; *Genesis* A 221; 1077; 1645; *Christ III* 1171; *Meters of Boethius* 20.59) and precedes in five (*Beowulf* 1458; *Andreas* 1104; 1495; *Christ III* 1268; *Meters of Boethius* 28.9). This great variability in the positions of 'an' is probably due to the fact that, unlike 'sum,' it is normally stressed and alliterates in all positions except when used dependently immediately before the noun in an uninflected form as in 'Him þa secg hraðe / gewat siðian, // an gara laf, / se ða guðe genæs' (*Genesis* A 2018–19); 'An wiht is on eorþan / wundrum acenned' (*Riddle* 84.1). The antepositive dependent 'an,' separated from the noun, is a particularly favoured structure in OE poetry: 'oð ðæt an ongan // fyrene fremman / feond on helle' (*Beowulf* 100-1); 'Ic ane geseah / idese sittan' (*Riddle* 76.1); 'him eac þær wæs // an on gesyhðe, / engel ælmihtiges' (*Daniel* 271-2); also *Beowulf* 2210; 2280; *Riddles* 9.3; 10.4; 52.5; 56.1; *Andreas* 475; 1555; 1647 etc.

THE NON-INDIVIDUALIZING USE OF 'SUM'

As mentioned above, the 'discourse-based' division into individualizing and non-individualizing uses of 'sum' seems more appropriate than the strictly grammatical division into specific and non-specific reference. The most typical non-individualizing use of 'sum' is the 'enumerative' one, in which 'sum' occurs in a sequence of parallel constructions, usually at the beginning of the clause or phrase. In most instances, 'sum' is independent and is not linked with a partitive genitive. There are two outstanding themes with which this enumerative 'sum' is inseparably connected: following the editorial titles of two *Exeter Book* poems, these themes could be called 'The Fortunes of Men' and 'The Gifts of Men':

17   God ana wat
    hwæt him weaxendum   winter bringað!
        Sumum þæt gegongeð   on geoguðfeore
    þæt se endestæf   earfeðmæcgum

wealic weorþeð.   Sceal hine wulf etan,
har hæðstapa;   hinsiþ þonne
modor bimurneð.   Ne bið swylc monnes geweald!
    Sumne sceal hungor ahiþan,   sumne sceal hreoh fordrifan,
sumne sceal gar agetan,   sumne guð abreotan.
Sum sceal leomena leas   lifes neotan,
folmum ætfeohtan,   sum on feðe lef,
seonobennum seoc,   sar cwanian,
murnan meotudgesceaft   mode gebysgad.
[etc]   (*Fortunes of Men* 8b-20)

18   se þe ah domes geweald,
missenlice   geond þisne middangeard
leoda leoþocræftas   londbuendum.
    Sumum her ofer eorþan   æhta onlihð,
woroldgestreona.   Sum bið wonspedig,
heardsælig hæle,   biþ hwæþre gleaw
modes cræfta.   Sum mægenstrengo
furþor onfehð.   Sum freolic bið
wlitig on wæstmum.   Sum biþ woðbora,
giedda giffæst.   Sum biþ gearuwyrdig.
Sum bið on huntoþe   hreoðeadigra
dora dræfend.   Sum dyre bið
woruldricum men.
[etc]   (*Gifts of Men* 27b-39a)

The theme of 'the fortunes of men' can also be found in *Wanderer* 80-4 (example 14 above) and, with the plural forms of 'sum,' in the following three passages:

19   ond ic sumra fet
forbræc bealosearwum   sume in bryne sende,
in liges locan,   þæt him lasta wearð
siþast gesyne.   Eac ic sume gedyde
þæt him banlocan   blode spiowedan,
þæt hi færinga   feorh aleton
þurh ædra wylm.   Sume on yðfare
wurdon on wege   wætrum bisencte,
on mereflode,   minum cræftum
under reone stream.   Sume ic rode bifealh,
þæt hi hyra dreorge   on hean galgan

lif aletan.   Sume ic larum geteah,
to geflite fremede,   þæt hy færinga
ealde æfþoncan   edniwedan,
beore druncne.   (*Juliana* 472b-86a)

20   Wurdon heardingas
wide towrecene.   Sume wig fornam.
Sume unsofte   aldor generedon
on þam heresiðe.   Sume healfcwice
flugon on fæsten   ond feore burgon
æfter stanclifum,   stede weardedon
ymb Danubie.   Sume drenc fornam
on lagostreame   lifes æt ende.   (*Elene* 130b-7)

21 Ac Godwine hine þa gelette   and hine on hæft sette,
and his geferan he todraf,   and sume mislice ofsloh;
sume hi man wið feo sealde,   sume hreowlice acwealde
sume hi man bende,   sume hi man blende,
sume hamelode,   sume hættode.   (*Death of Alfred* 6-10)

These passages show how the theme can be applied not only to meditative
but also to narrative contexts. The plural 'sume' here refers to specific
individuals although with no purpose of individualization.

A version of 'the gifts of men' theme occurs in *Christ*:

22 Ða us geweorðade   se þas world gescop,
    godes gæstsunu,   ond us giefe sealde,
    uppe mid englum   ece staþelas,
    ond eac monigfealde   modes snyttru
    seow ond sette   geond sefan mionna.
    Sumum wordlaþe   wise sendeð
    on his modes gemynd   þurh his muþes gæst,
    æðele ondgiet.   Se mæg eal fela
    singan ond secgan   þam bið snyttru cræft
    bifolen on ferðe.   Sum mæg fingrum wel
    hlude fore hæleþum   hearpan stirgan,
    gleobeam gretan.   Sum mæg godcunde
    reccan ryhte æ.   Sum mæg ryne tungla
    secgan, side gesceaft.   Sum mæg searolice

wordcwide writan.   Sumum wiges sped
giefeð æt guþe,   þonne gargetrum
ofer scildhreadan   sceotend sendað,
flacor flangeweorc.   Sum mæg fromlice
ofer sealtne sæe   sundwudu drifan,
hreran holmþæce.   Sum mæg heanne beam
stælgne gestigan.   Sum mæg styled sweord,
wæpen gewyrcan.   Sum con wonga bigong,
wegas widgielle.   (*Christ II* 659-81a)

The passages dealing with these two themes, with 'sum' used enumeratively, account for 79 out of the 93 instances of the independent singular 'sum' without a partitive genitive in Old English poetry, and for 22 out of the 53 of the independent plural forms. The independent 'an' is not used in similar contexts. Owing to its numerical origin, the enumerative 'an' is mostly combined with 'oþer' ('-þridda') in Old English poetry. The only type in which the sequence 'an ... an' occurs in poetic texts is 'an æfter anum' (*Beowulf* 2461 etc).

Although it is impossible to estimate the popularity of these themes at various stages of the Old English period, it might not be too rash to suggest that the close association of the independent 'sum' with the theme of 'the fortunes of men,' in a variety of Old English poems, might be of importance in the interpretation of the following passages in which 'sum' is not enumerative:

23 Æt þæm ade wæs   eþgesyne
   swatfah syrce,   swyn ealgylden,
   eofer irenheard,   æþeling manig
   wundum awyrded;   sume on wæle crungon!   (*Beowulf* 1110-13)

Klaeber (Glossary sv 'sum') gives this passage as an example of 'sometimes, by litotes, "Many (a one),"' and Wrenn translates, 'notable men had fallen in the slaughter.' It seems to me that the real depth and emphasis of this expression can be appreciated if it is viewed against the background of 'the fortunes of men' theme which, as was shown above, is common in narrative contexts as well. 'Sume wig fornam' in *Wanderer* 80 and *Elene* 131, and 'sumne sceal gar agetan, / sumne guð abreotan' in *Fortunes of Men* 16, seem to offer close parallels to the *Beowulf* line. This simple comment would thus combine the ideas of a Christian belief in God's control over the fates of men – 'Swa missenlice / meahtig dryhten // geond eorþan sceat / eallum dæleð' (*Fortunes of Men* 64-5) – and the Germanic code of men being 'fæge.'

Klaeber also suggests the interpretation of 'sum' as 'many (a one)' in the following instance:

24 cwæð, he on mergenne   meces ecgum
  getan wolde,   sum[e] on galgtreowu[m]
  [fuglum] to gamene.   (*Beowulf* 2939-41)

A parallel to this passage can be found in *The Fortunes of Men*:

25   Sum sceal on geapum   gallgan ridan,
  seomian æt swylte,   oþþæt sawlhord,
  bancofa blodig,   abrocen weorþeð.
  Þær him hrefn nimeþ   heafodsyne,
  sliteð salwigpad   sawelleasne   (*Fortunes of Men* 33-7)

Against this background, it seems possible that the anticipatory allusion to Æschere's death, which begins the episode of Grendel's mother's raid to Heorot, had a deeper significance to the Anglo-Saxon audience than it has to a present-day reader:

26   Sigon þa to slæpe.   Sum sare angeald
  æfenræste,   swa him ful oft gelamp,
  siþðan goldsele   Grendel warode   (*Beowulf* 1251-3)

The immediate association of the independent 'sum' with the 'fortunes of men' theme would create a clear impression in the mind of the hearer of the kind of 'grievous penalty' one of the men had to pay for his night's sleep.

It is worth pointing out, though it may be a mere coincidence, that in four instances out of a total five (examples 1, 23, 24, 26, and 46) the independent 'sum' without a partitive genitive in *Beowulf* is associated with violent death. In *Beowulf* 1432 (example 1 above), 'sum' refers to the water-monster killed by Beowulf. The referent is, of course, quite different from the ones in the other passages quoted above, but the scene is elaborated in formulaic phrases echoing battle descriptions.

A variation of 'the gifts of men' theme can be traced in the following example in which 'sum' is not used enumeratively:

27 'Ac forhwan næron eorð[..]lan   ealle gedæled
   leodum gelice?   Sum to lyt hafað,
   godes grædig;   hine god seteð
   þurh geearnunga   eadgum to ræste.'   (*Solomon and Saturn* 344-7)

The following selection of examples gives an idea of the other types
of use of the non-individualizing 'sum.'
In parallel structures:

28 þa þær cwice meteð   cwelmende fyr,
   sume up, sume niþer,   ældes fulle.   (*Christ III* 958-9)

29 Weoxan word cwidum,   weras þeahtedon
   on healfa gehwær,   sume hyder, sume þyder,
   þrydedon ond þohton.   (*Elene* 547-9a)

30 Þonne is se finta   fægre gedæled,
   sum brun, sum basu,   sum blacum splottum
   searolice beseted.   (*Phoenix* 295-7a)

Also *Genesis* B 636 (example 4 above); *Guthlac II* 876; *Paris Psalter* 74.7;
Meters of Boethius 26.79-81; 28.7-8; 31.10-15.
    Indefinite non-specific reference is typical of the structure of the *Riddles*:

31 hwilum mægða sum   minne gefylleð
   bosm beaghroden;   (*Riddle* 14.8-9a)

32   Nu wile monna sum
   min flæsc fretan,   felles ne recceð,   (*Riddle* 77.4b-5)

Also *Riddles* 3.4; 14.15; 47.3; 73.23; 80.9.
    Non-specific reference is also common in the abstract philosophical
discourse to be found in *The Meters of Boethius*:

33 oþþe hi eft se reða   ren onhrereð
   sumes ymbhogan,   ungemet gemen.   (*Meters of Boethius* 7.27-8)

34 Ic ðe sæde ær   on ðisse selfan bec
   þæt sumes goodes   sidra gesceafta
   anlepra ælc   a wilnode   (*Meters of Boethius* 25.54-6)

Also *Meters of Boethius* 10.60; 22.37; 25.27; 25.50; 28.35.

The reference is non-specific when intention, fear, hypothesis, etc is expressed:

35 mynte se manscaða   manna cynnes
   sumne besyrwan   in sele þam hean   (*Beowulf* 712-13)

Even here, Klaeber's suggestion of a plural interpretation seems unnecessary.

36   Ic me onegan mæg
   þæt me wraðra sum   wæpnes ecge
   for freondmynde   feore beneote.   (*Genesis* A 1829a-31)

Also *Genesis* A 1034; 1828; 2701.

37 swa þæt wenaþ   wægliþende
   þæt hy on ealond sum   eagum wliten,   (*Whale* 11-12)

In the following instances, 'sum' refers to a number of alternatives enumerated in the context:

38 Simle þreora sum   þinga gehwylce,
   ær his tid aga,   to tweon weorþeð;
   adl oþþe yldo   oþþ ecghete
   fægum fromweardum   feorh oðþringeð.   (*Seafarer* 68-71)

39   Symble fyr oððe gar,
   sum heard geswinc   habban sceoldon.   (*Genesis* B 316b-17)

'An' is common in contexts with non-specific reference: 'Me bið gyrn witod, // gif mec onhæle / an onfindeð // wælgrim wiga' (*Riddle* 15.6-8); 'oft utan beweorpeð anre þecene' (*Riddle* 84.40); 'Ne gewuna wyrsa, / widan feore, // ængum eahta, / ac þu þe anne genim // to gesprecan symle / spella ond lara // rædhycgende' (*Precepts* 23-6); 'Ic eom anlic mid þe / anum neate' (*Paris Psalter* 72.18). Also *Solomon and Saturn* 393; *Paris Psalter* 78.2; 81.7. There seems to be little difference between the uses of 'sum' and 'an' in many of the instances quoted above, except that 'an' is more often used dependently. The uses of the non-specific or non-individualizing 'sum' are, however, more varied, and the number of the instances higher than with 'an.'

'Sum' and 'an' can be used side by side with words indicating a (period of) time in expressions meaning 'for a while,' 'for a certain period of time,' 'on some occasion.' 'Sum' is more frequent in this context, with eleven instances in poetry, most in *The Meters of Boethius*, as against the three instances of 'an.'

[40] We ðe gesawon   æt sumum cyrre,
þec gelegdon   on laðne bend
hæþene mid hondum;   (*Christ and Satan* 536-8a)

[41] þæt ðas gyldnan gatu   giet sume siþe
god sylf wile   gæstes mægne
gefælsian,   (*Christ I* 318-20a)

[42]   þeah hi sume hwile
gecure butan cræftum   cyninga dysegast,   (*Meters of Boethius* 15.10b-11)

Also *Elene* 479; *Meters of Boethius* 9.15; 9.23; 16.7; 22.6; 24.64; 28.21.

'An' occurs in 'Nu is þines mægnes blæd // ane hwile' (*Beowulf* 1761-2); *Descent into Hell* 5; *Genesis* b 369.

Finally, the reference is non-specific in negative clauses. Here the use of 'sum' or 'an' is of interest because 'ænig' is the pronoun normally used in these contexts. There are three instances with 'sum':

[43] Habbað we to þæm mæran   micel ærende
Deniga frean;   ne sceal þær dyrne sum
wesan, þæs ic wene.   (*Beowulf* 270-2a)

[44]   dytteð hyre earan,
þæt heo nele gehyran   heahgaldor sum
þæt snotre men   singað wið attrum.   (*Paris Psalter* 57.4, 3b-5)

[45] Hwy ge nu ne settan   on sume dune
fiscnet eowru,   þonne eow fon lysteð
leax oððe cyperan?   (*Meters of Boethius* 19.10-12a)

In the two last-quoted sentences, it seems that the use of 'some,' or an article, would be more appropriate than 'any' even in present-day English. This might imply that the utterances are basically assertive.[19]

The use of 'sum,' instead of 'ænig,' in *Beowulf* 271 is more problematic. The only explanation, though admittedly a rather lame one, is that 'ænig' would have made the line metrically unsatisfactory and the poet therefore resorted to 'sum.'

When 'an' is used in negative contexts, the meaning seems to be emphatic, 'not a single,' 'none at all': 'þæt þæra æfre ne com / an spell-boda' (*Paris Psalter* 105.10); *Guthlac I* 269; *Paris Psalter* 70.10; 72.11; 106.11; *Meters of Boethius* 10.38.

THE INDIVIDUALIZING USE OF 'SUM'

As mentioned above, the individualizing 'sum' singles out a person or thing that is of central importance to the discourse. A correspondence seems to exist between the syntactic structure and the individualizing function of 'sum' in Old English poetry. When 'sum' is used dependently, or independently without a partitive genitive, its function is seldom individualizing; this function is, on the other hand, typical of the construction in which 'sum' is preceded, or sometimes followed, by a partitive genitive.

In *Beowulf* 1432 (example 1 above), 'sum' is clearly individualizing. *Beowulf* 1251 (example 26 above) is less obvious in this respect. In addition to these two, there is only one instance in Old English poetry, again in *Beowulf*, in which the independent 'sum' without a partitive genitive is individualizing:

46 acigde of corðre   cyniges þegnas
   syfone (to)somne,   þa selestan
   eode eahta sum   under inwithrof
   hilderinc[a];   sum on handa bær
   æledleoman,   se ðe on orde geong.   (*Beowulf* 3121-5)

Attention is called to the second 'sum,' in line 3124. Even here, the need for individualization seems fairly weak.

The number of instances with the independent individualizing 'an' is also low, but the examples come from a variety of texts, and the individualizing force seems to be stronger than with 'sum': 'An wisode // mægenþrymmum mæst / þy he mære wearð' (*Exodus* 348b-9); 'Gesett hæfde he hie swa gesæliglice, / ænne hæfde he swa swiðne geworhtne, // swa mihtigne ... (*Genesis* B 252-3a); *Daniel* 91; *Battle of Maldon* 117.

In three instances, 'sum' is used dependently:

[47] Sum wæs æhtwelig   æþeles cynnes
rice gerefa.   Rondburgum weold,   (*Juliana* 18-19)

[48] Hyrde ic secgan gen   bi sumum fugle
wundorlicne[20]   (*Partridge* 1-2a)

Also *Christ I* 302, example 2 above.

The scantiness of the individualizing examples of dependent 'sum' is all the more noteworthy when it is compared with the richness of instances of the individualizing dependent 'an' (see Rissanen 295-9). It seems, indeed, that the construction partitive genitive + 'sum' was particularly favoured in contexts in which the need of individualization was strongly felt and the extra emphasis given to 'sum' by displacement most appropriate.

It is useful to divide the instances of partitive genitive + 'sum' according to whether the partitive genitive denotes a restricted group or refers to all individuals or the species or class in question.

In the following instances, the group is restricted:

[50] To raþe hine gelette   lidmanna sum
þa he þæs eorles   earm amyrde.   (*Battle of Maldon* 164-5)

[51] þa wearð sið ond late   sum to ðam arod
þara beadorinca,   þæt he in þæt burgeteld
niðheard neðde   (*Judith* 275-7a)

[52]   Þara is gehaten
Saturnus sum,   se hæfð ymb þritig
wintergerimes   weoruld ymbcirred.   (*Meters of Boethius* 28.25b-7)

[53] Bencþelu beredon;   hit geondbræded wearð
beddum ond bolstrum.   Beorscealca sum
fus on fæge   fletræste gebeag.   (*Beowulf* 1239-41)

Contrary to what Klaeber and Wrenn (notes) seem to think, nothing should prevent a simple interpretation of the last example, with the individualizing 'sum' in an anticipating expression so typical of the narrative technique of the *Beowulf* poet.[21] Æschere's fate is alluded to, for the second time, only a dozen lines later, in 'Sum sare angeald' (example 26 above).

A simple interpretation is also possible in the following passage:

54   Næfre ic maran geseah
    eorla ofer eorþan,   ðonne is eower sum,
    secg on searwum;   (*Beowulf* 247b-9a)

Wrenn (note) translates, 'a notable one among you,' interpreting 'sum' as an intensifying word. His translation need not be inaccurate, but it is difficult to see why this expression should have a basically different meaning from the others in which 'sum' singles out one member of a restricted group. The coastguard's oblique way of reference may well be in accordance with the code of polite conversation and address in Anglo-Saxon society, and the possible emphatic quality of the expression should be estimated against this background rather than be attributed to the intensifying capacity of 'sum' with the genitive of a pronoun. The coastguard continues with a third-person description: 'nis þæt seldguma, // wæpnum geweorðad, / næfne him his wite leoge, // ænlic ansyn.'

Also *Battle of Maldon* 149; *Andreas* 11; and, with weaker individualization, *Genesis* A 1093; *Judith* 148; *Paris Psalter* 134.11.

This use of 'an' is also fairly common (twelve instances): 'hraðe heo æþelinga / anne hæfde // fæste befangen' (*Beowulf* 1294-5); 'Ða se tan gehwearf // efne ofer ænne / ealdgesiða, // se wæs ...' (*Andreas* 1103-5). The numerical meaning of 'an' is often present. In four examples, 'an' is used in contrast with 'oþer' ('-þridda'): 'Hwæt, þu, wuldres god, // þone anne naman / eft todældes, // fæder, on feower; / wæs þara folde an // and wæter oðer ...' (*Meters of Boethius* 20.57-60); *Genesis* A 221; *Christ III* 1268; *Meters of Boethius* 28.9. In three examples, the partitive genitive is a pronoun referring to a preceding numeral or quantifier: 'eahta mearas // ... þara anum stod // sadol searwum fah' (*Beowulf* 1035-8); *Genesis* A 1077; *Christ III* 1171.

In the following instances, 'sum' occurs in a non-referring expression, as a predicate complement:[22]

55   He wæs þeara sum;
    ne won he æfter worulde,   ac he in wuldre ahof
    modes wynne.   (*Guthlac I* 398b-400)

56   þanon woc fela
    geosceaftgasta;   wæs þæra Grendel sum,
    heorowearh hetelic,   (*Beowulf* 1265b-7)

A special use of 'sum' with a partitive genitive indicating a restricted group is the combination of a numeral or quantifier ('manig,' 'feawa') and 'sum.' This construction, and the question whether the individual referred to is included in the number expressed by the numeral or not, has been amply discussed in the past.[23] There is no need to repeat that discussion here; it is worth pointing out, however, that 'sum' can occur in subject, object, complement, or appositive position, and that, in most cases, the referent is familiar, ie, it has been defined earlier in the context.

57 Hæfde se goda   Geata leoda
    cempan gecorone   þara þe he cenoste
    findan mihte;   fiftyna sum
    sundwudu sohte,   (*Beowulf* 205-8a)

58 Gewat þa twelfa sum   torne gebolgen
    dryhten Geata   dracan sceawian;   (*Beowulf* 2401-2)

59 Huru se snotra   sunu Wihstanes
    acigde of corðre   cyniges þegnas
    syfone (to)somne,   þa selestan,
    eode eahta sum   under inwithrof
    hilderinc[a]   (*Beowulf* 3120-4a)

60 He mec þær on innan   unsynnigne,
    dior dædfruma   gedon wolde
    manigra sumne;   (*Beowulf* 2089-91a)

61 Ofereode þa   æþelinga bearn
    steap stanhliðo,
    . . .
    he feara sum   beforan gengde
    wisra monna wong sceawian   (*Beowulf* 1408-13)

Also *Beowulf* 3061; *Genesis* A 2203; *Andreas* 1311; *Christ III* 1275; *Guthlac I* 173; 709.
In a number of instances, the group denoted by the partitive genitive

is not restricted but comprises all individuals of the class or species in question. This construction is thus roughly equivalent in meaning to the dependent use of 'sum' – 'gumena sum' meaning 'a man,' and 'wundra sum' 'a wonder.' A similar use of 'an' cannot be found in Old English poetry. Many scholars, most notably Wrenn in his *Beowulf* edition, believe that 'sum' is here strongly emphatic and intensifying. The combination with 'sum' is certainly more emphatic than the use of the noun without 'sum,' and the displacement adds to the weight of the phrase. But here we face the difficult problem whether we should treat 'sum' as intensifying in all instances of this type, or whether, following Wrenn, we should only do it when the meaning of the phrase seems to justify this interpretation. In the former case, we are compelled to read intensification into many passages which do not seem to deserve it; in the latter, we become victims of circular reasoning: the examples do not give evidence of an inherent intensifying force of 'sum.' The intensifying interpretation of 'sum' would seem to me justifiable mainly in those instances in which the use of 'sum' cannot be naturally explained in any other way, such as by the need of individualization.

In the following examples, 'sum' is individualizing and thus these instances cannot be used as evidence of the intensifying force of 'sum':

62   þa metodes ðegn
   ufan engla sum,   Abraham hlude
   stefne cygde   (*Genesis* A 2908-10a)

63 Her is gefered   ofer feorne weg
   æðelinga sum   innan ceastre,   (*Andreas* 1173-4)

64 Ða wæs ricra sum   on Rome byrig   (*Meters of Boethius* 1.46)

Also *Riddle* 26.1; *Andreas* 967; *Seasons for Fasting* 123; *Panther* 8.

The need for individualizing is less obvious when the referent is an inanimate noun:

65 Þa wæs be mæste   merehrægla sum,
   segl sale fæst;   (*Beowulf* 1905-6a)

66 Gespræc þa se goda   gylpworda sum   (*Beowulf* 675)

67   and seo byrne sang

gryreleoða sum.   (*Battle of Maldon* 284b–5a)

68 Ða ongon se wisdom   his gewuman fylgan,
gliowordum gol,   gyd æfter spelle,
song soðcwida   sumne þa geta,   (*Meters of Boethius* 7.1–3)

But the lack of the need for individualizing does not, in itself, offer
conclusive evidence of the intensifying force of 'sum,' cf examples 31
and 32 above.

The intensifying quality of 'sum' is more likely when 'sum' is used
in a predicative expression:

69   Þa þæt sweord ongan
æfter heaþoswate   hildegicelum,
wigbil wanian;   þæt wæs wundra sum,
þæt hit eal gemealt   ise gelicost.   (*Beowulf* 1605b–8)

70   Nu sceal heard and steap
on þam wicum   wyrde bidan,
drihtnes domes,   hwonne dogora rim,
woruld gewite.   Þæt is wundra sum,
þara ðe geworhte   wuldres aldor.   (*Genesis* A 2571–5)

71 Ða cwæð se ðe wæs   cyninges ræswa,
wis and wordgleaw: 'Þæt is wundra sum
þæt we ðær eagum   on lociað....'   (*Daniel* 416–18)

72   Hwæt, þæt wundra sum
monnum þuhte,   þæt he ma wolde
afrum onfengum   earme gæstas
hrinan leton,   ond þæt hwæþre gelomp!   (*Guthlac I* 517b–20)

73 [Tir] biþ tacna sum,   healdeð trywa wel
wiþ æþelingas,   a biþ on færylde,
ofer nihta genipu   næfre swiceþ.   (*Rune Poem* 48–50)

74   Nu earttu sceaðana sum,[24]
in fyrlocan   feste gebunden.   (*Christ and Satan* 57b–8)

In the last two examples, 'tacna' and 'sceaðana' may also indicate restricted groups of signs (or heavenly bodies) and fallen angels.[25] Cf, also

75 Hwæt, ge nu eagum to   on lociað
    folca leofost,   færwundra sum,
    hu ic sylfa sloh   and þeos swiðre hand
    grene tacne   garsecges deop.   (*Exodus* 278–81)

In Old English prose, in which the article-like use of 'an' and 'sum' is very common, the noun in a complement position was normally used without a determiner.[26] In poetry, in addition to the examples quoted above, the singular 'sum' occurs as a predicate complement only when the expression indicates membership of a restricted group (examples 55 and 56 above). Consequently, in the examples quoted above, 'sum' may well have been used mainly for intensification. This suggestion is supported by the meaning of the noun in genitive plural and perhaps even by the fact that three of the passages occur in direct speech.[27]

The two poetical occurrences of 'an' in a complement position are regarded as intensifying by Klaeber (Glossary, sv 'an'): 'þæt wæs an foran / ealdgestreona' (*Beowulf* 1458); 'þæt wæs an cyning // æghwæs orleahtre' (*Beowulf* 1885-6).

Following the same line of argumentation, the non-referring 'sum' could be intensifying when the expression stands in variation:

76   Dægwoma becwom
    ofer garsecge,   godes beacna sum,
    morgen mæretorht;   mægen forð gewat,   (*Exodus* 344–6)

77 [yr] byþ æþelinga   and eorla gehwæs
    wyn and wyrþmynd,   byþ on wicge fæger,
    fæstlic on færelde,   fyrdgeatewa sum.   (*Rune Poem* 84-6)

But see my note on examples 73 and 74 above.

Finally, there are a few instances in which 'sum' occurs in subject or object position, referring to a person or thing that has been defined earlier in the context, and thus might appear to be used for a definite reference.

78 Sona þæt onfunde   se ðe floda begong
    heorogifre beheold   hund missera,
    grim ond grædig,   þæt þær gumena sum

ælwihta eard   ufan cunnode.   (*Beowulf* 1497-1500)

79   he þæt sona onfand,
ðæt hæfde gumena sum   goldes gefandod,
heahgestreona.   (*Beowulf* 2300b-2a)

80 Swa se ðeodsceaða   þreo hund wintra
heold on hrusan   hordærna sum
eacencræftig,   (*Beowulf* 2278-80a)

81 Hraþe wæs to bure   Beowulf fetod,
sigoreadig secg.   Samod ærdæge
eode eorla sum,   æþele cempa
self mid gesiðum   þær se snotera bad,
hwæþer him Alwalda   æfre wille
æfter weaspelle   wyrpe gefremman.   (*Beowulf* 1310-15)

82 Him þa hildedeor   [h]of modigra
torht getæhte,   þæt hie him to mihton
gegnum gangan;   guðbeorna sum
wicg gewende,   word æfter cwæð: (*Beowulf* 312-15)

In the first and second examples, to my mind, the use of 'sum' stands as evidence of the *Beowulf* poet's narrative and dramatic skill. The events have been described from the point of view of Grendel's mother and the dragon: for them, the identity of the intruder is not known. The wording of the passages is strikingly similar. The use of 'an' in 'Ða ic on hlæwe gefrægn / hord reafian, // eald enta geweorc / anne mannan' (*Beowulf* 2773-4) seems to belong to the same class of vividly descriptive expression. In this example it is also possible that a kind of generic contrast 'ent' / 'mann' is implied.

In *Beowulf* 2279, the most plausible explanation is that offered by Klaeber for the use of 'an' in some passages: 'It looks as if the poet, after a digression, were starting afresh' (Note on *Beowulf* 100). The sentence begins with the adverbial 'swa,' a marker of a new episode in *Beowulf*.

But (contrary to Klaeber's opinion expressed in the note on *Beowulf* 100), these suggestions do not explain satisfactorily the use of 'sum' in *Beowulf* 1312 and 314. The standard explanations have been that 'sum' is used either as a demonstrative pronoun (Heyne-Schücking-v. Schaubert) or as an intensifying word (Wrenn). Neither of these suggestions is supported by the uses of 'sum' described in this article or by later evidence of the development of the word. To attribute to 'sum' a capacity of definite reference in referring expressions would run counter to its inherent functions of indefinite reference and specification or individualization. It is highly unlikely that the mere purpose of intensification would justify such a deviation from the system of indefinite pronouns in Old English. There are no traces of this kind of use of 'sum' in Old English prose or in the later stages of the English language.[28]

Thus, if 'sum' is demonstrative or intensifying in these two examples, the use must be attributed to the freedom of poetic syntax or to the loose use of formulaic expressions to fill in a half-line. Both explanations are possible but not particularly attractive. A more satisfactory interpretation can be found if we have a look at the other constructions in which 'sum' in a subject position, preceded by a partitive genitive, refers to a person defined in the immediately preceding context. These features occur in the combination of a numeral or quantifier and 'sum,' the type 'fiftyna sum,' 'manigra sum.' This construction is particularly common in *Beowulf* as is shown by examples 57 to 61 above. It is not impossible that the same syntactic arrangement might be extended to contexts in which the group is indicated by a noun instead of a numeral or quantifier. If this is the case, 'eorla' and 'guðbeorna' do not denote all warriors but a restricted group – a retinue or a band of soldiers.

In *Beowulf* 1312, the meaning '(as?) one of the warriors,' 'with his retinue,' fits in with the context excellently: in fact, 'self mid gesiðum' in the following line offers an exact variant to 'eorla sum' interpreted in this way. Although the scene is described in less explicit terms in the other passage under discussion, a close reading supports the suggestion that the coastguard was not alone but leader of a small troop. His arrogant first address to Beowulf and his men displays self-confidence and strength:

[83] Hwæt syndon ge   searohæbbendra,
     byrnum werede,   þe þus brontne ceol
     ofer lagustræte   lædan cwomon,
     hider ofer holmas?   [Hwæt, ic hwi]le wæs
     endesæta,   ægwearde heold,
     þe on land Dena   laðra nænig
     mid scipherge   sceðþan ne meahte.
     No her cuðlicor   cuman ongunnon
     lindhæbbende,   ne ge leafnesword

guðfremmendra　gearwe ne wisson,
maga gemedu.　(*Beowulf* 327-47)

Had the coastguard been alone, his duty would no doubt have been to ride immediately to Heorot to warn Hrothgar of the intruders rather than stay to inquire who they were. In addition, lines 293-6 'swylcne ic maguþegnas / mine hate // wið feonda gehwone / flotan eowerne // ... arum healdan,' imply the presence of a band of men. According to this interpretation, the coastguard escorts Beowulf and his men until they can see Heorot and then turns back with his fellow warriors – 'guðbeorna sum' – to guard Beowulf's ship.

My interpretation of these two passages is hypothetical, but it saves us from a reading which would violate the basic type of reference of 'sum.' In *Beowulf* there are half-lines which very closely correspond to the structures dicussed: the most obvious parallels are 3123a 'eode eahta sum' and 207b 'fiftyna sum,' examples 59 and 57 above. Furthermore, there is one passage in Old English poetry in which 'sum' in a subject position, preceded by a partitive genitive denoting a restricted group, refers to an individual defined in the immediately preceding context:

84　　　　　　　　Him wæs an fæder,
　　leof leodfruma,　landriht geþah,
　　frod on ferhðe,　freomagum leof.
　　Cende cneowsibbe　cenra manna
　　heahfædera sum,　halige þeode,
　　Israela cyn,　onriht godes,　(*Exodus* 353b-8)

Whether 'sum' in the two *Beowulf* passages is the subject of the sentence or a kind of appositive expression, with the subject pronoun understood, is a question that must be left unanswered in the present context. As can be seen from examples 57 to 61, both alternatives seem possible when 'sum' is appended to a numeral or quantifier in the genitive plural.

CONCLUDING REMARKS

In this article, it has been my intention to show how 'sum' and 'an' compete as pronouns of indefinite, non-generic reference in Old English poetry, just as they do in the prose. The other pronouns ('nathwylc,' etc) are of little significance as variants of 'an' and 'sum': 'ænig' and the pronouns of the 'hw-' paradigm are clearly restricted to their own typical functions (non-assertive expressions, generic reference) even at this early stage of the development of the English language. Perhaps owing to its numeral origin and its readiness to carry stress and alliteration, the uses of 'an' seem more varied and flexible than those of 'sum.' But 'sum' possesses a number of uses in which it is, generally speaking, not replaceable by 'an,' most notably as an independent pronoun with non-specific reference, and with a partitive genitive which does not denote a restricted group but refers to all members of a species or class.

The particular attraction of the study of 'sum' (like other pronominal words) lies in the fact that it gains its real significance from the context, from its referent and from the words it is linked with. As these words are often the most central elements of the text, they may render even 'sum' a kind of relevance which makes it as interesting a topic for analysis as are the words which have greater semantic content in isolation.

NOTES

1 The most exhaustive survey of the uses of 'sum' is Peter Süsskand *Geschichte des umbestimmten Artikels im Alt- und Frühmittelenglischen* (Halle 1935). Eugen Einenkel's many writings, notably 'Das englische Indefinitum' *Anglia* 26 and 27 (1903-4) 461-572; 1-204, contain interesting observations on the uses of Old English indefinite pronouns. See also Matti Rissanen *The Uses of 'One' in Old and Early Middle English* (Helsinki 1967). I am indebted to Dr Bruce Mitchell for allowing me to see the page proofs of the chapters on 'sum' and other indefinite pronouns before the publication of his *Old English Syntax* (Oxford 1985). I am also most grateful to Dr Mitchell and to Professor Fred C. Robinson for their valuable comments on the typescript version of this article.

2 A good general survey of the main types of reference can be found in John Lyons *Semantics* 2 vols (Cambridge 1977) 1: 177-97. Poul Christophersen's *The Articles* (Copenhagen and London 1939) is still a useful basic work for the discussion of the questions of individualization from the point of view of the development of the English article system. See also M.V. Aldridge *English Quantifiers* (Amersham 1982).

   Randolph Quirk et al *A Grammar of Contemporary English* (London 1972) does not recognize the non-specific, non-generic indefinite reference, but includes cases of this type in the class of specific reference (149-50 §4.31). It is possible that this distinction is related to that of assertions and non-assertions because the non-specific indefinite reference typically occurs in negative, interrogative, conditional, or comparative clauses or in commands and requests. But it is also frequent in assertions (see examples 7 to 10 below). This distinction is of importance in the discussion of the development of the uses of the indefinite pronouns and the indefinite article (cf Süsskand 50-1 and Rissanen 53-4 and 268-74).

3 Interesting observations on degrees of specificity, with examples taken from a variety of languages, can be found in C.B. Comrie *Language Universals and Linguistic Typology* (London 1981) 128-31. I am indebted to Miss Terttu Nevalainen for this reference.

4 The use of 'sum,' in plural forms, before cardinal numerals ('sume hundred scipa') cannot be found in Old English poetry and, for this reason, it has not been discussed in the present article. See, for instance, Mitchell *Syntax* 153-5 §§389-92.

5 The references to *Beowulf* are from Fr. Klaeber's edition, *Beowulf and The Fight at Finnsburg* 3rd ed (Boston 1950). All other poetic passages are quoted from the *ASPR*.

6 See, in particular, C.L. Wrenn's *Beowulf with the Finnesburg Fragment* 3rd ed rev W.F. Bolton (New York 1973), Glossary sv 'sum.' Cf Mitchell *Syntax* 159 §401.

7 See Moritz Heyne and L.L. Schücking eds *Beowulf*. Mit ausführlichem Glossar, rev Else von Schaubert 18th ed (Paderborn 1963).

8 'Nat-'<'ne wat.' Alistair Campbell *Old English Grammar* (Oxford 1959) 294 §723 also mentions the form 'nathwa,' but no instances are recorded in *A Microfiche Concordance to Old English* compiled by Antonette diPaolo Healey and Richard L. Venezky (Toronto 1980).

9 See Süsskand 59; Rissanen 261-303.

10 See Rissanen 54-77.

11 An extensive comparative survey of the sets of pronominal forms with indefinite reference in a number of languages would further illustrate the subtleties of the early development of the pronominal and article system in Old English as well as in other languages (cf Comrie's findings referred to in n3 above). The uses of Finnish indefinite pronouns, for instance, show striking similarities to the Old English ones; the parallelism is of particular significance as Finnish has no articles.

12 In two articles – 'The Old English Appositional Construction Exemplified by *sume his geferan*' *ES* 50 (1969) 225-35, and 'Aspects of the Syntax of Quantifiers in Old English' *Norwegian Journal of Linguistics* 31 (1977) 47-94 – Trygve Heltveit discusses in detail the appositive use of 'sum.' This construction is also thoroughly dealt with by Mitchell (*Syntax* 159-69 §§402-16), whose views differ from Heltveit's in some essential points. As the type 'sume his geferan' does not occur in OE poetry, I have not discussed it in

this article. The type 'sume hie' can be occasionally found in poetic texts (*Christ and Satan* 540; *Meters of Boethius* 26.79; 28.5; *Death of Alfred* 8-9). 'Þa sume' occurs in *Seafarer* 56.

13 The figures for *Beowulf* are given separately to show the conspicuous frequency of the use with the partitive genitive and the infrequency of other constructions. Some other poems might show a similar tendency, but the figures are too low for comparisons. As will be shown below, the instances of the dependent use and of the independent use without a partitive genitive tend to cluster in a few poems.

In the plural, the independent use prevails (53 instances). There are six instances of the dependent use and only one of the partitive genitive.

The figures from *Bede* and from Ælfric's *Catholic Homilies* and *Lives of the Saints* are based on the fifty first instances of 'sum' from each text, as listed in the *Microfiche Concordance to Old English* (*Bede* 58-342; *Homilies* 42-400; *Lives* 4-348).

14 Hans Kuhn 'Zur wortstellung und -betonung im altgermanischen' *BGdSL* 57 (1933) 1-109; A.J. Bliss *The Metre of 'Beowulf'* rev ed (Oxford 1967) 6. Displacement has been recently discussed, eg, by Lydia Fakundiny 'The Art of Old English Verse Composition' *RES* ns 21 (1970) 129-42 and 257-66, and C.B. Kendall 'The Metrical Grammar of *Beowulf*: Displacement' *Speculum* 58 (1983) 1-30.

15 Cf D. Slay 'Some Aspects of the Technique of Composition of Old English Verse' *TPS* (1952) 1-14.

16 It is a matter of taste whether 'sumne' in 'simle suð oþþe norð / sumne gemetað// gydda gleawne, / geofum unhneawne // se þe ...' (Widsith 138-40) is regarded as independent or dependent. In table 1, this instance is included in the figure for independent use. There are two instances (*Solomon and Saturn* 183; *Riddle* 10.8) in which a plural form of 'sum' is separated from the following noun.

17 The only exception in the singular use is 'þonne ic winde sceal // sincfag swelgan / of sumes bosme' (*Riddle* 14.14b-15). There are a few examples in which the plural forms of 'sum' alliterate (*Meters of Boethius* 28.7; 28.8; 28.35; *Juliana* 472; 475; 490; *Seafarer* 56).

18 In the present article, the figures and other generalizations concerning 'an' only refer to those cases in which it is used in ways similar to the uses of 'sum' (the so-called individualizing use of 'an' referred to in Rissanen 1967).

19 Cf Quirk et al 224 §4.127.

20 There is a gap in the manuscript after 'wundorlicne,' but the general development of the theme can be guessed by the model offered by *The Panther*:

49   We bi sumum hyrdon

> wrætlice gecynd   wildra secgan
> firum freamærne   feorlondum on
> eard weardian,   edles neotan
> æfter dunscrafum.   Is þæt deor pandher
> bi noman haten,   (8b–13)

21 See also Mitchell 156 §395.

22 Cf Lyon's distinction between a referring expression and a predicative expression: 'The expression we use in order to refer to what we are talking about is typically the subject of the sentence, and this is combined with a predicative expression (which is typically the grammatical predicate)' (1:178).

23 See the standard dictionaries of Old English, and the notes and glossaries of the editions of Old English texts. See also J. Ernst Wülfing's articles 'Ae. *sum* mit dem genitiv einer grundzahl' in *E Stn* 17 (1892) 285-91; 24 (1898) 463 and 26 (1899) 455; and Mitchell 157-9 §§397-400.

24 The manuscript reads 'earm sceaða,' followed by 'na sum,' erased.

25 Wrenn, in his *Beowulf* edition (Glossary sv 'sum') and in *A Study of Old English Literature* (London 1967) 16, translates 'T is a most important symbol,' and T.A. Shippey *Poems of Wisdom and Learning in Old English* (Cambridge 1976) 83, 'Tir is a constellation'; see also his note on 'tacna.'

26 See Süsskand 53.

27 The intensifying use of 'sum' would be, at least to some extent, similar to the present-day (especially American) use of 'some' and 'one' in expressions of the type 'I call that some poem'; 'It's one grand and glorious feeling.' See, for instance, R.W. Zandvoort 'Pregnant *One*' *ES* 22 (1940) 199-200, and Fred C. Robinson 'The American Element in *Beowulf*' *ES* 49 (1968) 510.

28 Even in present-day English it does not seem possible to use the intensifying 'some' in referring expressions. Cf 'He beat me easily – (he is) some chess-player!' But in 'Some chess-player beat me easily' 'some' can only have indefinite specific reference.

PART IV

SOURCES AND WORDS

The distinction between literary and historical scholarship is not always clear.

A Bibliography of Publications on Old English Literature to the end of 1972 1980

JAMES E. CROSS

Identification:
Towards Criticism

I HAD THOUGHT that I could not, at present, contribute to a volume on critical method for Stanley Greenfield since I have been almost fully occupied in recent years with identification of sources for the 'narrative' *Old English Martyrology* (OEM). But I was reminded that any identification of thought in a work, or method of composition, is an aid to understanding, so to explication and, eventually, to evaluation. Recently published discussions of sections of OEM indicating attitudes of its composer, if accepted as valid, can be said to have made the martyrologist a different kind of writer from the one surmised by George Herzfeld.[1]

Relevant scholarship, for me, aids critical evaluation in limiting, although not entirely negating, personal and subjective reaction or choice. Such scholarship entails the understanding of the parts, or even single statements, against the discovered emphases of the whole, the comparison of the whole against works of similar function and kind (if they exist), and of similar style in order to recognize similarities but also differences,[2] and the consideration of the general thought or sequences of thought against those of the age. As a 'historical' critic I attempt to read and understand the work at centre against all that I know of and think to be relevant. This is not to say, as some have misunderstood, that one starts from the outside and moves inside. There should be a continual interplay in the critic's mind and memory between the thought in the studied work and those elsewhere.

My work on OEM began, in fact, with one of these critical principles. Some years ago I was asked some questions about the reading of the martyrologist for which I had no firm answer. Although I had noted a direct source for a section I had not then thoroughly considered the whole, but then began. For certain sections which already had clearly

signalled sources such as the named *Historia Ecclesiastica* of Bede and
Adómnan's *De Locis Sanctis*,[3] it soon became clear that the composer
understood his Latin sources, abstracting from these with echo of word
and phrase to form his own summary accounts. Such a conclusion also
obtained for entries in OEM without named source, but for which a 'vita,'
a 'passio' or other work such as Bede's *Historia Abbatum* or Gregory's
Homiliae in Evangelia[4] existed in a comparatively stable text, or in a
modern collated edition from many manuscripts such as the *Liber
Pontificalis* in Mommsen's edition.[5] For the last case it was apparent
that OEM sometimes equated words which were not those chosen for the
edited text, but which were extant in one or more of the variant texts.[6]
Nevertheless, it appeared that the composer followed closely *a* Latin text
before him, even though the actual manuscript(s) which he used may
not be extant now. The number of notices read was by now considerable
enough to indicate persistent attitudes or methods of the composer, in
other words, discovered emphases in the work. Yet many sources designated
by Herzfeld for other separate entries did not have the same echo of
significant detail (name, number, image, word, and phrase). Common
sense (and critical principle if need be) demanded that the composer's
method had not changed but that Herzfeld had, often, not been able
to see the appropriate Latin text in print at his time. In 1900 he was
limited for some saints' lives to texts in the earlier volumes of *Acta
Sanctorum* (some of which are printed from one manuscript only and
some from manuscripts which are difficult to trace and date), to texts
in Mombritius, *Sanctuarium seu Vitae sanctorum* (published about 1480)[7]
and to texts which he could find in other early printed editions. Nor
did Herzfeld have the advantage of the *Bibliotheca Hagiographica Latina*
(BHL),[8] published at the turn of the century, which distinguishes and
numbers different versions of saints' lives, and also subdivisions of
individual versions, with reference to the printings of these where they
occurred. Using BHL I began with some early printings unseen by Herzfeld
but soon realized for some entries that a comparison did not produce
the results that the discovered emphases demanded. Unpublished manuscript texts were clearly needed, preferably of the period before and during
the time when the ninth-century OEM was being composed. By collecting
manuscript texts[9] of individual saint's lives and noting variant readings
it could be possible to create the sequences of words which the martyrologist saw. My published results for certain entries indicate, to me
at least, that it was possible. These results have confirmed the persistent
emphases so that, now, where a sufficiently close attention to the extant

Latin texts (known to me) *cannot* be demonstrated, I believe it is because I have not found the Latin words which the martyrologist read. I illustrate success and present failure for a few entries one of which is a composite entry (another demonstrable habit of the composer).

PANCRAS (12 MAY)

OEM reads (with my itemization):[10]

(i) On ðone twelftan dæg þæs monðes bið Sancte Pancrates ðrowung þæs æþelan cnihtes, se wæs fiftene geara ða he for Cristes geleafan deað geðrowade. (ii) He wæs acenned on Frigia ceastre of æþelum cynne; his fæder nama wæs Cledones ond his modor noma wæs Cyriade, (iii) ac he wæs gefullwad æt Rome fram Sancte Cornelie ðæm papan. (iv) Ða ongan Dioclitsianus (variant: Dioclitianus) se hæþna casere hine læran þæt he Criste wiðsoce, (v) ond cwæð þæt he hine ðonne wolde swa weligne gedon swa he his sunu wære. (vi) Þa he þæt ne geþafade, ða het he hine beheafdian on ðæm wege ðe æt Rome is nemned Aurelia. Ðær is his lichoma bebyrged, (vii) ond his cirice getimbred oð þysne ondweardan dæg.

Significant details (apart from the obit)[11] within this notice form a pattern of information which allows rejection of some subdivisions of the *one version* of the *Passio S. Pancratii* noted as BHL 6240-27.[12] BHL 6427[13] names Valerianus as persecutor, instead of Diocletian (item iv), omits to name the mother (item ii) and does not have the image (item v). BHL 6425[14] omits the mother (item ii) and the pope's name (item iii). BHL 6420[15] does not mention the baptism or the pope (item iii). BHL 6422[16] (reputedly abbreviated) and BHL 6426[17] do not actually note the decollation, but have all other details and a decollation could be assumed from their statement: 'Tunc iussit Dioclitianus duci eum in viam Aureliam ibique capitalem subire sententiam.' But a more recent study of the cult of Pancras[18] has postulated a stemma for the texts of the legend and suggests that the text printed in A SS (BHL 6421)[19] was the nearest to the original. Variant texts of this edited text include all the details in OEM. Manuscript variants (BHL 6421) are: Graz, Universitäts-Bibliothek ms 412 fols 145r-146v (saec IX),[20] Brussels, Bollandist's Library Codex 14 fols 9v-10v (saec IX med-IX 3/4),[21] Vatican Regina lat ms 516 fols 95v-96v (saec IX/x)[22] and the English manuscript Oxford, Bodleian Library ms Fell 4 (saec XI ex, Salisbury).[23] For item ii A SS §1 tells us that the events happened: 'apud provinciam Phrygiam in civitate Synnada, post mortem Cleonii et coniugis eius Cyriadae, qui de nobile genere erant orti, quorum filius erat Pancratius' but Graz 412 reads: 'in civitate Frigia . . . Cleodonii . . . Cyriade . . .' almost to equate OEM. As A ss notes,[24] manuscripts which vary on the spelling of the names, include 'Cledonius' as in OEM. For item iii A ss §2 names the pope 'Caius' but Graz 412 and the others call him 'Cornelius' as OEM does. The persecutor (item iv) is 'Diocletianus' (Dioclicianus) in A ss §3 and variants as in OEM. For the place of execution (item vi) all texts of BHL 6421 read as BHL 6426 (cited above) does and all say that he was actually beheaded ('decollatus' A ss §4). and buried ('Octabilla . . . sepelivit in sepulcro novo quarto Idus Majas' A ss §4). That he was buried 'there' ('ðær') could have been assumed from the 'passio,' since there was no 'translatio,' but also from a recension of the *Liber Pontificalis* (a proven source for some notices in OEM)[25] which could also have been the basis for the extra statement (item vii) (not in any of the passiones) that 'his church is built up to the present day.' Among the events recorded during the pontificate of Honorius was that he 'fecit basilica beato Pancratio martyri via Aurelia miliario ab urbe Roma,'[26] and later Gregory the Great preached his *Homilia* 27 *in Evangelia* there.[27] Two items are left, (i) Pancratius' age at martyrdom and (v) Diocletian's blandishing offer to the saint. Item v reflects the ideas in 'te magnificentiorem et ditiorem faciam, ut a latere meo non sis alienus, sed veluti filium te habeam' (A ss §3 and manuscripts). Item i indicates that OEM did not use Bede's *Martyrology* on this occasion and it may also suggest an error of hasty reading. During the interrogation Diocletian speculates that Pancras' age 'non est plus quam ter quini anni' (A ss §3), and this becomes more precise in Graz 412 (and other mss): 'non est plus minus quam terquinos annos.' This is the basis for OEM's age of fifteen. But Pancras corrects Diocletian: 'Noli frustra errare, Domine Imperator, quod quasi videns puerum annorum quatuordecim' etc, from which Bede notes: 'qui cum esset annorum quatuordecim . . . martyrium complevit.'[28]

The variant manuscript-texts of BHL 6421 allow a close identification of this notice.

JULIAN AND BASILISSA (6 JANUARY)

OEM reads:[29]

On ðone ylcan dæg bið þæs æþelan weres þrowung se is nemned Sanctus Iulianus, þæs lichoma resteð in Antiochia þære ceastre; se sona on his cnihthade ðeowade

Gode on clænnesse. Ond his yldran hine þa genyddon on his geogoðe þæt he onfeng æþele bryd, seo wæs on naman Basilissa. Ond ða þære forman brydniht, þa hi twa wæron on ðæm brydbure, þa com þær ærest wundorlic stenc, ond æfter ðæm stence heofonlic leoht, ond æfter þæm leohte Crist self þær ætewde mid engla werede. Ond ða for þære gesihðe fægernesse ðe hi gesawon, ond ðæm wordum ðe hi gehyrdon, hi wunedan a clæne, he mid werum ond heo mid fæmnum. Þes Iulianus awehte hæþenne man of deaðe, ond se wæs siððan gefullad. Se man sæde fram helle siðfæte swylc sarspell swylce næfre ær on men ne becom, ne naht oft siððan.

There is no need to itemize this notice for discussion since the martyrologist has made a free summary, without noticeable verbal echo, of the only prose *Passio*. A sequence of BHL numbers 4529-32[30] merely refer to texts of this version which lack the prologue or certain sections or the final chapter, but OEM's summary does not allow us to distinguish one among these. Herzfeld[31] was inaccurate in referring to the printing by Mombritius which apparently was abstracted from the epitome made by Vincent of Beauvais, but Kotzor[32] refers correctly to A ss which prints the *Passio* 'ex aliquot veteribus mss.'[33] Some 'old' manuscripts known to me are Munich, Bayerische Staatsbibliothek ms clm 3514 pp 34-76 (saec VIII med)[34] with prologue but with folios missing and incomplete ending; Munich clm 4554, fol 94r seq (saec VIII ex or VIII/IX)[35] which begins imperfectly like A ss §4; Vatican Regina lat ms 516 fols 45r-59r (saec IX/X)[36] without prologue; Montpellier, Bibliothèque Interuniversitaire, Section Médecine H 156 fols 156v-186v (saec X in)[37] with prologue. There is now another printed edition of the 'passio' within the Spanish Passionary[38] which varies in phraseology from A ss, often in agreement with the early manuscripts, but since OEM has a free summary here, the most convenient printing, A ss, may be used.

Julian's noble parentage and his serving of God in youth are described in A ss §1, his parents' exhortations to marriage in §2, the choice of Basilissa in §5 ('nobilitate et genere coaequalis'). The miraculous events of the bridal night occupy A ss §§6,7, the 'wundorlic stenc' ('odor liliorum et rosarum' §6) the 'heofonlic leoht' ('lux inenarrabilis' §7) and Christ coming with a band of angels ('Dominus Christus, cum multitudine innumerabilium candidatorum; et . . . multitudo virginum' §7). As a result of that beautiful vision, says OEM, which they saw, and the words which they heard, they always remained chaste, he with men, and she with virgins, as noted in A ss §10.

But the entry concludes with a miracle, where one word in OEM demands comment in terms of the composer's attitude to his source-material. 'This Julian awoke a pagan man from death and he was baptized afterwards. The man told such a woeful tale ['sarspell'] about a hell-journey, such as had never befallen a man before nor often since.' The details of the event are found is A ss §§39,40 but the final comment is the martyrologist's own, especially 'oft' in the phrase 'ne naht oft siððan.' As I have noted elsewhere, the composer is a man of scholarly instincts, concerned to transmit the truth as he received it. He knows of no hell-journey before this one, but he does know of one, at least, afterwards, that of Furseus (16 January),[39] whose story he read both in Bede and the Anonymous Life, so 'oft' is inserted. In this volume to Stanley Greenfield we may be allowed to pursue the general critical point of considering individual words and phrases against persistent emphases or attitudes. In my view 'oft' in the majority of cases where it appears in Old English poetry may well not have to be specifically noted or carry the meaning 'many times,' since, in most cases, 'oft' is the main stave and the only alliterating word in the second half-line of whole lines linked by vowel-alliteration.[40] In my view the word mostly serves as does a rhyming-tag in later poetry. Each case, obviously, has to be tested in the immediate context but if there is no other indication of 'many times,' explication should not turn solely on this single word.

THE FORTY SOLDIERS OF SEBASTEA (9 MARCH)

OEM reads:[41]

(i) On ðone nygeðan dæg ðæs monðes bið feowertiges cæmpena ðrowung on Sebastia ðære ceastre on Licinis tidum ðæs cyninges; (ii) þæt wæron strange weras ond sigefæste on woroldgefeohtum ond hwæþre arwyrðlice Gode herdon. (iii) Ða ongan ðære burge gerefa, se wæs on naman Agriculaus, ond ðara cæmpena ealdorman, se wæs on naman Lyssiarchus, hi neddon þæt hi Criste wiðsocan. (iv) Þa hi þæt ne geðafedan, þa hetan hi on æfenne on swiðe cealdum winde weorpan hi on deopne mere. On ðæm mere wæs micel is ond yfel, ond þær wæs hat bæþ be þæm mere, þæt gif heora hwilc on his geleafan getweode, þæt he gebuge to þæm. (v) Þa on forewearde niht snað þæt is ðara haligra lichoman; þa getweode heora an on his mode ond arn to þæm hatan baðe ond wæs sona dead ond him þa lima ealle tofeollan. (vi) Ða on niht com leoht of heofonum, swa hat swa sunne bið on sumera, ond þæt is gemelte ond þæt wæter wearð wearm, (vii) ond þara wearda sum geseah ðæt of heofonum com an læs feowertig wuldorbeaga ofer þa cæmpan. Þa ongeat he þæt se wæs Gode wiðcoren se þe on þæt bæþ eode. (viii) Þa gecerde se weard to Criste ond awearp his hrægl him of ond hleop on ðone mere ond stod on ðara midle, ond mid him þurh martyrdom his gast to Gode onsænde.

Although two early[42] versions of this *Passio* are extant, which are thought to be different Latin translations of an original Greek 'passio,' our composer certainly saw *Passio* 2 (BHL 7539), printed in A ss,[43] but in a variant text of that edition as an early but important manuscript indicates. This variant is Paris, Bibliothèque Nationale ms lat 10861 fols 82v–87v (saec IX[1]) written in England and, indeed, the only English legendary still extant of the period of OEM.[44] The other 'passio' (1) is extant in early manuscripts[45] but omissions and differences of phrase from the words of OEM demonstrate that such a 'passio' was not consulted.

For item i compare A ss §1: 'in tempore ... Licinii regis' (he is 'imperator' in the other 'passio,'[46] although this is not an important difference). But *Passio* 1 omits the descriptive phrase in item ii, for which see A ss §1: 'quadraginta milites ... in numero uno viventes venerabiliter secundum Deum, invicti et fortissimi in bello.' The name Agricolaus in item iii is common to both 'passiones' but no text seen by me has exactly the name 'Lyssiarchus' as in OEM. *Passio* 2 (BHL 7539) in A ss §5 has 'Chiliarchus' but its variant in Paris 10861 reads: 'Siliarchus,' and this latter variant may have produced OEM's name in yet another variant by metathesis. But the composition of the name could have been influenced by names in texts of *Passio* 1: 'Lisia,' 'Lisias,' 'Lisie,' 'Lisies.'[47] Then follows the account of the immersion in the lake (item iv), where only *Passio* 2 (in A ss §7) has almost all the details: 'iubet ... adduci omnes [Paris 10861: 'et adducit totus'] ... in stagnum habentem aquam multam.... habebat glaciem magnam [Paris 10861: 'malam'].... Erat autem et ventus frigidus, et hora noctis proxima, ad vesperam enim erat.... Erat autem et lavacrum de quo calefierent [Paris 10861: 'calefacerentur'] ut si quis eorum voluisset praevaricari, refugeret ad lavacrum caloris, et calefaceret se.'[48] We note, however, an unusual extra adjective to describe the ice in OEM: 'micel is ond yfel'; but, for A ss: 'glaciem magnam,' Paris 10861 reads: 'glaciem malam,' and our composer surely had a text with both adjectives. *Passio* 2 (BHL 7539) does not actually say that the ice 'cut' them as OEM 'snað,' (item v), but abbreviation occurs here of A ss §8: 'Hora autem noctis prima constringebat glacies sanctos, et intumescentes carnes eorum disrumpebantur,' and for the comment on the man who doubted A ss §8 is close in word: 'Unus autem de numero ipsorum [Paris 10861 adds: xl] deficiens animo, dubitavit, et refugiens ad lavacrum cum attigisset [Paris 10861: 'tetegisset'] calorem, statim dissoluta sunt membra eius, et confestim reddidit spiritum.' For the heavenly light and the image of item vi compare A ss §9: 'Et cum facta esset hora tertia noctis, sol illuxit super eos sicut in aestate calidus, et soluta est glacies, et facta est aqua calida.' Within item vii we note the unusual way of presenting the number 39 and the reason, cf A ss §9: 'clauicularius. . . . vidit coronas descendentes de coelo numero triginta novem, et cogitabat intra se dicens: Quomodo cum sint quadraginta, una minus est corona? Et cognovit quia ille, qui refugerat ad lavacrum, reprobatus est, et non est annumeratus cum quadraginta.' A small problem needs comment for item viii in comparison with A ss §9: 'projecit [ie the one guard] eis [the other] res suas, salivitque introiens in stagnum clamans: Et ego Christianus sum. Et vadens in medio eorum [the martyrs] stetit et dixit: Domine Deus, credo in te . . .' (his death with the other martyrs is reported later). If the martyrologist was not certain what 'res suas' was at this point he could have taken his information from the report of the other guards in §11: 'ille . . . projiciens vestimenta.' But the problem was for me, and maybe others, how our composer obtained 'hleop on ðone mere' ('he leapt into the lake') from 'salivitque [Paris 10861: 'saliuit'], introiens in stagnum.' The other 'passio' does say 'exiliuit in stagnum' ('exsilio' 'spring out, leap up'), but our composer probably saw or reasonably understood 'saluit' ('salio ui' 'to leap'). All the echoes of idea and word in this close comparison indicate that the martyrologist used a variant text of *Passio* 2 (BHL 7539).

SOSIUS (23 SEPTEMBER)

OEM reads:[49]

On ðone .xxiii. dæg þæs monðes bið ðæs diacones gemynd se is nemned Sancti Sossy. He wæs in ðære ceastre Meselana, ond sume dæge þa he rædde godspell æt mæssan, ða scan him heofonlic leoht ymb ðæt heafod. Ða cwæð se biscop se ðe his lareow wæs: 'Ne bið þes diacon noht longe mid us, ac he sceal beon mid Criste.' Ond þa æfter feaw[um] dagum þa endode he his lif þurh martyrhad for Criste.

Sosius is a subordinate figure in the *Acta* of Januarius (19 September), bishop of Beneventum, for which there are several versions.[50] The entry in OEM is brief, as was Bede's notice on the saint which also tells the story about the sign of Sosius' martyrdom. Bede says:[51] 'Is cum, tempore quodam, Evangelium legeret in ecclesia Mesenatae civitatis praesente episcopo Ianuario . . . vidit subito idem episcopus de capite eius flammam exsurgere . . . et praenuntiavit eum martyrum futurum. Et post non multos dies' (he was thrown into prison with his companions) and 'occisi sunt,' and Ado and Hrabanus Maurus copied Bede verbatim.[52] Bede took information and echoed word and phrase from the *Acta* 5 (BHL 4132, *Passio S. Sosii*), according to Quentin.[53] We note some similarities between OEM and Bede (and in the designated *Passio*) but particular differences, notably that 'ða scan him heofonlic leoht ymb ðæt heafod' which does not equate: 'de capite eius flammam exsurgere' of Bede or of the named *Passio*: 'et subito de capite eius flamma exurexit' and that no direct speech, as in OEM, appears in Bede and the *Passio*.

We can get a little closer with manuscript-texts of *Acta* 3 (BHL 4124-5), which is not in print but is available in the following manuscripts: St Gall, Stiftsbibliothek ms 566 p 272 seq (saec x); Zurich, Zentralbibliothek ms Rh 81 p 208 seq (saec x) and Munich, Bayerische Staatsbibliothek ms clm 9506 (saec XII).[54] Although none of these manuscripts is of the period when OEM was written, their text is yet a little closer to what the martyrologist saw. St Gall 566 pp 286-7 reads:

Cui [ie Sosius] beatus Ianuarius longe ante de martyrio prophetauit. Nam cum eum uisitandum de Beneuentana ciuitate Mesenatam uenisset propter religionem ipsius et predictus Sossius in ecclesia, presente episcopo, euangelium legeret, idem episcopus super caput eius flammam non minimam effulgere conspexit. Solus autem hoc uidit statimque eum praenuntiauit martyrum futurum.

The flame here 'shines,' as in OEM, 'above' the head, not rises up from the head as in Bede and in *Acta* 5. But the direct speech of the bishop is as yet unidentified.

Over sixty entries in OEM include examples of direct speech, sometimes a phrase, on occasions a prayer of a few lines, or a curse, or an interchange of dialogue. Thirty-eight of these speeches have been compared with sources in print, some by the editors Herzfeld and Kotzor and others in more recent papers on groups of notices or on separate sections.[55] In these cases the martyrologist either translates closely, particularly brief phrases, or adapts so little that verbal echoes abound. To reinforce this statement two more examples are given here, both to indicate the probability of an unfound, but then extant, source for the speech in the notice for Sosius.

LUCY OF ROME (25 JUNE)

The notice is based on the brief *Passio* 1 (BHL 4980), as Herzfeld noted,[56] which is printed in A ss from two 'old' manuscripts, to which may be added: Turin, Biblioteca Nazionale ms D V 3 fols 76v–79r (saec VIII ex); St Gall Stiftsbibliothek ms 548 pp 167-72 (saec VIII ex); Montpellier Bibliothèque Interuniversitaire, Section Médecine, ms H 55 fols 200r–201v (saec VIII/IX or IX in); Zurich, Zentralbibliothek ms Car C 10 i fols 90v–91v (saec IX 2/4) and Rome, Cod Farfa 29, fols 225v–227r (saec IX med).[57] Obviously, the manuscript-readings vary but only differences are recorded which are relevant to the Old English text.

Lucy's speech to the pagan king Auceia (Turin: 'Aceia,' as OEM) reads: 'Ic hæbbe mycelne brydguman, þæt is Cryst, se gewrycð raðe mynne teonan on ðe,' cf A ss §1: '... magnum habeo sponsum, qui statim vindicet injurias meas de te' (Turin, St Gall: 'in te'),[58] and, in answer to the question, who is your bridegroom?, Lucy later says '... habeo Dominum Jesum Christum sponsum.' At the end of the notice comes the interchange between Auceia, now wishing to be martyred with Lucy, and his persecutor:[59]

Þa frægn se burhgerefa hyne hwæt he wære. 'Ic eom Aceia mynre þeode cyning.' Þa cwæð se gerefa: 'Hu miht þu for Cryste sweltan, nu ðu eart hæðen[?]' Þa cwæð se cyning: 'Ic gelyfe þæt mynes blodes agotenys me gelædde on Godes gesyhðe.'

cf A ss §5:

Praefectus interrogavit eum, quis esset. At ille respondit: Ego sum Auceia, Rex gentis meae ... Praefectus dixit: Quomodo sic, qui Christianus non es, pro nomine Dei ipsius poteris mori? Auceia Rex respondit: quod Effusio sanguinis mei credo faciet me Christianum, nec a conspectibus suis et ab ancilla [ie Lucy] sua faciet alienum.

Although the martyrologist has adapted some of the Latin dialogue, enough verbal echo remains to indicate a Latin basis for the Old English words.

MAMAS (MAMMES, MAMMAS) (17 AUGUST)

Mammas (OE Mommos) was notable for his friendly association with wild animals, as is described in OEM's anecdote. Theodosius, *De Situ Terrae* (520–30 AD), recorded: 'Caesaria Cappadociae, ibi est sanctus Mammes heremita et martyr, qui mulsit agrestia et fecit caseum,[60] and this curious fact impressed a composer of a question-and-answer list in two manuscripts of saec VIII/IX and saec IX who asked: 'Qui bestia mulsit?' and answered: 'Sanctus Mamas.'[61] References to his legend have been traced to the turn of the eighth/ninth century.[62] According to BHL,[63] five different versions are extant, but correspondence of significant detail indicates that OEM selects from a text of *Passio* 1 (BHL 5192-4), printed by Mombritius, whose text may be compared for many of the details[64] but not for the speeches towards the end of the notice in OEM. Fortunately, *Passio* 1 is available in Vienna, Österreichische Nationalbibliothek ms 371 fols 114r–118r (saec IX in); Paris, Bibliothèque Nationale ms Nouv Acq lat 2179 fols 258r–261v [P] (saec XI, but a manuscript of the Spanish Passionary); Montpellier, Bibliothèque Interuniversitaire, Section Médecine ms H 156 fols 30r–37v [Mt] (saec X in).[65] For the Latin, the earliest manuscript, Vienna 371, is cited, with variants only from the other manuscripts and Mombritius [Mo] which are relevant for the text of OEM.

The first speech reads in its context:[66]

ða com þær micel leo, se wæs ær mid þæm cnihte on þam wuda, ond se leo cwæð: 'Eala, Mommos, þu eart ure hyrde. Ic eom nu genyded from Godes englum þæt ic for ðe sprece from minre gecynde.' Ond þa abat se leo ðara hæþenra ond ðara Iudea, þara ðe hine bysmrodon, swa fela ðæt þæt blod arn of þære ylcan stowe swa flod. Ond þa bebead him se cniht þæt se leo hwurfe eft to his stowe.

Vienna 371 reads:

... leo illi qui prius [Mo, Mt, P omit] martyri fuerat uisus [Mo: 'missus'] ... ingressus est in [Mo, P omit] ciuitatem ... et respiciens sanctum Mamem [Mt: 'Mammen'; Mo: 'sanctus Mammes'] dixit: ... Ecce enim nunc [Mo, Mt omit] tui propter causam [Mo: 'propter te'; P: 'tui propter esse': Mt: 'tui causa'] cogor ab angelis contra naturam loqui. Tu enim est pastor noster [Mo, Mt, P omit: 'tu ... noster'] ... ascendens leo laniauit multitudinem paganorum et Iudaeorum ... de illorum autem laceratione facta est plenitudo sanguinis [Mo, Mt: 'sanguis'; P: 'sanguis multitudo'] in similitudinem [Mt: 'modum'] fluuii ... Tunc Mames leonem iussit ad propriam reuerti loco [Mo, Mt: 'locum'; P omits the phrase].

We note especially 'tu enim est pastor noster' of Vienna 371 only, but as OEM, and Mombritius 'propter te' as OEM, although here considerable manuscript variation indicates that OEM could have seen the phrase in an earlier text.

The second speech is by a voice from heaven, in OEM:[67]

Ða com stefn of heofonum ond seo cwæþ: 'Cum, Mommos, heofenas ðe synt mid gefean ontynede; ond Crist stondeð æt þam ærestan gete, ond ðe gelædeþ in his neorxnawang.'

Vienna 371 reads:

et uox ... facta est de caelo ... Ueni, aperte sunt tibi caeli congaude [Mt, P: 'congaudet pater'] in paradiso. Stat [Mt, P: 'adstat'] Dei filius ... ad primam portam ... et sanctus spiritus deducens [Mt, P: 'deducet'; Mo omits this phrase] te.

If OEM read 'congaude' as 'with joy' ('mid gefean'), a text of the *Passio* could have provided all the words in the slightly adapted speech.

One could continue with illustration, since OEM is a very full 'narrative' martyrology and a repository of many fascinating anecdotes, but, in terms of this volume, we should sum up that source-analysis (if possible) and criticism agree on one basic principle: 'know your writer.'

NOTES

1 *An Old English Martyrology* ed George Herzfeld EETS OS 116 (London 1900). Herzfeld comments (xxxiii), for example, that 'the compiler of the OE text has occasionally misunderstood the Latin of his source, and . . . he has evidently translated it in a negligent manner,' and (xxxvi) 'his knowledge of Latin is not beyond doubt, as some curious mistakes occur.' Almost every demonstration of an accurate source in early Latin manuscripts opposes this conclusion, but, for a discussion see J.E. Cross 'The Latinity of the ninth-century Old English martyrologist' in *Studies in Earlier Old English Prose* ed Paul Szarmach (Binghamton New York 1986) 275-99.

2 In his *A Preface to Chaucer: Studies in Medieval Perspectives* (Princeton 1962) D.W. Robertson, Jr conveniently assembles protestations of love (or death) from a number of Chaucerian characters (47). We immediately note the difference of Nicholas (*Miller's Tale*) with his delimiting adjective: 'For deerne love of thee, lemman, I spille.'

3 See Herzfeld xxxiii and xxxvi–xlii, for a note of these sources, and for detailed

presentation of the parallel texts see *Das altenglische Martyrologium* ed Günter Kotzor, Abhandlungen der Bayer Akad der Wiss, *Phil-Hist Kl* NF 88 (Munich 1981) 2:277-375, under the relevant days.

4 See Herzfeld xxxvi–xlii for a note of the sources and Kotzor, under the relevant days, for presentation of the Latin texts.

5 See J.E. Cross 'Popes of Rome in the *Old English Martyrology*' ARCA: Classical and Medieval Texts, Papers and Monographs 3. *Papers of the Liverpool Latin Seminar* 2, ed Francis Cairns (Liverpool 1979) 191-211 for a discussion of notices on Popes, and reference to Mommsen's edition.

6 See Cross 'Popes' 192-3 for some examples with discussion.

7 Boninus Mombritius *Sanctuarium seu Vitae Sanctorum*. Herzfeld used the first edition but a second edition appeared in Paris, 1910, where the anonymous editors compared the texts of Mombritius with manuscript texts and other editions and also identified some sources. Herzfeld was sometimes in error since he did not know that certain sections in Mombritius were taken from Vincent of Beauvais.

8 *Bibliotheca Hagiographica Latina Antiquae et Mediae Aetatis* ed Socii Bollandiani (*Subsidia Hagiographica* 6) 2 vols (Brussels 1898-9, 1900-1); *Supplementi* (1911)

9 For manuscripts written up to the turn of the ninth century see E.A. Lowe ed *Codices Latini Antiquiores* (*CLA*) 11 vols (Oxford 1934–66) and Supplement (1971); 2nd ed part II (1972). For later manuscripts an investigator has to read individual library catalogues where they have been completed. I have been vastly aided in my work by the generosity of Bernhard Bischoff of Munich who has been willing to confirm or re-date manuscripts noted in early catalogues.

10 Text from Kotzor 2:102; cf Herzfeld 80. A translation reads: '(i) On the twelfth day of the month is the passion of the noble youth Saint Pancras, who was fifteen years old when he suffered death for the faith of Christ. (ii) He was born in the city of Frigia of noble lineage; his father's name was Cledones and his mother's name was Cyriade, (iii) but he was baptized at Rome by the pope, Saint Cornelius. (iv) Then the pagan emperor Diocletianus advised him to forsake Christ, (v) and said that he would make him as wealthy as if he were his own son. (vi) When he would not consent to that, he ordered him to be beheaded on the road at Rome that is called Aurelia. There his body is buried (vii) and his church is built up to the present day.'

11 The obit (12 May) is common. It is in the printed texts of various subdivisions of the 'passio' (BHL 6420, 6421, 6426, 6427). Bede, Hrabanus Maurus, Ado, and the Hieronymian Martyrology all record Pancras on the day, 12 May. For Bede and the Hieronymian, see Henri Quentin *Les Martyrologes His-*

toriques du Moyen Âge 2nd ed (Paris 1908) 87; for Hrabanus, see *Rabani Mauri Martyrologium* ed John McCulloh, CC Continuatio Mediaevalis 44 (Turnhout 1979) 45; for Ado see PL 123 col 265.

12 BHL 2:928-9

13 Printed in *Analecta Bollandiana* 2 (1882) 289-91

14 Printed in 'Florilegia' in the *Bibliotheca Casinensis* 4 vols (Casinensi 1873-94) 3:349-50

15 Printed in *Analecta Bollandiana* 10 (1891) 53-6

16 Printed in an inaccessible edition but seen in a variant text within Stuttgart, Württembergischen Landesbibliothek ms HB XIV, 14 (saec IX[2]) fols 169v-171r, which is described in MS Buhl and L. Kurras *Die Handschriften der Württembergischen Landesbibliothek Stuttgart* (Wiesbaden 1969) 4, part 2:106-7

17 Mombritius 2:342

18 A.Z. Huizman *Die Verehrung des heiligen Pancratius in West- und Mitteleuropa* (Haarlem 1938) 14-15

19 A ss Maii III; 21

20 Described in Anton Kern *Die Handschriften der Universitäts-bibliothek Graz* 3 vols (Leipzig 1942-67) 1:241-3 and dated saec IX[1]. Bernhard Bischoff *Die Südostdeutschen Schreibschulen und Bibliotheken in der Karolingerzeit: Teil II; Die Vorwiegend Österreichischen Diözesen* (Wiesbaden 1980) 175 dates it saec IX 3/4.

21 Described in *Analecta Bollandiana* 24 (1905) 432-9 and there dated saec x. My dating is from Bernhard Bischoff.

22 Described in Albert Poncelet *Catalogus Codicum Hagiographicum Latinorum Bibliothecae Vaticanae* (Brussels 1910) 344-6 and there dated saec IX ex. My dating is from Bernhard Bischoff.

23 Printed by Huizman 16-18. My dating is from Helmut Gnuess 'A preliminary list of manuscripts written or owned in England up to 1100' *Anglo-Saxon England* 9 (1981) 39.

24 A ss 21 note c

25 See Cross 'Popes' passim.

26 *Gestorum Pontificum Romanorum* I *Libri Pontificalis pars prior* ed Theodor Mommsen MGH (Berlin 1898) 172

27 PL 76 col 1204

28 Bede in Quentin 87

29 Kotzor 2:12-13 cf Herzfeld 14-16. A translation reads: 'On the same day is the passion of the noble man who is called St Julian, whose body rests in the city of Antioch; immediately in his youth he served God in chastity. And his parents compelled him then in his youth to take a noble bride, Basilissa by name. And on the first bridal-night, when these two were in the bridal

chamber, then first came there a marvellous smell, and after the smell a heavenly light, and after the light Christ himself appeared there with a band of angels. And then because of the beauty of the vision which they saw and the words which they heard, they always remained chaste, he with men and she with virgins. This Julian awoke a pagan from death and he was baptized afterwards. The man told such a woeful tale about a hell-journey, such as had never befallen a man before nor often since.'

30 BHL 1:671-2

31 Herzfeld xxxvii

32 Kotzor 2:281

33 A SS Ian I 575-87

34 See E.A. Lowe *CLA* (Oxford 1959) 9:no1238.

35 Lowe *CLA* 9:no1242

36 See above n22 for comment on the manuscript.

37 Described in *Analecta Bollandiana* 34/35 (1915-16) 261-3. My dating is from Bernhard Bischoff.

38 Ángel Fábrega Grau *Pasionario Hispánico* Monumenta Hispaniae Sacra: serie litúrgica 6 (Madrid-Barcelona 1955) 118-44

39 Kotzor 2:16-17; Herzfeld 20. For a discussion of the sources for this notice see J.E. Cross 'The influence of Irish texts and traditions on the *Old English Martyrology*' PRIA 81C (1981) 178-80.

40 See my review of Bernard F. Huppé *Doctrine and Poetry* in *JEGP* 59 (1960) 563.

41 Kotzor 2:31 cf Herzfeld 36-8. A translation reads: '(i) On the ninth day of the month is the passion of the forty soldiers in the city of Sebastia in the times of King Licinius; (ii) these were strong and victorious men in worldly battles, and, however, they obeyed God honourably. (iii) Then the governor of the town [Latin: 'praesul,' 'praeses'], Agricolaus by name, and the commander of the soldiers [Latin: 'dux'] Lyssiarchus by name, forced them to deny Christ. (iv) When they would not consent they ordered them to be thrown into a deep lake in the evening in a very cold wind. In the lake there was much and bad ice, and there was a hot bath by the lake so that if any one of them doubted in his faith he might turn to this. (v) When the ice cut the bodies of the saints in the early part of the night, one of them doubted in his mind and ran to the hot bath and immediately died and all his limbs fell away. (vi) Then a light came from heaven in the night, as hot as the sun is in summer, and the ice melted and the water became warm, (vii) and one of the guards saw that from heaven came forty less one crowns above the soldiers. Then he saw that he who went into the bath was rejected by God. (viii) Then the guard was converted to Christ and threw his garments

from him and leapt into the lake and stood in the middle, and sent his spirit to God with them through martyrdom.'

42 BHL 2:1092-3, on *Passio* 1 and 2. There is a third by John the Deacon which was not used.

43 A ss Mart II; 19-21

44 Described in *Catalogus Codicum Hagiographicorum Latinorum ... Bibliotheca Nationali Parisiensi* ed *Hagiographi Bollandiani* 3 vols (Brussels 1889-93) 2:605-6. The place and date of origin are recorded by Gneuss *ASE* 9 (1981) 57.

45 One text is printed in 'Florilegia' in the *Bibliotheca Casinensis* 3:58-61 (n14 above). I have also seen manuscript-variants.

46 *Bibliotheca Casinensis* 3:58

47 *Bibliotheca Casinensis* 3:59. Others from manuscripts of *Passio* 1

48 Old English 'tweogan, tweode' means 'to doubt' and does not equate 'praevaricor' but later in A ss §8 when the man defects the word is 'dubitavit,' as cited in the text of this paper.

49 Kotzor 2:215 cf Herzfeld 174-6. A translation reads: 'On the twenty-third day of the month is the commemoration ['memoria'] of the deacon who is named Saint Sosius. He was in the city of Miseno and one day, when he read the gospel at mass, a heavenly light shone around his head. The bishop who was his teacher then said: "This deacon will not be long with us but he shall be with Christ." And after a few days he then ended his life through martyrdom for Christ.'

50 BHL 1:613-15

51 Quentin 75-6

52 Ado in PL 123 col 364; Hrabanus Maurus in McCulloh 96-7

53 Quentin cites from *Acta* 5 (BHL 4132) 76.

54 St Gall 566 is noted in *Verzeichniss der Handschriften der Stiftsbibliothek von Sankt Gallen* (Halle 1875) 181 under its number. The dating is from Professor Bischoff. Zurich Rh 81 is described and dated in L.C. Mohlberg *Katalog der Handschriften der Zentralbibliothek Zürich* 1: *Mittelalterliche Handschriften* (Zurich 1951), under the number 449. Munich 9506 is noted and dated in vol 2 (1874) of the *Catalogus Codicum Manu Scriptorum Bibliothecae Regiae Monacensis* (Munich 1868 seq) 94.

55 It would be too tedious to record the individual papers under my name here, but if anyone is interested in an individual saint within OEM I am willing to give what information I have.

56 Herzfeld xxxix, referring to A ss (3rd ed) Iun VII; 11-12 (now BHL 4980)

57 Turin D V 3 is described in *Analecta Bollandiana* 28 (1909) 419-22, and dated in CLA 4 (1947), as no 446. St Gall 548 is described in the catalogue (see

n54) vol 1 (1875) 168, and dated in CLA 7 (1956) as no 940. Montpellier H
55 is described in *Analecta Bollandiana* 34/35 (1915-16) 251-5, and dated by
Bernhard Bischoff; Zurich Car C 10 i is listed in the catalogue (see n54) as
number 47 and dated by Bernhard Bischoff; and Farfa 29 is described in Albert
Poncelet *Catalogus Codicum Hagiographicorum Latinorum Bibliothecarum
Romanarum* (Brussels 1909) 118-23 and dated by Bernhard Bischoff.

58 The Old English in Kotzor 2:132 cf Herzfeld 106 translated as: 'I have a great
bridegroom, that is Christ, who will avenge my injuries on you.' We note
that 'in te' of the mss equates OE 'on ðe' but have also to record the only
error of transcription yet noted in Kotzor's edition, where he prints 'gewyrcð'
for ms 'gewrycð.' The latter word (OE 'gewrecan') equates 'vindicet.'

59 Kotzor 2:133 cf Herzfeld 106. A translation reads: 'Then the town-governor
asked what he was. "I am Aceia, king of my people." Then the governor
said: "How could you die for Christ, now you are a pagan?" Then the king
said: "I believe that the shedding (pouring out) of my blood will lead me
to the sight of God."'

60 Printed in PL *Supplementum* 4*** col 1460 §15

61 See Walther Suchier *Das mittellateinische Gespräch Adrian und Epictitus,
nebst verwandten Texten (Joca Monachorum)* (Tübingen 1955) 116.

62 See Günter Bernt 'Die Quellen zu Walafrids Mammes-Leben' in *Festschrift
Bernhard Bischoff* ed Johanne Autenrieth and Franz Brunhölzl (Stuttgart 1971)
148 and n32.

63 BHL 2:771-2

64 One other detail in OEM's notice for Mamas does not equate the *Passio* in
Mombritius 2:126-9 and manuscripts. In OEM 'the judge ordered him to be
stoned' but in the *Passio* the situation is opposite in that the people demand
that Mamas be stoned and then stone him without order. This change may
have been caused by abbreviation. We should note that the martyrology of
Hrabanus Maurus also abbreviates and notes: 'postea eum lapidare iussit'
(McCulloh 82) and then the people stone the saint.

65 Vienna 371 is noted in *Tabulae Codicum Manu Scriptorum ... in Bibliotheca
Palatina Vindobonensi* (Vienna 1864) 57 and was dated by Bernhard Bischoff.
Paris NA lat 2179 is described in the Paris catalogue (see n44) 3:476-87 and
there dated. On Montpellier H 156 see n37.

66 Kotzor 2:182-3 cf Herzfeld 148. A translation reads: 'Then a great lion came
there, who was with the youth before in the wood, and the lion said: 'Oh,
Mamas, you are our shepherd. I am now compelled by God's angels to speak
for you against my nature." And the the lion devoured so many of the pagans
and the Jews who had abused him that the blood ran from the same place
like a river. And then the youth ordered the lion to return to his place.'

67 Kotzor 2:183 cf Herzfeld 148. A translation reads: 'Then a voice came from heaven and it said: "Come Mamas the heavens are opened to you with joy; and Christ stands at the first gate, and leads you into his paradise."'

EARL R. ANDERSON
The Battle of Maldon:
A Reappraisal of Possible
Sources, Date, and Theme

THE BATTLE OF MALDON traditionally has been thought of as a poem
composed during the 990s by a poet who had first-hand knowledge about
Byrhtnoth's defeat by the Vikings early in that decade. Historians have
related the poem to the Viking activities of Olaf Tryggvason, and have
noted on the Anglo-Saxon side an ideal of suicidal loyalty reminiscent
of Tacitus' comments about the ideals of the Germanic comitatus in
his De Germania. Literary critics have spoken of a 'journalistic' element
in the style of the poem, as though the poet had been something like
a newspaper reporter. During the last ten years, however, there have been
challenges to this view of the poem. Rosemary Woolf, in 1976, revived
a suggestion originally put forward by Bertha Phillpotts in 1929, that
the Maldon poet was influenced by the Old Danish Bjarkamál: Woolf
proposed Bjarkamál as the source for the Maldon poet's ideal of men
dying with their lord, which (as she argued) was otherwise alien to
Germanic and Anglo-Saxon tradition.[1] John McKinnell, in 1975, noted
that the Maldon poet uses the word 'eorl' as an English title equivalent
to Old Norse 'jarl' (= OE 'ealdormann'), which suggests a date ca 1020
or later for the poem.[2] N.F. Blake, in 1978, accepted McKinnell's arguments
for a late date and proposed, further, that the Maldon poet got his
information about Byrhtnoth's death in battle from Byrhtferth's Vita
Oswaldi, which was composed ca 995–1005.[3] The similarities between
Maldon and the account of Byrhtnoth in the Vita Oswaldi are not detailed
enough to prove the dependence of one work upon the other; however,
our understanding about the place of Maldon in English literary history
has undergone much revision during the last decade – revision that was
anticipated, to a certain extent, by Stanley Greenfield in his comment
that 'though an historical battle was the occasion of the poem, under

the scop's handling of the traditional heroic formulas its real heroes merge with legendary ones.'⁴ *Maldon* must be regarded primarily as the work of a poetic imagination. John Scattergood recently has attempted to reassert the older view that the poem was composed shortly after the battle; the poem, he argues, belongs to 'a distinctively historical context because it deals with problems which were relevant to Englishmen in the reign of Æthelred – three problems in particular: what is it that makes a good leader, especially a good war-leader; whether it is better to confront the Vikings with military force or to pay them tribute; and whether it is better to fight battles through to the bitter end and risk one's life or to ensure safety by flight.'⁵ His evidence for these concerns includes *Anglo-Saxon Chronicle* entries dated as late as 1016; however, if he had wanted to he could have added *Chronicle* entries and charters for the years 1044–7 when rumours circulated in England that Magnus of Norway was planning an invasion. The invasion scare of 1044 was taken seriously by Edward the Confessor, who personally took charge of the naval fleet at Sandwich.⁶

Many questions about *Maldon* thus are left unanswered. If the poet was composing as late as the reign of Knútr, and had to rely on second-hand sources (literary or oral) for information about Byrhtnoth's death, where did he get his inspiration for the poem's battlefield details? Did he make them up? The battle of Maldon, after all, was only one of many military encounters during a period of constant conflict between the English and the Danes, and after thirty years or more its details would be at best a vague and distant memory. If the central theme of the poem – an affirmation of the ideal of men dying with their lord in battle – really came from *Bjarkamál*, why is it that except for this theme, the only evidence for the influence of *Bjarkamál* consists of a few inconsequential bits and pieces of detail – a word here, a phrase there – most of which are easily explained away as part of Anglo-Saxon or common Germanic heritage? Then, too, the argument for a late date based on 'eorl' is by no means certain, either: Cecily Clark, in 1983, noted that because we cannot be sure where or under what circumstances the poet was composing, the evidence of Scandinavian linguistic influence cannot help us date the poem as precisely as we might wish. As for the word 'eorl,' Clark argues, the poet could have had in mind not the technical sense of 'ealdormann,' but rather 'commander' or 'leader' in a more general sense such as was possible in the late ninth century alongside the older, poetic meaning 'noble warrior,' and she concludes, 'with the king-pin knocked out of [McKinnell's] argument, the whole question of dating

The Battle of Maldon is reopened.'[7] D.C. Scragg, in his 1981 edition of *Maldon*, also rejects McKinnell's arguments: he concedes that the poet's use of 'eorl' as a title seems unique and anachronistic, but argues that the poet was influenced by the frequent use of this word as a heroic epithet in Old English poetry.[8] Scragg's own conclusion, however – that 'Spelling, accidence, and vocabulary are so conservative in the text as a whole that a date late in the tenth century or early in the eleventh seems probable' – is open to serious question, for, as Ashley Amos has concluded in her admirable survey of the linguistic problems involved in dating Old English texts, 'Most of the linguistic tests ... are so limited by qualifications that they do not provide clear, unambiguous, objective evidence with respect to date.'[9] Among the few unambiguous tests there is one that points to a late date rather than an early one for *Maldon*: the poet avoids alliteration of palatal and velar 'g'; and at least in the case of line 192, 'God*w*ine and Godwig, guþe ne gymdon,' metrical correctness depends on the phonemic split of 'g' into /g/ and /j/ heard as distinct sounds.[10] But, of course, although this test suggests that *Maldon* is later than most other Old English poems, it cannot be used to decide between, say, an early- or a mid-eleventh-century date for the poem.

Along with the question of dating, there are questions about the poem's sources, and about the circumstances of its composition, that must also be reopened. In an effort to deal with these questions, I would like to continue the process of reappraisal of *Maldon* by attempting to establish the following five points: (1) The question of the poem's date must be left open not only because the linguistic evidence is inconclusive, but also because of literary evidence that could suggest a late date for the composition of *Maldon* – perhaps even as late as the reign of Edward the Confessor (1042–65) – although, as we shall see, the literary evidence is not really conclusive either. (2) I must reject Phillpotts' and Woolf's arguments for the influence of *Bjarkamál*. To my mind, the *Maldon* poet was not influenced by this or any other Scandinavian poem. The Scandinavian influence on the vocabulary of *Maldon* is considerable, but this is easily explained by reference to the linguistic history of England during its last Anglo-Saxon century. (3) The ideal of men dying with their lord in battle is found not only in *Bjarkamál*, but also in the *Encomium Emmae Reginae*, which was composed during the reign of Hörthaknútr (1040–2). (4) Much of the detail in the *Maldon* poet's battlefield narrative is similar to an account of the battle of Ashingdon which appears in the *Encomium Emmae Reginae*. Especially important is the Encomiast's account of the treachery of Eadric Streon, which resembles the *Maldon* poet's account of the flight of the sons of Odda. (5) If, as is possible, the *Maldon* poet was influenced by the *Encomium*, that influence would have far-reaching implications for our understanding of the poem's date and theme. Even if that influence cannot be demonstrated conclusively, however, a comparison of the relevant details in the *Encomium* and *Maldon* encourages a belief that the flight of the sons of Odda must be the turning-point and central issue in the poem. This, in turn, has a bearing on our interpretation of certain other details, such as the poet's comment about Byrhtnoth's 'ofermod.'

Bertha Phillpotts turned to the Old Danish *Bjarkamál* in an effort to explain certain stylistic features of *Maldon*: the poet's preference for end-stopped rather than caesura-stopped sentences, characteristic of Scandinavian poetry but not usually predominant in Old English poetry; the poet's use of negative comparison to describe heroic conduct, for example in his account of Æscferð the Northumbrian hostage – 'He ne wandode na æt þam wigplegan' (259); the use of certain phrases suggestive of *Bjarkamál*; and the use of Scandinavian loan words or phrases. It is impossible to undertake a close comparison between *Maldon* and *Bjarkamál*, of course, since *Bjarkamál* survives only in Saxo Grammaticus' translation of it (ca AD 1200) into Latin hexameters.[11] Nevertheless it is possible to dismiss Phillpotts' stylistic arguments point by point. End-stopped sentences are not predominant in most Old English poetry, but they are not unknown, either. Negative comparison is used often in heroic narrative, and the *Beowulf* poet often uses this device to define heroic conduct, as Edward B. Irving, Jr, has shown.[12] The phrases from Saxo that Phillpotts adduces for comparison with *Maldon* prove little except that *Maldon* and *Bjarkamál* share in a common Germanic tradition of heroic poetry. 'Nemo pedem referat' (Saxo 203), for example, in a command not to retreat a foot-space, according to Phillpotts (181) is echoed in Leofsunu's boast, 'ic heonon nelle // fleon fotes trym' (*Maldon* 246b–47a),[13] but the expression 'oferfleon fotes trem' is found in Beowulf's boast that he will not retreat a single foot-space from the fire dragon (*Beowulf* 2525a),[14] and the *Maldon* poet's use of the collocation a second time, in Eadweard the Long's boast that 'he nolde fleogan fotmæl landes' (275), should be enough to show that we are dealing with a native Anglo-Saxon verse formula, not with a quotation from a Danish poem. Finally, the presence of Danish words and phrases in *Maldon* cannot be denied,[15] but in view of a continued Danish presence in England in the tenth and eleventh centuries, this lexical influence need not have come from any one or another poetic source.

Rosemary Woolf, in her comments about 'the ideal of men dying with their lord,' extended the argument for the influence of *Bjarkamál* to include, also, a theme of fundamental importance in *Maldon*. She demonstrated quite convincingly that the ideal of men dying with their lord mentioned by Tacitus in *Germania*, and exemplified in *Maldon*, is *not* part of a continuous Germanic tradition. Its absence from *Beowulf* is especially noteworthy. It is possible, indeed, as Woolf pointed out, that Tacitus derived this supposedly 'Germanic' ideal not from information about Germanic tribes, but rather from Julius Caesar's description of the band of 'soldurii' in Aquitania of whom it could be said that 'neque adhuc hominum memoria repertus est quisquam, qui eo interfecto, cuius se amicitiae devovisset, mori recusaret' ('nor within human memory has anybody been found who has refused to die when he to whom he was bound by a vow of friendship had been killed'). Sallust, in his *Historiae*, had made a similar remark about the Celts in Spain, to judge from allusions to it in Plutarch's 'Life of Sertorius' and in Servius' commentary on Vergil's *Georgics*.[16] Besides these writers, Woolf mentions others to illustrate a classical tradition about the barbarian heroic ideal of men dying with their lord: Ammianus Marcellinus, a Byzantine Greek who wrote in Latin about the fourth-century wars in Gaul, and Agathias, a sixth-century Greek who wrote a continuation of Procopius' *History of the Goths*. As Woolf notes, none of the classical references that she adduces provides 'in context an actual example of such determination to die a suicidal death but only an example of less spectacular and more practical acts of loyalty' (64), except possibly for Agathias, though in his case the meaning of the text is unclear (66). What *is* clear from early historical accounts is that among the fourth-century Visigoths, as E.A. Thompson has shown, the 'comites' would remain loyal to their leader 'only so long as he could ensure a steady intake of plunder and fame'; and, in the alternative, they would desert him in cases of military failure, as Alaric had feared (Claudian, *vi cons Hon* 314ff), or in cases of idleness, as happened to Athanaric in 378 because he had remained at peace during the period of Fritigern's campaigns against the Empire in 377–80 (Ammianus Marcellinus, 27.5.10 and 31.4.13).[17]

Woolf overlooked one very important, and unambiguous, example of suicidal fighting in Quintus Curtius Rufus' *History of Alexander* 4.15.24.[18] In his description of the battle between Darius and Alexander at Arbela (= Gaugamela), Quintus Curtius writes,

Curru Dareus, Alexander equo vehebatur. Utrumque delecti tuebantur, sui immemores; quippe amisso rege nec volebant salvi esse nec poterant. Ante oculos sui quisque regis mortem occumbere ducebat egregium.

Darius rode in his chariot, Alexander on horseback. Both were defended by élite troops, unmindful of their own lives; for if their king were lost they did not wish to be saved, nor could they be. Each man thought it glorious to meet death before the eyes of his king.

In the course of the battle, the Macedonians got the upper hand, and many of the Persians thought that Darius had been killed; the left wing of the Persian army panicked in flight. Darius remained in battle with those of his élite warriors who remained loyal to him, until the battle turned into a massacre; then Darius also turned to flee (Quintus Curtius 4.15.28-32). The date and identity of Quintus Curtius Rufus is obscure; he could possibly be the Curtius Rufus mentioned by Tacitus in *Annales* 11.21, who was consul ca AD 43 and Legate of Upper Germany in AD 47; or he could be a writer whose career dates to the time of Vespasian (AD 69-79). In either case, Quintus Curtius Rufus is just as likely as Julius Caesar or Sallust to have been the source for the ideal of suicidal fighting which Tacitus describes in his *Germania*. The additional reference from Quintus Curtius, of course, serves to underscore one of Woolf's key points: that Tacitus probably had a literary source for the so-called Germanic ideal of men dying with their lord.

If the ideal of suicidal fighting for one's lord has any sort of *continuous* heritage, that heritage is to be found mainly in classical Latin and Greek histories and ethnographies, not in Germanic poetry. Nevertheless, it should not be forgotten that any military society founded on bonds of kinship or 'comitatus' is capable of developing, and from time to time acting upon, an ideal of loyalty that is expressed through suicidal fighting. That is perhaps the lesson we can learn from the *Anglo-Saxon Chronicle* account of events that occurred in Wessex in ca 786 (entered under the year 784 because of a two-year error on chronology, and told in detail in the entry for 755). According to the *Chronicle* account, Cynewulf, king of Wessex, was set upon and murdered by a dynastic rival, Cyneheard, while visiting a mistress at 'Merantun' (= Merton, in Devon). The lady's screams wakened Cynewulf's retainers, who fought with Cyneheard's followers and who, rejecting an offer of money and safe conduct, 'simle feohtende wæran oþ hie alle lægon butan anum Bryttiscum gisle, *and* se swiþe gewundad wæs' ('went on fighting continuously until they all lay [slain] except one Welsh hostage, and he was sorely wounded').[19]

Cyneheard's men, in turn, were then attacked by Cynewulf's ealdorman Osric and his thane Wigfrith. Cyneheard offered Osric and Wigfrith money and land according to 'hiera agenna dom' if they would recognize him as king, and he pointed out to them that there were kinsmen fighting on both sides in this conflict; but Osric and Wigfrith replied 'þæt him nænig mæg leofra nære þonne hiera hlaford' ('that no kinsman was dearer to them than their lord'). The kinsmen on Cyneheard's side, for their part, refused an offer of safe conduct. In the fighting that followed at the gates of 'Merantun,' Cyneheard was slain, together with all but one of his followers.

The story of Cynewulf, Cyneheard, and Osric is the most detailed narrative in the *Anglo-Saxon Chronicle*, and partly for this reason, scholars have attempted to associate it with Anglo-Saxon poetic or prose traditions. The argument for the influence of poetry on the story, developed most fully by Ruth Waterhouse, is based entirely on narrative structure – that is, on the use of repetition and symmetry of detail so as to emphasize the conflict between the claims of kinship and 'comitatus.'[20] This, without complementary stylistic evidence for the influence of poetry, is not convincing. R.W. McTurk has discussed most fully the view that the story of Cynewulf, Cyneheard, and Osric reflects an oral tradition of prose saga and thus is comparable to the Icelandic family sagas. The arguments here are (1) that stories about tragic conflicts among kinsmen are common also in the Icelandic sagas; and (2) that the prose style in the *Chronicle* entry, like that of the sagas, has characteristics usually found in oral narrative: editorial economy, repetition of subject and of certain phrases, frequent use of sentence connectors, certain types of ellipsis, and so forth.[21] The relevance for *Maldon* would be this: if the *Chronicle* story reflects a prose saga tradition, the ideal of suicidal fighting as an expression of 'comitatus'-loyalty may well have been part of that tradition. In McTurk's view, the narrative structure of the *Chronicle* story resembles that of oral narrative, but the argument for an 'oral' prose style is unconvincing; it might be noted, indeed, that the characteristics of 'oral narrative' found in the *Chronicle* are also to be found in the prose of Sir Thomas Malory, who, of course, worked mainly with French literary sources, not with a prose saga tradition.[22] As for the theme of tragic fighting among kinsmen torn by conflicting loyalties – that is what one expects to find in a story about dynastic conflict. Dynastic rivals usually are related to each other. Taking these various considerations into account, I find myself in agreement with the position advanced some fifty years ago by Francis P. Magoun, Jr, that although the *Chronicle* story resembles *Maldon* and other Old English heroic poems in some interesting details, it is 'the politico-historical aspect' that 'presses more and more to the fore.'[23] Ideals of 'comitatus'-loyalty and suicidal fighting are present in the *Chronicle* story – attenuated, however, by the realities of conflicting obligation and betrayal: loyalty to Cyneheard, for example, is possible only at the cost of disloyalty to Cynewulf, who has the better claim to loyalty.[24] The suicidal fighting at 'Merantun' should be seen not as evidence for a continuing Germanic tradition of warriors dying with their lord, but, rather, as an isolated example of the sort of thing that can take place in violent military societies.

If, as I believe, the *Maldon* poet got the ideal of suicidal fighting from some particular poetic or literary source, rather than from 'Germanic tradition' generally, another candidate is available besides the *Bjarkamál* proposed by Woolf: the ideal also appears in the *Encomium Emmae Reginae*, which was composed by a monk of either St Bertin's or St Omer's, Flanders, during the reign of Horthaknútr (1940-2). The Encomiast describes Knútr's father, Sveinn Forkbeard, as a Danish ruler who, because of his munificence, was able to command the loyalty of his retainers, and adds:

Atque ut scias, quantus suorum fuerit in precordiis, pro certo affirmare ualeam, quod nullus formidine mortis periculum refugeret, eiusque pro fidelitate hostibus innumeris solus, armatis etiam manibus nudis, inperterritus occurreret, si euntibus tantum regale premonstraretur signum.   (*Encomium* 1.1.22-5)

So that you may realise how highly he was regarded by his men, I can strongly affirm that not one of them would have recoiled from danger owing to fear of death, but, unafraid, would have gone out of loyalty to him against innumerable enemies alone, and even with bare hands against armed men, if only the royal signal should be given to them as they went.[25]

Rosemary Woolf was certainly right in claiming that the ideal of men dying with their lord 'was not an ancient and traditional commonplace of Old English heroic poetry but was new and strange.... Liberated from the view that it illustrates a central tenet of the heroic code *The Battle of Maldon* becomes more moving.'[26] The Encomiast, indeed, provides evidence in support of the strangeness of the idea, for after asserting that Sveinn's Danish retainers were willing to undertake suicidal fighting on his behalf, he addresses the unbelieving reader:

At ne me credat aliquis hec falsa fingendo alicuius amoris gratia compilare: recte animaduertenti in subsequentibus patebit, utrum uera dixerim an minime. Omnibus enim liquet procul dubio, quoniam humanitatis ita sese habeat consuetudo, ut plerumque ex rebus prospere cedentibus mentes quorumdam plus equo exagitet cogitationum aestus, atque ex nimia in ocio licentia aggrediuntur aliqui, quod uix cogitare nedum facere audent in aduersitate positi.   (*Encomium* 1.1.25-31)

And lest any man think that I am lying, and concocting what I say from regard for any person's favour, in what is to follow, it will be plain to any one paying due attention, whether I am telling the truth or not. For it is abundantly plain to all, that it is the habit of human nature that fervour of mental activity, arising from favourable circumstances, unduly stimulates the spirits of some, and that some will undertake matters owing to the excessive liberty which they enjoy in time of leisure, which they would hardly contemplate, much less perform, if placed in unfavourable circumstances.

The Encomiast is noted for his Latin learning. He refers to himself and his colleagues as 'nos Latini' (2.9.14: 'we Latinists'), and in the *Encomium* he quotes from, or is influenced by, the *Aeneid*, an unidentified biography of Virgil, Lucan, Sallust, and possibly Julius Caesar.[27] He could have borrowed the ideal of men fighting suicidally for their lord from a classical source, especially in view of his knowledge of Sallust and Julius Caesar; but since his remarks obviously allude to the Jómsvikings, a warrior brotherhood at Jómsborg founded by Sveinn's father Haraldr, it should not be ruled out that an ideal of suicidal fighting was maintained as part of this élite Scandinavian comitatus-cult.[28] Jómsviking influence would account for the presence of this ideal in *Bjarkamál* as well.

The similarities between the *Encomium* and *Maldon* go beyond the ideal of suicidal fighting to include, also, battlefield details: there are a number of parallels between the poet's account of the battle of Maldon and the Encomiast's account of the battle of Ashingdon, in 1016, when Knútr secured his claim to the English crown by means of an important military victory over the Anglo-Saxons. According to the Encomiast, Knútr, after the death of his father Sveinn, had reason to believe that his control of London was precarious, so in the winter of 1015-16 he retreated to the isle of Sheppey. Meanwhile Eadmund Ironside, the champion of the English, collected a force in London. During the winter, Eadmund attempted to draw Knútr into battle, even proposing a single combat between them, but the Danes bided their time until after Easter, when they crossed to the mainland and met the English at Ashingdon. During the fighting Eadmund's chief supporter, Eadric Streon, fled from the battle, and other Englishmen followed his example, causing a disruption of the English defences from which the Danes were able to obtain a military victory. The *Encomium* and *Maldon* have in common five clusters of detail, presented here in the order that they appear in both works:

1. A battle 'flyting': the hostile exchange of words between Byrhtnoth and the Viking messenger (*Maldon* 25-61) has its counterpart in Eadmund Ironside's challenge to fight Knútr in single combat, which Knútr, being 'sapiens,' refused, in a speech promising warfare between the English and Danish forces:

Ego tempus luctae prestolabor congruae, dum non casum suspectus certus fuero uictoriae; tu uero, qui aues duellum in hieme, caue ne deficias etiam aptiori tempore.   (*Encomium* 2.8.8-10)

I will await a time, when contest will be fitting, and when anticipating no misfortune, I shall be sure of victory; but as for you, who desire combat in the winter, beware lest you fail to appear even when the time is more appropriate.

The battle flyting, of course, is conventional in heroic poetry[29] and there is only a very general parallel between the *Encomium* and *Maldon* at this point.

2. Crossing from an island to the mainland, after a delay in fighting: Knútr and the Danes spent the winter on the isle of Sheppey, and soon after Easter, they got word that Eadmund's army was advancing to attack them, and 'puppibus posthabitis petunt arida, aptantes se excipere quaeque obuia' (*Encomium* 2.9.3-4: 'they left their ships and went ashore, preparing to receive whatever they should encounter'); they met the English at Ashingdon in Essex. In *Maldon* (84-99), the Vikings' crossing over a causeway from an island to the mainland likewise marks an end to the delay in fighting. The 'bricg' or causeway of *Maldon* 74 and 78 is found only in the poem, not in the *Encomium*. Since neither the *Vita Oswaldi* nor any other source except *Maldon* mentions the Danes landing on an island in 991, Blake imagines that the poet made up this detail, based partly on his knowledge of the Essex coastline and partly on his need to give Byrhtnoth an opportunity to express his resolution to fight in a heroic speech.[30] A literary source cannot be ruled out, however: the

Danes' crossing from Sheppey to the mainland in the *Encomium* shows that this sort of detail was not unique to *Maldon*.

3. The beasts of battle: the Encomiast makes use of a tradition of Viking raven-miracles that goes back to the ninth century or earlier:[31] he writes that the Danes had a banner of white silk with no image inserted into it, but a raven appeared as if embroidered on the silk during time of war, subdued and drooping if the Danes were to be defeated, but restive and flapping its wings if the Danes were to be victorious. The restive raven appeared just as the Danes had crossed to the mainland (*Encomium* 2.9.5-12). Later, after the battle of Ashingdon, we are told that the Danes buried their dead, and, having despoiled the corpses of the English, 'bestiis et auibus eorum relinquentes morticina' (*Encomium* 2.11.6-7: 'left their bodies to the beasts and birds'). The beasts of battle topos, of course, is conventional in Old English and Old Norse poetry; in this tradition, the wolf, raven, and eagle accompany the victors to battle, like the restive raven on Knútr's banner, and/or remain on the battlefield afterward to feed on the corpses of the slain warriors.[32] The *Maldon* poet, like the Encomiast, introduces the beasts of battle as an omen of Viking victory in connection with the Danes' crossing to the mainland. The Vikings are called 'wælwulfas' as they cross 'west ofer Pantan' (96-7), and above them, 'Hremmas wundon, // earn æses georn' (106b-7a): 'Ravens circled, the eagle eager for food').

4. Flight of traitors from the battlefield: during the battle at Ashingdon, Eadric Streon concealed the battle-standard which he carried in his right hand, and 'dans tergum hostibus magnam partem militum bello fraudabat' (*Encomium* 2.9.18-19: 'he turned his back on the enemy, and caused the withdrawal of a large part of the soldiers from battle'). The *Maldon* poet does not mention a battle-standard, but he does describe the defection of a core of traitors (the sons of Odda) which causes many other men to withdraw from the battle:

> Hi bugon þa fram beaduwe   þe þær beon noldon:
> þær wurdon[33] Oddan bearn   ærest on fleame,
> Godric fram guþe,   and þone godan forlet,
> þe him mænigne oft   mear gesealde;
> he gehleop þone eoh   þe ahte his hlaford,
> on þam gerædum   þe hit riht ne wæs,
> and his broðru mid him   begen ærndon,
> Godwine and Godwig,   guþe ne gymdon,

ac wendon fram þam wige   and þone wudu sohton,
flugon on þæt fæsten   and hyra feore burgon,
and manna ma   þonne hit ænig mæð wære,
gyf hi þa geearnunga   ealle gemundon,
þe he him to duguþe   gedon hæfde.   (*Maldon* 185-97)

Then they who did not wish to be there turned from the battle. There the sons of Odda were first in flight, Godric from the battle, and abandoned the good [man] who often gave him many a horse. He leaped on the horse that belonged to his lord, on those trappings which it was not right [to mount on], and his brothers with him both galloped [away], Godwine and Godwig cared not for battle, but turned from the battle and sought the wood, fled to the place of safety and saved their lives, and more men [with them] than was at all fitting, if they had remembered then all the favours that he had done as a benefit for them.

The phrase 'ærest on fleame' (186b) appears several times in the *Anglo-Saxon Chronicle*, including one time in the entry for AD 1016 where Eadric's flight at Ashingdon is reported: 'Ða dyde Eadric ealdormann swa he oftor ær dyde . astealde þone fleam ærest mid Mage sæton . swa aswac his cynehlaforde.'[34] The Encomiast is in agreement with the *Chronicle* about Eadric's deception and disloyalty, but provides a more detailed account that resembles *Maldon* in presenting (a) the flight of a traitor (or traitors); (b) the consequent flight of other warriors as well, resulting in a disruption of the English defences; (c) suggestions that the traitor's defection was planned ahead of time; and (d) suggestions that the defection was motivated not by fear, but by disloyalty.

Eadric Streon, according to the Encomiast, had planned his defection beforehand and had urged his comrades, 'Fugiamus, o sotii, uitamque subtrahamus morti imminenti, alioquin occumbemus ilico; Danorum enim duritiam nosco' (*Encomiast* 2.9.16-17): 'Let us flee, oh comrades, and snatch our lives from imminent death, or else we will fall forthwith, for I know the hardihood of the Danes'); but while he may have tried to inspire fear in his comrades, for his own part 'ut quidam aiunt hoc (non) causa egit timoris sed dolositatis, ut postea claruit; quia hoc eum clam Danis promisisse, nescio quo pro beneficio, assertio multorum dicit' (*Encomium* 1.9.19-21: 'according to some, it was afterwards evident that he did this not out of fear but in guile; and what many assert is that he had promised this secretly to the Danes in return for some favour'). So, also, in the *Maldon* poet's description of the flight of Odda's sons. When the poet says that they turned from battle 'þe þær beon noldon'

(185) and that they 'guþe ne gymdon' (192b), he is not necessarily using litotes to suggest cowardice on their part; rather, the poet could be stating, quite literally, that the sons of Odda did not wish to fight Danes – perhaps because of their Danish family connections.

Godric, Godwine,[35] and Godwig are Anglo-Saxon names, but Odda is Danish; this suggests an English mother and a Danish father. The political ambiguities created by Anglo-Danish parentage are suggested by a tradition relating to the unsuccessful attempt of the English to marshal an army against the Danes in Lindsey and Northumbria in 993. The *Anglo-Saxon Chronicle* (Laud ms) for that year reports that the English leaders, Fræna, Godwine, and Frythegyst, 'onstealdon ... ærest þone fleam,' and Florence of Worcester, probably drawing on a phrase that has dropped out of the *Anglo-Saxon Chronicle* manuscripts that have come down to us, adds that these three defectors were Danes by their father's side.[36] The potential for political ambiguity among Anglo-Danes might also explain the presence in Byrhtnoth's retinue of Æscferth the Northumbrian hostage (*Maldon* 265–72). Dorothy Whitelock, in a survey of the difficulties that Anglo-Saxon kings had in maintaining authority in Northumbria, suggests that the presence of this hostage at Maldon 'is most easily accounted for on the assumption that the English government did not fully trust the Northumbrian Danes when Scandinavian invasions had recommenced.'[37] 'Æscferð,' of course, is an English name, but the name of the hostage's father, 'Ecglaf' (267a), in an eleventh-century Northumbrian context, would be ambiguously English[38] or an anglicized form of OSw or ODan 'Elaf,' own 'Eileifr,' 'Eilifr.'[39] To judge from his father's name, his aristocratic Northumbrian origin, and his status as a hostage, Æscferth was one of the Anglo-Danes in Byrhtnoth's retinue who remained loyal to the English. Two other loyal Anglo-Danes, to judge from their Scandinavian names, were Maccus (70; Sc 'Magnus') and Wistan (Sc 'Wistæin') son of Thurstan (Sc 'Þurstæin') (297–8).[40] Thus three loyal Anglo-Danes, Æscferth, Maccus, and Wistan, contrast with the three disloyal sons of Odda.

Shortly before the battle, Byrhtnoth's chief adviser, Offa, had warned Byrhtnoth, in the counsel-place,

> þæt þær modelice[41]   manega spræcon
> þe eft æt þearfe   þolian noldon   (*Maldon* 200–1)

that many spoke bravely there who would not hold out afterward at [time of] need.

It may be that Offa, aware of the Anglo-Danish connections among Byrhtnoth's followers, suspects a conspiracy, or fears the potential for one, and thus warns about the possibility of defection 'æt þearfe,' that is, at some critical moment in the battle, although, of course, Offa's counsel cautions Byrhtnoth more generally to take into account the potential for cowardice among his men. This dual concern for cowardice and betrayal – the two possible motives for defection from battle – appears later when Offa says that 'Us Godric hæfð // earh Oddan bearn, / ealle beswicene' (237b–38: 'Godric, the cowardly son of Odda, has betrayed us all'). Offa explains further that many of the English, when they saw Byrhtnoth's horse turn from battle, assumed that Byrhtnoth had taken flight; thus deceived, many of the English also turned from battle (239–42a). We are reminded of another supposed exploit of Eadric Streon, during a battle between Knútr and Eadmund at Scearstan in late summer 1016, when Eadric struck off the head of Osmær, an 'Eadmund Ironside look-alike,' held it up for display, and admonished the English to flee because their leader was slain.[42] Concerning the defection of Odda's sons, Offa adds, 'Abreoðe his angin, // þæt he her swa manigne / man aflymde!' (242b–43): 'May his [Godric's] enterprise fail,[43] that he here caused so many men to take flight'). So far as the motives of the defectors from battle are concerned, the *Maldon* poet maintains a dual and at times ambiguous interest in both cowardice and betrayal. As we have seen, the Encomiast, likewise, maintains a dual interest in cowardice and betrayal as possible motives for defection from the battle of Ashingdon.

5. The pattern of heroic speeches and warriors advancing to battle: immediately after the defection of Odda's sons, Ælfwine makes a speech stating his resolve to continue fighting (209–24), then advances to battle (225–9). The same pattern is followed by Offa, Leofsunu, Dunnere,[44] and others, as each faithful warrior encourages the others by words and deeds. This pattern appears also in the *Encomium*: immediately after the defection of Eadric Streon, Eadmund makes a heroic speech –

O Angli ... aut hodie bellabitis, aut omnes una in deditionem ibitis. Pugnate ergo pro libertate et patria, uiri cordati; hi quippe qui fugiunt, utpote formidolosi, si non abirent, essent impedimento exercitui.   (*Encomium* 2.9.21-4)

Oh Englishmen, to-day you will fight or surrender yourselves all together. Therefore, fight for your liberty and your country, men of understanding; truly, those who are in flight, inasmuch as they are afraid, if they were not withdrawing, would be a hindrance to the army.

Then Eadmund advances to battle –

Et haec dicens in medios ingreditur hostes circumquaque caedens Danos, nobiles hoc exemplo suos reddens ad bellandum proniores.   (*Encomium* 2.9.24-6)

And as he said these things, he advanced into the midst of the enemy, cutting down the Danes on all sides, and by this example rendering his noble followers more inclined to fight.

Here and in the preceding incident of the traitor's defection, it would be difficult to imagine closer parallels between the Latin and the English, short of literal translation from one language into the other.

 There are five possible explanations for the parallels between *Maldon* and the *Encomium*. (1) One would be that the similarities are the result of chance or coincidence. It was inevitable that there would be similarities in detail among at least some of the many battles fought between the English and the Danes during the tenth and eleventh centuries, and this happened to be the case with the battles fought at Maldon and Ashingdon. (2) A second possibility would be that the Encomiast's account of the events at Ashingdon, and especially of Eadric Streon's conduct there, was essentially true, and generally known in England during the years after 1016; the *Maldon* poet could have based his own battlefield account, with its story of treachery at a crucial moment, on what was known about the battle of Ashingdon. This would explain at least some of the more important parallels between *Maldon* and the *Encomium*; it would imply a date of ca 1020 or later for *Maldon*. (3) A third possibility would be that *Maldon* influenced the *Encomium*. This seems to me to be very unlikely, however. We know for certain that the *Encomium* was composed in Flanders and circulated in England; it was, indeed, particularly intended for an English readership. On the other hand we have no reason to suppose that *Maldon* or any other English poem enjoyed a comparable circulation in Flanders. Of course, anything is possible. One could imagine, for example, that *Maldon* was composed around 1000 and was part of the repertoire of an unknown Anglo-Saxon scop who accompanied Queen Emma in her exile in Flanders, in 1037-40. Those who think so may explain why this great Norman magnate would employ an English minstrel in her retinue during the period when events had driven her to a long sojourn on the continent. I have tried to imagine other, similar scenarios and they all seem equally implausible to me. (4) A fourth possibility is that both *Maldon* and the *Encomium* were influenced by some unknown, lost source. It is pretty clear, however, that the Encomiast got his information about historical events in England under Sveinn and Knútr directly from Queen Emma or from members of her retinue, during the period of her exile in Flanders. It is very unlikely that the Encomiast had consulted some unknown literary source for his account of the battle of Ashingdon. (5) A fifth possibility would be that the *Maldon* poet used the *Encomium* as a source for his battlefield details. This, of course, implies a date of ca 1042 or later for the composition of the poem; however, there is no linguistic, stylistic, or historical reason why *Maldon* could not have been composed sometime after ca 1040.

If *Maldon* was composed at a relatively early date, it may be that its parallels with the *Encomium* are only a coincidence, and that the details in the poem correspond, to some extent at least, with what actually happened in 991 – difficult as it is to imagine what historical events might lie behind details in the poem that are obviously the work of a poetic imagination: the sequence of faithful warriors making heroic speeches and stepping into battle, for example. If *Maldon* was composed at a relatively late date, the circumstances of its composition might be partially reconstructed with reference to the *Vita Oswaldi* and the *Encomium*. It is difficult to say how much the poet might have known about the battle of Maldon or about Byrhtnoth from oral or written sources, but if the *Vita Oswaldi* is any indication, from local history he could have got some hints about Byrhtnoth's age, stature, leadership abilities, and pious character; he could have learned that Byrhtnoth fought and died in a battle against Danes; that a number of Englishmen fled from the battle after his death; and (not in the poem) that 'the Danes were so mauled that they could hardly man their ships after the battle.'[45] Neither the extant poem nor the *Vita Oswaldi* mentions the town of Maldon (named in the *Anglo-Saxon Chronicle*), but the poet does mention the river Pante[46] and thus locates the battle near Maldon. Probably the poet did not know of a tradition, some would say reliable, reported in the *Liber Eliensis*, according to which Byrhtnoth's body was decapitated by the Vikings during the battle.[47] Certainly he understood the topography of the Essex shore, and he may well have had a particular location in mind, such as Northey Island near the Blackwater estuary,[48] although the location chosen for the poem need not have been the site of the historical battle. When it came to battlefield details, the poet's knowledge was limited to what he could glean from traditional poetry or from written sources. *If* the poem was a very late composition (after ca 1042), the *Encomium Emmae Reginae* recently promulgated by Queen Emma, which circulated in courtly[49] and perhaps in monastic[50] circles, with its relatively detailed account of the battle of Ashingdon, could have offered a welcome source of inspiration to a poet who was striving to compose a credible battlefield narrative. But, of course, this is only one of several possibilities, as we have indicated above.

The *Maldon* poet's artistic resources included a command of traditional formulaic verse,[51] and also a sensitivity to dialect differences. Against the background of his southeastern dialect,[52] he uses words and phrases of Scandinavian origin in strategic places to reflect a foreign intrusion on England's language and land. Most striking is his use of Scandinavian locutions in the Viking messenger's speech (29-41), which Robinson has noted: 'griŏ' (25); 'garræs' (32, ON 'geirras'); 'þon' meaning 'than' (33); 'most' (30); 'hilde dælan' (33, ON 'deila heiptir,' 'deila sakar'); 'syllan ... sylfra dom' (38; ON 'selja sjalfdœmi'): *Maldon* seems to be the first English poem to exploit dialect differences for artistic purposes.[53] The use of dialect differences in speech is extended to indirect discourse in the Vikings' request for 'upgangan' (87a: 'a landing,' 'a passage up on land'). Most editors emend to 'upgang' because, as Gordon explains in his edition (49n), 'no weak form of this word is known elsewhere in OE'; but in view of the poet's Scandinavianisms elsewhere, a weak form based on ON 'ganga' seems probable, especially since the Norse word is used in compounds that have a military context: 'herganga' ('war-march'), and 'holmganga' ('duel,' literally 'island-going').[54] Besides these there is the use of personal names of Scandinavian origin, discussed above, and also the use of Scandinavian words that reflect Viking military activity: 'wicing' (26, 73, sqq); 'æschere' (69: ON 'askr' + 'here' 'ship army'); 'dreng' (149); the verb 'ceallian' (91).[55] The noun 'lidmen' (99a), gen pl 'lidmanna sum' (164b) in a phrase parallel to 'drenga sum' fourteen lines earlier (149a), in *Beowulf* (1623) means 'sailors' 'men of the fleet,' but by the time of Knútr the more usual meaning of 'lidmen' must have been 'men of the "liŏ" [army],' referring specifically to Sveinn's and Knútr's 'þinga-mannaliŏ' which was the military basis of these kings' rule in England.[56] The poet's use of Scandinavian words to refer to the Vikings (with the exception of 'ceallian,' which refers to Byrhtnoth's reply to the Viking request for 'upganga') is similar to Wulfstan's practice in *Sermo Lupi ad Anglos*: there, Scandinavian words are used heavily in those parts of the homily that deal with the relationships between the English and the Danes.[57]

In language as in content, then, *Maldon* combines the old and the new: traditional verse formulas but with occasional Scandinavian loan words; conventional battlefield activity associated not with an ancient hero like Hengest or Ingeld, but with a comparatively recent one, Byrhtnoth – yet one not so recent as to limit the poet's options in the creative process of composition. The poet exercises his creative options in many incidental details (such as the names of the English fighters) and also in developing the poem's central theme: the ideal of suicidal fighting as an expression of loyalty, seen in contrast with flight from battle as an expression of either cowardice or disloyalty. The ideal of suicidal fighting, seen also in *Bjarkamál* and in the *Encomium*, is unique in Old English poetry; it is a tribute to the poet's artistry in combining the old and the new that for many years, commentators on *Maldon*, captivated by the poem's illusion of familiarity and strangeness, assumed that its theme reflected traditional military values. Similarities between the Encomiast's account of the defection of Eadric Streon at Ashingdon, and the defection of the sons of Odda at Maldon, encourage the belief, argued by George Clark, that the turning-point of the poem is the moment of defection, not Byrhtnoth's earlier decision to allow the Vikings to cross the causeway to the mainland.[58]

This is not to say that Byrhtnoth's decision to grant 'upganga,' to the Vikings is unimportant: for while the defection of Odda's sons explains the circumstances that led to the English defeat, as Offa's commentary (230-43) makes explicit, the decision to grant 'upganga' explains the circumstances that led to Byrhtnoth's death, and with regard to that decision, the poet offers a commentary (84-90) that is parallel to Offa's later on. He says that the Vikings, finding the 'bricgweardas' too hard for them, 'longunnon lytegian' (86a: 'resorted to strategem') and requested 'upgangan' (87a);

> Ða se eorl ongan   for his ofermode
> alyfan landes to fela   laþere ðeode.   (*Maldon* 89-90)

Then the earl, because of his 'ofermod,' began to give too much land to the hostile people.

I have no contribution to make to the debate about 'ofermod,' except to note my agreement with Professor Gneuss that a word that almost always means 'pride' probably ought to be translated as 'pride' in *Maldon*;[59] but for reasons presented above I must also agree with Professor Clark that the 'ofermod' passage cannot be considered the 'touchstone' for criticism of the poem. I translate 'ongunnon lytegian' in as neutral a sense as possible, 'resorted to strategem,' perhaps better 'began to strategize' on the principle that a verb should not be translated as a noun; however, in contrast with Clark's view that the phrase means something like 'acted prudently' with ironic overtones of obsequious behaviour,[60] I believe that 'lytegian,' a class II consonantal verb Gmc '*leut-,' Gothic 'luton,'[61] has the basic sense 'deceive.' There is no basis for the suggestion in the OED, s v 'lout,' that the primary sense of '*leut-' was 'bow, bend, make obeisance.'[62] Gothic 'luton, usluton' in every occurrence means 'deceive' and in one instance is used (as is 'lytegian' in *Maldon*) to contrast strategem with force: 'Jabai auk diabulau fram anastodeinai nih nauþjandin, ak uslotondin mannan ...' (*Skeireins* I.b: 'for inasmuch as the devil from the beginning not forcing but deceiving man ...').[63] Unlike 'usluton' in *Skeireins* I.b, however, 'lytegian' in *Maldon* is used intransitively;[64] the poet does not state that Byrhtnoth was tricked, only that the Vikings resorted to strategem – successfully. Byrhtnoth concedes 'upgangan,' 'landes to fela.' 'Upganga,' besides being provocatively Scandinavian in morphology, through its prefix 'up-' implies that Byrhtnoth is conceding a tactical advantage not only because of the narrowness of the easily defended causeway, but also because the English, prior to this concession, had been able to fight from the vantage of a higher elevation.

Thus in the poet's view, Byrhtnoth contributed to the circumstances that led to his death; but it was the defection of Odda's sons, not Byrhtnoth's 'ofermod,' that led to the defeat of the English. *Maldon* is not fundamentally a tragedy of 'ofermod' (although 'ofermod,' courage, and cowardice are secondary issues in the poem); *Maldon* is, rather, a heroic poem about loyalty, which finds its expression in the ideal of suicidal fighting, in contrast to defection from battle, which may be an expression of either cowardice or disloyalty.

NOTES

1 Rosemary Woolf 'The ideal of men dying with their lord in the *Germania* and in *The Battle of Maldon*' *ASE* 5 (1976) 63-81; Bertha Phillpotts ' "The Battle of Maldon": Some Danish Affinities' *MLR* 24 (1929) 172-90

2 John McKinnell 'On the Date of *The Battle of Maldon*' *MÆ* 44 (1975) 121-36

3 N.F. Blake 'The genesis of *The Battle of Maldon*' *ASE* 7 (1978) 119-29. For Byrtferth of Ramsey's authorship of the *Vita Oswaldi*, see Michael Lapidge 'The hermeneutic style in tenth-century Anglo-Latin literature' *ASE* 4 (1975)

91-3.

4 Stanley B. Greenfield *A Critical History of Old English Literature* (New York: 1965) 99; Greenfield cites with approval Jess B. Bessinger's caveat against the 'equation of poetic verisimilitude to historical verity'; Bessinger '*Maldon* and the *Óláfsdrápa*: An Historical Caveat' *CL* 14 (1962) 23-35.

5 John Scattergood '*The Battle of Maldon* and History' in *Literature and Learning in Medieval and Renaissance England: Essays presented to Fitzroy Pyle* ed Scattergood (Dublin 1984) 11-24

6 For the military situation in 1044-7 see Frank Barlow *Edward the Confessor* (Berkeley 1970) 79-80

7 Cecily Clark 'On Dating *The Battle of Maldon*: Certain Evidence Reviewed' *Nottingham Medieval Studies* 27 (1983) 1-22; quotations from 2, 22

8 D.C. Scragg ed *The Battle of Maldon* (Manchester 1981) 26-7; 23-8 for discussion of language and date. For a similar argument about 'eorl' see Scattergood '*The Battle of Maldon* and History' 15-16.

9 Ashley Crandell Amos *Linguistic Means of Determining the Dates of Old English Literary Texts* (Cambridge, Mass 1980) 167

10 Amos *Linguistic Means* 94 and 101-2. Scragg, ed, *Maldon* 29 and 52n, recognizes this phonemic split but does not include it as evidence in his discussion of the poem's date.

11 *Saxonis Grammatici Gesta Danorvm* ed Alfred Holder (Strassburg 1886); in particular, Woolf (79-80) cites a speech by Hjalti (Holder ed 61); Bjarki's and Hjalti's resolve to lie beside their lord Hrolfr in death (Holder ed 66); and Saxo's comment on their loyalty (67).

12 Edward B. Irving, Jr *A Reading of Beowulf* (New Haven 1968) 2-15. Negative comparison is used to define the heroic more often in *Beowulf* than in *Maldon*; indeed, Irving does not call attention to this device in his 'The Heroic Style in *The Battle of Maldon*' *SP* 58 (1961) 457-67. For negative comparison generally see George Kurman 'Negative Comparison in Literary Epic Narrative' *CL* 21 (1969) 337-47.

13 For the text of *Maldon* I am using *The Anglo-Saxon Minor Poems*, ed Elliott Van Kirk Dobbie, ASPR 6 (New York 1942), with occasional deviations from Dobbie's punctuation, and I do not always agree with Dobbie's emendations when they reflect seemingly unnecessary departures from the manuscript.

14 Sophus Bugge 'Studien über das Beowulfepos' *Paul und Braunes Beiträge* 12 (1887) 104 called attention to the similarity of *Bjarkamál* 203 and *Beowulf* 2525. Phillpotts acknowledges this similarity but argues that *Maldon* 'corresponds almost word for word with *Bjarkamál*' (185). The presence of a verse formula seems to me far more likely than the influence of *Bjarkamál* on both *Beowulf* and *Maldon*. Scragg ed *The Battle of Maldon* points out that

Florence of Worcester, in his account of the battle, mentions Byrhtnoth's refusal to give up 'unum passum pedis' to the Danes.

15 For Danish lexical influence see Phillpotts 'Danish Affinities' 187-8, and Fred C. Robinson 'Some Aspects of the *Maldon* Poet's Artistry' *JEGP* 75 (1976) 25-8.

16 For Julius Caesar, *De Bello Gallico* 3.22; Woolf's translation 64. For Sallust and Servius, Woolf 65 nn3 and 5 refers to the 'Life of Sertorius' in *Plutarch's Lives* ed Bernadotte Perrin (Cambridge, Mass [Loeb Classical Library] 1919), and to *Servii Grammatici qui feruntur in Vergilii Carmina Commentarii* ed G. Thilo and H. Hagen, 3.1 (Leipzig 1887) 336.

17 E.A. Thompson *The Visigoths in the Time of Ulfila* (Oxford 1966) 52

18 Quintus Curtius *History of Alexander* ed John C. Rolfe (Cambridge, Mass [Loeb Classical Library] 1946)

19 *Two of the Saxon Chronicles Parallel* ed Charles Plummer (Oxford 1892) 1:48; for the identification of '*Merantun*' with Merton in Devon, see C.L. Wrenn 'A Saga of the Anglo-Saxons' *History* ns 25 (1940) 214.

20 Ruth Waterhouse 'The Theme and Structure of 755 *Anglo-Saxon Chronicle*' *NM* 70 (1969) 630-40

21 R.W. McTurk '"Cynewulf and Cyneheard" and the Icelandic Sagas' *Leeds SE* 12 (1981) 81-127

22 See especially Mark Lambert *Malory: Style and Vision in Le Morte Darthur* (New Haven 1975) 1-55.

23 Francis P. Magoun, Jr 'Cynewulf, Cyneheard, and Osric' *Anglia* 57 (1933) 374

24 The language of the *Chronicle* story is ambiguous at times, especially in pronoun reference, and consequently there has been controversy about the details of the conflict; besides Magoun (n 23 above) 361-76, see Charles Moorman 'The "Anglo-Saxon Chronicle" for 755' *N&Q* 199 (March 1954) 94-8; Tom H. Towers 'Thematic Unity in the Story of Cynewulf and Cyneheard' *JEGP* 62 (1963) 310-16; and Francis J. Battaglia '*Anglo-Saxon Chronicle* for 755: The Missing Evidence for a Traditional Reading' *PMLA* 81 (1966) 173-8. Despite disagreements over details, there is general agreement that the story involves conflicts between the obligations of kinship and retainership.

25 *Encomium Emmae Reginae* ed Alistair Campbell, Royal Historical Society, Camden Third Series, 72 (London 1949); Campbell's translation. For a discussion of the date and circumstances of composition, see Campbell xix-xxiii.

26 Woolf 'The ideal of men dying with their lord' 81

27 For the Encomiast's Latin learning, see Campbell ed *Encomium* xxiii-xl.

28 The *Encomium* should, perhaps, be added to the primary sources normally

cited in discussions of the Jómsvikings, although it must be admitted that, with his ideal of suicidal fighting and his Viking raven-miracle (discussed below), the Encomiast perhaps offers a view as romanticized as that in the *Jómsvikingasaga*, for which see N.F. Blake trans *The Saga of the Jomsvikings* (London 1962). Lauritz Weibull has argued in several places that neither the Jómsvikings nor Jómsborg ever existed: in *Kritiska undersökningar i Nordens historia omkring år 1000* (Lund 1911); in *Historisk-kritisk metod och nordisk medeltidsforskning* (Lund 1913); with arguments in these works reprinted in *Nordisk Historia. Forskningar och undersökningar, I, Forntid och Vikingatid* (Stockholm 1948) 313-30 and 440-8. For a brief survey of Jómsborg problems see Gwyn Jones *A History of the Vikings* (London 1968) 127-30.

29 Various conventional or literary features of the flyting match in *Maldon* are discussed by Irving 'Heroic Style in "The Battle of Maldon"' 460-1; Ralph W.V. Elliott 'Byrhtnoth and Hildebrand: A Study in Heroic Technique' *CL* 14 (1962) 57-8; George Clark '*The Battle of Maldon*: A Heroic Poem' *Speculum* 43 (1968) 58 and 64-5; Earl R. Anderson 'Flyting in *The Battle of Maldon*' *NM* 71 (1970) 197-202; N.F. Blake 'The Flyting in *The Battle of Maldon*' *ELN* 13 (1976) 242-4; Fred Robinson 'Some Aspects of the *Maldon* Poet's Artistry' 25-8.

It should be noted, incidentally, that in the twelfth-century *Chronicle* of Henry of Huntingdon, Knútr and Eadmund Ironside are represented as fighting in single combat at 'Olanie' (possibly referring to an island in the Severn, which would make the episode consistent with the Icelandic practice of 'holmganga'); T. Arnold ed, Rolls Series (London 1879) 185 (book 6). Henry of Huntingdon's account is repeated by other chroniclers. Margaret Ashdown, in 'The Single Combat in Certain Cycles of English and Scandinavian Tradition and Romance' *MLR* 17 (1922) 112-30, proposes an elaborate theory for the origin of this non-historical episode, relating it to the Havelok tradition. It seems to me a much simpler matter to imagine that Henry of Huntingdon, or his source, knew of Knútr's refusal to fight in single combat in the *Encomium*, and created, in contradiction to the Encomiast's account, a 'holmganga' episode that presented both Eadmund and Knútr in a more heroic light.

30 Blake 'The Genesis of "The Battle of Maldon"' 122-3.

31 N. Lukman 'The Raven Banner and the Changing Ravens' *Classica et Mediaevalia* 19 (1958) 133-51, 139-40 for the *Encomium*; for this tradition in English see Kathryn Hume 'The Function of the *Hrefn Blaca: Beowulf* 1801' *MP* 67 (1969-70) 60-3; Sylvia Huntley Horowitz 'The Ravens in *Beowulf*' *JEGP* 80 (1981) 502-11.

The literary transmission of the detail about the raven-banner is summarized by Campbell ed *Encomium* xxxvii: the Encomiast found such a banner described in his manuscript of Asser's *Life of Alfred*; Asser's work was also the source for the miraculous raven-banner mentioned in the *Annals of St. Neot's*. Campbell 96–7 also discusses briefly the cultural background of raven-banners.

32 For the beasts of battle topos, see Francis P. Magoun, Jr 'The Theme of the Beasts of Battle in Anglo-Saxon Poetry' *NM* 56 (1955) 81-90, and Adrien Bonjour '*Beowulf* and the Beasts of Battle' *PMLA* 72 (1957) 563-72. E.D. Laborde, 'The Style of "The Battle of Maldon"' *MLR* 19 (1924) 412, notes that raven and eagles are shown hovering over the battle at Hastings in the Bayeux Tapestry.

33 Dobbie ed line 186a alters ms 'wurdon' to 'wearð' but his only argument is that the singular form of the verb 'seems much more natural' (144n).

In line 190b below 'þe' could possibly be emended to 'þeh': 'þeh hit riht ne waes' ('although it was not right'): see Elizabeth Suddaby 'Three Notes on Old English Texts' *MLN* 69 (1954) 466-7.

34 *Two of the Saxon Chronicles Parallel* ed Plummer, 1:152

35 Ms 'Godrine' (192a) is otherwise unknown, and unlikely, as an Anglo-Saxon name; other possibilities are 'Godryne,' 'Godrinc' (see Dobbie ed 145n). The *Maldon* poet made up most of the names (as noted by Blake 'Genesis of "The Battle of Maldon"' 126), a circumstance that makes 'Godwine' seem most likely because of its frequency as an Anglo-Saxon name.

36 *Two of the Saxon Chronicles Parallel* ed Plummer 1:127; *The Chronicle of Florence of Worcester with Two Continuations* ed Thomas Forester (London 1854) 110

37 Dorothy Whitelock 'The Dealings of the Kings of England with Northumbria in the Tenth and Eleventh Centuries' in *The Anglo-Saxons: Studies in Some Aspects of their History and Culture presented to Bruce Dickins* ed Peter Clemoes (London 1959) 87. I do not agree with Blake's assertion, 'The genesis of "The Battle of Maldon"' 127, that 'no one has yet explained convincingly why a hostage from Northumbria should be among Byrthnoth's followers. Historically it seems most improbable;' I do agree with Blake, however, that the poet invented the hostage.

38 'Ecglaf' appears in charters in *Cartularium Saxonicum* ed Walter de Gray Birch, 4 vols (London 1893) nos 162, 538, 574 (dated AD 742, 874, 896); 'Ecglaf' is the name of Unferth's father in *Beowulf*.

39 Erik Björkman *Nordische Personnamen in England in alt- und fruhmittelenglischer Zeit* (Halle 1910), 'Eʒlaf': Assar Janzén, *Personnamn* (Stockholm 1948), cites runic 'ailaif' (69), 'Eileifr,' etc, 25, 67, 69, 71, 107, 109, 120, 122, 272. For Eʒlaf, chief of Sweinn's 'þingamannalið' in London, 'dux' under Knútr, and confraternal member of Thorney Abbey along with others of Knútr's

jarls, see Dorothy Whitelock 'Scandinavian Personal Names in the *Liber Vitae* of Thorney Abbey' *Saga-Book of the Viking Society* 12 (1940) 132, 134-5, 139, 142, 152-3.

40 For the Scandinavian background of Wistan and Thurstan, see E.V. Gordon ed *The Battle of Maldon* (London 1937) 84-5; for Maccus, see Blake 'Genesis of "The Battle of Maldon"' 126.

41 Dobbie ed emends to 'modiglice,' calling 'modelice' 'an impossible form' (145n), but in view of the adjective 'modi' at line 147a, 'modelice' is possible.

42 *Chronicle of Florence of Worcester* 127-9; Forester trans 128-9n notes that Henry of Huntingdon transfers this ruse to the battle of Offington, fought shortly afterward. The *Anglo-Saxon Chronicle* for 1016 (Laud ms) mentions Eadric Streon's treachery at Sceorstan but gives no details about it (Plummer ed 1:149-50).

43 Gordon ed *The Battle of Maldon* translates line 242b 'may his conduct have an evil end' or 'curse him for behaving thus.' Scragg ed *The Battle of Maldon* in his glossary, 89 sv 'ābrēoðan,' translates 'may his enterprise fail (*a curse*).'

44 The inclusion of Dunnere, the 'unorne ceorl' (*Maldon* 255-6: 'simple yeoman') and some others is best explained as an artistic attempt to represent the warriors as a microcosm of English society, representing various localities, age groups, and social classes: see N.F. Blake 'The Battle of Maldon' *Neophil* 49 (1965) 337-8. McKinnell, 'Date of *The Battle of Maldon*' 130, notes that 'it is easy to cite other examples of heroic behaviour from lower-class characters in Germanic literature' (and he mentions examples from the *Njáls saga, Gísla saga,* and *Laxdæla saga*). As a type of the 'rustic warrior,' Dunnere has a venerable classical heritage as well. According to Pausanias, one of the heroes worshipped at Marathon after the Athenian victory over the Persians in 490 BC was Echetlaeus ('he of the plough-tail'), 'a man of rustic appearance and dress' who was present in the battle and 'slaughtered many of the foreigners with a plow'; he mysteriously disappeared and his cult was then ordered by the Delphian oracle: Pausanias 1.32.5

45 Blake 'Genesis of "The Battle of Maldon"' 122

46 According to [Eilert] Ekwall, *English River-Names* (Oxford 1928) 319, 'The old name Pant (pronounced Pont) is still applied to the river below Maldon'; so noted in Gordon ed *The Battle of Maldon* 85. The river-name 'Pante,' 'Panta,' it should be added, may well be related etymologically to a Germanic adjective root '-panta' ('slow' 'sluggish'), otherwise unattested except in Jordanes *Getica* 17:95; see Theodor Mommsen ed MGH *Auctores Antiquissimi* 5 (Berlin 1882), and for English translation, Charles Christopher Mierow, *The Gothic History of Jordanes* 2nd ed (Princeton 1915). There, Jordanes derives the tribal name 'Gepidae' from the Gothic adjective 'gepanta' and

reports a legend according to which the ship carrying these people, one of the three ships of 'Getae' migrating from Scandza to Gothiscandza, was the last to reach its destination. Although 'gepanta' will hardly do as an etymology for 'Gepidae,' it is very plausible as a source for OE 'Pante,' 'Panta' as a river-name.

47 On this see Gordon ed *The Battle of Maldon* 8-9 and 20-1. Robinson, 'Some Aspects of the *Maldon* Poet's Artistry' 37-8, suggests that the poet knew of the decapitation but suppressed it except for hints in the word 'forheawen,' lines 223 and 314.

48 Originally proposed by E.D. Laborde 'The Site of the Battle of Maldon' *EHR* 40 (1925) 161-73; reviewed most importantly by O.D. Macrae-Gibson 'How Historical is *The Battle of Maldon?*' *MÆ* 39 (1970) 89-107, and George R. Petty, Jr and Susan Petty 'Geology and *The Battle of Maldon*' *Speculum* 51 (1976) 435-46

49 BM Additional 33241, the earliest and most authoritative manuscript and the one closest to the author's copy (and perhaps closest to Emma's copy), is illuminated with a tableau showing the author, kneeling, presenting his book to Queen Emma enthroned, with her sons Hörthaknútr and Eadweard standing at her side. This tableau certainly illustrates the theme of the last section of the *Encomium* (3.14) where the claim is made that 'Hic fides habetur regni sotiis' ('Here there is loyalty among sharers of rule'), adapted from Lucan 1.92 as a way of contrasting the tranquillity of Emma's England with the chaos of triumvirate Rome. Here as throughout the *Encomium* the propagandist objectives are obvious; no doubt Emma had a courtly readership primarily in mind when she commissioned the work.

50 In the *Encomium* 2.19-21 Knútr is praised for his gifts to churches and monasteries and for his piety, in a panegyric that seems to provide assurance to religious readers, as well as to encourage secular rulers to follow his example.

51 Important discussions of style are Laborde 'The Style of "The Battle of Maldon"' *MLR* 19 (1924) 401–17; Irving 'Heroic Style in *The Battle of Maldon*' (n 12 above); Greenfield *The Interpretation of Old English Poems* (London 1972) 55-8 and 110-11; Elizabeth S. Sklar '*The Battle of Maldon* and the Popular Tradition: Some Rhymed Formulas' *PQ* 59 (1975) 663-70.

52 The southeastern dialect features of the poem are discussed by Helmut Gneuss *Die Battle of Maldon als historisches und literarisches Zeugnis* Bayer Akad der Wiss, Phil-Hist Kl, NF 5 (Munich 1976) 55-8; and for discussion to the effect that the dialect evidence is not conclusive, see F. Wenisch 'Sächsische Dialektwörter in *The Battle of Maldon*' *Indogermansiche Forschungen* 81 (1976) 181-203.

53 Robinson 'Some Aspects of the *Maldon* Poet's Artistry' 25-8

54 For 'holmganga' see Marlene Ciclimini 'The Old Icelandic Duel' *Scandinavian Studies* 25 (1963) 175-94

55 See Phillpotts 'Danish Affinities' 187-9; Gordon ed 45n, 49n, 53n.

56 See C. Warren Hollister *Anglo-Saxon Military Institutions on the Eve of the Norman Conquest* (Oxford 1962) 16-18. The absence of Scandinavian influence on the language of *Beowulf*, it seems to me, creates a problem for proponents of an eleventh-century date for that poem – a problem not considered by Kevin S. Kiernan *Beowulf and the Beowulf Manuscript* (New Brunswick, NJ 1981).

57 Wulfstan *Sermo Lupi ad Anglos* ed Dorothy Whitelock (London 1938), 'unlaga' (14); 'lage' (24); 'lage,' 'griðian' (36); 'griðlease' (40); 'griðe' (84); and especially, in 104-18, 'wicinge,' 'þegengylde,' 'laga,' 'nydgyld,' 'feseð,' 'nydmagan'; see Whitelock's notes to these passages, and also her discussion of Wulfstan's language, 44-5. For 'lagu,' 'unlagu' see further A.G. Kennedy 'Cnut's law code of 1018' *ASE* 11 (1983) 67-70.

58 George Clark '*The Battle of Maldon*: A Heroic Poem' *Speculum* 43 (1968) 52-71; Clark 'The Battle in *The Battle of Maldon*' *NM* 69 (1968) 374-9; Clark 'The Hero of *Maldon*: Vir pius et strenuus' *Speculum* 54 (1979) 257-82

59 Helmut Gneuss '*The Battle of Maldon* 89: Byrhtnoð's *ofermod* Once Again' *SP* 72 (1976) 117-37; and see Gneuss's notes for earlier discussions of this problem.

60 George Clark '*The Battle of Maldon*: A Heroic Poem' 52-4

61 On the morphology of class II consonantals see now Gerald Lee Fullerton *Historical Germanic Verb Morphology* (Berlin 1977) 45-54.

62 George Clark '*The Battle of Maldon*: A Heroic Poem' 68, cites the OED comment on 'lout.' J.E. Cross 'Mainly on Philology and the Interpretative Criticism of *Maldon*' in *Old English Studies in Honor of John C. Pope* ed Robert B. Burlin and Edward B. Irving, Jr (Toronto 1974) 235-53, argues for 'lytegian' ('act cunningly, practise deception'); my discussion here is restricted to a point that does not overlap with Cross's.

63 *Stamm-Heyne's Ulfilas* ed Moritz Heyne (Paderborn 1874)

64 A point made by George Clark '*The Battle of Maldon*: A Heroic Poem' 53, and again in 'The Hero of *Maldon*' 269-71; Clark goes on to cite Kentish glosses of Proverbs that associate 'letig,' 'leti' with 'astutus,' 'callidus,' 'versutus' (273), which shows that, whatever may be said about the verb, the adjective need not always have a pejorative connotation.

MORTON W. BLOOMFIELD
Deor Revisited

*A*FTER AN ABSENCE of over twenty years from thinking and writing about *Deor*, I believe it is time to return again to this same topic. The occasion of the celebration of Stanley Greenfield's lengthy and productive period as a distinguished scholar and critic, especially but not exclusively of much early English literature, seems to be appropriate for such a return. Although it is not correct to say that many discoveries of fact or new interpretations have been made since 'The Form of *Deor*' appeared in *PMLA* 79 (1964), it is the case that some notable contributions, some helpful and some less so, have been made in that period. *Deor* invites speculation and is not easily open to definitive answers. We must rely on probableness.

In 1964, I suggested that the form of *Deor* had been influenced by the structure in both form and content of the charm, which in many cases uses the 'as x, so y,' format in order to bring about a desired action. It is obvious, as I wrote then, that the poem is not a charm, but it does bear some remarkable similarities to many charms. *Deor* has a tighter structure than any charm I know of. Its aim, like that of many charms, is to bring about a certain goal (in this case either a new minstrel position, a return to the old one or to his 'landright' ['londryht'], which the speaker believes to have been taken away from him). We find the desire to realize a practical goal in all charms. The traditional form frequently contains inter alia a certain 'as x, so y' pattern to remind the gods or God or Fortune that they, or he or it, have brought about such transformations in the past and hence perhaps he, they, or it may do so again.

This formula is found in charms all over the world. Its existence rests upon the widespread notion that if something has occurred or has been brought about once, it may be brought about again. Repetition is believed,

as Kirkegaard, Eliade, and Kawin[1] have suggested, to be a major force
in life and to bring things and events back and to 'lock together the
past and the present.'[2] Repetitions are always only near repetitions,[3]
though the heart of the event must remain the same. The horse whose
limp has been cured in the past is usually no longer the horse now before
one whom one desires to heal by the charm. It is, however, similar (if
not the same) to the antecedent horse. A charm attempts to recreate again
a past event, to bring back the admired past.

II

Although there have been since my article appeared several different
analyses of the poem, most of them have not been mainly concerned
with the overall structure of the poem, with the possible exception of
that put forth by Murray F. Markland entitled 'Boethius, Alfred, and
Deor,'[4] and even more to the point James L. Boren's 'The Design of
the Old English *Deor.*' Boren's we shall discuss below. Markland's is
at present our concern. In his article, he argues that *Deor* is simply a
development of a notion put forth in Boethius' *Consolation of Philosophy*
II, part 2. In that prose section, Markland writes, 'Philosophy speaks
in imitation of Fortune defending herself against Boethius' complaints';
she points out that since past happiness has vanished, it is also likely
that present unhappiness will also pass.[5] Markland finds Alfred's (or one
of his subordinates') translation a little more satisfactory than Boethius'
own words to support this interpretation.

There are some parallels, of course, between the Boethius reference
and the theme of the poem, but none is really close, even to Alfred's
translation. The notion of the transience of the world, life, and good
and bad fortune is a commonplace: Tyche and Fortuna are very ancient
Greek and Roman goddesses who give both good and bad and often
both at different times. Heraclitus and Plato (in book 10 of the *Laws*
– claiming that everything is due to three causes of which Chance is
one) accept the notion of the caprices of these goddesses. We don't have,
of course, enough material from early Germanic to be able to make this
generalization clearly applicable to the early Anglo-Saxons, but it would
indeed be surprising if they and most peoples at all times were not aware
of the fickleness of fortune both for good and for evil. One has simply
to be alive and perceptive to be aware of the whims of fortune.

Furthermore it is very difficult to conceive of a minstrel who would
be learned in Boethius, especially when all one had to do to write of

the vagaries of fortune was to look around him. It is extremely unlikely that Deor was a cleric or monastic minstrel who knew his Germanic tradition well. It is by no means certain that there were actually clerical minstrels (not even Cædmon) as opposed to secular minstrels in Anglo-Saxon times. Even if there were such, I can hardly conceive of them spending their time reading Boethius in Latin or even Old English. If Deor did read Boethius, he would surely have Christianized his poem, in as much as Boethius was assumed to be and indeed probably was Christian. The personal reference at the end of the poem would make his interest in Boethius very unlikely. *Deor* is not a romantic poem; it must obviously refer to a real situation, here most likely in the past. It is true that some scholars have assumed that the minstreal was a cleric or monk,[6] but I find it hard to believe. He may have been a Christian layman, but I doubt this as well.

There is also no evidence that Boethius was known in England (except perhaps by a few learned monks like Bede, and even that is uncertain) in Latin or the vernacular before Alfred's time, and it is extremely unlikely that Deor lived as late as the beginning of the tenth century. Of course, I am assuming that the poem was composed by a minstrel named Deor, another unprovable point but more likely than not. Such a poem demands a composer who had experienced a calamity similar to the one he refers to at the end of the poem. Although Deor and Heorrenda are pretty clearly masking names, the experience described must have been at least partially real. The specificity of the experience can hardly have been made up.

If the poet had wished to write a pure Boethian poem, I cannot conceive why he would have picked a commonplace from Boethius when the demand to wipe out a loss was so strong in him. He is not merely, as is Boethius, consoling himself philosophically, although that is no doubt one of his purposes, but he wishes to bring to pass, by reminding Fortune of her up-and-down mode of movement, the destruction of a foe and the return of a stolen or lost land right. Piling up cases of the appearance and disappearance of the misfortunes of others would hardly have had much of a rationale unless uttered to take misfortunes away and bring good fortune in its place. It is difficult to conceive of a philosophical Deor who had no desire but a calm philosophical hope.

Further, the notion of the transience of everything is by no means an original insight of Boethius. The notion that everything passes is a commonplace applied to both good and bad fortune. It is widespread in many traditions, beliefs, and writings. That Deor knew either the Bible or Greek philosophy where the notion may be found more than once is extremely unlikely. The Germanic tradition, like most ancient traditions, would almost certainly have contained the notion, as some of its extant literature shows. In Old English, we have *The Wanderer* and *The Seafarer*, not to speak of other references, where the world's transience is pointed to. The poet or minstrel need have gone no further than his own native tradition to hit upon the idea of the exchange of good and bad fortune, even if this exchange is not always presented in concentrated form. We have evidence in *Beowulf* to this effect, as L. Whitbread has pointed out.[7] The total Germanic references in the poem itself give evidence that the minstrel of Deor knew the Germanic tradition but no evidence whatsoever that he knew any classical or even biblical literature.

Markland stumbled upon or perhaps knew a concise example of this commonplace in Boethius and insists that the poem is about the transience of good and evil delivered by a minstrel who needed Boethius to learn of this commonplace. There is no specific reference in Boethius to substantiate Deor's use of Boethius except perhaps for one word. There is of course a similar idea in Boethius and *Deor*, but the common notion of the changeability of Fortune alone cannot prove any source whatsoever.

Though Markland rejects my explanation of the poem's structure, certainly Boethius and Plato and so forth cannot explain the structure of *Deor*. Although I cannot claim that I have solved all its structural and ideational elements, my concern was with the structure as well as the idea of the poem. As we shall see below, others recently have to some extent made contributions to our understanding of the structure of *Deor*. Although the heyday of structuralism came to America in the late sixties and early seventies, it was well known in France and to some extent America when I was writing my article in 1962-3. Markland's chief difference from my approach is his ignoring of structuralism.

I have argued, as stated above, that a common form of the *Consolatio* notion is to be found in traditional charms and that this structure stimulated Deor (whoever he may be) to cast his 'complaint' in a charm-like form. Reminders to God of his kindnesses in the past in order to obtain his aid again are not unknown in ancient Jewish and Christian prayer and liturgy. As he saved us (or brought rain or raised someone from the dead or brought about other special desires) in the past, so may he do at present. This 'as x, so y' formula is very common in most traditions, most of which do not refer to divine action, though some do. The ancient oral Germanic tradition no doubt contained many examples of this formula and would be more available to an English minstrel or scop than Boethius or the Bible in the eighth or ninth centuries.

The Exeter ms which provides us with the sole surviving text of the poem is not of course written in verse lines such as we find in modern books which print a text in poetic form when poetry is being presented, no matter when or how the original (if known) was written. Manuscript material was too precious and expensive to leave many empty spaces on each page. Yet looking at the Exeter ms again, one must note that the five cases of misfortune followed by a long paragraph in the ms are clearly delineated as separate. Capital letters begin the six sections, and the manuscript leaves spaces between them, which implies a deliberate formalizing.

Now neither Boethius nor the charm in Old English, as far as I am aware, lists misfortunes followed by good fortune in regimented order. Nor do charms end with a personal description or expression of personal woe. Nor does the form of the *Consolation* correspond formally in any way to that of *Deor*, although the *Consolation* like many other works does in one section express a similar idea to that of *Deor*. Many other parallels may be found in other Old English poems, several in the same Exeter ms in which we find *Deor*. These notions and many others are all commonplaces in Old English (and indeed in other) wisdom literature.

The only way that I could be convinced that the *Deor*-poet used Boethius as his source would be if Deor referred to Croesus as Boethius does. The general theme of *Deor*, that just as good times will give way to bad times so bad will also give way to good, is too much of a commonplace to serve as proof of Boethian influence, especially as *Deor* is about pagan Germanic history and pseudo-history which present events quoted in the distant past. The similarities to Alfred's translation and modifications of the *De Consolatione* are simply not convincing. The use of the same common verb ('ofereode') proves nothing.

III

After having shown how shaky the Boethius theory is, I now wish to discuss briefly the refrain, 'þaes ofereode, þisses swa maeg,' which is found six times in the poem, including the last line. It obviously occupies an important role in the poem. Its brevity and its emphasis upon hope make it the ideal 'sententia' to conclude each of the examples culled from the past and the poem as a whole. It provides the forms for the moral of the poem. If something has occurred in the past more than once or twice, it is likely to occur again. This is the theme of the poem:

'that [event] has passed, this [present misfortune and/or unhappiness] will also pass.'

The use of this refrain at the end of the poem seems to bother certain commentators.[8] Although Markland[9] points out quite clearly and in agreement with the text that 'in the first five stanzas the referent of *þæs* is obviously the misfortune (or event described), and the referent of *þisses* is each time the speaker's unidentified [sic] misery,' he seems upset because 'the poet [in the last stanza] does not set forth a misfortune for *þæs* to refer to.' He attempts to explain this so-called shift by the parallel with the *Consolation of Philosophy* he has been pushing. 'The referent of *þæs* becomes the good fortune he has lost'(4). It would be much better, I think, to particularize it to the position he has just lost. According to Markland, 'þisses' refers to the 'current misery' Deor is in. The difficulty with this interpretation of the last refrain is that it separates the current misery Deor is in from the good fortune he has lost. His current misery *is* the good fortune he has lost.

There is no good reason why 'þæs' should not have a plural rather than a singular referent in the last stanza. 'Þæs' ('that' in the genitive singular case) and its nominative 'þæt,' like most demonstrative pronouns, can indicate a collective singular (eg 'that sort of thing'). Misfortune, unhappiness, etc can be and here are collective nouns which imply a group of misfortunes. A demonstrative can represent a group of items, as is the case occasionally in Latin.[10]

This interpretation takes us back to the traditional translation, 'That passed, so may this,' with 'that' referring to the collective past misfortune (which has just been referred to), and 'this' referring to the outcome, the rescue from trouble and misfortune. Deor could only be reciting these examples in order to remind the gods or God that great heroes or heroines have in the past been rescued from misfortune and thus there is a chance for a notable minstrel too.

IV

In any discussion about the form and structure of *Deor*, it must be emphasized that there is no one form of a charm. I did not make it clear in my 1964 article on the form of *Deor* that not all charms use the 'as x, so y' formula. It is in fact very common, but it does not cover all of the many charms which exist all over the world.[11] Furthermore it often appears as a part of a charm and rarely as a whole one. When it does appear, and it does in many charms, it is usually a part of a poem or, more rarely, the dominant structure throughout. Charms are forms of prayer for certain results, and frequently the good deeds of the deity or of the gods are called up to remind the almighty power of what it has achieved in the past so that it may be again achieved.

'As x, so y' is, as noted, a common organizational principle of charms. I have read a good many charms in the languages I know and don't hesitate to claim the phrase as the most common of all the verbal structural forms found in charms. It is a mode of asking for divine or diabolic powers in order to produce a practical effect. Charms are not philosophical poems but plea and prayer poems aimed at producing some particular goal. In Deor's case, he wishes to regain his lost land right and presumably a position at court.

Deor is obviously a Christian poem in as much as it refers to God (32), and yet all the examples (except Theodoric) are pagan historical or mythical figures, and the speaker clothes himself as a minstrel who was displaced by Heorrenda the ideal Norse (and presumably Germanic) minstrel. This shift to the immediate past after a long description of past figures, all Germanic great men,[12] is a kind of consolation and hope, bringing the speaker into the past under the name Deor. Deor may have been well known or may not have been. We do not know.

The presence of the word God, 'dryhten' (32), and the type of language used in the poem would tend to indicate that it is an early Anglo-Saxon poem that displays various older Germanic names, all of which except Deor are known. It is true that the third stanza may be an exception to this rule, but I think not. It is even possible that the poet in *Deor* was not a minstrel or scop, but the restrained emotion of the poem and its allusiveness argue for a minstrel author.

The form of the poem, however, can be looked upon from a structural point of view as strongly emphasizing the brief Theodoric stanza which occurs in the centre of *Deor*. This structural fact (along with others) was first pointed out by James L. Boren in 1975.[13] Some of his interpretations are debatable, but on the whole his structural analysis is impressive. A student of mine, Sara Blair, has also written an interesting but unpublished paper entitled 'A Reading of *Deor*: Episodic Nature and Design,' indebted to Boren but carrying his argument further. She refers to the form of the stanzas in *Deor* as 'the hour-glass shape' and notes that the centre of the poem concerning Theodoric is created 'by understatement and ellipsis rather than elaboration.' The movement of the first five stanzas is from myth and legend to ancient history. We then move into the poem's present – the plight of Deor after a generalized out-of-time statement about misfortune and God's role in bringing it on and removing it from men.

Needless to say, much more could be written about the structure of *Deor*; here only some of the main lines can be discussed. The term 'structure' itself is loosely used in literary scholarship and criticism (not to speak of theory), largely because distinctions have still to be made in the study of its various meanings. Often, for instance, as here, the term is used to indicate the line of meaning of the work. I have, however, concentrated on what one might call the physical structure of a poem. The form the words assume – whether in sentences, paragraphs, divisions (here because of the refrain easy to establish in manuscript where usually no divisions are made within poems), their length and frequency – is my main concern. Other investigations need to be done, but the best piece of news we could possibly hear about *Deor* (and which is extremely unlikely to occur) is the discovery of a new manuscript containing a new version of *Deor* or a poem on the same basic topic. Alas, we cannot depend on such a discovery unless a miracle happens.

v

Where do we go from here? No further discoveries are likely, although one can never tell. We must stick to our Exeter ms text. The poem is presented as an outburst of both grief and jealousy in rather rigid form, especially for an Old English poem or for a philosophic poem urging hope and comfort. It is in standard Old English metrical alliterative pattern except for the short refrain, which has only one pair of initial alliterating sounds. The refrain, however, sets it apart from almost all other alliterative poems. I don't believe we have another example of a refrain poem preserved in Old English, although we do find occasional repetitions, as in *Wulf and Eadwacer*. The brevity of the whole poem adds to its unusual qualities.

As Petrarch some seven or eight hundred years later put it in his title *De Remediis utriusque Fortunae*, both success and failure need remedies. There can also be too much of a good thing. When caught in misfortune one needs good fortune as most understand it, but when good fortune prevails misfortune is also needed to provide us with some caution. The lower universe ruled by Fortune is not just a jumble of events but has some kind of pattern or patterns. *Deor* is concerned with the inevitability of the wheel of Fortune. Misery changes to joy and joy to misery. The poem makes use of the past in order to support hope to overcome the current misery of Deor. The past offers examples of misery overcome; why not, then, this present misery which is pressing on the minstrel?

NOTES

1 See Søren Kierkegaard *Repetition: An Essay in Experimental Psychology* trans Walter Lourie (Princeton 1941); Mircea Eliade *The Myth of the Eternal Return* trans Willard R. Trask (New York 1954) rpt as *Cosmos and History: The Myth of the Eternal Return* (1959); and Bruce F. Kawin *Telling It Again and Again: Repetition in Literature and Film* (Ithaca 1972). None of these writers write of the desire to bring about a repetition of an event or related events, whereby the present is transcended by bringing about again through word magic an event or situation in the past which you hope or wish for. Repetition is a (perhaps the) major factor in magical or miraculous recurrences.

2 Kawin 83

3 Kawin 182

4 *MP* 66 (1968-9) 1-4 and an addendum entitled '*Deor*: þæs ofereode: þisses swa mæg' *American Notes & Queries* 11 (1972-3) 35-6

5 *MP* 66 (1968-9) 1

6 Note Karl Jost's assumption that there is no question but that the composer of *Deor* was a monk or priest. See 'Welund und Samson' in *Festschrift zum 75. Geburtstag von Theodor Spira* ed H. Viebrock and W. Erzgräber (Heidelberg 1961) 86-7. See also Whitbread 'The Pattern of Misfortune in *Deor* and Other Old English Poems' *Neophil* 54 (1970) 176.

7 Whitbread 170 and 173-4 (for *The Wanderer*)

8 See Bloomfield 'The Form of *Deor*' *PMLA* 79 (1964) 535-7 and very recently Jerome Mandel 'Audience Response Strategies in the Opening of *Deor*' *Mosaic* 15:4 (1983) 127-32. Mandel's 'Exemplum and Refrain: The Meaning of *Deor*' *YES* 7 (1977) 1-9 contains a lengthy and important discussion of the refrain.

9 See his *MP* article 3-4.

10 See J.H. Allen and James B Greenough *Latin Grammar* rev Greenough and Kittredge (Boston 1901) 195.

11 For a recent article on the form of a special type of charm, the journey charm, see Heather Stuart, 'Ic Me on þisse Gyrde Beluce: The Structure and Meaning of the Old English *Journey Charm*' *MÆ* 50 (1981) 259-73. Stuart does refer to the 'as x, so y' formula (without using the algebraic symbols) on p 261. For a general treatment of charms, see Northrop Frye 'Charms and Riddles' in *Spiritus Mundi: Essays on Literature, Myth and Society* (Bloomington 1976) 123-47.

12 Except perhaps the third stanza in the poem about Mæðhilde and Geat if

Kemp Malone is right in his edition of the poem in Methuen's Old English Library, 4th ed (London 1966) 8-9 and 24-5n; or if Thomas T. Tuggle in 'The Structure of *Deor*' *SP* 74 (1977) 230ff is right, 'hilde' may refer not to a name but to the Old English word for 'battle' and 'Geat' to Niðhad.

13 See 'The Design of the Old English *Deor*' in *Anglo-Saxon Poetry: Essays in Appreciation for John C. McGalliard* ed Lewis E. Nicholson and Dolores Warwick Frese (Notre Dame 1975) 265-72. The final part of his paper is devoted to a fairly widely accepted notion: that *Deor* is a wisdom poem.

Publications of Stanley B. Greenfield, 1951 to the Present; Awards and Honours

BOOKS

A Critical History of Old English Literature. New York: New York University Press 1965. London: University of London Press 1966

The Interpretation of Old English Poems. London and Boston: Routledge and Kegan Paul 1972

A Readable Beowulf: The Old English Epic Newly Translated, with an Introduction by Alain Renoir. Carbondale: Southern Illinois University Press 1982

A New Critical History of Old English Literature, with Daniel G. Calder; with an Introductory Essay on Anglo-Latin Literature by Michael Lapidge. New York: New York University Press 1986

BIBLIOGRAPHIES

Annual Old English Bibliographies for the Old English Group of the MLA 1951-62

Annotated bibliographies in David M. Zesmer's *Guide to English Literature from Beowulf through Chaucer and Medieval Drama*. College Outline Series. New York: Barnes and Noble 1961. Rpt 1972. 292-381

'Old English Poetry' in *The New Cambridge Bibliography of English Literature*. Ed George Watson. Cambridge: Cambridge University Press 1974. Vol I, cols 225-312

A Bibliography of Publications on Old English Literature to the end of 1972, with Fred C. Robinson. Toronto: University of Toronto Press 1980

EDITIONS

Studies in Old English Literature in Honor of Arthur G. Brodeur. Eugene,

Oregon: University of Oregon Books 1963. Rpt New York: Russell and Russell 1973

The Poem: An Anthology, with A. Kingsley Weatherhead. New York: Appleton Century Crofts 1968. 2nd ed 1972

Pacific Coast Philology 17 (Nov 1982)

SCHOLARLY ARTICLES

'*The Wanderer*: A Reconsideration of Theme and Structure.' *JEGP* 50 (1951) 451-65

'Of Locks and Keys: Line 19a of the o.e. *Christ*.' *MLN* 67 (1952) 238-40

'Sittingbourne and the Order of *The Canterbury Tales*.' *MLR* 48 (1953) 51-2

'The Theme of Spiritual Exile in *Christ I*.' *PQ* 32 (1953) 321-28

'*The Wife's Lament* Reconsidered.' *PMLA* 68 (1953) 907-12

'Attitudes and Values in *The Seafarer*.' *SP* 51 (1954) 15-20

'Moth's *L'Envoy* and the Courtiers in *Love's Labour's Lost*.' *RES* 5 (1954) 167-8

'The Formulaic Expression of the Theme of "Exile" in Anglo-Saxon Poetry.' *Speculum* 30 (1955) 200-6

'Mansfield's *The Fly*.' *Explicator* 17 (1958) item 2

'The Unmistakable Stephen Crane.' *PMLA* 73 (1958) 562-72

'*Pastors and Masters*: The Spoils of Genius.' *Criticism* 2 (1960) 66-80

'*Paradise Lost* XII, 629-632.' *Explicator* (1961) item 57

'*Beowulf* and Epic Tragedy.' *CL* 14 (1962) 91-105. Rpt in *Studies in Old English Literature in Honor of Arthur G. Brodeur*

'Syntactical Analysis and Old English Poetry.' *NM* 64 (1963) 373-8

'Geatish History: Poetic Art and Epic Quality in *Beowulf*.' *Neophil* 47 (1963) 211-17

'*Beowulf* 207b-228: Narrative and Descriptive Art.' *N&Q* 211 (1966) 86-90

'The Old English Elegies.' In *Continuations and Beginnings: Studies in Old English Literature*. Ed E.G. Stanley. London: Thomas Nelson and Sons 1966

'Grendel's Approach to Heorot: Syntax and Poetry.' In *Old English Poetry: Fifteen Essays*. Ed Robert P. Creed. Providence: Brown University Press 1967

'The Canons of Old English Criticism.' *ELH* 34 (1967) 141-55

'Grammar and Meaning in Poetry.' *PMLA* 82 (1967) 377-87

'The Role of Calkas in *Troilus and Criseyde*.' *MÆ* 36 (1967) 141-51

'*Mīn, Sylf*, and "Dramatic Voices in *The Wanderer* and *The Seafarer*."' *JEGP* 68 (1969) 212-20

'Ellipsis and Meaning in Poetry.' *TSLL* 13 (1971) 137-47

'*Folces Hyrde, Finnsburh* 46b.' *NM* 73 (1972) 97-102

'*Gifstol* and Goldhoard in *Beowulf*.' In *Old English Studies in Honour of John*

C. Pope. Ed Robert B. Burlin and Edward B. Irving, Jr. Toronto: University of Toronto Press 1974

'*Maxims II*: Gnome and Poem,' with Richard Evert. In *Anglo-Saxon Poetry: Essays in Appreciation for John C. McGalliard*. Ed Lewis E. Nicholson and Dolores Warwick Frese. Notre Dame: Notre Dame University Press 1975

'The authenticating voice in *Beowulf*.' *ASE* 5 (1976) 51-62

'Three *Beowulf* Notes.' In *Medieval Studies in Honor of Lillian Herlands Hornstein*. Ed Jess B. Bessinger, Jr, and Robert R. Raymo. New York: New York University Press 1976

'OE Words and Patristic Exegesis – *hwyrftum scrifað*: A Caveat.' *MP* 75 (1977) 44-8

'OE *Exodus* 33a, MS. *ingere*: A New Suggestion.' *N&Q* 224 (1979) 296-7

'Esthetics and Meaning and the Translation of Old English Poetry.' In *Old English Poetry: Essays on Style*. Ed Daniel G. Calder. Berkeley: University of California Press 1979. 91-110

'The Extremities of the *Beowulf*ian Body Politic.' In *Saints, Scholars, and Heroes: Studies in Medieval Culture in Honor of Charles W. Jones*. 2 vols. Ed Margot H. King and Wesley M. Stevens. Collegeville, Minn: Saint John's Abbey and Univ Press 1979 1:1-14

'Old English Riddle 39 Clear and Visible.' *Anglia* 98 (1980) 95-100

'Sylf, seasons, structure and genre in *The Seafarer*.' *ASE* 9 (1980) 199-211

'A Touch of the Monstrous in the Hero, or Beowulf Remarvellized.' *ES* 63 (1982) 294-300

'Of Words and Deeds – The Coastguard's Maxim Once More.' In *The Wisdom of Poetry: Essays in Early English Literature in Honor of Morton W. Bloomfield*. Ed Larry D. Benson and Siegfried Wenzel. Kalamazoo: Medieval Institute Publications 1982

'President's Address: Filling in the Blanks.' *Pacific Coast Philology* 18 (1983) 7-13

'Beowulf and the judgment of the righteous.' In *Learning and Literature in Anglo-Saxon England: Studies Presented to Peter Clemoes*. Ed Michael Lapidge and Helmut Gneuss. Cambridge: Cambridge University Press 1985. 393-407

'*Þancword* for John C. Pope: *Advent Lyric II* Again.' *MP* 83 (1985) 166-8

'The Petitions of the *Advent Lyrics* and the Question of Unity.' Forthcoming

'*Wulf and Eadwacer*: All Passion Pent.' Forthcoming

REVIEWS

J.W. Clark *Early English*. *MLN* 74 (1959) 59-60

A.G. Brodeur *The Art of Beowulf. CL* 12 (1960) 73-8

S.B. Meech *Design in Chaucer's Troilus. CL* 12 (1960) 360-4

Burton Raffel *Poems from the Old English. Northwest Review* (Fall 1961) 124-6

Morton Bloomfield *Piers Plowman as a Fourteenth-Century Apocalypse. CL* 15 (1963) 374-6

John H. Fisher *John Gower: Moral Philosopher and Friend of Chaucer. CL* 18 (1966) 81-3

George Williams *A New View of Chaucer. ELN* 3 (1966) 300-3

Edward B. Irving, Jr *A Reading of Beowulf. Speculum* 44 (1969) 301-4

Neil D. Isaacs *Structural Principles in Old English Poetry. JEGP* 68 (1969) 496-9

P.M. Kean *The Pearl: An Interpretation. CL* 21 (1969) 164-6

T.P. Dunning and A.J. Bliss, eds *The Wanderer. N&Q* 218 (1973) 24-6

Edward B. Irving, Jr *Introduction to Beowulf. Speculum* 45 (1970) 301-2

Ann Chalmers Watt *The Lyre and the Harp: A Comparative Reconsideration of Oral Tradition in Homer and Old English Epic Poetry*, and William Whalon, *Formula, Character, and Context: Studies in Homeric, Old English, and Old Testament Poetry. JEGP* 70 (1971) 279-83

Alvin A. Lee *The Guest-Hall of Eden. JEGP* 72 (1973) 122-6

Thomas A. Shippey *Old English Verse. N&Q* 218 (1973) 24-6

John Gardner *The Construction of Christian Poetry in Old English. MLQ* 36 (1975) 426-8

Theodore M. Andersson *Early Epic Scenery: Homer, Virgil, and the Medieval Legacy. JEGP* 76 (1977) 537-9

Walter H. Beale *Old and Middle English Poetry to 1500. Literary Research Newsletter* 3 (1978) 75-8

James H. Wilson *Christian Theology and Old English Poetry. MÆ* 46 (1977) 290-2

Donald R. Howard *The Idea of the Canterbury Tales. CL* 30 (1978) 72-7

A.N. Doane *Genesis A: A New Edition. JEGP* 78 (1979) 244-8

Derek Pearsall *Old English and Middle English Poetry. MP* 77 (1979) 188-91

Barbara Raw *The Art and Background of Old English Poetry. Speculum* 54 (1979) 417-20

Herbert Pilch and Hildegard Tristram *Altenglische Literatur. Anglia* 99 (1981) 487-90

Michael Swanton *Beowulf, edited with an introduction, notes and new prose translation. Anglia* 100 (1982) 168-72

David Williams *Cain and Beowulf. MP* 81 (1983) 191-4

Jeff Opland *Anglo-Saxon Oral Poetry: A Study of the Traditions. CL* 34 (1982) 67-70

John D. Niles *Beowulf: The Poem and Its Tradition. CL* 38 (1986) 98-100

AWARDS AND HONOURS

Among the many awards and honours Stanley B. Greenfield has received are Phi Beta Kappa and Phi Kappa Phi, Cornell University, 1942; Ersted Award for Distinguished Teaching, University of Oregon, 1963; Guggenheim Fellow, 1965-6; Annual Prize for Outstanding Article in *PMLA*, 1968; NEH Senior Fellow, 1970-1; Fulbright Fellow, University of Regensburg, 1974-5. He has been a visiting Professor or Fellow at University of California, Los Angeles (1976-7) and Berkeley (1981), and Emmanuel College, Cambridge (1979). He has given invitational lectures in London, Dublin, Leeds, Aachen, Bonn, Heidelberg, Mannheim, Munich, Lausanne, Geneva, Cambridge, Keele, Kent, Oxford, and at many universities in the United States including Wisconsin, Berkeley, UCLA, and Pennsylvania.

Professor Greenfield was chairman of the Old English Bibliography Committee of the Old English Group, MLA (1951-62), on the Executive Committee of the Old English Group, MLA (1968-73; 1979-83) - chairman in 1972 and 1982, on NEH Fellowship Selection Panels (1971-6), on the Editorial Committee of *PMLA* (1971-4), on the MLA Executive Council (1974-7), Co-founder and Editorial Board Member of *Anglo-Saxon England* (since 1972), on the Advisory Board of the Medieval Association of the Pacific (1974-7), on the Editorial Board of *Speculum* (1978-82), Vice President and President of the Philological Association of the Pacific Coast (1980-2), on the Editorial Board of *Viator* (1980-2), founding member and Vice President of the International Society of Anglo-Saxonists (1983-5).

Index

Tabula Gratulatoria

Ashley Crandell Amos
Dictionary of Old English
University of Toronto

Ruth apRoberts
Robert apRoberts
Riverside, California

Roland Bartel
University of Oregon

Carol Bensick
University of Oregon

Carl T. Berkhout
University of Arizona

Robert E. Bjork
Arizona State University

Constance Bordwell
University of Oregon

James L. Boren
University of Oregon

Richard Maxwell Brown
University of Oregon

William Calin
University of Oregon

Jackson J. Campbell
University of Illinois

Fredi Chiappelli
University of California
Los Angeles

Howell Chickering
Amherst College

Herbert E. Childs
Corvallis, Oregon

George Clark
Queen's University
Kingston, Ontario, Canada

Robert D. Clark
University of Oregon

Frances B. Cogan
University of Oregon

Helen Damico
University of New Mexico

Ann Dobyns
The Ohio State University

E. Talbot Donaldson
Bloomington, Indiana

Sigmund Eisner
University of Arizona

Ralph W.V. Elliott
Australian National University
Canberra

Arthur Frietzsche
California Polytechnic State University
San Luis Obispo

R.D. Fulk
Indiana University

Thomas J. Garbáty
University of Michigan

Walter Goffart
University of Toronto

Dr Karen Gould
Dr Lewis L. Gould
Department of History
University of Texas, Austin

Richard H. Green
Professor Emeritus
University of Florida

Sidney Greenbaum
University College
London

Thelma N. Greenfield
University of Oregon

Hoyt S. Greeson
Department of English
Laurentian University
Sudbury, Ontario, Canada

Michaela Grudin
Robert Grudin
University of Oregon

Renate Haas
University of Duisburg
West Germany

Antonette diPaolo Healey
Dictionary of Old English
University of Toronto

Paul S. Holbo
University of Oregon

Gloria Johnson
University of Oregon

Miriam M. Johnson
G. Benton Johnson, Jr
University of Oregon

Stanley J. Kahrl
Department of English
The Ohio State University

Henry Ansgar Kelly
Department of English
University of California
Los Angeles

Kevin S. Kiernan
University of Kentucky

Albert R. Kitzhaber
University of Oregon

Dominic A. LaRusso
University of Oregon

Roy F. Leslie
Department of English
University of Victoria
British Columbia, Canada

Glen A. Love
University of Oregon

Charles D. Ludlum
Department of English
San Jose State University
San Jose, California

John C. McGalliard
Senior Associate Editor
Dictionary of American Regional
    English
University of Wisconsin, Madison

Grant McKernie
University of Oregon

Waldo F. McNeir
Houston, Texas

Daniel F. Melia
University of California
Berkeley

Ernest G. Moll
Oroville, California

Carlisle Moore
University of Oregon

John D. Niles
University of California
Berkeley

Michiko Ogura
Tsuru University
Tokyo, Japan

Teresa Pàroli
Facoltà di Lettere
Università di Roma 'La Sapienza'

Carol Braun Pasternack
University of Winsconsin
Madison

Helmut R. Plant
University of Oregon

Earl Pomeroy
University of Oregon

Robert C. Rice
Christendom College

Janette Richardson
University of California
Berkeley

Florence H. Ridley
University of California
Los Angeles

William Rockett
University of Oregon

George E. Rowe
University of Oregon

Steven Shankman
University of Oregon

George J. Sheridan, Jr
University of Oregon

Glenn Starlin
University of Oregon

Barrie Ruth Straus
University of Florida

Donald S. Tull
University of Oregon

Linda Ehrsam Voigts
University of Missouri
Kansas City

Ingrid Weatherhead
Kingsley Weatherhead
University of Oregon

Christof Wegelin
University of Oregon

Horst Weinstock
Technical University of Aachen
West Germany

Louise Westling
University of Oregon

George Wickes
University of Oregon

Oliver M. Willard
University of Oregon